TITLED TRAINS

OF

GREAT BRITAIN

TITLED TRAINS
OF
GREAT BRITAIN

Cecil J. Allen
FRSA, MInstT, AILocoE

Revised by: B. K. Cooper

LONDON

IAN ALLAN LTD

First published 1946
Second edition 1947
Third edition 1953
Fourth edition 1955
Fifth edition 1967
Sixth edition 1983

ISBN 0 7110 1309 8

Published by Ian Allan Ltd, Shepperton, Surrey; and printed by Ian Allan Printing Ltd at their works at Coombelands in Runnymede, England

Index
OF TRAINS IN ALPHABETICAL ORDER

*Title now extinct

†Unofficial title or nickname

Foreword
TO THE FIFTH EDITION

Nothing ever remains static for any length of time so far as passenger train services are concerned; and to me the preparation of the fifth edition of this book has stressed the astonishing changes which have taken place on British railways over a period of little more than twenty years. The first and second editions appeared in 1946 and 1947, in the days of the four main line railways; by the emergence of the third edition in 1953, nationalisation had taken place; to-day, though speeds in general are far higher, with the gradual disappearance of steam power much of the romance that attached to the famous named trains of the past has vanished also.

During World War 1 four trains only retained their distinctive titles — the 'Flying Scotsman', the 'Cornish Riviera Express', the 'Aberdonian', and the 'Night Scotsman'. When the first edition of this book was published, many of the pre-war names had been restored, and the past and present titles required descriptions of 70 trains; by the publication of the second edition the number had grown to 79; while the third and fourth editions described 108 titled trains. There is a further increase in the present edition to over 120 titles, but of these 69 — more than half — are no longer in use, and in a number of cases the trains concerned, some of them in the past quite famous services, have ceased to run.

It is remarkable that at the present time, when all the principal trains in countries like France and Germany bear titles, and passenger train naming is the universal practice in the United States, British railway authorities are setting their face against the practice, and steadily removing train names rather than adding to them. The excuse offered is that the higher speeds of to-day make it possible for the same sets of coaches to be used on three or four long-distance runs on the one day, so that the continued use of names would involve fitting or removing carriage name-boards to a troublesome extent; moreover, the tendency is towards standard schedules and equipment rather than to the running of expresses of exceptional speed or luxury. But one cannot help feeling that public attraction as well as romance are being lost in this way.

In the preface to the third and fourth editions I remarked that the overall times of some titled trains had receded from the fastest since World War 2, and that at the time very few expresses had reattained the speed levels that prevailed in the halcyon days of steam, in the later 1930s. But such a criticism could certainly not be levelled to-day, when the London Midland Region electric service alone is responsible for 12 daily runs timed at over 80mph from start to stop, 107 at over 75mph and no fewer than 165, with an aggregate mileage of 13,775, at over 72mph, not to mention the numerous high-speed runs with diesel power on the other Regions.

I added in 1953 my hope that the Coronation year, at a time when British punctuality as well as speed was at a low ebb, might see some revival of British prestige in these matters, and that before long we might be able once again to take justifiable pride, on every count, in the express passenger train services of these islands. That hope, I think, has now been fulfilled; as to aggregate high-speed mileage, at long last we have both France and Germany beaten, and so far at least as second-class accommodation is concerned, no country on the mainland of Europe can show a standard equal to that of Great Britain.

It has been a pleasure to me to write this book. During the course of some 60 years of continuous travelling, to a total distance by now well in excess of two million miles, there is scarcely one of the trains described on which I have not travelled at some time or other; some, indeed, I have used to such an extent that they have become almost like second homes. And even to-day, whether the train concerned carries a title or not, to settle down in the corner of a first-class compartment, to record the work of the locomotive at the head of the train, even if it be a soulless diesel or electric machine, and to view the passing scenery of our loved country, is still to me one of the most congenial of all ways of spending my time.

Cecil J. Allen

The Aberdonian

Lineal descendant of the East Coast flyer which in 1895 raced the West Coast train to be the first from London to reach Aberdeen, the 'Aberdonian' since that day fell somewhat from grace in the matter of speed, though what it had lost up to the outbreak of World War 2 it had far more than gained in comfort. With comfort came vastly increased weight, and the weight in part provided the reason for the deceleration. Apart from that, however, slower running at night was justifiable for few night passengers wanted to arrive at their destinations in the 'small hours'.

The 1895 'Race' began with the modest announcement that from 1 July the West Coast Companies — London & North Western and Caledonian — would bring their 8pm express from Euston to Aberdeen at 7.40am, 15min earlier than before, and only 5min behind the corresponding train from King's Cross of the East Coast Companies — Great Northern, North Eastern and North British. Seven weeks later, the West Coast schedule had been cut by 2¼hr, and the East Coast by 1hr 55min, but the racing trains, which had been running well ahead of time, continued to do so.

On the East Coast side the record achievement was that of the night of 21-22 August, when the King's Cross train rolled into Aberdeen at 4.40am, having covered the entire 523.7 miles, stops included, in 520min. The train, weighing 105 tons, had been worked over the 105.5 miles from King's Cross to Grantham by a GNR Stirling 8ft single in 101min; another engine of the same type continued over the 82.7 miles to York in 76min; there the North Eastern took charge, and ran the 80.5 miles to Newcastle in 78min, with a 4-4-0 of the then NER Class M; following this run a sister engine covered the 124.5 miles from Newcastle to Edinburgh in 114½min.

In view of the difficulties of grading and curvature north of Edinburgh, it was a fine feat for the North British 4-4-0s to take the train first over the 59.2 miles to Dundee in 60min, and then from Dundee to Aberdeen, 71.3 miles, in 77min. The actual running times thus added up to no more than 506½min, and had the East Coast been as free from scruples as the West Coast about leaving intermediate stops before time, the final outcome of the race might have been different. As it was, the rivals 'won' on the following night with their amazing time of 8hr 32min (512min for 540 miles), including three stops, and by common consent the 'Race' was then at an end.

But the night Highland 'sleeper' from King's Cross still continued for years as the fastest train on the service. Up to the time of World War 1, while the 'Flying Scotsman', bound by agreement, still pottered from London to Edinburgh in 8¼hr, the 8.15 or 8pm from King's Cross (the times varied in different years) took from 7hr 45min to 50min. After the war, in 1923, the first year of the LNER, the working time from King's Cross to Edinburgh had crept back to 7¾hr, and Aberdeen was reached in 11hr 5min, but by 1924 the decline in speed had begun again.

In 1939 the 'Aberdonian', which had received its name in 1927, was making a much more stately pilgrimage to the North. Its starting time had been advanced to 7.30pm, and it had acquired, on the rear, a composite restaurant car, which provided sustenance for its passengers as far as York. The timetable allowed 124min to Grantham, and 96min on to York, reached at 11.15pm; here the dining car was detached. Leaving York 10min later, the express was allowed 101min to Newcastle, and spending 8min there, the longest non-stop run of the journey — 124.5 miles to Edinburgh — was begun at 1.14am and completed at 3.50am. At Edinburgh Waverley the train was split up; and sleeping cars and through coaches for Fort William, Perth and Inverness were detached.

The Fort William section was scheduled to wait 40min, till 4.30am, and then to be worked across to Glasgow in exactly one hour, for attachment to the 5.50am from Queen Street through the wild West Highlands to Fort William and Mallaig. The comfort of passengers on this long and mountainous run was assured by a restaurant car from Glasgow, and Fort William, 562½ miles from King's Cross, was reached at 9.54am. Meantime, the Perth and Inverness section had been taken out of Edinburgh at 4.20am, and worked non-stop over the 47¾ miles of extremely difficult grades to Perth, arriving at 5.28am, to wait the arrival of the 'Royal Highlander' from Euston. After 57min at Perth, the combined train was away at 6.25am, and the Inverness sleeping cars reached that city at 9.50am — almost a 'dead-heat' with the Fort William vehicles, and over an almost identical distance, actually 4 miles less in 4min less running time.

Long before this the 'Aberdonian' proper, which had left Edinburgh at 4.15am, and made calls at Dundee, Arbroath, Montrose and Stonehaven, had come to rest in the Granite City. Scheduled time of arrival was 7.30am, precisely 12 hours from London, 55min more than in 1923, and 3hr 20min slower than the best racing time in 1895! But by 1939, as previously mentioned, the 'Aberdonian' had become an extremely heavy train. Fort William was content with a composite sleeping car and a composite brake; Inverness usually required a first-class car, a third-class car and a composite brake; to Aberdeen there were first- and third-class cars (the former an articulated twin), a composite and a third-classs brake; and various vans distributed about the train, with the dining car, made the customary formation at least 500 tons in weight from London.

In summer the train ran nightly in two sections, and often in three. At 7.25pm the first train, given the name of 'Highlandman', left King's Cross, with the Fort William and Inverness sections, and an additional sleeping car portion for Nairn (detached from the Inverness cars at Aviemore); while the 'Aberdonian', at 7.40pm, was the main Aberdeen train, with a through section for Elgin and Lossiemouth, taken forward over the old Great North of Scotland line from Aberdeen and, very likely, by a 4-6-0 locomotive of the former Great Eastern Railway. South of Aberdeen, Pacific haulage was invariable between London and Edinburgh, but between Edinburgh and Aberdeen there was generally provided one of the fine Class P2 2-8-2 locomotives of the 'Cock o' the North' type, specially designed by the late Sir Nigel Gresley for this difficult route, but later unhappily converted to Pacifics by Gresley's successor, Edward Thompson.

In the southbound direction the departure of the 'Aberdonian' from Aberdeen, complete with dining cars to Edinburgh, had by 1939 become standardised at 7.35pm, and the run to London took 10min under the 12hr. With the same stops as in the reverse direction, Edinburgh was reached at 10.55pm. Long before the start from Aberdeen, the portion from Fort William was under way, at 4.07pm, and as this collected additional sleeping cars before leaving Glasgow at 10pm, the southbound Inverness cars were worked to King's Cross on a preceding express from Edinburgh. South of Edinburgh, the 'Aberdonian' made the same stops as the northbound train to York, but then exchanged the Grantham stop for halts at Doncaster and Peterbrough. It was due in London at 7.25am.

This important service continued throughout World War 2, but between King's Cross, Edinburgh and Aberdeen only, with a connection to Fort William. Leaving King's Cross at 7pm, the 'Aberdonian' — one of the only four British trains to retain its title throughout the war — was allowed 13½hr to complete its run to Aberdeen, and, leaving there at 6pm, 13hr 35min up to London.

Speed recovery was considerably slower after World War 2 than after World War 1, but the advent of the 3,300hp 'Deltic' diesels in replacement of the steam Pacifics made possible a considerable reduction in journey time. The main section of the 'Aberdonian', due out of King's Cross at 7.40pm reached Aberdeen at 6.50am, in 11hr 10min, or 50min less than its 1939 allowance. With 112½min for the 105.5 miles to Grantham, and 87½min for the 82.7 miles on to York, some fast running was needed with what was the heaviest passenger train worked regularly out of King's Cross. This comprised four sleeping cars, three passenger coaches and three vans for Aberdeen; two sleeping cars and a composite brake for Fort William (reached at 10.14am); and the restaurant car as far as York, 14 coaches in all with a tare weight of 518 tons.

The postwar years also saw an addition to the King's Cross-Aberdeen night service in a train leaving London at 10.15pm and making no advertised passenger stops south of Inverkeithing although stopping at Newcastle and Edinburgh for locomotive changes. The corresponding up service left Aberdeen at 8.30pm and had the same pattern of stops. In the 1960s the name 'Aberdonian' was transferred to this southbound train. The 10.15pm from King's Cross became the 'Night Aberdonian' in 1971 and the up train was named similarly. This name was dropped in the revised ECML service of October 1982.

The 'Aberdonian' name was transferred in 1972 to the 12 noon from King's Cross and the 10.30am from Aberdeen. The down train was accelerated by 36min, omitting stops at Darlington, Berwick and Dunbar and reaching Aberdeen at 9.09pm. This overall time of 9hr 9min was the best ever from London to Aberdeen up to then.

Introduction of HSTs on the East Coast main line began in 1978. The 'Aberdonian' became an HST Class 254 unit in the summer timetable of 1979. Again a new best time from London to Aberdeen was established, the train arriving in the northern city at 7.27pm after stopping at Darlington, Newcastle, Edinburgh and Dundee. The up 'Aberdonian' now left at 10.35am and with stops at Stonehaven, Montrose, Arbroath, Dundee, and Edinburgh fitted into a standard pattern of hourly departures from Edinburgh to King's Cross. Yet another change came three years later, and one which broke a long tradition. In the 1982 timetable the down 'Aberdonian' took over the 10am departure from King's Cross so long associated with the 'Flying Scotsman'. Its time to Edinburgh, with stops at Doncaster, York, Darlington and Newcastle, was 4hr 51min (compared with 4hr 43min by the 10am 'Scotsman' of the previous year); Aberdeen was reached in 7hr 21min from London after further stops at Dundee, Arbroath, Montrose and Stonehaven. The up 'Aberdonian' at 7.30am again took up the 10am departure from Edinburgh and stopping only at Berwick, Newcastle, Darlington and York reached King's Cross at 2.48pm in 7hr 18min from Aberdeen.

Revised East Coast main line timetables introduced on 4 October 1982 brought yet another change to the up 'Aberdonian'. The 7.30am from Aberdeen became the 'Flying Scotsman' and the 'Aberdonian' title was transferred to the 8.40am, which stopped only at Dundee en route to Edinburgh. Leaving the Scottish capital at 11am the 'Aberdonian' called at Newcastle, York, Darlington and Peterborough, reaching King's Cross at 3.52pm, the overall time from Aberdeen being 6min less than in the previous timetable.

The Atlantic Coast Express

Though for many years past, back into London & South Western days, an express had left Waterloo for the West of England at about 11am, it was not until 1926 that the Southern Railway introduced the title of 'Atlantic Coast Express' for this service — the Southern 'ACE', as it has sometimes been called. The 'Atlantic Coast Express' became the most multi-portioned train in the country. Nine different sections were included in the formation.

The leading end of the train comprised the Ilfracombe portion, of two third-class brakes and a composite coach between, together with composite brakes for Torrington, Padstow, Bude and Plymouth. After these the restaurant cars — first-class and kitchen car with open third-class car — could be classed as a 'portion', for they were detached at Exeter. Then followed composite brakes for Exmouth, Sidmouth and for stations between Salisbury and Seaton, the last-mentioned detached at Salisbury. In the days of the keenest competition between the LSWR and the GWR for the traffic to and from the West of England, the predecessor of the 'Atlantic Coast Express' was regarded as being a Plymouth train, with a connection for Ilfracombe; but the opening of the GWR Westbury route enabled the latter company to accelerate its Plymouth services to such a degree that the SR fell into the background as a route from London to Plymouth, and the Ilfracombe section of this train then assumed the major importance.

Up to 1939 the 'Atlantic Coast Express' was booked to leave Waterloo at 11am, and to make its first stop at Salisbury at 12.26pm — 83.8 miles in 86min. Although the provision of water-troughs on this route had often been mooted, and years ago Dugald Drummond, then Locomotive Superintendent of the LSWR, even went to the length of fitting some of his tenders with water-scoops, the troughs never materialised. For reasons of water alone, therefore, it was never possible to run non-stop from Waterloo to Exeter, though the Salisbury stop was desirable for more reasons than locomotive requirements merely, as important connections were made there. Through locomotive running had been tried from Waterloo to Exeter, but a change of engine at Salisbury was preferred until the advent of the Bulleid Pacifics, with which from 1950 the through working became a regular practice.

West of Salisbury the locomotive running with steam power was always some of the most exciting in Great Britain. Nowhere else in the country were such high speeds run relative to the severity of the profile. The route was particularly well aligned and there was practically no limit to maximum speeds; in consequence the drivers made the utmost use of the falling gradients, in order that the impetus so gained might help them on the succeeding ascents. In the westbound direction, speeds of over 80mph were frequently attained at Gillingham, Sherborne, Axminster, Honiton and at Broad Clyst (between Sidmouth Junction and Exeter). The stiffest task set the locomotives in this direction was the ascent of Honiton bank; beginning just to the west of Axminster, this rises for 1½ miles at 1 in 100, then for 4½ miles at 1 in 80, and finally for ¾ mile at 1 in 132 through Honiton tunnel to the summit at the latter's western portal, 153½ miles from Waterloo.

At Salisbury, on the 1939 schedule of the 'Atlantic Coast Express', the rear coach, for Seaton, was detached and went forward with a stopping train that followed at 12.38pm. The main train left for the West at 12.31pm, and was booked to run the 75.8 miles to Sidmouth Junction in 83min. Here the Sidmouth and Exmouth coaches came off the rear of the train; a tank engine of the 0-4-4 type collected them and worked them to Tipton St Johns, continuing from there to Sidmouth with the Sidmouth coach, due at 2.23pm, while another 0-4-4 tank worked the other coach through

Budleigh Salterton to an arrival in Exmouth at 2.46pm. The express itself was booked to leave Sidmouth Junction at 1.58pm, and to run the 12.2 miles into Exeter Central in 14min. Arriving at 2.12pm, the 'Atlantic Coast Express' had come down from Waterloo in 3hr 12min.

Here a general break-up of the train occurred. The restaurant cars were detached from the rear, and the remaining coaches were divided into two parts. A Mogul backed on to the Ilfracombe and Torrington sections, and left with these coaches at 2.18pm, reaching Barnstaple Junction 62min later. Ten minutes before this, a Great Western Railway 'slow' from Taunton had put in an appearance at Barnstaple Junction with the through Ilfracombe coach off the 'Cornish Riviera Limited'; this the 'Atlantic Coast Express' added to its formation, while leaving the Torrington coach behind. From Barnstaple Junction, the Ilfracombe train then continued over some of the steepest main line gradients in Great Britain, climbing for $3\frac{1}{4}$ miles at 1 in 40 to Mortehoe, and finally dropping for $2\frac{1}{4}$ miles at 1 in 36 down into Ilfracombe. This popular coast resort, 226.5 miles from Waterloo, was reached at 4.06pm, 8min after the Torrington coach had arrived at its destination.

The three remaining portions of the 'Atlantic Coast Express' left Exeter in company at 2.23pm for Okehampton, usually with a three-coach corridor set added to the Waterloo-Plymouth coach. At Okehampton the Padstow and Bude coaches were detached for the journey over the North Cornwall line, and it was not until 5.37pm that the former ran into Padstow, 259.7 miles from Waterloo, after completing the longest daily through journey on Southern metals. The Bude coach, parting company with the Padstow portion at Halwill, reached Bude at 4.39pm. At Meldon Junction, where the Plymouth and Padstow lines separated to the west of Okehampton, after passing over a high lattice steel viaduct, the train attained the greatest altitude reached on the then Southern system, 950ft above sea level.

A striking feature of the working of the Plymouth portions of Southern trains from London was the way in which they almost boxed the compass in the course of their journeys. Through Exeter they ran for a short distance over GWR metals between St Davids station and Cowley Bridge junction, where trains from Waterloo were travelling due north; through North Road station at Plymouth, formerly joint GWR and SR property, they were running east; before reaching Plymouth Friary they had turned due west again. Moreover, twice in succession, both at Exeter St Davids and Plymouth North Road, they could meet the GWR expresses from Paddington to Plymouth travelling in the opposite direction! Up to World War 2, the Plymouth coach of the down 'Atlantic Coast Express' came to rest in Friary terminus, 234 miles from Waterloo, at 4.19pm.

In the height of the summer season, two daily down services were needed to carry the traffic, at 10.35am to Ilfracombe, Torrington, Bude and Padstow, and at 11am to Sidmouth, Exmouth and Plymouth. On Saturdays the two branched out into no fewer than *eight* complete restaurant car trains between 10.24am and 12.05pm — at 10.24 and 10.35am to Ilfracombe, 10.40am to Padstow, 10.54am to Bude, 11am to Plymouth, 11.45am to Sidmouth and Exmouth, 12 noon to Exeter, and 12.05pm to Salisbury and all stations from Axminster onwards. Similar arrangements were in force in the opposite direction.

The up winter working of the single 'Atlantic Coast Express' in 1939 involved departures from Padstow at 8.40am, Bude at 9.40am, and Plymouth Friary at 10.28am, joined at Okehampton and leaving there for Exeter at 11.26am. Exeter Central was reached at 12.12pm, 12min ahead of the Ilfracombe and Torrington sections, which had started at 10.30 and 10.28am respectively. Departure from Exeter was at 12.30pm, and from Sidmouth Junction, where the Exmouth and Sidmouth coaches came on, at 12.52pm. From here over the difficult gradients to Salisbury the allowance was only 84min for th 75.8 miles; and after stopping at Salisbury for 6min, the express finished with an 89min run over the 83.8 miles to Waterloo, arriving at 3.49pm.

As to locomotive power, until the middle of the war period it had been customary for some time to use 'Lord Nelson' four-cylinder 4-6-0s between Waterloo and Salisbury, and 'King Arthur' 4-6-0s between Salisbury and Exeter. The advent of the 'Merchant Navy' streamlined Pacifics, however, resulted in the taking over by these extremely capable locomotives of the Salisbury-Exeter workings in their entirety, and of the Waterloo-Salisbury workings also. The speeds run regularly by the 4-6-2s west of Salisbury were higher than those attained on any other British main line during the war, barely distinguishable from the speeds of peacetime. West of Exeter, Moguls shouldered the major proportion of the workings until the light 'West Country' Pacifics arrived to take over these duties.

During the war period, in common with other SR West of England expresses, the 'Atlantic Coast Express' stopped additionally at Woking; and long after the war had ended and the stop had been cut out, the increased 103min timing from Waterloo to Salisbury remained. Not until 1949 did it come down to 93min for the 83.7 miles, the up train being accelerated at the same time to make the run in 90min. But overall times of both workings were slower than before the war, particularly those of the up express, which as compared with prewar days, on the winter service, made additional stops at Axminster, Yeovil

Junction, Sherborne and Templecombe, and reached Waterloo at 4.20pm instead of 3.49pm. All the eight through portions from and to Waterloo once again had come into operation.

In the summer of 1952 a revolutionary speed-up of the Southern 'ACE' took place, not only bringing the train back to prewar times, but to times even faster than those booked in 1939, including the first run at over 60mph from start to stop to appear in the Southern Region timetable. The down train, leaving Waterloo at 11am, was booked over the 83.7 miles to Salisbury in 83min; then after 5min for station working and taking water (usually exceeded) came 80min for the 75.9 miles of very hard gradients to Sidmouth Junction, and, after a 3min stop there, 14min for the 12.2 miles to Exeter, reached at 2.06pm (public time 2.05pm). This, incidentally, beat the two-stop 11am from Paddington at that time by a clear half-hour! Arrivals were earlier than those before the war by 18min to Bude (4.21pm), 16min to Padstow (5.21pm), 6min to Exeter (2.06pm) and by smaller amounts to the other points served by through coaches.

Similarly in the reverse direction, all stops between Sidmouth Junction and Salisbury were cut out, bringing the arrival at Waterloo forward to 3.40 instead of 4.18pm; this included an easy booking of 18min from Exeter (12.30pm) to Sidmouth Junction (12.48-12.50pm); 79min from there to Salisbury (2.09-2.15pm), and 85min thence to Waterloo. In this direction the load was made up to 11 vehicles at Exeter (no Exmouth and Sidmouth coaches being attached at Sidmouth Junction), and 13 from Salisbury; going down the load was 12 (about 397 tons tare) from Waterloo, 11 (364 tons) from Salisbury, and nine (just under 300 tons) from Sidmouth Junction to Exeter.

The final phase was the most brilliant of all. From October 1961, times in both directions over the 83.8 miles between Waterloo and Salisbury were pared to 80min, but the most astonishing schedules were those over the 75.9 miles between Salisbury and Sidmouth Junction — 73min down and 74min up. Up to that time nothing as fast as this over comparable gradients had ever been scheduled in Great Britain, but the Bulleid Pacifics made light of these bookings, and gains on schedule were of constant occurrence. So, including Salisbury and Sidmouth Junction stops, the time of the 'Atlantic Coast Express' from Waterloo to Exeter Central came down finally to 2hr 56min, the fastest ever, and the 12.30pm from Exeter reached Waterloo at 3.28pm, in 2hr 58min.

But the 'ACE' was now rapidly approaching the end of its long and distinguished history. One by one the many through coaches were withdrawn until the Ilfracombe and Plymouth sections and the Exeter restaurant cars alone were left. And then in 1964 the Western Region took over the whole of the former Southern territory west of Salisbury. Western 'Warship' diesels replaced the Bulleid Pacifics for the working of the trains, not merely as far east as Salisbury, but right through to Waterloo. The expresses continued to run through between Waterloo and Exeter, though not beyond, and with the withdrawal of local services they acquired many additional stops in their schedules. The one train from Waterloo to have its journey cut short at Salisbury was the 11am down, the former 'Atlantic Coast Express'.

From Salisbury to Exeter much of the line was singled and the only branch retained was Exeter-Exmouth. Beyond Exeter local services at first ran to Okehampton, and to Barnstaple and Ilfracombe, although the only through London service for Ilfracombe was to and from Paddington. Later the Barnstaple-Ilfracombe section was closed and Ilfracombe was served by buses from Barnstaple. Okehampton also lost its passenger trains, although the line remained open to Meldon for traffic from the quarries. From Meldon to Bere Alston the old main line to Plymouth disappeared but the few remaining miles together with the branch to Gunnislake continued to be worked as a 'basic railway' providing a local service for Plymouth and Devonport.

The Waterloo-Exeter service continued, and gradually there were signs of reviving traffic. More travellers from south-west of London found it convenient to join the Exeter trains at Woking, while the Rail-Air link between Woking and Heathrow was a useful facility for passengers from the Salisbury/Andover area going further afield. Industrial development at Basingstoke also helped. As HSTs took over more West of England services on the Western Region, Class 50 diesel locomotives became available for the Waterloo-Exeter trains, on which Class 33s had succeeded the 'Warships' in October 1971, enabling Mk 2 stock with electric heating to be used. The advent of larger locomotives allowed accelerations of some 20min in the 1980 timetables, and at the same time more trains were put on between Waterloo and Salisbury. The 11.10am Waterloo-Exeter of 1980 may not have been quite the 'Atlantic Coast Express' of earlier years but it opened the new decade on a more hopeful note for what remained of the Southern's route to the West Country.

The Blackpool and Fylde Coast Express

Under the helpful stimulus of a well-known LMSR Vice-President who had a house near the popular resort of Blackpool, much was done after the grouping of the railways to improve the service between Euston and the Fylde coast. One of the trains put on in consequence was a morning express from Blackpool Central to Euston, giving passengers who so desired about four hours in London, with a swift and comfortable service back in the evening. Eventually these trains received the name 'Blackpool and Fylde Coast Express'.

The up service was fast. In the years before the outbreak of World War 2 it left Blackpool at 8.25am and called at the usual stations round the coast — Blackpool South, St Annes, Ansdell, and Lytham — from which it ran to Preston, reached at 9.08am. After standing 5min here, it made the run of 51 miles to Crewe in 59min, and then followed a high-speed break over the 158.1 miles from Crewe to Euston in 154min, at 61.6mph. Euston was reached at 12.50pm and the time from Blackpool was thus 4hr 25min. No additional sections were run in this direction, and a formation of seven or eight bogies, including restaurant cars, usually sufficed.

Going down, the 'Blackpool and Fylde Coast Express' had a heavier load and a more leisurely journey. Leaving Euston at 5.10pm, the engine had 165min at its disposal on the non-stop run to Crewe, and 40min for the 36 miles from there to Wigan, reached at 8.40pm. The stop here was to detach through coaches for Blackburn, Burnley and Colne, taken on by a most unusual route through Chorley, which was, however, the original LNWR route from Euston to Blackburn; Colne was reached at 10.21pm. All other through Colne services were routed via Manchester.

Meantime the express from London, Leaving Wigan at 8.44pm, was into Preston by 9.05pm, and here a second through section was detached, destined for Barrow-in-Furness; making its way along the main line to Carnforth, and then round the coast, this portion was into Barrow by 10.45pm. The main train, leaving Preston at 9.10pm, made the usual coastal stops and reached Blackpool Central at 9.57pm. This was a through locomotive working between London and Blackpool, usually with a 'Patriot' or 'Jubilee' 4-6-0, and run alternately by London and Blackpool engines and men; but whereas the Blackpool men obtained quite a pleasant turn-round time in London, their London colleagues were less fortunate, as their Blackpool arrival was too late in the evening for them to sample many of the attractions of this lively resort!

After the war, by October 1946, a recognisable post-war version of the 'Blackpool and Fylde Coast Express' was once again in operation, with restaurant cars complete. The down train left Euston at 5.05pm and reached Blackpool Central at 10.24pm; coming up, the train got away from Blackpool at 8am, and was into Euston by 1.10pm — a journey 45min slower than before the war, though with a considerably heavier load. But it was no longer a 'titled train'.

Electrification from Euston and the closure of lines and stations was to change the whole pattern of service. Blackpool Central is no more, and the through London trains run to and from Blackpool North, giving connections at Kirkham & Wesham for St Annes, Ansdell, and Lytham. Business travellers start their journeys earlier than they did, perhaps conditioned by inter-continental air travel and changing time zones. There is now (1982) a fast morning service from Blackpool to Euston at 6.15am, arriving at 9.48. Even if the traveller delays his departure until 9.20 he is still at Euston at 1.10pm, only 20min later than by the 'Blackpool and Fylde Coast Express', with a full afternoon for business in London before catching the 6.05pm from Euston for a quick run home, reaching Blackpool North at 9.54.

The Blue Pullmans, Western Region

The former Great Western Railway had no particular love for Pullman cars. It is true that in May 1929 an experiment was tried with the introduction of Pullmans on the Transatlantic boat trains from Plymouth to Paddington, run in connection with the French Line steamers, and that in July of the same year an all-

Pullman train began to run between Paddington and Paignton — the 'Torquay Pullman'. Going down, it left Paddington at 11am, covered the 193.9 miles to Newton Abbot non-stop in 205min, and reached Torquay at 2.40 and Paignton at 2.50pm. On the up journey, starting from Paignton at 4.30 and Torquay at 4.40pm, it was back into Paddington by 8.30pm. But it had to compete with the forerunner of the 'Torbay Express', which ran at more convenient times for the patrons of this route and which required no supplementary fare. In consequence the Pullman never reached adequate patronage, and was withdrawn in 1930, as also were the cars from the boat trains. All the cars involved moved to the Southern Railway, some from then on working in Transatlantic boat trains between Southampton and Waterloo, and others finding employment in the 'Bournemouth Belle'.

Not until the summer of 1955, after the Great Western Railway had become swallowed up in the nationalised British Railways, did Pullman cars reappear on Western metals. And not, this time, as an attraction for holidaymakers, but in recognition of the fact that a business clientele favours this kind of comfort and service. So it was the growing industrial and commercial importance of South Wales that suggested the South Wales main line as a suitable venue for a new Pullman venture, this time destined not merely to be permanent, but eventually to justify a Pullman service three times daily in each direction. The first 'South Wales Pullman' was an eight-coach train of standard cars, in the Pullman chocolate-and-cream livery, steam-hauled in each direction by a 'Castle' class 4-6-0. It left Paddington at 9.55am, ran non-stop to Newport and with halts after that at Cardiff and Port Talbot reached Swansea at 2pm. The return journey was begun at 4.35pm, and with the same stops Paddington was reached at 8.45pm.

Five years then elapsed before further Pullman train sets made their appearance at Paddington. By 1960 diesel traction was well under way in Great Britain, and three new trains, instead of being locomotive-hauled, had their diesel-electric power incorporated in the cars. Each of these Western Region trains comprised eight cars, first and second class, with diesel engines developing 2,000hp one service was to run between Paddington and Bristol and the other between Paddington and Wolverhampton. A distinctive livery was decided on for the new cars, of a brilliant blue in place of the former chocolate-and-cream shades. It was now realised that the more important business demand was to be brought up from the Provinces to the capital in the early morning, and to be taken back in the evening, rather than the other way round, and the trains were arranged accordingly.

First of the new train sets to take up service was the 'Bristol Pullman'. This left Temple Meads at 7.45am, and ran non-stop to London over the Badminton route, 117.65 miles in 110min. Instead of standing idle during the day, it then returned at 10.05am via Bath, running the 106.85 miles to Bath in 95min, and reaching Bristol at 12 noon. Thirty minutes later it was starting back to London, again making the run in 115min, and the final journey was from Paddington at 4.55pm, non-stop to Bristol via Badminton in 110min. Bath, however, was too important to be missed out on the up morning and down evening trips, and from mid-October the up Pullman started its day 5min earlier, and finished it 5min later, by reason of the diversion to the Bath route and a call there. It was a disappointment to many that the new Bristol service took longer on the journey than the 105min of the steam-hauled 'Bristolian', which by 1954 had been restored to its prewar schedule; the latter was certainly non-stop, but its point-to-point times were as fast as those of the Pullman.

It was equally disappointing to learn that the new 'Birmingham Pullman', the next to be introduced, was to take 5min over 2hr to run up to Paddington, with no more than two intermediate stops — one at Solihull to pick up residents living on the south side of the city, and the other at Leamington Spa. Wolverhampton patrons had to make an early start, at 7am; Birmingham Snow Hill was left at 7.30am, and with no less than 95min allowed for the 87.3 miles from Leamington the London terminus was reached at 9.35am, or at exactly the same time as the 'Bristol Pullman'. Indeed, on the first day of the new service the two trains most artistically dead-heated up the length of two adjacent arrival platforms at Paddington and came to a stand at precisely the same moment.

As with the Bristol train, the 'Birmingham Pullman' made a mid-day excursion as far as Snow Hill and back, and on the fastest timing scheduled up to that date over the former GWR route, 1hr 55min, but with only one intermediate stop, at Leamington. Leaving Paddington at 12.10pm the train reached Birmingham at 2.05pm, and with a quick turn round it was on its way back to London by 2.30pm, arriving at 4.25pm. Here there was an equally narrow turn-round time, for the final journey was begun at 4.50pm, Snow Hill being reached at 6.55 and Wolverhampton at 7.20pm.

In the following year, 1961, South Wales exchanged its steam-hauled Pullman train for one of the new 'Blue Pullman' diesel sets. For some time the former had been running an hour earlier in the down direction than when first introduced, leaving London at 8.50am, though the up working had been but little altered. But with the introduction of the new 8-car diesel train set in September 1961, as with the other WR 'Blue Pullmans' the working of the 'South Wales Pullman' was completely reversed. The new train started out of Swansea bright and early at 6.40am, added Bridgend to the Neath and Port Talbot stops, and after the customary halts at Cardiff and Newport ran the 133.4 miles from the latter town to Paddington in 127min, arriving at 10.15am. The down journey was begun at 4.55pm, and with a 127min timing to Newport and the same stops as coming up, Swansea was reached at 8.40pm. The 3hr 35min of the up journey was easily the fastest ever tabled between Swansea and London, and 35min quicker than that of the steam-hauled train.

In 1964 it was decided that just as with the other two 'Blue Pullmans' the 'South Wales Pullman' should no longer stand idle all day at Paddington, and that there was plenty of time available to make a midday run as far as Cardiff and back. So at 11am it started out on a non-stop timing of 122min to Newport, and reached Cardiff at 1.19pm; returning at 2.30pm, it was into London by 4.50pm, but this, of course, necessitated a later start of the final run, which was put back to 5.40pm, Swansea now being reached at 9.10pm. Later there were substantial accelerations. The Swansea start was made 15min later at 6.55am, and with a 2-hour run over the 133.4 miles from Newport the Pullman achieved a time of no more than 3hr 20min from Swansea to London; in the reverse direction the 5.40pm down took 3½hr. The 11am down 'Cardiff Pullman' and the 2.30pm up were allowed 2¼hr.

From the summer of 1967 a third 'Blue Pullman' began to serve South Wales, and was booked to make the run of 133.4 miles from Paddington to Newport in 113min, at an average of 70.8mph. It took its place at 9am in the sequence of even-hour departures from Paddington, and with stops at Newport, Cardiff, Bridgend and Neath was into Swansea by 12.20pm. It then provided an evening service from South Wales to London, at 4.20pm from Swansea, arriving at Paddington by 7.45pm. The set of 'Blue Pullmans' making the morning up and evening down runs, with the midday trip to Cardiff and back, covered no less than 672 miles each day.

Meantime various changes had taken place in the Bristol workings. With the introduction, in March 1967 of the full London Midland electric service between Euston and Birmingham, the service between Paddington, Birmingham and Wolverhampton was very severely pruned, and in the process Birmingham lost all its Pullman facilities. The only alteration that had been made in the 'Birmingham Pullman' workings up to the time of their disappearance was to put the midday down trip forward from 12.10pm to 10.10am, and that coming up from 2.30pm to 1pm out of Snow Hill. The release of the 'Blue Pullman' set, however, made possible the additional South Wales working and certain changes in the Bristol workings also.

Meanwhile the down midday 'Bristol Pullman' working had been changed, first from 10.05 to 10.45am out of Paddington; next came an alteration in the starting time to 12.45pm, with the introduction of a stop at Chippenham, and a fast time of 84min over this 94-mile stretch; the return from Bristol was at 3.15pm, and the Paddington arrival at 5.15pm, 30min before departure on the last down trip of the day. Later still, Reading was added as an intermediate stop.

In March 1967 yet another alteration took place in the midday working. The Paddington start went back to 10.45am, the Chippenham stop was cut out, and with Reading and Bath stops the booked time to Bristol became 2hr exactly. In the reverse direction, this way with a stop at Swindon as well as at Bath and Reading, the time went up to a rather indifferent 2hr 5min, though it must be added that all the main line times in the 1967 timetable were increased by an average of 5min or so because of delays likely to be experienced in the resignalling of Paddington station and its approaches.

Another change of note in 1967 concerned the morning and evening Paddington-Bristol 'Blue Pullman' workings. To such an extent had their patronage increased that with the help of the released 'Birmingham Pullmans' two six-car trains were made up, which were coupled to form a 12-car train on the 8.15am from Bristol, still stopping only at Bath and taking 1hr 50min to London. On arrival at Paddington the train was split into its two sections. One of these formed the 10.45am to Bristol. The other left at 12.15pm on an entirely new 60min run to Oxford — an experiment designed in particular to attract American visitors to the University city. Returning at 4.15pm, the 'Oxford Pullman' reached Paddington with a 30min margin for reunion with the other Bristol set, and the 12-car working back at 5.45pm to Bath and Bristol. The Oxford working was not a commercial success, however, and was discontinued in 1969 along with the other midday workings of the Pullman sets.

In 1968 the 'Bristol Pullman' had its time cut to 100min inclusive of the Bath stop, and when in 1972 a Chippenham stop was added the set had to cover the 94 miles from Paddington to Chippenham in 73min at an average speed of 77.3mph.

The end came for the 'Blue Pullmans' in 1973. Costs for maintaining the non-standard units were high and the introduction of air-conditioned stock with better riding qualities on other services blunted their competitiveness. All the trains were withdrawn.

The Bon Accord, The Grampian, The Granite City and The St Mungo

In 1905, as a result of spirited competition between the then Caledonian and North British Railways for the traffic between Glasgow and Edinburgh in the south, and Dundee and Aberdeen in the north, some magnificent new 12-wheeled 'Grampian Corridor' stock was introduced by the Caledonian for its principal services. This was formed into set trains; in general, four coaches worked between Glasgow and Aberdeen, with restaurant car; through coaches from Glasgow to Dundee, detached at Perth, were replaced there by through coaches from Edinburgh to Aberdeen. These morning and evening services both ways continued more or less unchanged, except for acceleration and the substitution of modern LMSR rolling stock, until the beginning of World War 2. Another pair of trains over the same route received the title 'Granite City' in 1906; but both names disappeared during World War 1.

In Caledonian days, the restaurant car catering was taken over by the Pullman Car Company, whose contract extended to 1933, well into the LMSR era; on its expiry, the LMSR bought the cars, and painted them in the LMSR crimson livery. Later on, standard LMSR cars of the latest type were substituted for the Pullman vehicles.

With the general outbreak of train naming on the LMSR, in 1933, the name 'Granite City' was revived; it was now given to the 10.05am express from Glasgow to Aberdeen, returning from the Granite City, as Aberdeen is often known, at 5.35 in the evening. As a result of acceleration, which eventually brought the Glasgow-Aberdeen time of the northbound train down to 3½hr, including eight intermediate stops in the 153 miles, some fairly tight point-to-point timings for the period were in force. For example, the 15.8 miles from Perth to Coupar Angus, with a steeply rising start, had to be run in 20min, the 16.7 miles from there to Forfar in 18min, and the 15.4 miles from Forfar to Bridge of Dun in 19min. Coming south, the 'Granite City' was expected to cover the 32.5 miles from Forfar to Perth in 35min; this train took 3hr 39min, reaching Buchanan Street Station in Glasgow at 9.14pm. It is of interest to recall that for many years the 5.30pm from Aberdeen (as it was then) ran round through Coatbridge into Glasgow Central Station, instead of into Buchanan Street.

These timings had to be maintained over a route with long and arduous gradients throughout its length, save only for the racing stretch between Perth and Forfar. Out of Buchanan Street there is a very steep climb of 2½ miles at 1 in 79-98 through St Rollox to Robroyston; between Cumbernauld and Larbert there are over 5 miles down at 1 in 98 to 1 in 128. Then from Stirling northwards the trains faced a 6½-mile climb mostly at 1 in 75-100 up to Kinbuck, with a corresponding seven-mile descent from Gleneagles northwards. From Bridge of Dun to Drumlithie, 10½ miles out of 17½ are uphill, followed by the steep 5-mile descent to and past Stonehaven; in addition to mounting the latter, southbound trains had the even worse start out of Aberdeen, beginning at 1 in 96, and continuing for 7 miles to milepost 234 beyond Newtonhill. From nearly all the principal starts — Glasgow, Stirling, Perth, Stonehaven and Aberdeen in particular — the engines were faced with steeply rising gradients, many of them lengthy and difficult.

During the last summer seasons before World War 1, some much more elaborate arrangements were brought into force over this route, and resulted both in the appearance in 1937 of two additional named trains and in the cutting of the Glasgow-Aberdeen time to the unprecedentedly low figure of 3hr flat. The trains concerned were the 'Bon Accord' and the 'St Mungo', strictly limited, because of their speed, to eight-coach formations, restaurant car included, weighing about 260 tons empty, and usually worked by 'Jubilee' 4-6-0 locomotives.

The northbound 'Bon Accord' went out of Buchanan Street at the winter 'Granite City's' time of 10.05am, and ran the difficult stretch of 63.2 miles non-stop to Perth in 77min. After a 5min halt there, it was allowed 76min for the 73.7 miles on to Stonehaven; the final scenic stretch of 16.1 miles round the rugged cliffs to Aberdeen was run in 21min, bringing the train into the Granite City at 1.05pm. After 2¼hr in Aberdeen, the 'Bon Accord' began the return journey at 3.20pm, and with the same stops reached Buchanan Street, Glasgow, at 6.20pm; the fastest run in this direction was over the 73.7 miles from Stonehaven to Perth in 76min. The 'St Mungo' began its working day at Aberdeen at 9.35 in the morning, and stopped at Forfar instead of Stonehaven, making a fast run over the 32.5 miles from there to Perth in 33 minutes. Reaching Glasgow at 12.35pm, it returned at 1.30pm, with the same stops and times on the northbound trip as the 'Bon Accord', and reached Aberdeen at 4.30pm. Neither the 'Bon Accord' nor the 'St Mungo' ran on Saturdays.

In the war timetables only the 'Granite City' workings survived, and without their names; the restaurant cars were continued up to the time of the general withdrawal. Scottish schedules in general suffered less than those in other parts of the country, and for a time certain point-to-point bookings of these trains were among the fastest wartime schedules in Great Britain. From Glasgow the northbound train continued to start at 10am, and was due in Aberdeen at 1.53pm; it returned at 5.30pm, reaching Buchanan Street at 9.37pm. Thus the overall timing was lengthened by 23min going north, and 28min coming south, over the normal peacetime figure. Restaurant cars returned on 1 October 1945.

In 1949 the three names were all revived, but two of them were transferred to other trains. The 10am from Buchanan Street and the 5.30pm from Aberdeen were still the 'Granite City'; but the old established 1.35pm from Glasgow to Aberdeen, with the 6.25am from Aberdeen to Glasgow, became the 'Bon Accord'; and the name 'St Mungo' was assumed by the 9.35am southbound and the 5pm northbound.

Since then the only changes of note have been accelerations. Buchanan Street terminus in Glasgow no longer exists; trains for the north start from Queen Street and use the former North British line up Cowlairs bank and as far as Greenhill Upper Junction, just beyond where this line crosses the main line from Carlisle to Aberdeen; here they diverge and run down to join the latter at Greenhill Lower Junction. Morning and evening 3hr schedules were revived in 1962 between Glasgow and Aberdeen, and now with four intermediate stops — Stirling, Perth, Forfar and Stonehaven. Some very smart point-to-point timings were involved, such as 32min for the 32.5 miles from Perth to Forfar and 31min in the reverse direction; while 42min northbound and 43min southbound for the heavily-graded 41.2 miles between Perth and Stonehaven did not leave much to spare. The loads, however, were light, generally not exceeding seven coaches. For some years Gresley 'A4' Pacifics brought their distinguished careers practically to an end on these trains, but later on the all-conquering diesels took the service over.

In 1967 the historic Caledonian main line to Aberdeen was closed to passenger traffic throughout from Stanley, where the Highland line diverges north of Perth, to Kinnaber Junction, where the East Coast main line is joined north of Montrose. The Glasgow-Aberdeen trains were therefore diverted to run from Perth to Kinnaber by way of Dundee, Arbroath and Montrose, and while the two last-mentioned towns gained new fast connections with Perth, Stirling and Glasgow, Coupar Angus and Forfar were deprived altogether of passenger trains.

The diversion took effect from September 1967. The addition to the distance from Glasgow to Inverness was no more than from $152\frac{1}{4}$ to $154\frac{1}{2}$ miles, but extra time was needed because of some severe speed restrictions between Dundee and Kinnaber. One train only, the 7.20am (former 7.10) 'Bon Accord' from Aberdeen to Glasgow, retained its 3 hour timing, inclusive of stops at Stonehaven, Dundee, Perth, Dunblane and Stirling, with some very smart point-to-point times because a Class 40 2,000hp diesel was rostered for the service. For the 24.5 miles from Stonehaven to Montrose only 24min were allowed, and the 21.5 miles from Dundee to Perth had to be covered in 21min.

Going north, the 8.15am 'Grampian', with the same stops, was slowed from 3 to $3\frac{1}{4}$hr; the 10.10am 'Granite City', in this direction, now nameless, terminated at Dundee at 11.56am; the 1.10pm 'Bon Accord', return working of the 2,000hp diesel, made the run in 3hr 10min, 20min less than before, though with nine intermediate stops; while the 5.35pm 'St Mungo', formerly a 3 hour train, now required $3\frac{1}{4}$hr, or on Fridays, when the load had to be increased, $3\frac{1}{2}$hr.

The southbound 9.10am 'St Mungo' left Aberdeen 10 minutes earlier, and was slowed by 10min to 3hr 35min, with nine stops; the $3\frac{1}{2}$hr 'Grampian', starting at 1.05 instead of 1.15pm, was unchanged in overall time; while the southbound 5.15pm, still called the 'Granite City', was another of the trains calling only at Stonehaven, Dundee, Perth and Stirling, but required $3\frac{1}{4}$hr for the run, increased on Fridays to $3\frac{1}{2}$hr. A new record was established for the East Coast route by two trains in each direction daily passing through Arbroath and Montrose without deigning to stop.

More powerful diesels have improved on these timings, and a regular interval timetable was introduced in 1977. Departures are now at two-hourly intervals at 25min past the hour from Glasgow and 55min past from Aberdeen. Journey times average 2hr 53min. Names in such a uniform service are superfluous and tradition has not been strong enough to save this colourful quartet from oblivion.

The Bournemouth Belle

Before the days of corridor trains, the London & South Western Railway used to include Pullman cars in the formation of its principal trains between Waterloo and Bournemouth. These 'Pullman Drawing Room Cars', as they were called officially in the timetables, were for the use of first class passengers only, who were required, of course, to pay the Pullman supplement in addition. The cars were attached to the 12.30, 2.00, 4.50 and 6.55pm trains from Waterloo, and to four corresponding expresses in the up direction. The introduction of restaurant cars, however, brought to an end this limited use of Pullmans on LSWR metals, and they were not seen again on the Bournemouth service until the introduction in 1931 of the 'Bournemouth Belle' by the Southern Railway. For some time this ran on Sundays only, but from the beginning of 1936 it became a daily service. Originally it was non-stop to Bournemouth.

There was nothing exceptional about the 'Bournemouth Belle' timing, which was but slightly faster than the general standard for the Bournemouth service (other than the 'Bournemouth Limited'). The down 'Belle' was booked to leave Waterloo at 10.30am, thus bridging the gap in the hourly morning Bournemouth departures between 9.30 and 11.30am. It made its first stop at Southampton Central, 79.2 miles from Waterloo, in 87min, at 11.57am, and after standing there three minutes, was timed to cover the 28.8 miles on to Bournemouth Central in 36min, arriving at 12.36pm. A wait of three minutes sufficed here, and the short run on to Bournemouth West was completed at 12.47pm.

In the up direction, departure from Bournemouth West was at 4.35pm, and after a stop of two minutes, the 'Belle' left Bournemouth Central at 4.45pm. From here to Southampton Central the time allowed was 33min, and the up 'Belle' then had the fastest start-to-stop timing of the day from Southampton Central to Waterloo, 79.2 miles in 85min, thus making a two-hour run from Bournemouth Central, including the Southampton stop. Actually, however, the working timetable showed an arrival at Waterloo a minute later than the public time, at 6.46pm.

The normal formation of the 'Bournemouth Belle' varied from 7 to 10 Pullmans, according to the season of the year. Two of these were first class cars; the two end ones were third class brake cars and the remainder were thirds. A number of the cars were twelve-wheelers, and the others were eight-wheel vehicles; the tare weight of the train was from 270 to 390 tons, and the working timetable limited the maximum load to 400 tons.

For the haulage of the 'Belle', Nine Elms shed invariably turned out a 'Lord Nelson' class 4-cylinder 4-6-0 locomotive, which made the round trip from Waterloo to Bournemouth West and back without change, so covering 222.8 miles in the day. The 'Lord Nelsons' did well on this train, and as it had no connections or through portions to or from other destinations, good time was kept. The train was withdrawn on the outbreak of World War 2. But it returned in all its glory on 7 October 1946, now with a 'Merchant Navy' Pacific at the head, and with ten Pullmans in the formation daily. Moreover, the fast prewar timings were restored, of 2hr 5min down and 2hr up between Waterloo and Bournemouth Central, both including the stop at Southampton Central. For a time, notwithstanding the use of 'Merchant Navy' Pacifics, the timings were eased to 2hr 10min down and 2hr 5min up, though eventually two-hour timings were restored in both directions between Waterloo and Bournemouth Central, and so remained until the decelerations caused by work on the electrification of this main line.

In its final years the load of the train often mounted to twelve Pullman cars, sometimes with a bogie brake in addition, and made this the heaviest passenger train working on the Western main lines of the SR. I once timed No 35002 *Union Castle*, a rebuilt 'Merchant Navy' Pacific, with a 72-axle 'Bournemouth Belle' weighing gross fully 565 tons, when the engine kept up a steady 56mph up the long 1 in 250 gradient past Winchester, touched 88mph after Woking, would have run the 79.2 miles from Southampton Central to Waterloo comfortably in 75min but for signal delays inwards from Earlsfield. Today Bournemouth West, the former terminal of the 'Bournemouth Belle', no longer exists, and with the introduction of the electrified service in the summer of 1967 the 'Belle' itself went out of existence also.

The Brighton Belle

About the beginning of the century, the popularity of Pullman accommodation on the London, Brighton & South Coast Railway suggested that something in the nature of a 'Pullman Excursion' between London and Brighton on Sundays would be a successful venture. So it proved; and in 1899 the 'Brighton Sunday Pullman Limited' came into all-the-year-round service. First class cars only were used, flanked at each end by six-wheel brakes provided specially with clerestory roofs to match the Pullman stock. Departure from Victoria was at 11am and 60min were allowed for the 51-mile run.

Billinton's 4-4-0 locomotives had come into use, and it was one of these, No 70 *Holyrood*, that was used on the occasion of a special test run on 26 July 1903. On this journey, the schedule was cut to 48min 41sec and a maximum speed of 90mph was reached at Haywards Heath. Coming back in the evening, *Holyrood* made a start-to-stop time of 50min 21sec. But these runs, remarkable as they were in relation to the modest dimensions of the locomotive used, were not followed by any regular acceleration of the express.

The success of the Sunday 'Pullman Limited' prompted the idea that it might be expanded to a daily service, and by November 1908 this materialised. A train of seven new 12-wheel cars was specially built, and received the attractive name of 'Southern Belle'. So that it might be put to adequate use, shortly after its introduction the service was doubled; the 'Southern Belle' went out of Victoria at 11am, and returned from Brighton at 12.20pm, so being back in London at 1.20pm; then it made a second trip to the coast at 3.10pm, and a final journey to Victoria at 5.45pm from Brighton — a total of 204 miles each day, covered in exactly four hours. For the weekday services, which like the Sunday services were still first class only, four cars often sufficed, but the number was increased at week-ends and on Sundays, when three trips in each direction were made. By now the Marsh Atlantics had appeared on the LB&SCR, and these frequently hauled the train, or the highly efficient 'I3' 4-4-2 superheater tanks, interspersed at times with 4-4-0 tender engines.

For some years third class coaches were run with the Pullmans on the midday workings; but after the formation of the Southern Railway it was decided that the 'Southern Belle' should include third class Pullmans with the first class cars in the formation of the train. This change entailed a considerable increase in weight, and shortly before electrification it was not unusual, at summer week-ends, for the 'Belle' to total as many as eleven or even twelve Pullmans, with a gross weight of fully 400 tons. Such a load provided quite a tough locomotive task, but in addition to the big Brighton 4-6-4 tanks, Grouping had introduced more powerful locomotives to the Brighton line, particularly the 4-6-0 'King Arthurs', so that the 60-minute schedule could still be observed. By now, also, as another 'Belle' had come into service on the Southern Railway, the 'Southern Belle' had had its name changed to the rather less euphonious 'Brighton Belle'.

The steam-hauled 'Southern Belle' made its last run on 31 December 1932. On the following day its place was taken by a brand-new electric train, which was distinguished by incorporating the only motor-driven Pullman cars in the world. The 'Brighton Belle' electric stock was in units of five cars, usually run in pairs, and thus making a ten-car all-Pullman train. Every day the 'Brighton Belle' now covered 306 miles by making three journeys in each direction, at 11am, 3pm, and 7pm from Victoria, and at 1.25pm 5.25pm, and 9.25pm from Brighton, but on Sundays the 3pm down and 1.25pm up workings were replaced by ordinary corridor sets with Pullmans included, instead of the all-Pullman train.

The 'Brighton Belle' was withdrawn on the outbreak of World War 2; the five-car Pullman sets reappeared in October 1946, attached to standard SR corridor sets, but shortly afterwards all-Pullman workings came once again into operation. By the middle 1960s the 'Brighton Belle' had increased its daily journeys to four each way, totalling 408 miles. Going down these were at 11am, 3pm 7pm and 11pm from Victoria, and coming up at 9.25am, 1.25pm, 5.25pm and 8.25pm from Brighton.

With the new timetable introduced in July 1967 in common with the other 60min trains the Victoria-Brighton time of the 'Belle' was cut to 55min in each direction. While starting times going down remained unchanged, those coming up were now 9.25am, 1.45,

5.45 and 8.45pm. The 'Brighton Belle' and the 'Golden Arrow' were the only trains on the Southern Region which still provided Pullman facilities.

In 1968-9 the 'Belle' sets were renovated internally and also exchanged their traditional umber and cream livery for the BR Pullman livery of blue and grey, reflecting the acquisition by BR of the shares of the Pullman company. They did not wear their new colours for long. The cars were nearing the end of their useful life, for refurbishing internally could not disguise ageing mechanical parts that gave a less than perfect ride. There was a local protest movement in Brighton among the regular patrons of the train, including some show business personalities, when hints of withdrawal were heard but the decision had been taken and the Pullman sets made their last scheduled journeys on 30 April 1972.

The Bristolian

To mark the centenary of the opening in 1835 of the Great Western main line between Paddington and Bristol, it was decided by the GWR management to put on a new express which would link the two cities in a shorter time than ever previously. There had been hopes that a schedule of 90min might have been tried, but eventually, in order that excessively high speed might not be necessary, a booking of 105min in each direction was brought into operation, 15min less than the previous best.

This required a slightly higher average speed on the down journey than on the up, for the down and the up trains took different routes. Brunel's original main line, 118.3 miles in length from Paddington to Temple Meads Station, Bristol, was used in the westbound direction, and the end-to-end average was thus 67.6mph; but on the up journey the train left Temple Meads by way of Stapleton Road, climbed the 1 in 75 of Ashley Hill bank (2¼ miles long), and from Filton Junction used the Badminton cut-off, which was opened in 1901, rejoining the older main line at Wootton Bassett. This reduced the distance to 117.6 miles, and the overall speed to 67.2mph. But because of the Ashley Hill bank, the slowing through Filton, and the long 1 in 300 climb to Badminton, the up journey was probably the harder of the two.

A seven-coach train sufficed for normal 'Bristolian' needs. This formation included two third class brakes, three composites, one third, and in the centre one of the latest buffet cars, with a counter along its full length, and pedestal seats for passengers taking refreshments. The coaches were of the latest wide type, with recessed end doors, and the weight of the seven-coach formation was 221 tons empty, or 235 tons with the normal passenger complement. In the first months of the 'Bristolian's' running, a 'King' class 4-6-0 was thought to be necessary, but it was soon found that the speed was well within the capacity of a 'Castle', and the working was turned over to the highly competent link of engines and crews at Old Oak Common shed that were responsible also for the working of the 'Cheltenham Flyer'.

Departure from Paddington was at 10am, and Bristol was reached at 11.45am. In the reverse direction, the 'Bristolian' left Temple Meads at 4.30pm, and was due in London at 6.15pm. This was probably the only express on Great Western metals which served two stations only — the starting point and the destination — without any intermediate stop. The down 'Bristolian' also could claim to have the most level main line in Britain on which to maintain its high speed.

When Brunel engineered his original line between Paddington and Bristol, by using the Thames Valley as far as Didcot, and curving across the flat country between there and Wootton Bassett, he contrived to keep his maximum steepness of gradient down to 1 in 754, and for the major part of the distance to work to nothing steeper than 1 in 1,320. West of Wootton Bassett he dropped down Dauntsey bank with 1½ miles at 1 in 100; and from Corsham he cut through to the Avon valley by means of the Box tunnel, with 1¾ miles down at 1 in 100 and ¾ mile at 1 in 120; but both these gradients are in favour of down trains, so that the down 'Bristolian' had no hindrance to speed whatever, other than the severe service slack through Bath. It was booked to pass Swindon, 77.3 miles, in 66½min. The fastest part of the journey was between Slough and Chippenham, a distance of 75.5 miles for which the timetable allowed only 61min; this entailed an average speed of 74.3mph.

On the up journey, after negotiating the gradients and slacks of the Badminton route to which reference has been made earlier, the train was allowed 62min from passing Swindon to Paddington, which called for roughly the same speeds as those of the 'Cheltenham Flyer'. Coming up, the fastest stretch was from Badminton to Southall, 91 miles allowed only 71min for an average of all but 77mph. The 'Bristolian' was withdrawn on the outbreak of war, and up to the winter of 1952-1953 no faster timing than 2hr 10min between Paddington and Bristol had appeared in the Western Region timetable.

But acceleration back to the old standards soon began, and by 1954 the 105-minute schedule in both directions between Paddington and Bristol had been restored. Five years later we had the electrifying announcement that the time was to be cut to 100min both ways, so requiring a start-to-stop average of 71mph going down and 70.6mph on the return journey. By this time the Western Region's 'Warship' diesel-hydraulic locomotives were available, and on the opening day of the summer service No D805 *Benbow*, with an 8-coach train of 300 tons gross, whirled us down to Bristol in 93min 48sec, or in 91min net, the latter representing a net average speed of 78mph from start to stop. However, shortly before this the double-chimney 4-6-0 *Drysllwyn Castle* had made the up run in 93min 50sec with steam power, so that such a timing would have had no terrors for a 'Castle' either. But the 100-minute schedule proved to be no more than a flash in the pan, and by the winter of 1959 the 'Bristolian' was back to its 105-minute timing once again.

So matters continued until the Western Region timetable revolution of 1961. In the summer of that year the Paddington-Bristol service was put on to an even-interval basis, with all the trains without exception, the 'Bristolian' among their number, calling at Bath, and as the loading of the train from now on might be increased to ten or eleven coaches, it was unhappy news that the schedule was to be increased by no less than 14min in each direction, to 119min.

By this time the more intensive use of rolling stock had led to the formations of named trains being used on other services as well. Removing and replacing nameboards had become a nuisance, and in June 1965 the 'Bristolian' lost its name. In April 1966 the 8.45am from Paddington to Bristol and the 4.15pm return train began to be worked by pairs of Class 37 diesel-electric locomotives specially geared for high speed and were given a 105min schedule with the Bath stop included. This was not an economic use of motive power and the duty was soon taken over by 'Western' class diesel-hydraulics. The train was now far heavier than formerly, particularly coming up, when the diesel had to handle a 12-coach load of 425 tons tare and 450 tons or so gross. In the summer of 1967 the times were eased by 5min both ways to allow for delays during resignalling at Paddington and in the Bristol area.

A new station called Bristol North with adequate parking space for cars was opened in 1972. The name was later changed to Bristol Parkway as being more representative of the new concept of encouraging motorists making long journeys to drive to a railhead and travel most of the distance by train. Bristol Parkway is on the line from Wootton Bassett via Badminton and several Bristol trains were rerouted to serve it. After Parkway they branched south at Stoke Gifford Junction to reach Temple Meads via Filton and Stapleton Road. Among the diverted services were the 8.40am from Paddington and the 4.40pm from Bristol, for both of which the 'Bristolian' title was revived. The time including the Parkway stop was 105min.

In its final years the 'Bristolian' was formed of air-conditioned and electrically-heated Mk 2d stock. Class 47s and Class 50s equipped to provide the necessary supplies took over from the 'Western' class diesel-hydraulics until they, too, were displaced by HSTs in the autumn of 1976 and the 'Bristolian' was no more.

It may be added that in 1950 another train over this route received a name, the 'Merchant Venturer'. This was the 11.15am from Paddington to Bath and Bristol, returning at 5.25pm. It was a train of less distinction than the 'Bristolian', but eventually graduated to a run at just over a mile-a-minute between Paddington and Bath, 106min each way for the 106.9 miles. In the general timetable reorganisation of 1965, however, the title 'Merchant Venturer' was withdrawn from both these trains.

The Caledonian

In the summer of 1957 the London Midland and Scottish Regions, following the success of the East Coast 'Talisman' introduced in the previous year, decided to revive a high speed service between Euston and Glasgow somewhat resembling the prewar 'Coronation Scot', but without any supplementary fare. The latter had left both London and Glasgow at 1.30pm, but with the new train a departure time in the down direction like that of the 'Talisman' was planned, at 4.15pm. Coming up, the train's course was to be at an entirely new time, 8.30am from Glasgow Central. As with the 'Coronation Scot', there would be one intermediate stop only, at Carlisle. The overall time of 6hr 40min was 10min more than the 'Coronation Scot' allowance, though the load of the new 1957 train was lighter — eight coaches of 264 tons as compared with nine of 297 tons. Between Euston and Carlisle the 'Duchess' Pacifics were allowed 291min for the 299.1 miles in each direction, for a start-to-stop average of 61.7mph, and the schedule for the 102.3 miles between Carlisle and Glasgow was 107 minutes each way.

In September 1957 a demonstration run was made with the up train from Carlisle to Euston, and it was very unfortunate that no advance information of what was planned was given to any competent recorder of locomotive performance; as a result, only the scantiest details became available afterwards as to what actually happened. The engine was 4-6-2 No 46244 *King George VI*, and with the normal eight-coach formation the gross load was 265 tons. No outstanding effort was made as far south as Crewe, but from there to Euston No 46244 tied with the 119min for the 158.1 miles that had been achieved twenty years before with an almost identical load by No 6220 *Coronation* on the Press trip of the 'Coronation Scot'. On this occasion the 'Caledonian' put in an appearance at Euston 37min ahead of time, the line having been kept clear throughout. But no acceleration of the train followed this startling performance.

In the summer of 1958, again following the lead of the Eastern, North Eastern and Scottish Regions, which had duplicated their 'Talisman' service between King's Cross and Edinburgh, the London Midland and Scottish Regions decided to do the same. They therefore put on a down morning 'Caledonian' from Euston at 7.45am, and a return train at 4pm from Glasgow. In the down direction a stop at Crewe was introduced in addition to Carlisle, doubtless in the hope of picking up traffic from the Midlands; the up express, with the same intent, called at Stafford in addition to Carlisle. From Euston the time allowed for the 158.1 miles to Crewe was 147min; coming up, the 2hr schedule for the 133.6 miles up from Stafford, averaging 66.8mph, was the fastest on the London Midland Region at that time. Overall, both expresses were allowed $6\frac{3}{4}$hr. The trains became known as the 'Morning Caledonian' and the 'Afternoon Caledonian' respectively. But the new 'Caledonian' workings failed to attract patronage, and within less than a year both had been withdrawn.

By 1962 the older 'Caledonians' had begun to acquire additional stops. From the summer of that year the down train, now leaving as early as 3.35pm — all expresses over this main line by now had been considerably decelerated because of engineering slacks due to electrification — was stopping at Stafford and not due in Glasgow till 11pm. The up morning 'Caledonian' had added both Preston and Stafford stops to its Carlisle halt, and was due in Euston at 3.55pm. Both trains were therefore taking 7hr 25min overall, $\frac{3}{4}$hr longer than when they were first put on. By the winter of 1963 the stops of the down train had increased to four — Stafford, Crewe, Wigan and Carlisle — but now with the help of diesel power Glasgow was being reached in $7\frac{1}{4}$hr. In the autumn of 1964, however, with the progressive reduction of train services between Euston and Crewe until the electrification work was completed, the 'Caledonians' in each direction disappeared altogether, and the name has not been revived since.

When at last the electric timetable was introduced, in April 1966, the Anglo-Scottish service by the West Coast route was transformed. Among the four day trains from Euston to Glasgow there was no counterpart of the down 'Morning Caledonian' that had such a brief history, but there was a departure at 4.05pm, similar to that of the afternoon down train; this express with electric haulage covered the 158.1 miles to Crewe non-stop in 121min, and after that, with a diesel at the head, called only at Wigan and Carlisle and reached Glasgow Central at 10.50pm — a time 5min slower than when the train was first put on in 1957. Coming up, the late afternoon up departure was also revived; an express at 4.15pm stopped at Carlisle, Preston, Crewe and Watford Junction, and arrived at 10.55pm. The allowance of $103\frac{1}{2}$min for the Crewe-Watford stage entailed a start-to-stop average of 81.5mph.

When the 1966 timetables were introduced, electrification through to Glasgow was being strongly urged but the work was not authorised until 1970. With its completion the timetables of 1974 brought in an LMR Anglo-Scottish service that eclipsed everything that had gone before, the average journey time between Euston and Glasgow coming down to a little over five hours.

The Cambrian Coast Express

In the summer of 1910 the Great Western Railway completed the last of four important cut-off routes by which the worst detours made by the original main lines from Paddington were eliminated. This was the main line from Paddington to the North. The original route, via Didcot and Oxford, following the Thames Valley, was almost perfect in its absence of gradients as far as Leamington Spa; but a distance of 129¼ miles from Paddington to Birmingham hampered the GWR considerably in competing with the then London & North Western Railway, with its 113-mile route, for the traffic from London to Birmingham and beyond. It was planned, therefore, to make a much more direct line from London to Banbury, and in the task the Great Western found an unexpected ally.

The Great Central Railway in 1899 had opened its London Extension into Marylebone terminus, to which access was obtained by using the then Metropolitan line from Quainton Road Junction, north of Aylesbury, to Harrow; from Harrow into Marylebone the GCR had independent tracks. But the Great Central soon found itself hampered both by the extremely heavy gradients and the dense occupation of the Metropolitan line; the latter affected chiefly the express passenger services, whereas the gradients severely limited the freight train loads. Consequently the Great Western and Great Central companies combined to build a new joint line, the one to shorten its distance and the other to ease its gradients to the North.

The project involved the construction of no less than 59 route-miles of new line. No existing route was used other than that of the GWR single-line branch from Maidenhead to Oxford via Thame; the course of this was followed roughly from High Wycombe to Princes Risborough, but actually complete reconstruction and realignment with doubling of the track were needed to adapt the earlier branch for high speed passenger work, so that to all intents and purposes this eight miles formed part of the new construction.

Of the whole line the portion actually joint — later, of course, between the Great Western and London & North Eastern Railways — was the 32¾ miles from Northolt Junction through High Wycombe and Princes Risborough to Ashendon Junction. Connecting with this, the GCR built a spur 6½ miles long from Neasden to Northolt, with the down line making a burrowing junction at Northolt, and another line 6 miles long from Ashendon to the company's existing main line at Grendon Underwood Junction, 9 miles north of Aylesbury. The new Great Western connections were from Old Oak Common West Junction, 3 miles out of Paddington, to Northolt (7 miles), with a spur from West Ealing to Greenford, and from Ashendon for 18¼ miles through Bicester to Aynho Junction, 5 miles south of Banbury. There was a flyover for the up GWR Bicester line at Ashendon, and for the down line at Aynho.

Until the opening of the Wycombe and Bicester route to Birmingham and the North in July 1910, the GWR had never ventured a shorter time than 2hr 17min for its 129¼ miles between Paddington and Birmingham, and no more than four trains made the journey in 2hr 20min or less. But with the distance cut to 110½ miles, the GWR immediately put into operation a series of two-hour trains in each direction, equalling the current London & North Western times, and over a considerably more difficult route. Considerable use was made of slip coaches, in order to avoid as many intermediate stops as possible; at different periods Princes Risborough, Bicester, Banbury, Leamington and Knowle were all served by various 'slips' going north, the last-mentioned in order to set down residents in the southern suburbs of Birmingham.

The principal destinations of northbound trains from Paddington was Birkenhead, though some of the Birmingham two-hour trains stopped short at Shrewsbury, and portions of them were detached at Wolverhampton. But the Bicester cut-off was also of considerable value to the Welsh coast resorts on Cardigan Bay, and in particular to Aberystwyth, reached by way of Shrewsbury, the then GW & LNWR joint line to Buttington, and what was the Cambrian Railways from there onwards through Welshpool and Machynlleth. From the beginning of 1923 the Cambrian became the property of the Great Western, and development of this seaside traffic soon began.

But before this date, in July 1921, the precursor of the 'Cambrian Coast Express' had been put into operation, as a restaurant car train from Paddington at

9.50am for Aberystwyth, Barmouth and Pwllheli, on every weekday during the summer season. By 1922 the start had been altered to 10.15am, and the train was travelling by way of Ealing, to pick up passengers at Ealing Broadway, and rejoining the Birmingham main line at Greenford. In 1923, when the GWR was fighting the LMSR strongly for the traffic between London, Shrewsbury, Chester and Birkenhead, the 10.20am from Paddington, as it was now, had become a Birkenhead express, non-stop to Birmingham in two hours, with an Aberystwyth portion detached at Snow Hill. The year 1924 saw the introduction of systematic departure times from Paddington, and the starting time was changed to 10.10am, thus splitting up the interval between the 9.10 and 11.10 Birkenhead departures. During these years departure of the up train from Aberystwyth had been at or about 12 noon.

The first appearance of the name 'Cambrian Coast Express' was in 1927, from which time this became the official title of the train; but by now the express, still leaving Paddington at 10.10am during the summer months, had become a Friday and Saturday working only. In the last summer before the outbreak of World War 2 the starting time from London had moved back to the 10.20am of 1923, while the working was restricted to Saturdays only. The 87.3 miles to Leamington were run in the fast time of 90½min, and after a stop of 3min there, 26½min were allowed for the 23.3 miles on to Birmingham, where the arrival at Snow Hill was at 12.20pm. The usual 19min for the difficult 12.4 miles to Wolverhampton brought the 'Cambrian Coast Express' into that town at 12.44pm.

Here the 'Castle' 4-6-0 which had brought the train from London was exchanged for motive power more suited to the light track and bridges of the Cambrian line — either one or two 'Duke' 4-4-0 locomotives, or latterly one of the 'Manor' 5ft 8in 4-6-0 engines, which were now permitted to run over the route. This engine change at Wolverhampton was necessary because the train avoided Shrewsbury, and used the Abbey Foregate curve in order to make a non-stop run from Wolverhampton to Welshpool, covering the 49.7 miles in 71½min. The remaining stops were at Machynlleth, Dovey Junction and Borth, and Aberystwyth was reached at 3.55pm. The up train now left the popular Welsh resort at 10am, made the same stops as on the down journey, with a conditional halt in addition at Newtown, and reached Wolverhampton, for the change of engine, at 1.28pm. After 7min there, and a 19min run to Birmingham, the 'Cambrian Coast Express' was ready to take its place at 2pm as one of the hourly departures for Paddington, calling at Leamington from 2.25 to 2.28pm, and due in London at 4pm. The up run thus took 25min longer than the down. The total distance was 234¾ miles.

There is little need to stress the difficulty of the running west of Welshpool. Much of the route is single track, and the gradients are very trying, especially the climb to Talerddig summit, between Moat Lane and Machynlleth, where the line is 693ft above sea level. From the Aberystwyth direction the ascent begins 3 miles from Machynlleth, and is unbroken for 10½ miles, finishing with 3¼ miles at 1 in 52 from Llanbrynmair to the top. From the east the difficulty is not so great, and is confined to short stretches at 1 in 71 and 1 in 80. There are also 6½ miles of 1 in 75 ups-and-downs between Borth and Aberystwyth. The locomotive or locomotives hauling the 'Cambrian Coast Express' over the 11¾ miles between Wolverhampton and Aberystwyth thus had quite a tough task before them.

Some of the most brilliant locomotive work on the entire Great Western system was done on the Birmingham two-hour trains. When the service began in 1910 the most powerful locomotives available were 2-cylinder 'Saint' and 4-cylinder 'Star' class 4-6-0s; from 1923 onwards the 'Castles' began to give much-needed relief, and it was not long after the introduction in 1927 of the 'Kings' that these, the most powerful express passenger class on the GWR, were drafted to the Birmingham route. From then on a number of these engines were stationed at Stafford Road shed, Wolverhampton, for this purpose, and shared the trains with 'Kings' stationed at Old Oak Common, and with occasional 'Castles'.

As compared with the LMSR, which had little or no difficulty other than the start out of Euston, GWR drivers en route to Birmingham had to reduce speed at Old Oak Common West Junction, High Wycombe and Leamington, and less severely at Ashendon and Aynho Junctions, and to master some long climbs, such as 7 miles at 1 in 175-264 from Denham; 5 miles at 1 in 179 to 1 in 164 past West Wycombe; 5½ miles at 1 in 200 past Bicester; and, worst of all, a bank which includes 3½ miles averaging 1 in 110 past Warwick up to Hatton. For a short time between the wars a 'Shakespeare Express' ran between Paddington and Stratford-on-Avon by this route, leaving the main line at Hatton. In 1951, the Festival of Britain year, the 10.10am to Wolverhampton and 7.50pm from Birmingham conveyed through coaches to and from Stratford-on-Avon and were named the 'William Shakespeare'.

There were correspondingly arduous grades on the up journey, all of which had to be covered at the high average speeds required by the two-hour schedules. Except for Hatton bank, most of the long inclines were surmounted regularly by the two-hour trains at speeds of over 50mph, even with trains up to 400 tons; and maximum speeds of 80 to 90mph were common north of Princes Risborough and approaching Leamington on the down journey, and near Warwick, Bicester and Denham coming up.

In the first summer after the war there was a revival of the Saturday 'Cambrian Coast Express' working, though without any distinctive name, and again on Saturdays only. The train left Paddington at 10.10am, and made the only non-stop run of the day to Birmingham, with an allowance of $2\frac{1}{4}$hr; with the same stops as before the war, and also Newtown in each direction, Aberystwyth was reached at 4.35pm. In the reverse direction, leaving Aberystwyth at 9.30am, the express called additionally at Leamington Spa, and reached Paddington at 4.10pm. By 1950 the down train was starting at 10.50am, and reaching Aberystywth at 5.15pm, but the up times remained unchanged.

In October 1950 another 'titled train' made its appearance on the Paddington-Birmingham main line, running daily. Since the war the 9.10am down Birkenhead express had become so popular that a regular relief train was run from Paddington at 9am, except on Saturdays, for Birmingham and Wolverhampton. This express, titled the 'Inter-City', could afford to miss Leamington, as the 9.10am down carried the Leamington traffic; though like the 9.10am, the 9am halted at High Wycombe to pick up passengers. It was due in Snow Hill, Birmingham, at 11.10am — this 130min was the nearest reached up till then to the prewar two hours — and in Wolverhampton at 11.35am. The stock, title included, returned from Wolverhampton at 4.25pm and Birmingham at 4.50pm; in this direction stops were made at both Leamington and High Wyucombe, and the 'Inter-City' was back in Paddington at 7.05pm.

By 1954 the down 'Inter-City' had become a two-hour train to Birmingham, and in the same year the 'Cambrian Coast Express', to which the name had been restored in 1951, became a daily two-hour working to Birmingham and resumed its 1924 start at 10.10am out of Paddington. Banbury instead of Leamington was now the only intermediate stop on this first stage; after Wolverhampton, instead of a non-stop run to Welshpool, the express halted at Shrewsbury, reversing there, and Aberystwyth was reached at 4.05pm, in just under 6hr from London. The train included a restaurant car throughout to Shrewsbury, and through coaches for Barmouth and Pwllheli were detached at Machynlleth. The up journey, starting at 11.15am, was less speedy by 45min, for the train stopped at all stations to Welshpool; but from Snow Hill, Birmingham, it took its place at 4pm in the hourly sequence of departures for Paddington, where 6pm was the scheduled arrival.

In 1963 the Paddington-Birmingham-Wolverhampton service underwent a complete revolution. This was due to the diversion of practically the whole of the London Midland Region Birmingham service to the Western Region, in order to relieve the former's main line to the utmost degree possible during the work of electrification. From that date, therefore, the WR for four years was to operate an hourly service of express trains throughout the day, loading in many cases up to 12, 13 and even 14 vehicles — a haulage proposition that this route had never had to face previously. At first the trains continued to be hauled by 'King' 4-6-0s, and with intermediate stops two-hour schedules between Paddington and Birmingham were very difficult to arrange; not until the advent of the 2,700hp 'Western' diesels, and later of the 2,750hp Brush Type 4 locomotives, did two-hour bookings reappear on an extensive scale, and some even in under two hours. The 2.10pm from Paddington, indeed, was booked non-stop over the 110.6 miles in 110min — the shortest time between London and Birmingham tabled by either route up to that time. The 'Inter-City' now lost its name.

In the final phase the only remaining 'titled train' over this route, apart from the Pullmans, was the 'Cambrian Coast Express'. After being displaced by the midday Pullman from its 10.10am departure in the down direction, the train became the 11.10am down, calling at Banbury, Leamington, Birmingham and Wolverhampton to Shrewsbury, and at principal stations from there to Aberystwyth, reached in exactly 6hr from Paddington. The return journey, begun at 9.45am, formed the 2pm from Birmingham, with a two-hour run to London including Leamington and Banbury stops. A portion of the down train, including the restaurant car, now came off at Wolverhampton, and as the stock of this express had to form the very popular 5.10pm from Paddington to the North, the load was made up daily at Wolverhampton to 14 coaches, with a gross weight of fully 500 tons — an exacting task of haulage indeed.

This was the end, not merely of the 'Cambrian Coast Express' but also of all but a limited express service, with numerous intermediate stops between Paddington and Birmingham. And not even to and from Snow Hill, for from March 1967 the trains from Paddington were diverted to New Street. As to Aberystwyth, a through service to and from London was confined to Saturdays in summer and was provided no longer from Paddington, but from Euston via Wolverhampton and Shrewsbury.

The Cambridge Buffet Expresses

In May 1932 a remarkable experiment was inaugurated by the LNER. It was realised that additional traffic might be created between London and Cambridge if there were a better train service; but the route principally used, to and from Liverpool Street, was so congested and difficult at the London end as to constitute a serious difficulty. It was therefore decided that an attempt should be made to popularise the slightly longer route between Cambridge and King's Cross; and for this purpose five new expresses were put on in each direction.

Each one included third class corridor coaches with armrests dividing the seats into three — a novelty at that time — and an open car with buffet counter at one end and seating for those taking meals or refreshments. Intermediate stops were made in each direction at Welwyn Garden City and Letchworth — hence the words 'Garden Cities' in the titles of these trains — and at Hitchin. At first the times were fixed at 82min down and 77min up, but the following year saw these curtailed to 75 and 72min respectively.

Success was immediate. So much so, indeed, that in a very short time the original three-coach formations had doubled in length and at times the loads grew to nine or ten vehicles, in which event the locomotive work required became exceedingly difficult. Light-hearted Cambridge undergraduates soon found a much shorter soubriquet for the service than the official mouthful, 'Garden Cities and Cambridge Buffet Expresses'; it was, *tout court*, the 'Beer Trains'. By 1939 the King's Cross departures had stabilised at 9.35am, 12.40, 2.10, 8.10 and 11.40pm, with slight alterations on Saturdays. Coming up, the trains left Cambridge at 9.25am, 12.30, 3.30, 5.25 and 10.10pm.

Going down, the engines had to face the climb out of King's Cross, and then 8 miles at 1 in 200 up to Potters Bar, and to stop at Welwyn Garden City, 20.3 miles, in 25min. Next the 11.6 miles on to Hitchin, with a start on a 1 in 200 up grade, had to be completed in 14min. For the short run of 2.6 miles from Hitchin to Letchworth the allowance was 5½min; and the final 23.4 miles from Letchworth into Cambridge were allowed 28min, including the slack round the curve at Shepreth Branch Junction. Two of the trains were allowed 2min extra — all too little — for an additional stop at Royston.

Coming up, the junction slack above-mentioned, and the 7-mile climb from Meldreth to Ashwell (5 miles at between 1 in 100 and 1 in 183), made it hard going to reach Letchworth in 28½min; from there to Hitchin was allowed 5min. Hardest of all the point-to-point bookings in this direction, probably, was 14min for the 11.6 miles from Hitchin to Welwyn Garden City, for it began with 3½ miles up at 1 in 200. Then the last stage was a lightning run from Welwyn Garden City into King's Cross, allowed 22min only for the 20.3 miles, on which speed often rose well above the 80mph mark down from Potters Bar to Wood Green. In this direction also two trains had 2min extra for a stop at Royston.

A great variety of engines was used on these trains, including Great Northern 'C1' class Atlantics and an occasional 'C6' from the Great Central line; Great Eastern 'B12' and 'Sandringham' (B17) 4-6-0s; Great Eastern 'Claud Hamilton' 4-4-0s, and other classes at times. With the heavier loads the running on these expresses, which ceased to operate with the outbreak of war, was of outstanding quality. Soon after the war four of these trains were back in the timetable, with the simpler title 'Cambridge Buffet Express'. In line with the systematic ER departure scheme inaugurated in October, 1950, they left King's Cross at 9.05am, 12.05noon, 2.05 and 8.05pm, and returned at 9.10am, 12.10, 3.10 and 6.10pm. Several of the trains made additional stops, and as at that time speed between King's Cross and Hatfield was limited to 60mph, and there were also a number of restrictions between Hitchin and Cambridge, overall times were considerably eased out, to between 80 and 93min. Class B1 4-6-0s supplied most of the motive power, though B17 4-6-0s also took a substantial share.

By the 1960s the service was taken over by diesel power, chiefly Type 2 Brush A1A-A1A units, and although each train made five intermediate stops — at Welwyn Garden City, Stevenage, Hitchin, Letchworth and Royston — with several smart point-to-point allowances — the overall times in most cases were no more than 81min. Though no longer carrying titles, the original workings were still clearly recognisable, at 9.05 and 11.35am, 1.35 and 8pm from King's Cross, plus new departures at 3.34 and 5.10pm; the last-named differed from the remainder by being non-stop to Hitchin but calling also at Ashwell. Coming up, the departures from Cambridge were at 9.32 and 11.40am, 1.40, 3.40 and 5.40pm, with an additional 8.15pm which was rather slower. With two exceptions, which had miniature buffets only, all these trains continued to provide full buffet facilities.

King's Cross-Cambridge buffet car trains continued until 5 February 1978. On the following day the second stage of the King's Cross suburban electrification came into operation, with through electric trains between King's Cross and Royston. A diesel shuttle ran between Royston and Cambridge. At the same time the speed and frequency of the Liverpool Street-Cambridge service were improved.

The Car-carriers

Great Britain may justifiably be proud of having given to the whole of Western Europe the idea of the 'Car-Sleeper' train. Originating in 1955 at the former headquarters of the Eastern Region at Liverpool Street, the idea was readily agreed when put to the administrations of the North Eastern and Scottish Regions. The plan was to run a night express between London and Scotland for motorists and their cars so that after their overnight journey they could drive into the Highlands first thing in the morning. The route chosen was between King's Cross and Perth and when introduced in 1955 the new trains ran twice weekly. The sleeping accommodation at first was in couchette berths, and the cars were conveyed in vans, but the popularity of the service soon led to full sleeping accommodation being provided. The train was loaded in the horse/motor loading bay at King's Cross.

The Perth train skirted Edinburgh to the south by using a suburban line (now freight-only) but in 1960 a daytime service to Edinburgh was put on, starting from Holloway.

Car-carrier trains ran to the West of England from the Midlands and North from 1956 onwards but the cars of motorists from London were first sent ahead of them by special freight trains starting from Westbourne Park on the Western Region and Nine Elms on the Southern. The first service conveying both cars and passengers from London to the West was launched by the Southern with a Saturdays-only Surbiton-Okehampton train in 1960.

In the Midlands a car-carrier terminal was established at Sutton Coldfield in 1958, and in 1965 Newton-le-Willows became the base for the North-West. Services from London began operating from Kensington Olympia in 1966. This was the former Kensington Addison Road station on the West London line and was given a face-lift, with waiting rooms and refreshment facilities to cater for the car-carrying services. In the same year the brand name 'Motorail' was chosen as a collective title for all these trains.

There have been many changes in services and terminals since those days. Motorail trains have often been notable for unusual routes, two examples of which may be mentioned. Glasgow-Newhaven Motorail began in 1964, starting from St Enoch, but when that terminus was closed in 1966 the starting point was changed to Stirling. The train followed the Midland line from Carlisle to Brent Junction, Cricklewood, where it branched to the North & South Western Junction line. From here the normal route to the Central Section of the SR would be via the junctions at Kew, Ludgate Junction, Factory Junction, and the curve between Herne Hill and Tulse Hill. This curve, however, was too sharp for the Class 45 and 46 diesels working the train and so at Acton Wells Junction it was switched on to the Western Region. As it was now travelling towards the west, it was sent round the Ealing-Greenford loop so as to approach the connection with the West London line at North Pole Junction in the west-to-east direction.

Another curiosity was the Stirling-Marylebone Motorail in the early 1960s. In order that the cars should be facing in the right direction for driving off on arrival, the train stopped at Neasden and another engine came on the rear to haul it round the Stadium loop and into the terminus 'back-to-front'.

In steam days cars were conveyed in covered vans but with the end of steam open vehicles became acceptable for day trains although cars still travelled in vans at night. The standard open car-carrier became the bogie Carflat accommodating four cars of average size. For a time in the mid-1960s double-deck Cartics as used for car deliveries were tried but presented various problems in loading.

Motorways began to have an impact on Motorail by removing some of the bottlenecks which had turned motorists towards the railway for reaching their chosen holiday area. The peak of Motorail traffic was reached in the 1970s. As passenger numbers declined it was decided to concentrate traffic at fewer terminals. Kensington Olympia has not been used since 1981 and by 1983 the number of Motorail terminals had been reduced to 14 as compared with a maximum of 57 at one time.

By the 1980s it was becoming difficult to fit daytime Motorail trains into the schedules of main lines operated by HSTs, while the search for operating economies inevitably led to a closer scrutiny of costs. In 1982 there was a switch to the policy of transporting cars separately from their passengers, who on the day routes were directed to Inter-City 125 services or other Inter-City trains. For overnight travel a 'tail' of Motorail vans was attached to certain regular sleeping car services although one or two exclusively Motorail night services continued. The daytime Motorail formed of ordinary coaches and Cartic flat wagons faded temporarily from the British Railways scene. It reappeared in 1983 in the 'Motorail Limited', a new Euston-Stirling service with a mid-morning departure which replaced the former arrangement of sending passengers north on the 9.35am 'Clansman', their cars following separately at 9.40.

The Cathedrals Express

One train alone in Great Britain can claim the distinction of having carried a representation of a bishop's mitre on its engine headboard. It was the short-lived 'Cathedrals Express' of the Western Region of British Railways, running between London, Oxford, Worcester and Hereford — four cathedral cities. The Worcester main line of the former Great Western Railway was one over which overall times had improved but little since the beginning of the century. In 1904, for example, it was possible to leave Paddington at 4.45pm and to be hurried non-stop over the 120 miles to Worcester in 2¼hr; and to come up from Worcester at 8.55am in the same time. These were the two trains on which in 1957 the title 'Cathedrals Express' was conferred.

But by that time it was no longer possible to give such a city as Oxford the 'go-by', and other stops had been introduced also. By 1939 the 12.45pm from Paddington, though stopping at Oxford, was still reaching Worcester in 2hr 10min, but the 4.45pm was stopping also at Moreton-in-Marsh and Evesham and taking 2hr 21min. The 8.55am up, however, with the help of a 60min sprint over the 63.4 miles from Oxford to Paddington, was making the same three stops but running up from Worcester in 2¼hr.

By the time the 2,750hp Brush diesels (Class 47) had taken over the service, in 1965, four stops — Oxford, Kingham, Moreton-in-Marsh and Evesham — were included in the schedule of the down train, now leaving Paddington at 5.15pm; while the up train, now at 9am from Worcester, was needing 2hr 25min, with additional halts at Charlbury and Reading. In this same year the 'Cathedrals Express' lost its title. In 1967 the Paddington-Worcester time at last was brought down to 2hr 5min by new trains at 6.15pm down and 7.50am up, calling at Oxford and Kingham in the former case and Evesham and Oxford in the latter, and these, though nameless, could perhaps be regarded as the logical successors of the former 'Cathedrals Express'.

The line from Oxford to Worcester has seen some fast running in the past. It was here on 31 July 1939 that No 4086 *Builth Castle* was timed by the late R. E. Charlewood to attain 100mph between mileposts 101 and 102 while descending the 1 in 100 gradient from Campden to Honeybourne with the 12.45pm Paddington to Worcester, a train which in those days stopped only at Kingham en route. In recent years, however, economic problems have struck the route, which is now single-track with passing loops from Moreton-in-Marsh to Norton Junction, Worcester; and from Wolvercot Junction, Oxford, to Ascott-under-Wychwood. It was proposed to defer track renewals by withdrawing locomotive-hauled trains, thus reducing wear and tear associated with the heavy locomotives of Classes 47 and 50, and to substitute diesel multiple-units running between Oxford and Worcester. At the present time (1983), however, two through London-Hereford locomotive-hauled trains catering for morning and evening business traffic, have been retained in each direction, and in the off-peak hours the service is provided by dmus connecting with Inter-City services at Oxford. The last day before the cut-back was also the last day of Class 50 workings on the route, 15 May 1982. Memories die hard, and a 'Cathedrals Express' headboard adorned the Class 50 on the last down evening train for part of the trip.

The Diesel Pullmans

British Rail's diesel Pullman sets were introduced as a foretaste of new standards in speed and comfort to come when the modernisation plan had had time to take effect.

Above: The up 'Midland Pullman' from Manchester Central to St Pancras passes Chinley North on 20 April 1965. *John Clarke*

Below: The Western Region's diesel Pullmans were eight-car sets with first and second class seating. Here an up Birmingham service speeds south near High Wycombe. *H. Harman*

Above: Leaving Bristol Temple Meads on 19 July 1968, the up 'Bristol Pullman' is in BR's blue and grey Pullman livery. A Class 35 ('Hymek') B-B diesel-hydraulic locomotive stands on the right.
G. R. Hounsell

Right: The down 'South Wales Pullman' between Tilehurst and Pangbourne on 10 October 1968.
J. H. Cooper-Smith

The Swindon Main Line

Until the 'Bristolian' was put on in the GWR Centenary Year, 1935, the Westbury and Bicester cut-off lines had almost monopolised the company's named trains. The original main line via Swindon, with its Bristol and South Wales services, tended to be overshadowed in the public mind. It came to the fore again in 1976 when Bristol and South Wales were given the first HST services, and there were hints that it might usurp the role of the Berks & Hants line via Westbury in the West of England timetable.

Above: The 11.45am Bristol-Paddington non-stop passes Badminton on 6 June 1951 with 'Castle' class 4-6-0 No 5064 *Bishops Castle* in charge. *G. J. Jefferson*

Centre left: The up 'Bristolian' is headed by standard Pacific No 70017 *Ariel* at Cholsey on 31 August 1951. *A. C. Cawston*

Bottom left: Seventeenth Century enterprise in opening up trade with the East was commemorated in the name of the 'Merchant Venturer' Paddington-Bristol express. Standard Pacific No 70020 *Mercury* leads the down train at Langley Crossing on 29 August 1951. *G. J. Jefferson*

Above right: The up 'Red Dragon' (10.00 ex-Cardiff) meets flood conditions at Chipping Sodbury on 27 November 1954. The locomotive is No 7020 *Gloucester Castle*. *A. Phipps*

Right: An HST to Swansea passes the junction between the Swindon and Westbury lines at Reading. *D. E. Canning*

Below: 'Cheltenham Flyer' was an unofficial title for a train more formally known as the 'Cheltenham Spa Express'. This name was revived by British Railways, and the postwar 'Cheltenham Spa Express' is seen passing Kemble in 1960 with 'Castle' class 4-6-0 No 5017 *The Gloucestershire Regiment 28th 61st*. It has left the Paddington-Bristol/South Wales main line at Swindon. *R. W. Hinton*

Serving the West Midlands

Ambridge and the Archers remind us that there is more to the West Midlands than the industrial belt. There is plenty of variety in the scenery and the train services.

Above: 'Castle' class 4-6-0 No 7007 *Great Western* wheels the up 'Cathedrals Express' past Norton Junction, Worcester, on 7 April 1962. The line turning away to the left joins the North East-South West route at Abbotswood Junction. *Anthony A. Vickers*

Below: Class 47 No 47.513 is on the singled section of the Oxford-Worcester line at Charlbury on 22 May 1980 with the 12.55 Paddington-Worcester.

Left: The Great Western through service from London to the West Midlands continued past Worcester to Malvern and Hereford, as well as detaching coaches at Worcester for Droitwich, Kidderminster and Stourbridge Junction. In Western Region days, on 6 December 1961, a Hereford-Paddington express hurries past Oxford behind 'Castle' class 4-6-0 No 7011 *Banbury Castle*. *Rev R. T. Hughes*

Below: Class 47 No 47.555 *The Commonwealth Spirit* leaves Birmingham New Street for Worcester with the 8.00 from Paddington on 21 April 1979. *C. J. Tuffs*

Right: 'Castle' No 5085 *Evesham Abbey* is ready to leave Oxford with a Worcester-Paddington train on 9 January 1961. *B. H. Jackson*

5085

Above: Two hours between London and Birmingham was long the accepted time for the principal trains by both routes. Rebuilt 'Scot' No 6146 *The Rifle Brigade* romps over Tring summit with an LMS two-hour up Birmingham express.
F. R. Hebron/Rail Archive Stephenson

Below: The 'Classic' Birmingham timings were slashed by the LMR electrification. No 86.228 heads past Tile Hill box towards Coventry with a Euston express on 21 May 1977. *G. O. Swain*

Some 1930s 'Classics'

The second half of the 1930s was the era of the first streamlined trains and locomotives. The high-speed diesel train was making its appearance in Germany and diesel performance was studied by a visiting LNER team which included H. N. (later Sir Nigel) Gresley, but there were doubts over reliability of the diesel engines of the day. Gresley considered that steam could do better, hauling trains with more passenger capacity and a higher standard of comfort than the German diesel sets. The streamliner period began with the LNER 'Silver Jubilee' (King's Cross-Newcastle) in 1935. In 1937, when the LNER 'Coronation' (King's Cross-Edinburgh) was introduced, the LMS joined the trend with the Euston-Glasgow 'Coronation Scot'.

Above: Streamlined Pacific No 4491 *Commonwealth of Australia* heads the up 'Coronation' at Cockburnspath on 20 August 1937. *E. R. Wethersett*

Left: The first of the LMS streamlined Pacifics, No 6220 *Coronation*, at Elvanfoot with the up 'Coronation Scot'.

Above: 'Frozen' speed in a broadside view of No 6224 *Princess Alexandra* on the down 'Coronation Scot'. *E. R. Wethersett*

Below: Another LNER streamliner of 1937 was the 'West Riding Limited' between King's Cross, Leeds and Bradford. The up train runs into King's Cross behind No 4491 *Commonwealth of Australia*. Two of the streamlined Pacifics were named *Golden Fleece* and *Golden Shuttle* to symbolise the woollen trade of the West Riding. *H. Gordon Tidey/Real Photos*

Top: Two Class B17 'Sandringham' 4-6-0s were streamlined for working the 'East Anglian' express between Liverpool Street and Norwich. No 2859 *East Anglian* poses at the head of its special set of rolling stock. *LPC*

Above: 'Land Cruises' by the LNER 'Northern Belle' cruising train were popular before World War 2. No 4467 *Wild Swan* 'sets sail' from King's Cross. *LPC*

North East-South West

Cross-country traffic between the South-West and the North of England is concentrated on the former Midland Bristol-Birmingham-Derby line, now generally known as the North East-South West Route. HSTs began working on this cross-country main line in 1982, when a Penzance-Edinburgh service revived something like the celebrated Penzance-Aberdeen through coaches of earlier years by the Great Central route.

Above: The 'Cornishman' (Penzance-Leeds) emerges from Mutley Tunnel, Plymouth, behind Class 47 No 47.138 on 3 December 1976. *Les Bertram*

Centre right: Window 'stickers' have their uses if less elegant than destination boards. The route of the 'Devonian' is clearly shown as the train stands at Bristol Temple Meads on 9 May 1974. *P. J. Fowler*

Bottom right: The 'Port-to-Port Express' of earlier days is gone but a Plymouth-Liverpool service could qualify for the title. No 50.005 *Achilles* takes the 13.30 Plymouth-Liverpool past Aller Junction on 18 October 1981. *Les Bertram*

The Channel Islands Boat Express

From the end of the 'Brighton Belle' in 1971 the columns of the Southern Region timetable remained bare of train names until the 1981/2 issue. Then the 'Channel Islands Boat Express' appeared in the Waterloo-Bournemouth pages. Previously the times of this seasonal train had been shown only among the shipping services at the back of the book.

'Channel Islands Boat Train' headboards were among the longest survivors of their kind on British Railways. For a time after they went the train could be recognised by its vans, but with the decline of van traffic they were dropped as well and the train might have been any locomotive-hauled special, apart from the fact that other specials were more likely to have a Class 33 diesel at the head than the Class 73 electro-diesel that has become the normal power.

Public attention was drawn to the 'Channel Islands Boat Express' in 1979 by promotion of low-priced off-peak holidays in the Channel Islands by Sealink UK. They were publicised by a ceremony at Waterloo on 12 October in which 'Miss Jersey' unveiled an 'Isle of Jersey' headboard on the locomotive, No 73.142, heading the boat train. Then anonymity returned until the name of the train appeared in the timetable. This signalled the availability of the service for ordinary passengers between Waterloo and Bournemouth. It was not shown in the Bournemouth-Weymouth section of the book.

The 'Channel Islands Boat Express' schedules are complicated, because although there are sailings throughout the year, the train only runs daily at certain periods. In 1982, for example, the morning train (9.54 from Waterloo) ran from 17 May (when the summer timetable began) until 1 October. From 16 July to 24 September it was supplemented by an evening service at 8.05pm for the overnight sailing. Before this train came into operation the Weymouth portion of the regular 7.35pm Waterloo-Weymouth train was worked through to Weymouth Quay on 28 May (the Friday of the Spring Bank Holiday), 4 June, and from 11 June to 15 July.

After the day boat train had ceased to run, daytime passengers could travel until 29 October by the 9.35am Bournemouth-Weymouth and take a connecting coach from Weymouth station to Weymouth Quay. The night service by the through portion to Weymouth Quay on the 7.35pm from Waterloo continued to be provided, but on Tuesday and Fridays only, from 2 November. It is not surprising that a timetable folder for the service has been produced in the form of a calendar showing what trains and boats were operating on any day in the year.

The through boat trains are worked to Bournemouth by the electro-diesel. Here a Class 33 diesel takes over and there is no scheduled stop until Weymouth Quay, reached by the day train at 1pm and by the night service at 11.20pm. In fact, however, the trains stop at Weymouth for the locomotive to be fitted with the flashing lamp and bell unit which it carries while travelling with its train along the Weymouth street to the quayside. Both trains call at Basingstoke and Southampton for the convenience of ordinary passengers. Services similar to those described operate in the inwards direction.

The 'Channel Islands Boat Express' has the distinction of being the only locomotive-hauled electric passenger train in the daylight hours on the old South Western main line, although electro-diesels work some late night services which carry mail and parcels traffic as well as passengers.

The Cheltenham Spa Express

It was as a very ordinary train that the 'Cheltenham Spa Express' began its course. After World War 1 an afternoon service was put on from Cheltenham and Gloucester to Paddington, due shortly after 5pm. But in 1923 the Great Western Railway, which had been steadily speeding up its long-distance services, decided to lay claim to the blue riband of railway speed in Great Britain, held until then by the North Eastern Railway — and later the London & North Eastern — with its 43min run over the 44.1 miles from Darlington to York. The almost perfectly level and well-aligned stretch from Swindon to Paddington was ideal for the purpose and the Cheltenham train was selected to make the new record. Its timing over the 77.3 miles from Swindon was cut to 75min, and now required a start-to-stop average of 61.8mph.

The first step had thus been taken to turn the 'Cheltenham Spa Express' into the 'Cheltenham Flyer' — the nickname by which this train was always known in later years, though it never came into official use. Railway speeds all over the world were advancing rapidly, and the 75min schedule was not destined to remain in force for long. Six years later, in July 1929, the timing was cut to 70min, and the booked speed rose to 66.2mph; at the time this was the fastest regular railway run in the world. Then the supremacy was challenged from an unexpected quarter. In 1931 the Canadian Pacific and Canadian National Railways were fighting for the traffic between Montreal and Toronto, and the competition grew so vigorous that the CPR cut the time of its fastest service to 108min for the 124 miles from Montreal West to Smiths Falls, which called for an average of 68.9mph from start to stop. In September 1931 therefore, the GWR accelerated the 'Cheltenham Flyer' to a 67min run from Swindon, so bringing the average speed up to 69.2mph. Finally, in order to reduce the schedule to a round figure, there came, in September 1932, the cut to 65min, and the raising of the start-to-stop average to 71.4mph.

After this final acceleration, the 'Cheltenham Flyer' was still the fastest train in the world. But from then onwards the march in world railway speed became so extraordinarily rapid that the 'Cheltenham Flyer', though still running on its 71.4mph schedule, by 1939 had to be content with a place well below the one-hundredth among the world's fastest runs, largely, of course, owing to the introduction of diesel-electric streamline trains in Germany and the United States. In Great Britain the 'Cheltenham Flyer's' speed was just beaten by the 71.9mph of the LNER 'Coronation' streamliner between London and York.

The best recorded journey of the 'Cheltenham Flyer' was made on 6 June 1932, when the 77.3 miles from Swindon to Paddington were covered in 56min 47sec, at an average of 81.7mph — the fastest start-to-stop speed achieved in Great Britain up till then and for a good many years afterwards. For 70 miles on end, between mileposts 72 and 2, an average rate of 87.5mph was maintained, though this feat was beaten by the 70 miles covered at 91.8mph on 27 September 1935 by the LNER 'Silver Jubilee' streamliner. On the GWR run the engine was No 5006, *Tregenna Castle*, a 4-cylinder 4-6-0 'Castle' of the class which was always responsible for working the train; the load was six bogie vehicles, weighing 186 tons empty, and 195 tons gross.

It was only between Swindon and Paddington that the 'Cheltenham Flyer' developed any turn of speed, and over this section the schedule demanded a sustained 80mph, or something closely approaching that figure, for most of the distance. The main train, which consisted usually of a six-coach set, was made up of third-class brake, corridor composite, restaurant car, corridor composite, third class, and third-class brake. Leaving St James station at Cheltenham Spa at 2.40pm, and calling at Malvern Road, it ran down to Gloucester, 7½ miles, in 13min. Here reversal was necessary; the engine for the run to London was attached to what had been the rear of the train, at the other end a through composite brake coach which left Hereford at 1.15pm, and had come across to Gloucester *via* Ross, calling at all stations. Previously, for some years, the main train avoided Gloucester, running direct from Engine Shed Junction to Gloucester South Junction, where the Hereford coach was attached.

Departure from Gloucester was at 2.58pm, and between there and Swindon stops were made at Stroud and Kemble; also on this length the 'Castle' had to tackle the stiff climb up 4 miles at 1 in 60-90 from Brimscombe to the summit at the east end of Sapperton tunnel. The 44¼ miles from Cheltenham to Swindon thus took 71min, by contrast with the high speed from Swindon onwards. Swindon was left at 3.55pm and Paddington was reached at 5pm. There was no corresponding down service. The stock of the main train, including the engine, went down from Paddington daily at 10.45am, but this was a semi-fast train of no distinctive speed.

On the day of the record 1932 run referred to earlier, arrangements were made for an extremely fast run in the opposite direction on the 5pm down 'Cheltenham Spa Express', which normally was non-stop to Kemble; on this trip, 'Castle' class 4-6-0 No 5005 *Manorbier Castle* with a load of 205 tons, worked the train to a special stop at Swindon in one second over the hour. The 5.15pm non-stop two-hour express from Bristol to Paddington was then stopped specially at Swindon to pick up those who had been recording the test journeys, and brought them back to Paddington in 66½min. Between 3.48 and 7.12pm, these recorders made *three* journeys over this 77.3 miles of line, so covering 232 miles in 3hr 24min, and in an actual running time of 3min over 3hr.

After the war the 'Cheltenham Flyer' never reappeared, and the fastest train from Swindon to Paddington was allowed 74min; it was possible, however, to make the run in the opposite direction in 70min. The 70min run was by the down 'Cheltenham Spa Express' of the period, the former 5pm down referred to in the last paragraph, which now started at 4.50pm, and called at Swindon daily instead of being non-stop to Kemble as in prewar days. By a new connection laid in at Standish Junction in 1964 it became possible for trains from Paddington to run direct into the former Midland Railway Eastgate Station at Gloucester, so that they proceeded direct to Cheltenham without reversal. The down 'Cheltenham Spa Express' then reached Gloucester at 6.56 and Cheltenham at 7.16pm, stopping at the ex-Midland Landsdown Station instead of the former terminal at St James. In the up direction the starts from Cheltenham and Gloucester were at 8.10 and 8.21am respectively, and the arrival at Paddington was at 10.35am. In 1939 the overall allowance was 2½hr each way, so that this particular service had seen but little improvement.

The City Limited

It was a tradition that the 'City Limited' of the London, Brighton & South Coast Railway would always run, notwithstanding fog, strike, war, or Act of God, and for over a century this famous train and its predecessors kept the tradition in being. So much so, indeed, that during World War 2, almost alone among British express trains, the 'City Limited' maintained its 60min schedule from London Bridge to Brighton, even though a considerable part of London Bridge terminus disappeared in the blitz, and the track at the London end of the journey suffered greatly from bomb damage. In the up direction the only alteration was a trifling addition of two minutes to cover an intermediate stop at Haywards Heath, but despite further stops at Preston Park and East Croydon the timing later came back to 60min. The Pullman cars in the train were withdrawn during the war.

The forerunner of the 'City Limited' came into operation on 21 September 1841, leaving Brighton for London Bridge at 8.30am, and returning at 4.45pm. In the up direction the time allowed was 1¾hr, and in the down 2hr; the only advertised stop was Croydon, though additional stops may have been needed to take water. By the beginning of 1850, the time had come down to 75min, and the London Bridge departure had been altered to the time-honoured 5pm. The 8.45am departure from Brighton had come into force in 1844.

In 1862, with the opening of Victoria, West End portions were added to both trains, but by 1865 the 5pm down was running from London Bridge only, and a year later was slipping a portion for Tunbridge Wells at Three Bridges. In the following decade the slip portion was for Eastbourne, and was detached at Haywards Heath, while the up train was slipping its Victoria portion at East Croydon, instead of stopping there. The up express also had come down to a 70min run to London Bridge. It was in the summer of 1912 that the 5pm down first became a 60min train, and after the interlude of the first world war, when the schedule went back to 75min, and 82min in the reverse direction, the 60min timing was restored in February 1921. The up express, now for London Bridge only, was cut to 62min at the same date, and to the even hour from July, 1928.

At the beginning of the present century, the up 'City Limited' was one of the heaviest trains in the country, notwithstanding the fact that it carried first-class passengers only. From 1901 onwards, the London Bridge portion consisted of six-wheeled brakes at each end, six bogie firsts, and three eight-wheel Pullmans in the centre, with a Victoria 'slip' composed of six-wheel brake, two bogie firsts and a twelve-wheel Pullman. On Mondays each section contained an additional bogie first, and the entire train then comprised 17 vehicles (67 axles) weighing 348 tons empty and at least 370 tons with passengers and luggage; it is no small tribute to the small London, Brighton & South Coast engines of the period that such a load could be worked single-headed.

New stock 9ft wide, introduced in 1907, made it possible to cut the London Bridge formation to nine bogies, weighing 217 tons; in the reverse direction, with the Victoria portion, the load was twelve bogies weighing 304 tons. In the entire train, which was still first class only, there were four Pullmans as before. This was the first LBSCR train to be steam-heated throughout. It was not until 1919, when the up Victoria portion began to run as a separate train, that third class passengers were admitted on weekdays to the 'City Limited', but the predominance of first class passengers made it necessary, when electric haulage was introduced in 1933, to build special sets of coaches for the working, owing to the unusually large proportion of first-class accommodation required. In 1924 standard Southern Railway corridor stock replaced the previous compartment stock in a train of eleven bogies, one only of which was now a Pullman car. The total weight was about 360 tons.

From Stroudley days many special locomotive classes that were built at Brighton were designed in the first instance to work the 'City Limited', such as the first Stroudley 0-4-2 express engines *Richmond* and *Cornwall* in 1878 and 1879, the 'Gladstone' 0-4-2s in the early 1880s, and the Billinton 4-4-0s *Siemens, Sirdar* and *Empress* in 1899. Then came the turn of the Marsh Atlantics, and of the Lawson Billinton 4-6-2 and 4-6-4 tanks. The final run of the 'City Limited' with steam power, made on Friday 30 December 1932, was by 4-6-4 tank No 332, which, with a gross load of 385 tons, ran the 50.9 miles in 57¾min.

For the electric working, as previously mentioned, special six-car sets were built. Each comprised two centre-corridor third-class motor brakes, three side-corridor firsts, and a composite Pullman. The entire twelve-coach train seated 276 first- and 240 third-class passengers, and weighed 526 tons empty, and about 565 tons with all seats occupied and a small amount of luggage. In the last years before World War 2 the down 'City Limited', though nominally a 60-minute train was scheduled in the working timetables to reach Brighton at 5.56pm, and so to maintain an overall average of 54.2mph. On the outbreak of war the Brighton arrival reverted to 6pm.

The name 'City Limited' appeared in the 'Southern Railway' timetables in the early 1930s but had been dropped by the time of World War 2. After the war a 5pm departure from London Bridge continued. Stops at Hassocks and Preston Park were added in later years but the train actually reached Brighton in 58min. The up train at 8.45am made the journey to London Bridge in 60min in spite of stops at Preston Park, Haywards Heath and East Croydon. The traditional departure times were closely adhered to until 1976, when the recognisable descendants of the 'City Limited' were withdrawn.

The Clansman

The Trent Valley line of the London & North Western Railway was opened between Rugby and Stafford in 1847, in time for the first through trains between Euston and Glasgow, which began running on 1 March 1848. The old route to the North via Birmingham was not used regularly again by these services until 1974 when London Midland Region trains began running between Euston and Glasgow with electric haulage throughout. Higher speeds with electric traction were seen to open up the possibility of daytime travel between London and Inverness, traditionally an overnight journey, and this could be achieved even with the longer journey via Birmingham.

By 1974 the remaining train names on the LMR were being retained largely to preserve traditions but it was decided that the only through daytime train from London to the West Midlands and the north of Scotland deserved a name to identify it as a new product in the Inter-City market. The name 'Clansman' was decided on jointly by representatives of the London Midland and the Scottish Regions.

The 'Clansman' was introduced in the first all-electric timetable of 1974. Originally the stops south of Birmingham New Street were at Watford (to pick up) and Coventry, but when the Birmingham International station was opened in 1976, serving the Exhibition Centre, the train called there as well.

In the present timetable (1982) the 'Clansman' leaves Euston at 9.35, picks up at Watford at 9.51, and after calling at Coventry and Birmingham International arrives in Birmingham New Street at 11.14. Departure is 2min later, the train calls at Wolverhampton and is then non-stop to Crewe, reached at 12.17pm. Subsequent stops are at Preston, Carlisle and Motherwell, where the 'Clansman' is due at 3.35pm.

At Motherwell the train diverges from the main line to Glasgow Central to skirt round the east of the city. Its next stop is only some two miles further on, in Mossend Yard, where electric traction ends and a Scottish Region diesel-electric locomotive, usually a Class 47, is waiting to take over from the electric locomotive of Class 86 or 87 which has worked through from Euston. The diesel will normally be in charge for the rest of the journey to Inverness.

Under diesel power the 'Clansman' continues its journey, calling at Coatbridge before joining the main line from Glasgow Queen Street to Perth and the North near Larbert. It is at Stirling at 4.30pm, Gleneagles at 4.53, and into Perth at 5.11.

After a stop of 3min the final stage of the journey

begins. The present main line to Aberdeen branches eastward at Perth and the 'Clansman' continues along the old Caledonian line to Stanley Junction, where the former route to Aberdeen via Forfar bore away to the east. After Stanley Junction the 'Clansman' is on the main line of the former Highland Railway. Its last stops are at Pitlochry, Newtonmore, Kingussie and Aviemore before running into Inverness at 8.15pm. For a railway enthusiast the 10hr 40min of travel (if the journey is made in summer) are unforgettable, taking him over the classic heights of Shap, Beattock, Druimuachdar and Slochd summits in daylight.

The up train, with similar stops, leaves Inverness at 10.30am and reaches Euston at 9.11pm. Most rolling stock workings today are complex, but the 'Clansman' has two sets of coaches allotted to it exclusively, each making the outward journey one day and returning the next. The usual formation is 12 coaches (11 in winter) as follows: Bogie brake, seven open seconds (six in winter), restaurant/buffet car, open first, brake first, corridor first.

The Comet

It was doubtless the up working of this express that suggested as distinctive a name as the 'Comet', for the down train carrying the same name did not lay quite the same claim to speed. For a good many years there had been a fast evening service from Manchester to Euston, which passed through various changes; at one time it left Manchester as late as 6.15pm, and for some time through Manchester coaches were attached at Crewe to the rear of the up 'Midday Scot'. Finally, however, Manchester had its up direct evening express once again, with a journey time cut to 3¼hr, similar to that of the up 'Mancunian' and the down 'Lancastrian'.

When the 'Comet' first received its name, in 1932, it left Manchester London Road (now Piccadilly) at 5.40pm, but this was altered later to 5.45pm, with an arrival in Euston at 9pm. The train travelled by the Styal line, passed Crewe without stopping, and made its only intermediate halt at Stafford, from 6.49 to 6.52pm (54.9 miles in 64min). From here the 133.6 miles to Euston had to be covered in 128min, at an average speed of 62.6mph, and this was one of the fastest scheduled runs on the LMSR. The train was very popular, and always ran filled to capacity; on Fridays a relief express left Manchester at 5.40pm, and ran non-stop to Euston, arriving at 8.57pm.

A 'Royal Scot' 4-6-0 was used invariably on the 'Comet' workings, both up and down, and in either case the working of the train was a severe test of locomotive capacity. The up train consisted of a set of six coaches — first-class brake, open first, third and kitchen car (a 12-wheeler), open third, third and third brake — to which was attached, in front, the set of cars which had worked down the same day on the 8.30am from London — third brake, third restaurant car, kitchen car, and first restaurant car — making a minimum of 11 vehicles, and a mimimum tare weight of about 340 tons. Extra vehicles were frequently attached, and if the load was 13 bogies or more, the 4-6-0 was allowed a pilot, usually a 4-4-0 three-cylinder compound.

In the down direction the 'Comet' left Euston at 11.50am, and was the lineal descendant of the 12.10pm express from Euston to Liverpool and Manchester that ran up to World War 1. The down 'Comet' ran non-stop over the 158.1 miles from Euston to Crewe, for which 165min were allowed (57.5mph); a stop of three minutes was allowed at Crewe for division of the train, after which the 'Comet' was booked to cover the 24.9 miles to Stockport in 29min. At Stockport a three-minute stop sufficed, and the final 5.9 miles into London Road took 10min, for an arrival at 3.20pm.

The down 'Comet' left London with the six-coach set including 12-wheel restaurant car, to which reference has already been made, and this formed the complete train from Crewe onwards. To Crewe there was attached on rear a seven-coach set for Liverpool — third brake, third, third restaurant, kitchen, first restaurant, and first brake — with a through composite brake for Birkenhead as the rearmost vehicle. This made a minimum load of 14 bogies, and a substantial tare load of about 430 tons for the 'Royal Scot' locomotive to work to Crewe at 57.5mph.

To Liverpool, departure from Crewe was at 2.42pm, and after a non-stop run Liverpool Lime Street was reached at 3.25pm. The Birkenhead coach was attached to a train made up at Crewe, and leaving at 2.43pm; with intermediate stops at Chester, Hooton, and Rock Ferry, this reached Birkenhead Woodside at 3.40pm, and gave Birkenhead passengers the fastest service of the day from London.

With postwar conditions the 'Comet' reappeared, leaving Manchester at 5.50pm, stopping at Stockport and Crewe in place of Stafford, but not due in Euston till 9.36pm — a journey of just over $3\frac{3}{4}$hr as compared with the prewar $3\frac{1}{2}$hr. By the 1952 winter the Euston arrival had advanced to 9.25pm. The stock used went down on the 9.45am from Euston to Manchester (instead of the prewar 11.50am), and the former therefore assumed the name 'Comet'. It was non-stop from Euston to Stoke and after that made the usual calls at Macclesfield and Stockport, reaching London Road at 1.40pm, except on Saturdays. On that day the unhappy train, after getting down the main line at its usual speed as far as Colwich, was compelled to hang about for half-an-hour between Colwich and Stoke, because of the difficulty of finding a path through the Saturday workmen's traffic of the Potteries, so not reaching Manchester until 2.12pm — a very far from 'Comet'-like proceeding!

In the summer of 1954, however, a considerable acceleration took place. The 10am 'Royal Scot' was put on to an 'XL Limit' timing from Euston, and in order to keep the 9.45am 'Comet' well clear, the latter was accelerated similarly as far as Colwich. It was now therefore booked over the 145.8 miles from Euston to Stoke-on-Trent in 146min, a run escaping mile-a-minute status by the narrowest of margins, and Manchester was reached once again in $3\frac{1}{2}$hr, as before the war. In the autumn of the same year the up 'Comet' also was accelerated to a $3\frac{1}{2}$hr run, including stops at Stockport and Crewe and a newly-introduced one to set down passengers at Watford Junction. From Crewe to Watford this express did get into the mile-a-minute category with a booking of 137min for the 140.7 miles, at a start-to-stop average of 61.6mph. The start from Manchester was now at 5.50pm, and the Euston arrival at 9.20pm.

In the succeeding years there were many alterations in the 'Comet's' running times, but these gradually worsened as engineering slacks due to electrification increased, and finally, in the autumn of 1962, there came the transfer of practically all the London-Manchester traffic to the Midland route — a temporary measure which lasted until March 1966, when the full electric service was brought into operation between Euston and Manchester. But the 'Comet' disappeared, and the name has not been revived since.

The Continentals, Eastern Region

It is generally agreed that the highest level of achievement of the one-time Great Eastern Railway, before its absorption into the London & North Eastern, was reached in its Continental boat services. Of all these the most important was the Hook of Holland service, principal means of communication between England and the whole of North Germany and beyond. To this there was added later the Antwerp service, very popular as a route to and from Belgium because of the smooth stretch along the River Schedlt, on the Continental side, in which the passenger could breakfast in comfort on the way over, or dine on the way back. These services were rendered the more attractive by the miniature ocean liners that the GER built for the service, on which very comfortable sleeping accommodation was provided. They made possible a mid-evening departure from Liverpool Street, and on the return journey a morning arrival at the very start of the business day.

After World War 1, in order further to popularise the Belgian coast resorts, a service was established between Parkeston Quay and the Belgian port of Zeebrugge. This ran during the summer season only, but it heralded the opening of the all-the-year-round freight ferry service between a new terminal at Harwich and Zeebrugge.

In 1927 another development of great importance took place at Parkeston Quay. The fine steamers of the Zeeland Shipping Company for many years had worked between the Dutch port of Flushing and Queenborough, near Sheerness. Later, to avoid the inconvenience of the latter and the fogs in the estuary they transferred to Folkestone. In 1927 they changed their port on the English side again, this time to Parkeston Quay. A fifth Continental passenger service that had begun to use Parkeston Quay was the Danish one operating to and from Esbjerg, on the western side of Jutland, which after the opening of the Little Belt Bridge in 1935 was provided with a high-speed diesel streamline train to make the connection between Esbjerg and Copenhagen.

All these flourishing services concentrated on Parkeston Quay required the provision of a fleet of connecting trains over the 69 miles between this Essex port and Liverpool Street. Here again the old Great Eastern Railway did well by putting on in 1904 a specially built corridor train for the Hook of Holland service, with restaurant cars in which there was established a catering tradition that became justly famed. The train of nine bogie vehicles, three six-wheelers, and a four-wheel truck for the registered luggage-boxes, weighed 287 tons. At first the time allowed for the journey in the down direction was 85min; then this was increased to 87min; but with the advent in 1912 of the first 4-6-0 locomotives of the '1500' class (later LNER Class B12) the time was cut to 82min.

In 1914 there came to the GER as General Manager Henry W. Thornton, who had been in the service of the Pennsylvania Railroad of the United States. An early result, when the necessary vehicles could be obtained after World War 1, was the introduction of Pullman cars on Great Eastern metals. Two first class Pullmans were attached to the Hook of Holland boat train, and continued to run in the formation until World War 2. In 1924 the LNER, as the GER had now become, built a new train of standard LNER stock for the Hook service, and the job of haulage now became one for expert enginemen only.

The train was of 13 bogie vehicles, including the Pullmans, and weighed about 430 tons empty. With passengers and luggage, a total weight of 455 tons had to be run from Liverpool Street to Parkeston Quay at an average speed of 50.4mph from start to stop. This included the initial climb to Bethnal Green, the long pull up Brentwood bank, the slacks through Stratford, Chelmsford and Colchester, and a dead slowing over the turnout from the main line at Manningtree, followed by a sharp incline up which to recover speed. Four engine-crews at Parkeston shed constituted the 'top link' responsible for these duties, and they were masters of their work. The '1500' class 4-6-0s were used exclusively.

In 1936 a new and still more luxurious train was built for the Hook of Holland service, and the weight was increased further to 443 tons tare. The formation in the outward direction, from the engine backwards, was third class brake, two second class compartment coaches, open second, second restaurant, kitchen car, first restaurant, semi-open first, compartment first, two Pullman cars and two bogie brakes, 13 vehicles in all, occasionally swollen to 14, with a gross weight of 500 tons.

By now, however, the timing had been eased, and was back at the earlier 87min. Also the three-cylinder Gresley 4-6-0s of the 'Sandringham' (B17) class had been introduced, though it is doubtful if the work they did was ever greatly superior to that of the capable GER '1500s', especially after the latter had been fitted with larger boilers, and had had their valve-setting improved on modern lines to allow of earlier cut-off working.

The down 'Hook Continental', as it became known officially from 1927 onwards, for many years was booked out of Liverpool Street at 8.30pm. In the heyday of its speed, it was scheduled to pass Colchester, 51.7 miles, in 61min, and to reach Parkeston Quay at 9.52pm; after the slowing, the start from Liverpool Street was altered to 8.15pm, and the Parkeston Quay arrival to 9.42pm. In the up direction the booked departure from Parkeston was at 6.20am, but the necessity for fitting the working into the dense suburban traffic from Gidea Park onwards made the up timing easier, and the 'Hook Continental' was not due in Liverpool Street until 7.53am. Various alternative paths were laid down in the working timetables for the up train, in the event of the steamer being delayed by bad weather.

The Antwerp train, which in later LNER days became the 'Antwerp Continental', used to follow the 'Hook Continental' out of Liverpool Street at an interval of 10min, at 8.40pm, and was allowed the same time to Parkeston Quay — an arrangement which meant smart work on the part of the station staff at Parkeston in getting the Hook train clear, as both normally used the same platform. But when the 'Hook' departure was altered to 8.15pm, the Antwerp train took the 8.30 path. The 'Antwerp Continental' continued to Dovercourt Bay and Harwich, and so carried ordinary as well as boat passengers. It was due at Harwich at 10.14pm.

In the morning the starting time from Parkeston Quay of the up 'Antwerp Continental' saw some variation, and was varied also between summer and winter. Immediately before World War 2 it left at 7am and reached Liverpool Street at 8.38am. When the Zeebrugge service was in operation, Zeebrugge passengers were carried on the 'Antwerp Continental'. At the depth of the depression period, one train, known as the 'Hook and Antwerp Continental', sufficed for both routes.

In 1905, the Great Eastern Railway also provided its Antwerp passengers with a corridor restaurant car train. In busy summer seasons, more particularly at weekends, the stock was used to form a restaurant car train from Liverpool Street to Clacton-on-Sea and back between its arrival from Parkeston and its return working at 8.40pm. In later LNER days catering on this train was turned over to the Pullman Car Company, and Pullman restaurant cars, three in number, were substituted for the LNER cars. A first class Pullman of the drawing-room type was also run on the train. The composition varied according to season, but rose to a maximum of 12 bogies in the summer, which including the four Pullmans weighed about 390 tons.

A similar formation, with first class Pullman car and Pullman restaurant cars, was run for the 'Flushing

Continental'. Of this train the running times varied considerably. In the last year before World War 2 it left Liverpool Street in winter at 9.30am, reaching Parkeston Quay West at 10.55am, and continuing to Parkeston main station. In summer departure was at 10am, and arrivals were at 11.30am and 11.38am respectively. On the up journey the train left Parkeston Quay at 6.30pm, and Parkeston Quay West 15min later, reaching Liverpool Street at 8.13pm in winter; the summer departures were 7.45 and 7.55pm, and arrival in London was not until 9.30pm.

During the winter months, passengers for Scandinavia via Esbjerg had to be content with a portion on the rear of the 3.10pm Yarmouth buffet car express from Liverpool Street, which was detached at Manningtree and run from there independently to Parkeston Quay West, arriving at 4.45pm. But in summer, before the war, the 'Scandinavian' blossomed out into an independent train with Pullman restaurant cars, due to depart from Liverpool Street at 4.10pm, reaching Parkeston Quay non-stop at 5.45pm, and running on with ordinary passengers to Harwich, where arrival was at 6.06pm. In the up direction the 'Scandinavian' left Parkeston Quay on one of the many 'conditional' paths arranged in the working timetables, according to the arrival of the boat.

All the LNER Continental services were withdrawn in 1939; the 'Hook Continental' was reinstated, three times weekly, in November 1945, and daily a year later. Departure from Liverpool Street had now become 8pm, and at first the allowance to Parkeston Quay was a leisurely 100min, but with the summer timetable of 1951, and with the new standard 'Britannia' class Pacifics replacing the B1 4-6-0s used until then, the journey time was reduced to 90min, which included a 3min recovery margin between Manningtree and Parkeston Quay. During the summer a relief train was run from Liverpool Street at 8.05pm, mainly for second class passengers who had overflowed from the 8pm; this had a buffet car in place of restaurant cars. In winter the main train had to leave London at 7.30pm, because of the difference between British and Continental time during this period.

Much of the prewar stock of the LNER streamliner type had reappeared. There were 13 vehicles, two of them bogie brakes (at the rear end from London), two combined kitchen and restaurant cars in the first and second class sections of the train, and the remainder mostly open stock, including the beautiful armchair 'Coronation' type open firsts, the whole forming one of the most palatial boat trains in the country. The empty weight was about 460 tons. Plenty of seating accommodation with tables was essential, for on the morning run in summer it was not unusual to serve between 150 and 200 breakfasts at one sitting. In 1952 the departure from Parkeston Quay on the inward run was put back to 7.42am, and the arrival in Liverpool Street became 9.14am.

Speeding up followed the replacement of the 'Britannia' Pacifics by diesel power. Classes 37 and 40 both worked on the 'Continentals' in the early years of the changeover but later Class 47 power was normal although Class 37 still appeared from time to time. The down 'Hook Continental' still started at 8pm but covered the 69 miles to Parkeston Quay in 80min; throughout the summer it was relieved nightly by an 8.10pm train which took 90min. In the up direction a 7.50am start from Parkeston Quay easily ensured continuation of the 9.14am Liverpool Street arrival. The up relief got away at 8.10am and was allowed 90min as in the opposite direction. The high standard of comfort and catering on the train remained unchanged.

On the day service the 'Day Continental' went down at 9.45am in winter and 10.45am in summer, and was the fastest train of the day, taking 75min only; it returned at 6pm in winter and 7pm in summer. The 'Scandinavian' was an afternoon service, at 3.05pm down in winter but 4.05pm in summer; it came up from Parkeston Quay at times varying from 12.30 to 1.20pm, according to the season.

At the time of writing (1982) the 'Day Continental' and 'Hook Continental' names are still current (both trains connect with Harwich-Hook of Holland sailings). There are three boat train services daily to and from Liverpool Street. The down 'Day Continental' leaves at 9.40am with a run of 78min to Parkeston Quay. Returning at 6pm, it is into Liverpool Street at 7.23pm. The 'Hook Continental' goes down at 7.40pm, arriving at the quayside at 8.56pm, and is followed by a relief at 8pm in summer. In the reverse direction the main train retains the long-established times of 7.50am departure and 9.14am arrival. The relief is away from Parkeston Quay at 8.15am and arrives at Liverpool Street at 9.47am. In addition to these services there is an unnamed boat train from Liverpool Street at 2.40pm with a corresponding service from Parkeston Quay at 12.10pm. These trains connect with sailings to and from Esbjerg and are successors to the 'Scandinavian'. On all trains full restaurant car service has been replaced by buffet cars.

The Cornish Riviera Express

It was in July 1904 that the forerunner of the 'Cornish Riviera Express' first made its appearance in the Great Western Railway timetables. Leaving Paddington at 10.10am, the new express, for the first time in GWR history, was booked to run daily to Plymouth without a stop; and as the Westbury route had not then come into use, it had to travel via Bath and the Pylle Hill avoiding line at Bristol, to avoid the small and congested Temple Meads station of those days. The Paddington-Plymouth run was therefore one of 245.7 miles, and by a considerable margin was the longest regular non-stop run in the world at that time.

A variety of engines was used; normally a 'City' class 4-4-0 appeared at the head of the train, but the locomotive might be one of the three French compound Atlantics; the first GWR 4-6-0s, and the 4-4-2s that were built for the purpose of direct comparison with the French engines, were also becoming available. The original 'Limited', at that time unnamed, was a train of seven vehicles — six clerestory-roofed eight-wheelers of the old GWR type, one of which ran through to Falmouth and the remainder to Penzance, with a new 68ft elliptical roofed dining car. The total was about 200 tons.

July 1906 saw the bringing into use of the shorter Westbury route, which cut the distance between Paddington and North Road, Plymouth, from 245.7 to 225.7 miles. The non-stop run to Plymouth was reintroduced, and from that date the train came into operation permanently, summer and winter alike. From Paddington the start was altered to the time-honoured hour of 10.30am, which continued unaltered for over sixty years. Arrival at Plymouth was fixed at 2.37pm, and at Penzance, including stops at the principal stations in Cornwall, at 5.05pm.

By now the Great Western Railway was bringing into use its 70ft coaching stock — the longest and most capacious corridor eight-wheelers that had ever been seen in Great Britain — and the 'Cornish Riviera Limited', as the train had become, was formed of these. Another new departure was the inclusion of slip portions for stations intermediate between Paddington and Plymouth; coaches were slipped at Westbury, Taunton and Exeter, and the 'Limited' thus created another new record by detaching three successive sections before the first stop was reached. Of these the innermost, or Exeter, slip carried the usual slip tail-lamps (red and white side by side); the Taunton slip showed a similar pair of lamps arranged vertically; and the outermost, or Westbury, slip had a special tail lamp indication, consisting of a triangle of lamps, two red and one white.

The effect of this slipping was nicely to proportion the load to the increasing severity of the gradients, as the train worked its way westwards. It would be difficult to find a single run anywhere else in the country with so great a variety of gradients within its length; from Paddington to Reading the course is virtually level; from there to Taunton the inclinations on the westbound journey are no more than moderate. But beyond Taunton there is first the 3-mile climb at 1 in 80-90-127 through the Blackdown Hills to Whiteball summit; and then, after Newton Abbot, there are the formidable ascents to Dainton summit, and from Totnes up to Brent, the former including a short stretch as steep as 1 in 36, and the latter $1\frac{1}{2}$ miles averaging 1 in 50, followed by the $2\frac{1}{4}$-mile descent at 1 in 42 from Hemerdon to Plympton.

Space does not permit a detailed description of the way in which the load of the 'Limited' had developed to the standard prevailing immediately before World War 2. By that time the traffic to Exeter, and the desirability of picking up passengers at Exeter for Cornwall, had resulted in the substitution of a stop at Exeter for the previous slip, leaving only the Westbury and Taunton slip portions, though these had expanded to two coaches each. In all, the 'Limited' now consisted of no fewer than eight through portions daily, except in the height of the summer; these were the main train, with the restaurant cars, for Penzance; a through coach for St Ives, detached at St Erth; one for Falmouth, detached at Truro; one for Newquay, detached at Par; one for Kingsbridge, detached at Exeter and worked forward by a stopping train; the Taunton slip, consisting of through coaches for both Ilfracombe and Minehead; and the two Weymouth coaches slipped at Westbury. At times of weekend pressure, an additional coach might be included for Plymouth, making a ninth portion.

Many different types of stock appeared in succession on the 'Cornish Riviera Limited' in the intervening years. The original 70ft coaches, with recessed end doors only, were succeeded by flush-sided 70ft cars with side doors, then by 60ft vehicles, and, finally, by some new and luxurious stock, introduced shortly before the war, again of maximum width and with recessed end doors. The original composite restaurant car and kitchen also had given place to an independent kitchen and first class car coupled to a third class open car, of very modern design. Again, the 'Star' class 4-cylinder 4-6-0s had been succeeded first by the 'Castles' in 1923, and then by the more powerful 'Kings' in 1926. At this period the empty weight of the 14-coach train out of Paddington had mounted to 498 tons, which meant a loaded weight of at least 530 tons.

By 1939 the winter weight of the down 'Limited' with lighter coaches had diminished to 468 tons empty and nearly 500 tons with a normal complement of passengers and luggage, but on its accelerated schedule the haulage had become one of the most exacting locomotive tasks in the country. New cut-off routes had been built to avoid both Westbury and Frome, so cutting out the service speed restrictions through both stations (incidentally, the Westbury cut-off now made it necessary to detach the Weymouth slip portion at Heywood Road Junction, and to work it over the mile from there into Westbury with a shunting engine), thus slightly reducing the Paddington-Exeter distance to 173.5 miles, but this was scheduled in the working timetable to be covered in 169min start-to-stop, so involving an average speed of 61.6mph throughout. For the 52 miles from Exeter to Plymouth 72min were allowed, and at North Road station, where engines were changed, the booked arrival was 2.35pm. Stopping after that at Par, Truro, Gwinear Road and St Erth, the 'Limited' reached Penzance at 5pm. Through Cornwall the train was usually worked by a 'Castle' class 4-6-0, as this was the heaviest type permitted to work over Saltash bridge. Later the high-pressure 'Counties' became available for the run through Cornwall.

During the currency of the summer timetable, the 'Limited' reverted to a nominal non-stop run between Paddington and Plymouth, covering the distance in 4hr 2min, and reaching Penzance at 4.55pm. In the working timetable, however, a stop was shown at Newton Abbot from 1.43 to 1.47pm to take an assisting engine between there and Plymouth. The summer formation consisted only of sections for Penzance, St Ives, Falmouth, Newquay and Weymouth; the other through portions of the normal winter load were run on additional trains which operated during the summer season only. The summer load of the 'Limited' was normally 12 to 15 bogies to Westbury and two less from there.

For most of its history the 'Cornish Riviera Limited' was an easier working in the up direction than in the down; the up schedule has not been quite so fast, and the absence of Ilfracombe, Minehead and Weymouth portions lightened the load to some degree. On its peacetime schedule, for many years the departure from Penzance was at 10am, and from North Road, Plymouth, at 12.30pm; in the summer the train ran non-stop from here to Paddington, with an allowance of 4¼hr, but during the remaining nine months a stop at Exeter was included, and the train was booked to run up from there in 2hr 55min, arriving at 4.45pm.

One of the most remarkable happenings in the history of this famous train occurred for a week in May 1925 when on the Monday, Wednesday and Friday in the down direction and the Tuesday, Thursday and Saturday in the up, it was worked by the LNER Class A1 Pacific No 4474 *Victor Wild*, turn-and-turn-about with the GWR 4-6-0 No 4074 *Caldicot Castle*. In this exchange trial, which was not without its effect on later LNER locomotive design, the 'Castle' made the better times, and did so on a lower fuel consumption.

When World War 2 broke out, the 10.30am down at first was altered to travel via Bath and Bristol, combining the work of the previous 10am, 10.30am, 11.15am and 12noon trains, but it was soon found impossible to accommodate all these passengers in a single service. So a combined 'Cornish Riviera' and 'Torbay' service via Westbury reappeared at 10.30am, and soon the 'Torbay' was split off as a separate train at 10.40am, leaving the 10.30am as a recognisable wartime edition of its peacetime self, non-stop between Paddington and Exeter, even to the extent of being one of the very few trains in the country still to carry its name on the carriage headboards.

There were no through portions other than the main train from Paddington to Penzance, but as many additional coaches for Plymouth were run on the rear as required, and because of the number of Servicemen travelling, a formation of 14 coaches was usually needed over this stage. The allowance to Exeter was 3½hr (a slowing of 41min); Plymouth was reched at 3.25pm, and Penzance at 6.25pm. In the up direction departure from Penzance was at 9.30am, from Plymouth 12.30pm, and from Exeter 1.55pm, and Paddington was reached at 5.30pm. After the war a cut of 15min each way between Paddington and Exeter was made from 1 October 1945. The allowance over the 173.5 miles from Paddington to Exeter came down to 195min (53.4mph), and Penzance was reached 35min earlier, at 5.50pm, in 7hr 20min from London. Restaurant cars, of an entirely new internal design, reappeared on the last day of 1945.

The summer of 1946 saw a further improvement, with a non-stop run in each direction between Paddington and Plymouth (4½hr down and 4hr 40min up), and the London-Penzance time cut to 6hr 55min down and 7¼hr up. With the winter timetables of

1950-51, the Westbury slip portion was restored to the train.

The summer timetables of 1952 showed another substantial speed-up of the 'Cornish Riviera Express', with $4\frac{1}{4}$hr now allowed in both directions for the 225.5 miles between Paddington and Plymouth, and no stop other than that required for attaching and detaching the assisting locomotive at Newton Abbot. In the 1952-1953 winter timetables the Exeter stop was not reinstated; from then on the time of 6hr 40min from London to Penzance was only 10min slower than that of prewar winters, while the Penzance to London time of $6\frac{3}{4}$hr (the arrival in Paddington was now 4.30pm) was right back to the prewar figure. But the train was lighter in weight, for none of the old through portions were carried, other than the Weymouth slip on the down journey. For a time the 4hr booking from Paddington to Plymouth was restored, but a gradual falling off of traffic made it necessary to increase the usefulness of the train by stopping once again at Exeter.

Then, in 1961, there came a complete recasting of the Western Region timetable which affected the 'Cornish Riviera Express' considerably. Between 1958 and 1960 diesel-hydraulic locomotives had replaced the 'King' 4-6-0s on these workings; first there were the 2,200hp 'Warships', but no acceleration of any note had taken place as yet. In the new timetable every West of England express combined a portion for Penzance or Plymouth with Torbay, and this included the 'Cornish Riviera Express'; also a stop at Taunton as well as Exeter was to be made by each express. Instead of the non-stop run to Plymouth, therefore, the 'Riviera' now had to stop twice *en route* in each direction, and its allowance from Paddington to Plymouth accordingly was increased to $4\frac{1}{4}$hr; as had always been customary, though for no understandable reason, the journey up from Plymouth was allowed 10min more. But better times lay ahead. In this same year there appeared from Swindon Works the first of the 2,700hp 'Western' diesels, which eventually were to make possible times undreamed of previously.

From that time the 'Cornish Riviera Express', still proudly carrying its name and still starting out of Paddington at 10.30am, now had to cover the 142.7 miles to Taunton in 124min, at an average of 69mph. Then, and including the steep climb to Whiteball summit, the 30.8 miles to Exeter were allowed 33min, and here the Torbay portion was detached. Great respect was still paid to the tremendous gradients west of Newton Abbot, the 51 miles from Exeter to Plymouth being allowed as much as 75min, but even so the stop at Plymouth was effected in 4hr from London. At Plymouth the restaurant cars were detached, and from there onwards the train, without any refreshments on the remaining journey of nearly $2\frac{1}{2}$hr, now had ten intermediate stops before finally running into Penzance at 5pm.

Coming up, departure from Penzance was at 10am, and arrival in London at 4.35pm. In the height of the summer the 'Cornish Riviera' omitted the Taunton call, and the Torbay portion ran as a separate train. The nominal limit of load for 'Western' diesels on the winter working was 420 tons tare, but in summer, without the Taunton stop but with the same time to Exeter, 525 tons might be taken. One interesting outcome of the Taunton stop was that, with a change of engine-crew there, the same crew could now work both the down and up 'Limiteds' (the nickname by which this famous train was still known by the staff) to Taunton and back — a coveted assignment! The 1968 timetables saw the train accelerated by 30min down and 35min up. A year later a further acceleration of 25min gave a time to Penzance of 5hr 35min. To meet the new schedule the train was double-headed by two 'Warship' class diesel-hydraulic locomotives.

It may be added that in the spate of train naming by the Western Region between the years 1955 and 1957, partly as an excuse by that Region for painting set trains in the former Great Western Railway chocolate-and-cream colours, two expresses over the West of England main line received names, though neither train was of anything like the same distinction as the 'Cornish Riviera Express'. One was the 1.30pm from Paddington to Penzance, returning at 11am from Penzance to London, which in January 1955, became the 'Royal Duchy', a title which, incidentally, required the consent of Her Majesty the Queen. The locomotives used on these trains carried headboards on which were displayed the arms of the Duchy of Cornwall. The other was the 8.30am from Plymouth to Paddington, and the 5.30pm back, which six months later, because of the association of Plymouth with that famous vessel, were given the title 'Mayflower'. These names survived until 1965, when on the reorganisation of the Western Region main line services, with more intensive rolling stock working than before, there was a general holocaust of WR train names, these among them. There was a brief revival of the 'Mayflower' title in 1970 to mark the 350th anniversary of the Pilgrim Fathers' sailing from Plymouth to America. The name was given to the 7.30am from Paddington, calling at Reading, Taunton, Exeter and Newton Abbot and arriving at Plymouth at 11.28am. The up train left Plymouth at 4.30pm, made the same stops plus Totnes and was at Paddington at 8.30pm. The Reading stops enabled contemporary pilgrims to make their way between Plymouth and the USA by using the Reading-Heathrow Railair Link.

The 'Cornish Riviera' has lived on, but in 1977 compulsory seat reservation was abolished and the 'Limited' was dropped from the title. Class 47 diesel-electric locomotives took over in 1970 after a period of working the train double-headed with diesel-hydraulic B-B 'Warships'. Air-conditioned stock appeared on the principal services to and from Plymouth in the spring of 1972. The Class 47s were succeeded by Class 50s made redundant on the West Coast main line by electrification.

In 1972 the 'Riviera's' departure from Paddington was changed to 11.30am. The 1977 timetable saw it making the fastest run yet between Paddington and Plymouth (3hr 40min down and 3hr 33min up). This was also the year of HSTs on the South Wales and Bristol services. The 'Cornish Riviera' became an HST working in October 1979. Leaving Paddington at 11.40am, it was accelerated by 15min to Exeter (1.54pm), 20min to Plymouth (2.53pm) and 29min to Penzance (4.48pm).

By 1982, with departure from Paddington from Mondays to Fridays at 10.25am, the time to Exeter had been cut to 2hr 10min, to Plymouth to 3hr 7min, and to Penzance to 4hr 57min, including a stop at Reading to pick up only. On Saturdays the Reading stop was omitted, the train left at 11.25am, and the time of 3hr 3min to Plymouth had all but achieved the goal of Plymouth in 3hr from London. The train today is a standard Western Region HST formation, but passengers joining it are reminded that they are about to ride in one of the 'classic' British expresses by 'Cornish Riviera' labels in the windows.

The Cornishman

Among well-known titled trains of the past, the 'Cornishman' of the GWR, though this title was never official enough to appear in timetables or other railway literature of the period, certainly was of sufficient note to deserve a place. It began its career in the days when the main line from Paddington to Penzance was still being operated on Brunel's 7ft gauge, and on 20 May 1892, had the distinction of being the last broad gauge express to leave London for stations in Cornwall before the final change of gauge from 7ft to 4ft 8½in was made.

When the 'Cornishman' came into operation in the summer of 1890, it was the fastest train between London and the West of England, and one of the fastest in the country. Leaving Paddington at 10.15am, it reached Bristol at 12.45pm, Exeter at 2.20pm, Plymouth at 3.50pm, and Penzance at 6.57pm; but contrary to present practice the up run was faster, and with departure from Penzance at 11.15am and arrival in Paddington at 7.50pm the overall time was reduced to 8hr 35min. This, of course, was via Bristol, and over a total distance of 325¼ miles, as compared with the present 305 miles via Westbury. A popular feature of this express was that it deigned to carry third class passengers, at a time when not a few important trains were still first and second only.

In those days the agreement between the GWR and the company controlling the hotel and refreshment rooms at Swindon station made it compulsory to stop every express at Swindon for at least 10 minutes to give passengers time to obtain refreshments. It was not until 1895 that the railway, by paying the large sum of £100,000, obtained release from its engagement, and until 1895, therefore, the 'Cornishman' stopped at Swindon in both directions. The time allowed for the 77.3 miles from Paddington to Swindon was 87min, calling for an average speed of 53.3mph from start to stop over this length.

By 1895 the GWR, now on the standard 4ft 8½in gauge throughout from Paddington to Penzance, had laid down water-troughs near Goring and at Keynsham, between Bath and Bristol, so that with the abolition of the Swindon stop from 1 October 1895, the 'Cornishman' was able to make the first regular non-stop runs between Paddington and Bristol. Departure from London was altered from 10.15 to 10.30am, and the time allowed for the 118.3 miles was cut to 135min, calling for an average speed of 52.6mph. By a further cut of 15min in 1903 the down 'Cornishman' became the first train on record to put Bristol within 2hrs of Paddington daily; the average of 59.2mph start-to-stop still kept this express in the front rank of the fastest British trains.

Well before this date a division into two parts of the 'Cornishman' in each direction, during the height of the summer season, had earned a new record. A relief section for Newquay, timed to leave Paddington at 10.25am, was booked to run the 193.6 miles from Paddington to Exeter without a stop, from 20 July 1896. The running times as far as Bath were unchanged; the train avoided Temple Meads station at Bristol by the relief line, and was due in Exeter at 2.10pm, in 3¾hr from London. Average speed for the run was thus 51.6mph, but the load was five bogie vehicles only. The 10.25am from Paddington reached Plymouth at 3.37pm, and stood there 5min; the next stop was at Par at 4.45pm, and arrival in Newquay was at 5.47pm. In the reverse direction, leaving Newquay at 11.05am, calling at all stations up to Par and after that at Liskeard, Devonport, Plymouth, Exeter and Bristol, the up express was due in Paddington at 6.48pm.

By an easy margin the run between Paddington and Exeter at that time was the longest in the world without intermediate stop. From 1899 non-stop running in the up direction became regular throughout the year, and from 1902 in the down direction also; then, from 1 July 1904, came the complete eclipse of the 'Cornishman' by the new 'Cornish Riviera Limited' express, with its daily runs of 245.6 miles in each direction between Paddington and North Road station at Plymouth. From then on, even as an unofficial nickname, no more was heard of the 'Cornishman'.

In the summer of 1952, however, the name 'Cornishman' was revived, but this time officially, and applied to an entirely different service — that running daily between Wolverhampton, Birmingham, Plymouth and Penzance by way of Stratford-on-Avon and Cheltenham. In the earlier years of Great Western history, GWR communication between the Midlands and the West of England had to be made circuitously by Oxford and the west curve at Didcot on to the Bristol main line. Then, in 1908, the GWR opened a new and costly direct route which enabled this company to compete much more effectively than before with the Midland Birmingham-Bristol route through Cheltenham. The new Great Western line took off from the London main line at Tyseley, 3 miles south of Birmingham (Snow Hill), cut in a south-westerly direction through Stratford-on-Avon to the northern fringes of the Cotswolds, connecting with the Oxford-Worcester main line at Honeybourne, and then continuing through Broadway to a new station at Cheltenham called Malvern Road.

The express next used the joint Midland-Great Western line from Cheltenham to Gloucester, but left it just short of Gloucester to join the GWR Gloucester-London line, so by-passing Gloucester to the east. At Standish Junction the trains of the Great Western Birmingham-Bristol service crossed over to the parallel Midland line, and with the aid of running powers made use of the latter as far south as Yate. There they branched off, to run up a short spur to the Swindon-South Wales main line of the GWR, which they followed to Stoke Gifford, then branching through Filton and Stapleton Road into Temple Meads station at Bristol.

At first, several through services in each direction daily were established, but in the course of years their number diminished, until by 1939 only one through service continued to run throughout the year, at 10.40am from Wolverhampton and 11.20am from Birmingham, reaching Bristol at 1.35pm, Plymouth at 4.52pm and Penzance at 7.45pm. It returned from Penzance at 10.45am, Plymouth at 1.40pm and Bristol at 4.45pm, reaching Birmingham at 7pm and Wolverhampton at 7.30pm.

This train was suspended during World War 2, but subsequently reappeared, running in much the same times until the summer of 1952, when its timing was altered completely and, as previously mentioned, it received the title of 'Cornishman'. The new 'Cornishman' left Wolverhampton at 9.15am and Birmingham (Snow Hill) at 9.50am. Calling after that at Stratford-on-Avon and Cheltenham (Malvern Road), it diverted from the previous Gloucester by-pass to stop in the one-time Midland station, before resuming its journey to Bristol, which was reached at 12.28pm. Restarting 7min later, it served Taunton by means of a slip-coach, and ran into Exeter at 2.08pm. The next stop was Plymouth (3.30pm-3.35pm), and after calls at principal stations in Cornwall, Penzance was reached at 5.55pm.

The return journey began from Penzance at 10.30am; stops were made at St Erth, Truro, St Austell and Par (not at Bodmin Road or Liskeard in this direction), and Plymouth was left at 12.58pm. The Exeter stop was at 2.19pm-2.22pm and that at Bristol at 3.56pm-4.02pm, and with the same stops beyond as on the reverse run, Birmingham was reached at 6.38pm and Wolverhampton at 7.28pm. Refreshment facilities were available for the entire journey, and through coaches, detached and attached at Exeter, were run between Wolverhampton, Torquay and Kingswear.

Later the 'Cornishman' underwent a number of changes. When almost all the passenger traffic was withdrawn from the Honeybourne-Cheltenham line, it was decided to transfer the train to the former Midland line between Birmingham and Cheltenham, which meant using New Street instead of Snow Hill station at Birmingham. It could have been run on, of course, to the High Level instead of the Low Level station at Wolverhampton, but it was decided instead greatly to increase the train's usefulness by continuing it over the former Midland line to Derby and Sheffield. The final stage was a further extension to Leeds and Bradford, so that the 'Cornishman' provided a daily through service between Bradford and Penzance.

Until the end of April 1967 Forster Square station at Bradford was the starting-point, and the former Midland line was used, not merely from there into the City station at Leeds, but after reversal at Leeds on by the Midland route through Normanton to Sheffield.

From 1 May 1967, however, in common with almost all other trains for the Midland line, the 'Cornishman' started from Bradford Exchange, called at New Pudsey, and took the new spur line into Leeds City, from which after reversal it proceeded to Wakefield Westgate, giving through facilities from Wakefield to the West of England for the first time. Out of Wakefield it travelled over the former Great Northern main line to Moorthorpe, where it ran up the spur to what was the Swinton & Knottingley Joint Line, regaining the Midland line at Swinton. Departure from Bradford was at 7.06am and from Leeds at 7.36am; Birmingham was left at 10.25am, and at the other end of the journey Plymouth was reached at 3.08 and Penzance at 5.55pm. In the reverse direction departure from Penzance was at 11am and from Plymouth at 1.30pm, Leeds City being reached at 9.31 and Bradford Exchange at 10.07pm. A restaurant car was provided, though between Sheffield and Plymouth only. Torbay had a through portion to and from Sheffield, but in the height of the season this was run as a separate train. Bradford connections with the 'Cornishman' were broken on Saturdays in 1971.

The name 'Cornishman' was discarded in 1975. The train had foreshadowed the development of the former Midland Railway's Derby-Bristol main line as a principal cross-country artery which began with planning in the mid-1960s. By October 1981 the first HST sets were being phased in, beginning with a Leeds-Plymouth and a Leeds-Bristol train in each direction. In the summer timetable of 1982 a through HST service between Penzance and Edinburgh echoed the 'Cornishman' in its later years, although serving Leeds and Bradford only by connections. The Penzance-Sheffield journey was now reduced to 6hr 47min in each direction.

The Coronation

Experience with the 'Silver Jubilee' having proved that the British public both wanted high speed and was prepared to pay for it, the LNER management decided in 1936 to add to its streamline trains. The second LNER streamliner thus to come into service, in July 1937, was the 'Coronation', so named in honour of the Coronation in that year of King George VI and Queen Elizabeth.

The 'Silver Jubilee' had shown that time could be maintained without difficulty on a 4hr schedule over the 268.4 miles between King's Cross and Newcastle; a further 2hr over the 124.5 miles between Newcastle and Edinburgh would put the Scottish capital within 6hr of London. Such a time had not been dreamed of since the 'Race to Aberdeen' in 1895, when the quickest time from King's Cross to Edinburgh Waverley came down to 6hr 19min.

But that was with a train weighing 105 tons only; and when the new 'Coronation' apeared, in all its glory, it was found that the weight of the nine coaches complete was no less than 312 tons, or 42% more than the original 'Silver Jubilee' seven-car train. It was over 26% heavier than the 'Jubilee' as rebuilt with eight cars. This difference was destined to influence the locomotive performance considerably, and the 'Coronation' was always a very much harder locomotive working than its predecessor, especially as the streamlined 'A4' Pacific locomotive was required to work through between London and Edinburgh.

The new 'Coronation' set consisted of nine cars, of very striking appearance both outside and inside. The exterior had an enamelled motorcar body finish in two shades of blue, with light blue upper panels, and a dark shade, known as 'Garter blue', for the lower panels. The set of nine cars consisted of four articulated 'twins', with a tail car that was unique in British coachbuilding practice.

The rear end, of 'beaver tail' design, reversed the wedge front of the streamlined locomotive, and was designed to reduce the air resistance caused by the suction of a normal square coach-end on the back of a train travelling at high speed. Further, this rear coach was designed as an observation car — the first of its kind since the building of the Pullman observation car, *Maid of Morven*, for the Glasgow-Oban service — and so was equipped with loose armchairs, and was available to passengers of both classes on payment of a small fee of 1s (5p) for one hour's stay.

The rest of the train, from south to north, comprised third-class brake, third and kitchen, two firsts, third, third and kitchen, third and third brake. Two kitchens were provided in order that passengers might be served without leaving their seats, as in Pullman practice. For the first time in Great Britain, electrically operated pressure ventilation was provided throughout the train, changing the air in each coach automatically every three minutes.

This made it possible to provide each coach with

double windows, permanently closed, and with the help of acoustic blankets, something as nearly approaching silent travel as could be hoped for, together with an equable temperature and complete absence of draughts, was actually achieved. Even the cutlery was provided with flat handles, so that the quietness might not be disturbed by rattling when the tables were laid! Each first-class seat was arranged in an alcove, and had a swivelling chair and a table tapering outwards towards the window, so permitting the traveller to turn his chair towards the window, and enjoy the view to better advantage. The decorations, in aluminium and colour throughout the train, were very original, and the vista along the central aisle, through the succession of partition openings framed in their aluminium architraves, was most attractive.

A long-felt need was met by starting the down 'Coronation' from King's Cross at 4 o'clock in the afternoon, so permitting a business man to have almost the entire day in London, and yet to be in Edinburgh by 10pm. In order not to interfere with the existing 4pm down Leeds express, the timetable authorities arranged for the two trains to start simultaneously, the 'Coronation' from No 5 platform, and the Leeds train from No 10; the latter took the slow road, and followed the 'Coronation' on the main line from No 5 box at the north end of Finsbury Park.

From King's Cross to York the 'Coronation' was booked to cover the 188.2 miles in 157min, and the start-to-stop average speed of 71.9mph so entailed made this the fastest regularly scheduled run in the British Empire. The train passed Peterborough, 76.4 miles, in 64min; Grantham, 105.5 miles, in 88min; and Doncaster, 156 miles, in 128½min. York was reached at 6.37pm; and here a stop of 3min was made.

At first the run of 204.7 miles from York to Edinburgh was made non-stop, but as the up 'Coronation' called at Newcastle, it was soon realised that, even allowing for the 'Silver Jubilee' 1½hr later, the potential Newcastle traffic on the down journey was too important to be overlooked. It was therefore arranged that the down 'Coronation' should make two stops, at both York and Newcastle, within the compass of its 6hr allowance, and from then on the 80.2 miles from York to Newcastle were run in 77min, and the Tyneside city was reached at 7.57pm. Leaving Newcastle at 8pm, the 'Coronation' had two hours left for the final 124.5 miles.

In the up direction, departure from Edinburgh was fixed half an hour later than in the down, at 4.30pm. This brought the 'Coronation' into Newcastle at 6.30pm, and it left at 6.33pm on a non-stop journey of 268.4 miles to King's Cross, reached at 10.30pm. Newcastle was therefore in the enviable position of having two streamline trains in each direction to and from London, down at 4pm and 5.30pm in 3hr 57min and 4hr respectively, and up at 10am and 6.33pm

The 'Coronation' soon became as popular as the 'Silver Jubilee' and began to run daily filled to capacity. For the through journey between London and Edinburgh the supplementary fare charged was 6s (30p) first class and 4s (20p) third class. In the winter, as most of the journey was made after dark, it was decided to detach the observation car, and this had the effect of reducing the weight behind the locomotive to 278 tons tare, which was particularly advantageous when weather conditions were at their worst. The full 312-ton load, which with passengers and luggage made about 330 tons with all seats occupied, ultimately was run during the height of the summer season only.

Unlike the 'Silver Jubilee' and the 'West Riding Limited', the 'Coronation' required two complete trains for the maintenance of daily service, and a fifth set of streamline cars was built to be used as a substitute for any of the regular streamline sets when they went into the works for overhaul. On the outbreak of war all the streamliners were withdrawn and the five trains were stored in remote places, where they would be unlikely to suffer damage, to wait for the return of peace. After that the sets of cars were split up, and used for ordinary passenger purposes. In the years after the war the place of the 'Coronation' was taken by the 'Talisman', which ultimately made a faster run with a considerably heavier load.

Five streamlined 'A4' Pacifics were specially allocated to the 'Coronation' service — Nos 4488 *Union of South Africa*; 4489 *Dominion of Canada*; 4490 *Empire of India*; 4491 *Commonwealth of Australia*; and 4492 *Dominion of New Zealand*. Other engines of the same class took their turns in the working, however, when occasion required.

The Coronation Scot

After the days of West Coast and East Coast competition, which reached its culmination in the 'Race to Edinburgh' of 1888 and the still more exciting 'Race to Aberdeen' in 1895, the railways up the two sides of the country worked in a certain measure of harmony, and declared to one another in advance any plans they might be making for improvements of their service. When the LNER, in the autumn of 1936, announced its intention of celebrating the Coronation year by introducing in the summer of 1937 a streamline high-speed train between London and Edinburgh, it seemed highly probable that the LMSR would follow suit.

Probability changed to certainty in November 1936 when the LMSR staged an unprecedented test journey from Euston to Glasgow and back. On 7 November, the non-streamlined Pacific No 6201 *Princess Elizabeth* (no streamlined 4-6-2s had been built to that date), was attached to a train of seven coaches, and worked non-stop over the 401.4 miles from Euston to Glasgow Central in 5hr 53½min. On the following day, in rain and high wind, the same locomotive, with one coach more, ran from Glasgow to Euston, again non-stop, in the astonishing time of 5hr 44¼min, so completing the entire run at an average speed of precisely 70mph. It has to be remembered that this remarkable feat of locomotive endurance included lifting the train in succession to the summits at Beatock and Shap, respectively 1,015 and 915ft above the sea, with a drop intermediately to sea level north of Carlisle.

The feasibility of high-speed schedules having been demonstrated in this striking way, it was, perhaps, a little disappointing that the booking of the 'Coronation Scot' was fixed at 6½hr in each direction, inclusive of a two-minute stop at Carlisle; even if a 6hr overall time, like that of the LNER 'Coronation' over a distance 8.7 miles less, were cutting it fine, one of 6¼hr might well have been tried, especially now that the first streamlined Pacifics were available. A later afternoon departure had also been confidently expected, but it was held that this would cause too much interference with the night freight trains, and the start from both terminals was therefore fixed at 1.30pm.

Before the 'Coronation Scot' began its regular running, a test trip took place on 29 June 1937 from Euston to Crewe and back. On the down journey the point-to-point bookings of the new schedule were worked as far as Stafford, but the engine, *Coronation*, was then opened out, and at the foot of the 1 in 177 past Madeley reached 114mph. On the return journey the 270-ton train was worked from Crewe to Euston, 158.1 miles, in the record time of 119min, at an average speed of 79.7mph from start to stop, reaching 100mph at Castlethorpe. The fact that 25min were gained on the 'Coronation Scot' schedule from Crewe once again demonstrated how ample a margin of time the new train would have on its booking in day-to-day running.

The original 'Coronation Scot' train consisted of nine bogie vehicles weighing 297 tons. Actually it was not a streamlined train but consisted of standard stock adapted for the purpose, and painted blue, with horizontal white lines which continued the white lines carried by the streamlined blue locomotive and tender. On the northbound journey, from the engine backwards, the train consisted of corridor third class brake, open third class, kitchen car, two open thirds, kitchen car, open first, corridor first, and corridor first brake.

In 1939 the first vehicles of a new and more luxurious 'Coronation Scot' train were built, including a first class buffet lounge of novel design; externally, instead of the original blue, the new coaches were painted standard LMSR red, with horizontal gold lines, and most of the streamlined Pacifics were painted to match. The new vehicles were sent to New York for exhibition at the New York World's Fair in 1939, with the locomotive *Coronation*; the latter returned to this country during the war, but in view of the risks of sea transport, the coaches were loaned by the LMSR to the United States, to serve as a rest train for officers until after the war, when they also returned to England.

The 'Coronation Scot' departure from Euston at 1.30pm displaced the 'Midday Scot', which for more than 10 years previously had left at that time. The 'Scot' was booked to pass Rugby at 2.46pm, and Crewe at 3.54pm, reaching Carlisle at 6.13pm. The 299.1 miles had thus to be covered in 283min at an average speed of 63.4mph. Departure from Carlisle was at 6.15pm, and the remaining 102.3 miles over Beattock Summit to Glasgow had to be run in 105min, with an arrival at 8pm.

In the reverse direction the 'Coronation Scot' left Glasgow Central at 1.30pm, called at Carlisle from 3.15 to 3.17pm, and was due in Euston at 8pm. The two trains were booked to pass each other at Preston; the northbound train was due through this Lancashire city at 4.44pm, and the southbound at 4.45pm. A seat charge of 2s 6d (12½p) was required of both first class and third class passengers.

The locomotive was invariably one of the streamlined Pacifics, which worked through between Euston and Glasgow in both directions, with a change of crew at Carlisle. On one or two occasions an extra coach was run in the train for some special purpose, but normally the nine-coach formation was strictly adhered to. In signalling the 'Coronation Scot' a special 'Is line clear?' bell was used: this was 4-4-4, or four beats repeated three times. The 'Coronation Scot' was not reinstated after the war.

The Devon Belle

On 16 June 1947 the Southern Railway, as it then still was, broke some entirely new ground by instituting an all-Pullman service between London and Devonshire. Pullman cars had been seen previously in the county of cream and cider, during the short-lived reign of the Great Western 'Torquay Pullman' in 1929, but never west of Basingstoke on the Southern line. The main objective of the new train — the 'Devon Belle' — was Ilfracombe, but it was decided to add a through portion for Plymouth also. At first six cars for Ilfracombe and four for Plymouth were thought to be adequate, but it soon became apparent, especially at the height of the season, that the Ilfracombe section was nothing like capacious enough, and the 'Devon Belle' frequently was increased at weekends to a total of 14 cars. This was a train of 545 tons tare, or 575 tons with passengers and luggage — a tremendous load to work over the heavy gradients west of Salisbury, especially up the long 1 in 80 from Seaton Junction to Honiton Tunnel, but one for which the 'Merchant Navy' Pacifics proved themselves thoroughly adequate.

It was hoped, when the advent of the new train was announced, that the schedule would enable the Bulleid Pacifics to display their real powers, and it was a disappointment to discover that the new train was to amble down from Waterloo to Salisbury in almost exactly the same time as the 'Atlantic Coast Express' (actually 102min), while the up train would have the same allowance (96min) as the up 'Atlantic Coast Express'. As it was not intended to pick up or set down passengers at Salisbury, it was decided not to obstruct the platforms by changing engines there — a non-stop run of 159¾ miles from Waterloo to Sidmouth Junction was, of course, impossible, as the engine tenders could not carry anything like enough water for the purpose — but to make the change at the next station, Wilton, instead. In all the history of the SR and its predecessors, no trains had ever previously run through Salisbury without stopping, apart from the Plymouth-Waterloo boat trains of 1903-1904, which were non-stop from Templecombe to Waterloo, but these ran at intermittent intervals only; the 'Devon Belle' was the only train ever to do so regularly.

The 'Devon Belle' was booked to leave Waterloo at 12 noon, and to run the 86.3 miles to Wilton in 107min, arriving at 1.47pm. After a six-minute halt, the 'Belle' then had to cover the 73.3 miles to Sidmouth Junction in 83min — a vastly harder proposition than the initial stage. After a stop from 3.16 to 3.20pm at Sidmouth Junction (to connect with Sidmouth and Budleigh Salterton) a 16min run over the 12.2 miles brought the 'Belle' into Exeter Central at 3.36pm. Here the train was split into its two sections. The Plymouth section left first, at 3.41pm in charge of a 'West Country' Pacific. After stopping at Exeter St Davids it carried on over the top of Dartmoor and stopping at Okehampton and Devonport, made its way into Plymouth North Road at 5.25pm and Friary at 5.36pm. The Ilfracombe section got away from Exeter Central at 3.48pm, and after a stop at St Davids ran the 39.1 miles to Barnstaple Junction, largely single line, in 56min. Subsequent stops were at Barnstaple Town, Braunton, and Mortehoe, and banking assistance was essential up the 1 in 40 from Heddon Mill to Mortehoe. After the abrupt drop into Ilfracombe, the popular Devon resort was reached at 5.33pm, in just over 5½hr from Waterloo.

The up 'Devon Belle' had a better timing from Ilfracombe of 5hr 20min partly because of following the Plymouth portion into Exeter, and thus having a shorter stop at Central. So, whereas the Plymouth and Ilfracombe times from Waterloo more or less tied, the Plymouth portion coming up made its exit from Friary station at 11.30am, half-an-hour before the Ilfracombe departure at 12 noon. The Ilfracombe section, very likely with a 'West Country' Pacific at the rear as well as one in front, had to start by tackling the steepest main line gradient in Great Britain, 2¼ miles at 1 in 36 up to Mortehoe. The 1 in 37 from Exeter St Davids up to Central demanded a couple of *ex*-Brighton 0-6-2 tank bankers, and very likely a similar engine as pilot, if the full 10 cars were in the Ilfracombe section. Leaving Exeter Central at 1.44pm, and Sidmouth Junction at 2.04pm, the 'Devon Belle' ran the difficult 73.3 miles to Wilton in 89min, and then, after a six-minute stop to change engines, from 3.33 to 3.39pm, the 'Devon Belle' was into Waterloo by 5.20pm.

Two vehicles of a very original description in the 'Devon Belle' formations were the observation cars. These were two third class cars, Nos 13 and 14, which were completely rebuilt in the Pullman shops for service on these trains. They were not the first observation cars in Great Britain, as they were long preceded by the first class Pullman observation car, *Maid of Morven*, run for years during the summer season, originally by the Caledonian Railway and later by the LMSR, between Glasgow and Oban. The 'Coronation' streamline trains of the LNER between King's Cross and Edinburgh also had their beaver-tail observation cars. But the 'Devon Belle' cars were the first ever to run on Southern metals. Rather more than half of each car was given over to observation, with an almost unbroken range of windows along each side and across the back end. The seating was of an 'occasional' type, in comfortable single armchairs and double settees that could be swung to any angle. The other end of the car was occupied by a refreshment buffet, with small kitchen and pantry.

Complicated car-turning and re-marshalling arrangements were necessary at both the London and Ilfracombe ends of the journey to ensure that the observation car was always on the rear of the train, with the observation end outward. As for the remainder of the 'Devon Belle', there were two first class cars in the Ilfracombe portion, and one in the Plymouth portion; the rest of the train was third class, except for the space taken up by kitchens and pantries of which there were two, so that passengers might be served with meals and refreshments at their own seats throughout the length of the train. At first the 'Devon Belle' operated at weekends only, but in the summer of 1949 it was altered to run five days a week each way — Thursdays to Mondays inclusive in the down direction, and Fridays to Tuesdays in the up, Sundays included, and during the currency of the summer timetable only, from June to September inclusive.

The summer of 1950 saw a considerable change in the working, for the Plymouth section was withdrawn, and what had been the Plymouth cars were detached at Exeter Central on the down journey, and attached there on the up. The stop of the Ilfracombe section at Exeter was curtailed accordingly, and Ilfracombe was reached 6min earlier than previously, at 5.27pm. No change was made in the up schedule, other than a slight adjustment of station times at Exeter. In 1952 it was decided at first to withdraw the 'Devon Belle', owing to lack of patronage, except on Saturdays, but eventually it was reinstated, down on Fridays, Saturdays and Sundays, and up on Saturdays, Sundays and Mondays, during the summer season. Owing to still declining custom, however, it was withdrawn at the end of the 1954 summer season.

The Devonian

Strictly speaking, for more than half of each year 'Devonian', when first introduced, was almost a misnomer for the train of which it was the title. For the express proper ran over LMSR metals between Bradford and Bristol, and did not actually touch Devonshire. A set of three coaches, however, was handed over to the Great Western Railway at Temple Meads station, Bristol, and was worked through by that company to Torquay and Paignton, and it was this through coach working that justified the name.

The trains on which the through Bradford-Paignton coaches worked were of old standing, and had seen little change up to the time when the title 'Devonian' was conferred in 1927. After that they participated in the general Midland Division accelerations of 1937, and became very fast over the Birmingham-Bristol section.

The southbound 'Devonian' was due to leave Bradford at 10.25am, to reverse in Leeds City station and leave at 10.52am on a 50-minute run to Sheffield. After 5min there, the express made a non-stop run to Derby in 53min. Here the train dropped a through coach from Bradford to Bournemouth and acquired a Newcastle-Bristol coach which had come south on the 10.20am from York. For the 41.3 miles from Derby to Birmingham the allowance was 47min, and a wait of 6min was imposed at the great Midland city.

With the compass of 53min allowed from Birmingham to Cheltenham, 45.5 miles, the 'Devonian' had to climb to Barnt Green and make a service stop at Blackwell before descending the Lickey incline, after which it travelled at over a mile a minute all the way to Cheltenham. The stops here and at the closely adjacent town of Gloucester, with the short run between, took up 16min, and the concluding run on LMSR metals was over the 37 miles from Gloucester to Bristol in 44min. For cross-country running of this description over a hard road, with numerous stops, the time of 4hr 40min for the 206 miles from Leeds to Bristol was an excellent one; it was the best of the day. The through Paignton coaches waited at Temple Meads from 3.32 to 3.50pm, and then left on a Great

Western express of no special distinction, making numerous intermediate stops and reaching Torquay at 6.44 and Paignton at 6.51pm. The entire journey of 323 miles from Bradford to Paignton thus took 8hr 26min, but the GWR section lowered the average speed considerably.

Northbound, the through coaches of the 'Devonian' left Paignton at 9.15 and Torquay at 9.22am for a similarly leisurely run to Bristol, reached at 12.13pm. From here the 'Devonian', with its restaurant cars, was timed to start at 12.35pm. First came a 43min run to Gloucester, beginning with the tremendous pull up to Fishponds, 2 miles at between 1 in 69 and 1 in 90, so that high-speed travelling was necessary from Yate onwards to maintain this timing over a 37-mile run. After Cheltenham, too, this train was one of those booked to cover the 31.1 miles from Cheltenham to Bromsgrove in 3min start-to-stop, before attaching the 'banker' required for assistance up the Lickey incline. Yet the 45.5 miles from Cheltenham to Birmingham were run in 54min.

The rest of the journey needs little description; there was an additional stop at Burton-on-Trent, and leaving Birmingham New Street at 2.37pm, the 'Devonian' was in Derby at 3.25pm, Sheffield at 4.25pm, Leeds at 5.24pm and Bradford at 5.54pm, 8hr 39min after leaving Paignton. Between Leeds and Bristol the engines used were almost invariably of the 'Jubilee' 3-cylinder 4-6-0 type, though a Class 5 4-6-0 might appear at times, and would prove an adequate substitute. From May to September inclusive the entire train, including LMSR stock and restaurant cars, ran through between Bradford and Kingswear. On Saturdays it divided into several parts.

The through service came to an end on the outbreak of World War 2, but was restored in October 1946 with a time of $8\frac{3}{4}$hr from Bradford to Torquay and 8hr 57min back.

After that there was a considerable deterioration, the overall time in 1947 increasing to 9hr 48min from Bradford to Kingswear and 9hr 37min in the reverse direction, while during the winter the train operated to and from Bristol only and was nameless. In the succeeding years it was subject of numerous changes, and the last of them, from 1 May 1967, was the transfer of the northern starting point from Bradford Forster Square to Exchange, and, after reversal at Leeds City, from the Normanton to the Wakefield Westgate (with a stop there) route and by the Moorthorpe spur to the Swinton & Knottingley line, regaining the former Midland route at Swinton. Throughout the year the 'Devonian' then ran between Bradford and Paignton (not Kingswear), and was considerably accelerated. It had the special distinction of being the only non-stop train between Birmingham and Bristol, southbound in 105min and northbound in 110min for the 88.9 miles, including the steep climbs out of both New Street and Temple Meads, the Lickey incline, and a number of speed restrictions.

Leaving Bradford at 10.05 and Leeds at 10.35am, the 'Devonian' got away from Sheffield at 11.52am; Derby was the only stop between there and Birmingham, from which departure in the even-interval sequence was at 1.25pm, Bristol being reached at 3.10pm. After this the stops were at Weston-super-Mare, Taunton, Exeter, Dawlish, Teignmouth and Newton Abbot to Torquay, 5.48, and Paignton, 5.55pm. At that time, usually with 'Peak' diesel power, the time of 4hr 35min from Leeds to Bristol was 5min less than the 4hr 40min with steam power in 1937; overall, the time from Bradford to Paignton was 7hr 50min. In the northbound direction, with departure from Paignton at 9.55 and Torquay at 10.03am, the 'Devonian' made the same stops and was into Leeds by 5.22pm, but 36min more were needed before the Bradford arrival at 5.58pm, a total journey of 8hr 3min. The 'Devonian' provided one of the best examples in Great Britain of a fast cross-country service providing valuable facilities throughout its course. It carried a restaurant car between Leeds and Paignton. The name was dropped in 1975. Briefly in 1970 a Paignton-Newcastle service (7.20am northbound and 12.05pm return) carried 'Torbay-Tyne' headboards, while the 7am Weston-super-Mare to Newcastle and 4.20pm return was labelled 'Severn-Tyne', but these names did not appear in the timetable.

A through Bradford/Leeds-Paignton service featured in the first full HST timetables over the North-east-South-west route in 1982, with the uncomfortably early departure times of 6.15am from Bradford and 6.46 from Leeds, but a journey of 6hr 40min from Bradford to Paignton may be considered a compensation. The northbound train left Paignton at 1.34pm was at Leeds in 5hr 39min (with a connection to Bradford), and continued to Newcastle.

The East Anglian, The Norfolkman and The Broadsman

In the Coronation year, 1937, when new streamline trains were being put on between London and Edinburgh, and London, Leeds and Bradford, the LNER authorities thought the time opportune for extending somewhat similar facilities to East Anglia. It was therefore decided to build a new six-coach train with interior furnishing similar to that of the streamliners, and to install it on the Liverpool Street-Norwich service. For the working of the train, two B17 three-cylinder 4-6-0 engines, Nos 2859 and 2870, were specially streamlined, and received the names *East Anglian* and *City of London* respectively.

But when the new schedules were made public, they proved, by comparison with the streamline achievements elsewhere, to be somewhat of an anti-climax. The down 'East Anglian' was to start from Liverpool Street at 6.40pm, call at Ipswich from 8.00 to 8.04pm, and reach Norwich Thorpe at 8.55pm. This entailed average start-to-stop speeds of 51.5 and 54.5mph respectively over the two stages. In the up direction, departure from Norwich was at 11.55am, a stop was made at Ipswich from 12.46 to 12.50pm, and Liverpool Street was reached at 2.10pm.

A year later the schedule was reduced from $2\frac{1}{4}$hr to 2hr 10min, with 2min cut from the Ipswich stop and 3min from the Ipswich-Norwich timing; the latter became 48min for 46.3 miles, and required a start-to-stop average of 57.9mph — the fastest known until then on Great Eastern metals. The 'East Anglian' now left Norwich at 12 noon, and was back into Thorpe Station at 8.50pm. Nevertheless, recalling the fact that the 50-ton Great Eastern 'Claud Hamilton' 4-4-0s used to get the 'Norfolk Coast Express', made up to 12, 13, and even 14 bogies, through Ipswich in 83min, and past Trowse, a mile outside Norwich, in 2hr 14min, many felt that with a streamlined 4-6-0 and a six-coach train a two-hour timing to and from Norwich might have been reasonably possible. Actually this ideal was not destined to be realised until 15 years after the 'East Anglian' first came into service.

The formation of the 'East Anglian' on the down journey, from the engine backwards, was third class brake, first class and kitchen, open first, open third, third and kitchen, and third brake; the entire train was of centre corridor stock, and passengers were served with meals and refreshments without leaving their seats. The tare weight of the six cars was 219 tons, and the normal full weight 235 tons. As the speed was far from reaching the recognised streamline level it was not thought advisable to make any supplementary charge for the use of the train, which was therefore open to ordinary ticket-holders without restriction.

At times there was some lively running, especially north of Ipswich. Actual times were recorded of $44\frac{1}{2}$min from Norwich to Ipswich and 42min in the reverse direction for the 46.3 miles, and between Ipswich and Liverpool Street there were net times as little as 72min up and $70\frac{1}{4}$min down, so demonstrating the feasibility of a two-hour schedule, despite the difficulties of the route. The 'East Anglian', which was withdrawn on the outbreak of war, ran from Mondays to Fridays inclusive, but not on Saturdays.

It was restored to the timetable on 7 October 1946, at the old starting times of 6.40pm down and 11.50am up (later 11.40am), and on a schedule of 2hr 20min. Also, in October 1948, the 'East Anglian' was joined by a new express called the 'Norfolkman', designed to give exactly the same facilities between Liverpool Street, Ipswich and Norwich down in the morning and up in the evening as the 'East Anglian' gave in the reverse direction. The 'Norfolkman' left Liverpool Street at 10am, reaching Norwich Thorpe at 12.20pm; return was at 5pm and Liverpool Street was reached at 7.20pm. In the summer service, the 'Norfolkman' prolonged its journey to Cromer, with a time of 3hr 22min down and 3hr 20min up, including a wait of 15min at Norwich. Stops were made at Wroxham and North Walsham. Normally the 'East Anglian' and the 'Norfolkman' were loaded to eight bogie vehicles apiece, and were worked by B1 4-6-0s between London and Norwich.

In the summer of 1951, with the arrival of the new 'Britannia' class Pacific engines at Stratford and Norwich sheds, a complete recasting of the Great Eastern timetable took place. Uniformly with the other principal expresses, the down 'Norfolkman' and 'East Anglian' were altered to start at 30min past the hour — 9.30am in the former case and 6.30pm in the latter — and had their London-Norwich times cut to 2hr 10min each (76min Liverpool Street to Ipswich and 51min thence to Norwich). In the reverse direction, to conform to the 45-minute departures from Norwich, the up 'East Anglian' was moved to 11.45am, and the up 'Norfolkman' to 5.45pm, with 51min allowed to Ipswich, 77min thence to Liverpool Street, and again an overall time of 2hr 10min.

The 'Broadsman', when its title was first conferred in 1950, made a not very exciting journey from Cromer at 6.28am and Norwich at 7.30am, to reach Liverpool Street at 10.16am; returning at 3.40pm, the train was into Norwich by 6.16pm and Cromer by 7.15pm. But in the summer of 1951 the 'Broadsman' shared in the tremendous speed-up which followed the introduction of the 'Britannia' class Pacifics between Liverpool Street and Norwich. The start of the Sheringham coaches was altered from 6.03 to 6.20am, and of the main train from Cromer to 6.45am; from Norwich the train got away at 7.45am, to reach Liverpool Street 9min earlier, at 10.07am. This meant an acceleration of 26min on the run. The down 'Broadsman' joined the fleet of 130min expresses between London and Norwich, now leaving Liverpool Street at 3.30pm, and getting into Norwich by 5.40pm, Cromer by 6.40pm and Sheringham by 7.06pm, a cut of 26min in this direction also.

But in mid-September, 1952, a more startling acceleration of the 'Broadsman' took place, introducing the first mile-a-minute timing on record in East Anglia. For the down train from then on was booked to reach Norwich in the even 2hr from Liverpool Street, divided in the proportion of 73min for the 68.7 miles to Ipswich, and 45min only for the 46.3 miles from there to Norwich Thorpe. The up 'Broadsman' also was speeded up, and with stops at Diss, Stowmarket and Ipswich had to make the 115-mile run in 2¼hr, reaching Liverpool Street at 10am. Both trains were limited to a maximum load of nine bogies, weighing about 300 tons tare.

In the summer of 1953, to allow three instead of two minutes at the Ispwich stop, the allowance of the down 'Broadsman' from Ipswich to Norwich was cut to 44min, raising the start-to-stop speed to 63.1mph. But of this schedule the 'Britannia' Pacifics could make light, as on the day when No 70035 *Rudyard Kipling*, with a train of 310 tons tare and 325 tons gross, covered the distance in 39min 7sec, reeling off 26½ miles at an average of 84.4mph and touching 94mph at Diss. Incidentally, by now Cromer High station, the old Great Eastern terminus, had been closed, and with the concentration of all traffic at the former Midland & Great Northern Cromer Beach, the 'Broadsman' had ceased to call at Cromer Junction to detach the Sheringham portion, but did so at Cromer Beach instead.

With the advent of diesel power, in the form of Class 40 2,000hp 1Co-Co1 units the 'Broadsman' lost its speed supremacy, for two hours now became the standard time in each direction for all the faster Liverpool Street-Norwich trains. A second intermediate stop was introduced at Colchester, without any increase in the two-hour time. So now these expresses had to cover the 51.7 miles from Liverpool Street to Colchester in 50min, and the steeply graded 17 miles from there to Ipswich in 17min; the time over the 46.3 miles from Ipswich to Norwich was temporarily increased to 49min however, to allow a recovery margin for time lost by slacks while continuous rail-welding was in progress. In the up direction 43min for the 46.3 miles from Norwich to Ipswich called for some lively running; from there the times, including recovery allowances were 21min from Ipswich to Colchester and 54min on to London.

The 'East Anglian', 'Norfolkman' and 'Broadsman' had all lost their names by the late 1960s but the 'East Anglian' title reappeared in May 1980. The name was applied to the 8am from Norwich, due Liverpool Street 9.52, and the 4.20pm from Liverpool Street, arriving Norwich at 6.12. Both trains called only at Ipswich between London and Norwich, and ran through to and from Yarmouth.

Eastern Region 'Executives' and others

Cold logic does not explain why named trains still run in a period of uniform formations, standardised departure times and schedules varying by only a few minutes. Yet visitors from the USA still enthuse at a journey in the 'Flying Scotsman', and in the USA Amtrak has retained the 'Broadway Limited' title among other classics, and has created new ones. Many train names on the Eastern Region disappeared after the 1967-68 timetable but some old-established ones were retained and others were restored later. New ones have joined them. There may still be good commercial reasons for naming a train. Replying to a questionnaire circulated to 4,600 passengers on the German Federal Railway, 87% wished names to be retained, only 8% thought them superfluous, and the remainder had no views on the matter.

In another chapter the revival of the 'East Anglian' title for a Norwich-Ipswich-London service is recorded. The timetable provided convenient fast trains for passengers from East Anglia wishing to have a full day in London and be home in the early evening, but a return train at 4.30pm which called at Colchester was attracting a large number of Essex commuters. A service specifically for the Ipswich and Norwich traffic was therefore put on at 4.20pm and together with the corresponding up train from Norwich at 8am was named the 'East Anglian' to identify it with a particular sector of the travel market. The trains are through to and from Yarmouth, and call only at Norwich and Ipswich.

The Eastern Region had a number of Pullman services, all named as was traditional for the all-Pullman train. The names survived the inclusion of ordinary stock in later years and only vanished with the trains themselves, the last going at the end of the 1977-78 timetable when the 'Hull Pullman' and the 'Yorkshire Pullman' were withdrawn. In the meantime the Region had introduced its 'Executive' trains, the name being given to services at times particularly suitable for businessmen in the North East and West Riding wishing to travel to and from London in a day, with ample time for their business in the capital. The first of the 'family' were the Leeds, Bradford, and Newcastle Executives and their origin can be traced back to the fast 'Deltic'-hauled eight-coach trains which in the 1968 timetable had been described laconically as 'High Speed'. Air-conditioned stock was introduced in 1971 and in 1973 three business services were named respectively the 'Leeds Executive', 'Bradford Executive' and 'Newcastle Executive'. The 'Hull Executive' followed in 1978, replacing the 'Hull Pullman', and in January 1981 the 'Cleveland Executive' began operation between Middlesbrough and King's Cross.

All the 'Executives' except the 'Cleveland Executive' began their careers as 'Deltic'-hauled eight-coach trains following the pattern of the services designated 'High Speed' in 1968. Heavier loads were hauled in later years. In 1978, its last year of 'Deltic' working, the 'Leeds Executive' was running non-stop to King's Cross in 2hr 28min and returning to Leeds in 2hr 26min. The 'Hull Executive' was also 'Deltic'-hauled on its introduction in the same year and made the journey to London in 3hr 4min. In 1979 its was accelerated, the 'Deltic' bringing its train into London in 2hr 57min with stops at Brough, Goole, Doncaster and Retford. The northbound journey took 2hr 50min with the same stops. Retford, 138½ miles from King's Cross was reached in 91min at an average speed of 91.32mph, the fastest locomotive-hauled timing, diesel or electric, ever scheduled on BR. This train was the last of the 'Executives' to go 'Inter-City 125' (HST), being locomotive hauled until 2 January 1981.

The Leeds, Bradford, and Newcastle 'Executives' were operated by Class 254 HSTs from the 1979 timetable. In 1982 the Leeds train was running to King's Cross non-stop in 2hr 7min to give a 9.42am arrival and was the fastest train of the day on that route. The return service, at 4.50pm, called at Wakefield, reached Leeds in 2hr 10min, and continued to Harrogate, arriving at 7.34pm. The first through train from Harrogate to King's Cross was at 8.07am, arriving at 11.13am, but passengers requiring an earlier arrival could take the 6.46am from Harrogate and change into the up 'Leeds Executive' at Leeds.

The up 'Bradford Executive' left at 7.36am, called at New Pudsey, Wakefield, Doncaster and Peterborough, and was into King's Cross at 10.12am. At the beginning of the HST era the name had been carried by a northbound service at 3.55pm from King's Cross but in 1982 there was no 'Bradford Executive' in that direction; a 3.50pm provided a similar service to Wakefield, New Pudsey and Bradford, but an 'Executive' title would have been inappropriate for a train leaving London at an hour when executives like to be thought of as being still at their desks.

Times of the 'Newcastle Executive' in 1982 were 7.40am from Newcastle, calling at Durham, Darlington and York, and arriving King's Cross at 10.48am; and 5.30pm from King's Cross, arriving at Newcastle at 8.51pm after similar stops plus Retford and Doncaster. The 'Hull Executive' was at 7am from Hull, calling at Doncaster and Retford to King's Cross, reached at 9.37am. The return service at 5.38pm called at Newark and Doncaster, arriving Hull at 8.12pm.

Youngest of the 'Executives' is the 'Cleveland Executive' from Middlesbrough. On its introduction in January 1981 it left Middlesbrough at 7.08am and with stops at Eaglescliffe (to pick up), Northallerton, York and Stevenage arrived in King's Cross at 10.11am. The northbound train left King's Cross at 4.40pm and calling at the same points arrived in Middlesbrough at 7.38pm. In 1982 the up departure was put back to 6.54am, giving a King's Cross arrival at 9.53am. The down train left at 4.37pm and with an additional stop at Newark reached Middlesborough at 7.38pm. In May 1983 the service was extended to Newcastle, calling at Sunderland, Hartlepool and Stockton in each direction.

The Eastern Region Class 254 HSTs forming the 'Executives' and other principal services are 10-car sets consisting of two 2,250hp power cars and eight trailers. There is parcels space in one power car and a guard's compartment in a second class trailer. There are two basic formations, providing alternative catering services, as follows:

(a)
Power car
2 open first (FO)
Kitchen/dining car (TRUK)
Buffet bar 125 (TRSB)
4 open seconds
Power car

(b)
Power car
2 open firsts
Buffet bar 125 (TRUB)
5 open seconds
Power car

In (a) above the TRUK (trailer restaurant unclassed kitchen) is a kitchen/dining car with 24 seats available to passengers of both classes taking meals. Waiter service can also be provided to certain seats in the adjacent first class coach but passengers occupying these seats are under no obligation to take a meal. Demand on the up Leeds and Hull 'Executives' has sometimes made it necessary to serve meals in both firsts. The TRSB (trailer restaurant second buffet) is a buffet car with 35 second class seats forming part of the ordinary second class seating on the train.

In formation (b) the TRUB (trailer restaurant unclassed buffet) has a kitchen and 17 seats with waiter meal service, also a buffet section. As in the TRUK the seats are available to both classes and must be vacated after a meal to allow for further sittings.

Travel in the 'Executives' can be sold as a 'package' covering items such as car parking, travel ticket, seat reservation, meal-at-seat reservation if required, and car hire at destination. Travel documents are supplied in a wallet bearing the name of the train, and the name also appears on train staff lapel badges, menu covers, and destination labels and indicators on the carriages. It is accompanied by an appropriate symbol; for example, a design representing mechanical and civil engineering and ship-building appears with the 'Cleveland Executive' name. Names and symbols also appear with the train times on station notices, including electronic departure indicators.

Train naming is seen as a marketing device, and it extends to the promotion of special rail trips. Some have echoed the 'Flying Scotsman' with titles like the 'Melton Mowbray Pieman', an excursion organised by the ER's Sheffield Division with the attraction of haulage by a Class 56 heavy freight diesel from Sheffield to Melton Mowbray, where there were trips on a nearby miniature railway. Steam-hauled excursions on BR routes have some former main-line train names found elsewhere in this book. A 'White Rose' has run between Crewe and York, and a 'Red Rose' between York and Skipton. The 'Scarborough Spa Express' from York to Harrogate, Leeds, and back via York to Scarborough must have stirred memories of the 'Scarborough Flier'. With the 'Cumbrian Coast Express' and the 'Cumbrian Mountain Express' the steam excursions have found titles that might well have been used effectively in earlier years for promoting regular services.

Names have also been used to draw attention to special cheap travel facilities. A group of overnight trains available to holders of cheap tickets received the name 'Starlight Specials' in the early days of British Railways, carrying on an idea which had originated on the LNER for travellers between Newcastle, Teesside and London in the late 1930s. There was another venture of a similar kind in 1970 when on 4 May the Eastern Region put on a day train between Newcastle and Finsbury Park with a single fare offer of only 35 shillings (£1.75) between any northern and southern stations. Departure was at 9.15am from Newcastle, and with stops at Sunderland, Hartlepool, Stockton, Eaglescliffe, Stevenage and Potters Bar the train was due at Finsbury Park at 3.12pm. The northbound train left Finsbury Park at 9.25am and was into Newcastle with the same stops at 3.18pm. Known as the 'Highwayman', the trains ran from Mondays to Saturdays between May and October (departing southbound at 3.13pm and northbound at 3.20pm on Saturdays). There was a buffet car in each direction. The 'Highwayman' ran for two seasons and was withdrawn in October 1971. It was advertised as a service 'for the traveller who puts cost before speed and frequency'. Tickets had to be booked in advance, three days before travel by personal application and a week before by post.

A more 'upmarket' reduced fare venture brought a new titled train to British Railways in 1982. The 'Nightrider' overnight express from King's Cross to Edinburgh, Glasgow and Aberdeen was introduced with the new timetables on 17 May although the name did not appear in the timetable columns until the amendments of 4 October. The 'Nightrider' was a reply to long-distance coach competition, designed to attract 'night-seated' passengers seeking maximum comfort without the expense of a sleeping berth. First class throughout, the train was formed of air-conditioned coaches of Mk 2d or 2e. Single fares from King's Cross were as low as £12 to Edinburgh or Glasgow and £16 for Aberdeen, including a reserved seat. Only passengers holding special 'Nightrider' tickets were admitted to the train. When introduced the formation, from the locomotive, was a first brake, five open firsts, and a restaurant-buffet car for Edinburgh and Aberdeen; and five open firsts and a first brake for Glasgow. The buffet was available all night. On the down journey the train left King's Cross at 10.05pm and after stops at Peterborough, York and Newcastle, arrived at Edinburgh at 5.42am. The front portion proceeded to Kirkcaldy, Dundee and Aberdeen, arriving at 8.31am. The Glasgow coaches called at Falkirk and reached their destination at 7am. Departures on the return journey were at 8.30pm from Aberdeen, 10.25pm from Glasgow, and 11.40pm from Edinburgh, giving a King's Cross arrival at 6.37am.

The Elizabethan

In former years it was always the practice in the height of summer to run the 'Flying Scotsman' in two sections between London and Edinburgh, and to cope with the traffic both parts, with certain variations, made almost all the same stops. Then in 1927 it was decided during the summer to run the main train non-stop between King's Cross and Newcastle, and in 1928, with the help of the corridor tenders specially built at Doncaster to Gresley's designs, to extend the non-stop run to the 392.9 miles between King's Cross and Edinburgh — the longest regular non-stop run in any part of the world. At first the time allowed was the $8\frac{1}{4}$hr laid down as the minimum by the East Coast-West Coast agreement of 1896, but when the 1932 accelerations began, the time was cut at one stroke to $7\frac{1}{2}$hr, and in two later stages it had come down to no more than 7hr by 1939.

It was some time after World War 2 before non-stop running was resumed, and from 1949 the 'Flying Scotsman' was no longer the train concerned. For it was felt that the 'Flying Scotsman' ought to run throughout the year to the same times and stops, and that the relief train should have different starting times and a different name. So for the non-stop the prewar 9.30am from King's Cross and 9.45am from Edinburgh were reverted to; and these were both given the name 'Capitals Limited'. The East Coast main line was still suffering from the disastrous wash-outs between Berkwick and Dunbar following on the cloud-burst of the previous summer, and the task of replacing with permanent structures the bridges which had been washed away, so as yet it was not possible to cut the overall time below 8hr. But as soon as these replacements were complete, acceleration began in earnest. The 'Capitals Limited' carried through coaches between London and Aberdeen, in the north-bound direction taken on from Edinburgh Waverley by a special additional summer train at 5.45pm, and reaching Aberdeen at 9.20pm; while the start from Aberdeen to the south was at the uncomfortably early hour of 5.55am, in order to reach Edinburgh in good time (9.28am) for attachment to the southbound 'Capitals Limited'. For the first time since the war these schedules brought London and Aberdeen within less than 12hr of each other — actually 11hr 50min each way.

The 'Capitals Limited' (and winter 'Flying Scotsman') set of cars, apart from all-Pullman trains, at that time was the heaviest in the country in relation to the number of vehicles composing it. The 13 cars had a tare weight of 473 tons. Of this, no less than 158 tons was contributed by the heavy kitchen car, the buffet car, and the two open restaurant cars. These and other amenities entailed a rigid limitation of seating in the rest of the train, from which first class passengers were the worst sufferers; on the up journey, owing to the provision of a ladies' retiring room, the only full length first had no more than five compartments; there were three more in the Aberdeen portion — 48 seats all told — and passengers were allowed to occupy seats in the three end bays of the first class restaurant, bringing the total up to 66. In the summer this accommodation at times was inadequate, and disappointed passengers who could not obtain seats had to use the 'Flying Scotsman' instead, losing half-an-hour in the process.

By the summer of 1950 the 'Capitals Limited' was into Edinburgh by 5.10pm, in 7hr 40min from King's Cross, and the up train was reaching King's Cross at 5.30pm, in $7\frac{3}{4}$hr. The Aberdeen connection also had been speeded-up to an overall time of 11hr 35min from and to London. The 1951 summer saw a further cut to 7hr 20min both ways, and by 1952 times were further reduced to 7hr 6min northbound (with the King's Cross start altered to 9.35am) and to 7hr 7min southbound — very nearly back to the prewar 7hr. But the reduction in time was accompanied by restriction in the load to 12 vehicles in 1951, and no more than 11 (400 tons maximum) in 1952. Again it was the first class end of the train that suffered, for the first class restaurant accommodation was pared ruthlessly to 18 seats in a combined restaurant and kitchen car, and the total first class compartment seating in the train from 66 to 42 places. The London-Aberdeen times by this service in 1952 were 11hr 1min north-bound and 11hr 2min southbound.

Then, in 1953, in honour of the Coronation of Queen Elizabeth, there came a notable change of name; it was from 'Capitals Limited' to 'Elizabethan'. With this came a further cut in time, to $6\frac{3}{4}$hr in each direction. Finally, in 1964, the time was cut to $6\frac{1}{2}$hr — 390min for a distance of 392.9 miles, which brought this express into the mile-a-minute category. From then on the working of the 'Elizabethan', with a tare load of just over 400 tons and a gross load normally of about 420 to 425 tons, became one of the most exacting duties ever required of a steam locomotive in Great Britain; it was entrusted, of course, to a Gresley A4 Pacific.

But eventually the all-conquering diesels took over. So in 1962 3,300hp 'Deltics' assumed control, and as this substitution did away with the corridor tenders of the Pacifics, which had permitted a change of crew *en route*, a stop at Newcastle became necessary, and as had previously been customary for a few weeks towards the close of each summer, passengers from now on were picked up and set down daily at the Tyneside city. Finally, in 1963, with the 'Flying Scotsman' itself accelerated to a 6hr London-Edinburgh run, Newcastle stop included, the name 'Elizabethan' disappeared, and the train that had carried it once again became a relief to the former, following it out of King's Cross at 10.10am and preceding it from Edinburgh at 9am, with a heavier load and on a slower timing both ways. In its heyday, with A4 steam power, the 'Elizabethan' certainly wrote a chapter in British railway history with its 425-ton mile-a-minute 393-mile non-stop run.

In 1971 the 'Capitals' name reappeared in the form of the 'Night Capitals', bestowed on the 11.10pm King's Cross to Edinburgh and the 10.30pm Edinburgh to King's Cross sleepers but it was dropped.

The Emerald Isle Express

With the ample sleeping accommodation provided on the night steamers between Holyhead and Dun Laoghaire in mind, knowledgeable passengers were in the habit of getting down to Holyhead before midnight, in order to have a good night's rest on board, instead of having to change from train to steamer in the small hours of the morning, as was necessary with those travelling down by the 8.45pm 'Irish Mail'. So after World War 2, passengers with this intention would take the express which at first left Euston at 5.15pm, but in the autumn of 1954 was altered to leave at 5.35pm, and to run non-stop over the 133.6 miles to Stafford in 140min, afterwards calling at Crewe, Chester and Llandudno Junction and getting to Holyhead by 10.55pm. A through portion for Birkenhead was detached from this train at Chester. With this speeding up the train received the name of 'Emerald Isle Express'. In the up direction the set of coaches with restaurant cars was returned by the old-established 7.30am from Holyhead, calling at principal stations to Crewe and picking up Llandudno and Birkenhead coaches at Llandudno Junction and Chester respectively; from Crewe there was a non-stop run to a set-down halt at Watford Junction and Euston was reached at 1.18pm.

In common with all the other LMR Western Division expresses, substantial recovery times caused a slowing down during the electrification period, but at the end of this the down 'Emerald Isle' was subjected to a remarkable diversion. From April 1966 it began to run from Rugby to Stafford via Birmingham and Wolverhampton. At first electric power was available round the loop as far as Coventry only; with a Euston start at 5.40pm the 'Emerald Isle' was run over the 94 miles to Coventry in 74min, and after a 10min halt there to change to diesel power, continued to Birmingham and Stafford, which was not reached until 8.35pm. After that the stops now were Crewe and Chester only, and the arrival at Holyhead was at 11.18pm. The journey had thus become 18min longer than previously. Between Rugby and Stafford the 'Emerald Isle' had been passed by the 6.00, 6.10, 6.30 and 6.50pm expresses from Euston.

With completion of electrification through Birmingham, however, a considerable improvement set in. The express now left Euston 55min later, at 6.35pm, and with the Coventry stop was into Birmingham by 8.13 and Stafford by 8.54pm. It had an additional stop at Bangor, but reached Holyhead by 11.27pm, so that even with the time-consuming Birmingham diversion the journey was still 28min quicker than in the former steam days. Curiously enough, the up 'Emerald Isle Express' did not copy the down train in the matter of route, though its schedule was considerably changed after electrification. It now left Holyhead at the rather uncomfortably early hour of 6.43am, stopped only at Bangor, Llandudno Junction and Chester to Crewe, and was then non-stop from Crewe to Euston on a standard 120-minute booking for the 158.1 miles, arriving at 11.05am. So the overall time of 4hr 22min was nearly $1\frac{1}{2}$hr shorter than the 5hr 48min of steam days — a very handsome improvement.

With further development of timetables under electrification all but the longest-established LMR train titles were dropped. The 'Emerald Isle Express' appeared for the last time in the timetable which ended on 4 May 1975 but the principle of a fast evening service to Holyhead in advance of the 'Irish Mail' has been maintained.

The Essex Coast Express

It was in 1910 that the former Great Eastern Railway first began to realise that a growing commuter traffic between the Essex Coast resorts and London might be developed, given better and faster trains. So in that year a breakfast car express was put on from Clacton-on-Sea at 7.03am, calling at Thorpe-le-Soken to attach a Walton portion and after that at Colchester, Chelmsford and Shenfield; Liverpool Street was reached at 8.52am. The return journey was begun at 5.06pm, following the 4.55pm to Cromer and the 5pm to Yarmouth; in this direction the only stops were at Colchester and Thorpe, the Clacton arrival being at 6.50pm. In the years between the wars the service was greatly improved and expanded until by 1939, although there was still a 6.50am breakfast car train from Clacton reaching London, with the same four stops, at 8.51am, there was also a much faster 8am from Clacton (of which the restaurant car portion rather oddly was that from Walton), non-stop from Thorpe-le-Soken and into Liverpool Street by 9.36am. Faster still was the 5.30pm down, again non-stop to Thorpe, and taking 94min to Clacton and 103min to Walton.

By now the Essex Coast commuter traffic had become extensive and remunerative, and postwar recovery of the service was fairly rapid. It was further accelerated after 'Britannia' Pacifics, displaced from the Norwich main line by diesels, took over in 1958. The 5.30pm down now had its starting time altered to 5.27pm, and although with a Colchester stop in addition to that at Thorpe-le-Soken for division, it was into Clacton by 6.53pm, in 86min from London, and there was a similar acceleration in the up direction, with the train stopping at Chelmsford in addition to Thorpe.

But the most revolutionary development of all was the extension in 1963 of the Great Eastern electrification throughout from Liverpool Street to Clacton and Walton. With three motorcoaches in each ten-coach train providing a total of no less than 3,384hp, electric traction permitted the tabling of the fastest point-to-point timings over short distances anywhere in Europe, let alone in Great Britain. Among them, for example, were such booked start-to-stop times as $8\frac{1}{2}$min for the $9\frac{1}{2}$ miles from Shenfield to Chelmsford and 9min in the reverse direction, which could only be maintained by lightning accelerations and maximum speeds up to 90mph — again an almost incredible transformation from former Great Eastern days. In addition, the new trains embodied an extremely high standard of comfort and smooth riding and the inducements to commuting from and to the Essex Coast resorts, with seven daily expresses up from Clacton between 6.13 and 8.48am, and six down between 4.34 and 6.20pm, were thus greater than ever.

Among these trains was the 'Essex Coast Express', one of the very few Great Eastern Section trains that retained the title conferred in the summer of 1958. In the up direction it left Walton at 7.59 and Clacton at 8.02am, called at Thorpe, Witham and Chelmsford, and arrived in Liverpool Street at 9.24am, in 82min from Clacton. Coastbound, it got away from London at 5.38pm, was non-stop to Colchester in $51\frac{1}{2}$min and stopped thereafter at Wivenhoe and Thorpe, depositing its commuters in Clacton at 6.58pm — an 80min run — and Walton at 7pm.

Although the name had been dropped in 1968, there was still an equivalent to the down 'Essex Coast Express' in the 1982 timetables, leaving Liverpool Street at 5.40pm and with the same stops reaching Clacton in 78min at 6.58pm. An up service leaving Walton at 7.46am and Clacton at 7.43am gave a Liverpool Street arrival at 9.06am with stops at Thorpe, Wivenhoe, Colchester and Kelvedon.

The Executive

As far back as 1902 the London & North Western Railway first timed a non-stop train to cover the 112.9 miles between London and Birmingham in the even two hours; this was the 5pm from New Street to Euston. The route was ideal for the purpose; apart from the initial climb of $1\frac{1}{4}$ miles from the platform end at Euston to Camden, at 1 in 70 to 1 in 105, and the short and sharp rise into New Street, Birmingham, the old London & Birmingham Railway was so magnificently engineered that there was no other gradient steeper than 1 in 330 throughout its length. Moreover, the only speed reduction enforced at any point was the 40mph through Rugby.

Within two years of the first 2hr timing, a complete service of two-hour trains, four in each direction daily, had come into existence. In these years, Coventry had not attained its motor manufacturing eminence, and before World War 1 it was sufficient for two of the down Birmingham two-hour trains (the 8.40am and the 6.55pm) to provide a service to Coventry by slip coaches, which were stopped clear of the platform loops and were then drawn into the platforms by waiting locomotives or horses. Eventually, in the last year before 1914, the LNWR specially built vestibuled slip coaches for this service, to give Coventry passengers access to the restaurant cars up to the moment of severing the train.

The most rapid development of the LNWR Birmingham and Wolverhampton service was during the years when the GWR was building its shortened Birmingham route via Bicester, and the former company thus was being threatened for the first time with competition for this important traffic on more or less equal terms. One striking LNWR experiment in 1910 was the introduction of a 'City-to-City' service between Birmingham and Broad Street, in the heart of the City of London, leaving New Street at 8.20am and reaching Broad Street at 10.35am; returning, the express left Broad Street at 5.25pm for a $2\frac{1}{4}$hr run back to Birmingham. The four-coach train included a restaurant car, and was worked by one of the rebuilt and simplified Webb compound 4-4-0s of the 'Renown' class. A typewriting compartment with typist was provided for businessmen desiring to dictate their correspondence en route (as also on the 4.45am from Euston to Birmingham and the 8.40am up express to Euston); intermediate stops were made at Willesden Junction and Coventry. But old customs are difficult to alter, and as the city magnates could not be induced in any numbers to change their custom from Euston to Broad Street, the 'City-to-City' disappeared on the outbreak of war in 1914.

After World War 1, the Coventry slip coaches were never restored, but as the importance of Coventry was increasing steadily, measures had to be taken to provide an adequate service. This had been done in part by running local trains over the short distance between Coventry and Rugby to connect at the latter station with expresses from and to the North, but by degrees Coventry stops began to appear also in the schedules of the Birmingham two-hour trains. As more powerful locomotives became available it was found that with faster running, notwithstanding the increased weight of the trains, an intermediate stop could be included in the two-hour schedule without any detriment to timekeeping. Among the earliest of the 2hr one-stop trains were the 9.10am from Euston and the 4.50pm from Birmingham, both of which called at Willesden Junction. Coventry stops then appeared in other 2hr schedules; and after the advent to the service of the 3-cylinder 'Jubilee' 4-6-0s, which ousted the 4-4-0 Midland compounds just as they, in their turn, had displaced the LNWR 'George the Fifth' 4-4-0s, the 2hr timing came down to 115min (all but a mile-a-minute for the 112.9 miles), Coventry stop included.

These timings meant a start-to-stop average of over 60mph between Euston and Coventry in both directions. Three down and three up expresses were booked to cover the 94 miles in 92min. The 4.50pm up contrived to cover the distance from Birmingham to Euston in two hours stopping at both Coventry and Willesden and running the 88.6 miles between them in 86min; the 9.15am down ran the 107.5 miles from Willesden to Birmingham in 104min, and the 8.10am down the 76.5 miles from Watford to Coventry in 73min. But the most outstanding performance was that of the 6.20pm up, which ran from New Street to Euston in two hours notwithstanding *three* intermediate stops — at Coventry, Rugby and Watford Junction. The 65.1mph timing of this express from Rugby to Watford — 65.1 miles in the hour exactly — was the fastest start-to-stop schedule in the LMSR timetables up to World War 2.

It should be added that all the Birmingham two-hour trains began or ended their journeys at Wolverhampton, some travelling via Dudley Port and stopping there to give communication to and from Dudley, and others by the heavily-graded and slightly longer route through Soho Road, Bescot and Darlaston. Some called at Bescot in order to connect to and from Walsall, and Walsall was served by one lone through coach attached to the 4.35pm from Euston and the 11.45am from Birmingham.

World War 2 wrought havoc with the LMSR Birmingham service, and recovery was slow. The trains were certainly a good deal heavier, loading as many of them now did to from 11 to 13 bogies regularly, but the one-stop trains, of which the best during the war (the 6pm down) was allowed 2hr 24min, had not got below 2hr 8min on the fastest service of 1950. This was the 'Midlander', the first train on the London-Birmingham service of the London Midland Region to earn a title, in the years between the wars. Reinstated in 1950, but on a different timing, it now left Euston at 5.45pm, called only at Coventry to Birmingham (7.53pm) and terminated at Wolverhampton at 8.27pm. The up journey, at 9.45am from Wolverhampton and 10.30am from Birmingham, was considerably slower, as the train took the Northampton loop and called at that town, and so was not due in Euston until 12.45pm.

By 1953, however, and largely with the help of 'Royal Scot' 4-6-0 haulage, two-hour Euston-Birmingham times had reappeared, and among the two-hour expresses was the 'Midlander', at 11am from Wolverhampton and 11.30am from Birmingham, reaching Euston at 1.30pm, while in the down direction the start from Euston was at 5.50pm, arrival at Birmingham being at 7.50pm and at Wolverhampton at 8.30pm. Each way the 94 miles between Euston and Coventry had to be covered in 94min. So matters went on until the electrification work between Euston and Rugby and beyond was well under way, and then in 1963 the well-nigh unbelievable happened. It was the almost entire suspension of the express service between Euston, Birmingham and Wolverhampton, and the transfer of this traffic to the Western Region between Snow Hill and Paddington. Birmingham did not suffer to any material extent, but Coventry most certainly did, for the whole of its non-stop service to and from Euston went, and, moreover, the first day of the withdrawal was a particularly bad one for British Railways, for it coincided with the opening of the M1 motorway. However, the loss was no more than temporary, until March 1967, when a total change set in with the introduction of the high speed electric service to and from Euston.

Now, at 15min past every hour from 8.15am to 8.15pm, and with additional peak hour services, an electrically-hauled express left Euston on a 73min timing over the 94 miles to Coventry, and with a time of 19min for the remaining 18.9 miles, stopped at Birmingham New Street in 94min from London. Moreover, these trains then continued from Birmingham as express services to Liverpool and Manchester, at alternate hours to each city. In the up direction the departures were also at 15min past each hour from Birmingham, each train having originated at either Liverpool or Manchester, and with timings of 18min from New Street to Coventry and 74min thence to Euston gave an overall time of 95min hourly from Birmingham to London.

Among the peak hour 'extras' was an express called the 'Executive'. This was a special train formation designed to give maximum meal accommodation. From the locomotive it comprised brake second, two open seconds, kitchen car, open firsts, another kitchen car, two open first, two compartment firsts, and brake first. For dining seats the users paid a 7s 6d (38p) first class supplement and 5s (25p) second class. The 'Executive' was intended to replace the blue 'Birmingham Pullman' which had been running between Snow Hill and Paddington. The up 'Executive' started from Wolverhampton at 7.30am and Birmingham New Street 20min later; it called, as did two other morning trains, at Hampton-in-Arden at 8.01am for passengers from the south-eastern suburbs of Birmingham, and at Coventry from 8.12 to 8.14am, bringing its passengers into Euston by 9.30am. The return journey was begun at the same hour, 5.50pm, as the former 'Midlander', but with 100mph travel was far quicker than the former; Coventry was reached at 7.03, Hampton at 7.14, Birmingham at 7.29 and Wolverhampton at 7.51pm — 1min over 2hr as compared with the 'Midlander's' 2hr 40min. The name 'Executive' did not appear after the 4 May 1970 to 2 May 1971 timetable.

There is an echo of the 'Executive' in the special facilities offered to first class travellers by the present 7.00, 7.30 and 8am expresses from Wolverhampton to Euston (7.18, 7.48 and 8.18am from Birmingham). For those wishing to take breakfast on the trains special 'meal at seat' reservations can be made at an inclusive fee. A stop at Birmingham International, the new station opened in 1974 to serve the exhibition centre and airport, has replaced the former Hampton-in-Arden stop.

Upmarket Travel

Like being bowed into a Rolls-Royce by a uniformed chauffeur, travel in one of the named Pullman trains was good for the ego. One might not aspire to a permanent Pullman lifestyle, but it was agreeable while it lasted.

Above: Marsh's Class J 4-6-2T *Bessborough* heads the 'Southern Belle' near Balham. *LPC*

Left: An all-Pullman train also ran to Eastbourne at one period of LBSC history but did not achieve the prestige or commercial success of its Brighton sister. R. J. Billinton's 'B4' class 4-4-0 *Marlborough* is at Stoats Nest with an Eastbourne Sunday Pullman working. *Wentworth S. Gray, courtsey J. H. Price*

Above: The 'Southern Belle' became an emu from 1 January 1933; the name was changed to 'Brighton Belle' in 1934. Two 'Belle' units forming a 10-car train cross the Ouse viaduct. *IAL*

Centre right: In BR Pullman livery and boldly labelled with the train name (which also appeared on the motorcoach ends), a first class car affords a glimpse of the traditional 'Belle' interior with tables and reading lamps. *J. Scrace*

Bottom right: The Southern Railway extended the 'Belle' title to the 'Bournemouth Belle', seen here approaching Clapham Junction in early Southern Region days on 18 June 1949. The locomotive is an unrebuilt 'Merchant Navy' Pacific. *C. C. B. Herbert*

Above: Great Western experience with Pullmans to Torbay had not been encouraging, but the Southern brought the cars to the West Country again with its 'Devon Belle'. Unrebuilt 'Merchant Navy' No 35015 passes Salisbury with the up train on 13 September 1952. *G. J. Jefferson*

Below: All-Pullman service for the North Kent Coast began with the Southern Region's 'Kentish Belle'. The down train is passing Bromley South in the summer of 1954 with 'Battle of Britain' Pacific No 34017 *Ilfracombe* at the head. *R. Russell*

YORKSHIRE PULLMAN
60062

THE QUEEN OF SCOTS

Top left: The Eastern Region carried on some well-known LNER Pullman titles. Class A3 Pacific No 60062 *Minoru* with 'cut-down' smoke deflectors whisks the down 'Yorkshire Pullman' through New Barnet on 2 August 1961. *R. S. Greenwood*

Centre left: 'B1' class 4-6-0 No 61180 adds to the murk of an overcast sky early in its journey from Glasgow to King's Cross. *E. R. Wethersett/LPC*

Bottom left: Pullman services to the north-west began when the London Midland Region electrification reached Euston. The 'Manchester Pullman' outlived all other BR Pullman trains. No 86.242 is beginning the descent of Camden bank into Euston with the up train on 12 July 1979. *J. G. Glover*

Top: No 86.225 hastens out of Kilsby Tunnel with the up afternoon 'Liverpool Pullman' on 11 July 1974. *John E. Oxley*

Above: 'Castle' class 4-6-0 No 7004 *Eastnor Castle* at Swindon on 21 June 1955 during a trial run with the 'South Wales Pullman'. *A. R. Carpenter*

Left: Class 40 No D246 emerges from the Oakleigh Park Tunnel with the down 'Tees-Tyne Pullman'. *Derek Cross*

Into East Anglia

The Eastern Region launched a number of named services with its 'Executives' on the East Coast main line, and in the 1980s revived the practice in East Anglia by restoring the 'East Anglian' title. A selection of named trains on what the LNER used to call 'the drier side of Britain' is illustrated.

Above: A 'Cambridge Buffet Express' from King's Cross approaches the University City in July 1973 behind Class 46 No D180. *IAL*

Right: No 47.100 waits to take the last 'Cambridge Buffet Express' out of King's Cross on 2 May 1978. The Cambridge buffet trains, popular both with the academic community and residents in the Garden Cities, were taken off when electrification from King's Cross reached Royston. A dmu service now links Royston and Cambridge. *David M. Scudamore*

Far right, top: A Liverpool Street-Kings Lynn/Hunstanton service was named the 'Fenman' by BR. The steam-hauled train with No 61617 at the head passes Littlebury on 12 August 1953. *E. R. Wethersett*

Far right, bottom: Class 37 No 6753 leaves Audley End with the down 'Fenman' on 23 July 1969. *R. Elsdon*

THE
FENMAN
61617

1L
20

Above: The 'Essex Coast Express' was a business service for residents in the Clacton/Walton area commuting to and from the City. No 70000 *Britannia*, first of the standard Pacifics, passes Brentwood with the inaugural train on 9 June 1959. *K. L. Cook*

Right: Class B1 No 61041 passes Trowse Yard, Norwich, with BR's 'East Anglian' on 6 September 1949. The name had been carried by an LNER Liverpool Street-Norwich service with streamlined locomotives shortly before World War 2. *E. Tuddenham*

Below right: The 'East Anglian' of the 1980s. Class 47 No 47.170 *County of Norfolk* leaves Ipswich with the down train on 22 May 1980, carrying a headboard to draw attention to the improved service which helped to separate shorter-distance commuters in the evening rush out of Liverpool Street from through travellers to Ipswich and Norwich. *I. P. Cowley*

Anglo-Scottish from King's Cross

The East Coast Route to Scotland was once prolific in named trains. Only the 'Flying Scotsman' and 'Aberdonian' titles have survived in the Anglo-Scottish daytime services.

Above: Class A4 Pacific No 60011 *Empire of India* crosses Welwyn Viaduct with the 'Elizabethan' non-stop King's Cross-Edinburgh express on 24 June 1959. *BR*

Below: Another non-stop King's Cross-Edinburgh service was the 'Capitals Limited', seen near Hadley Wood in September 1952 with 'A4' No 60034 *Lord Faringdon* in charge.

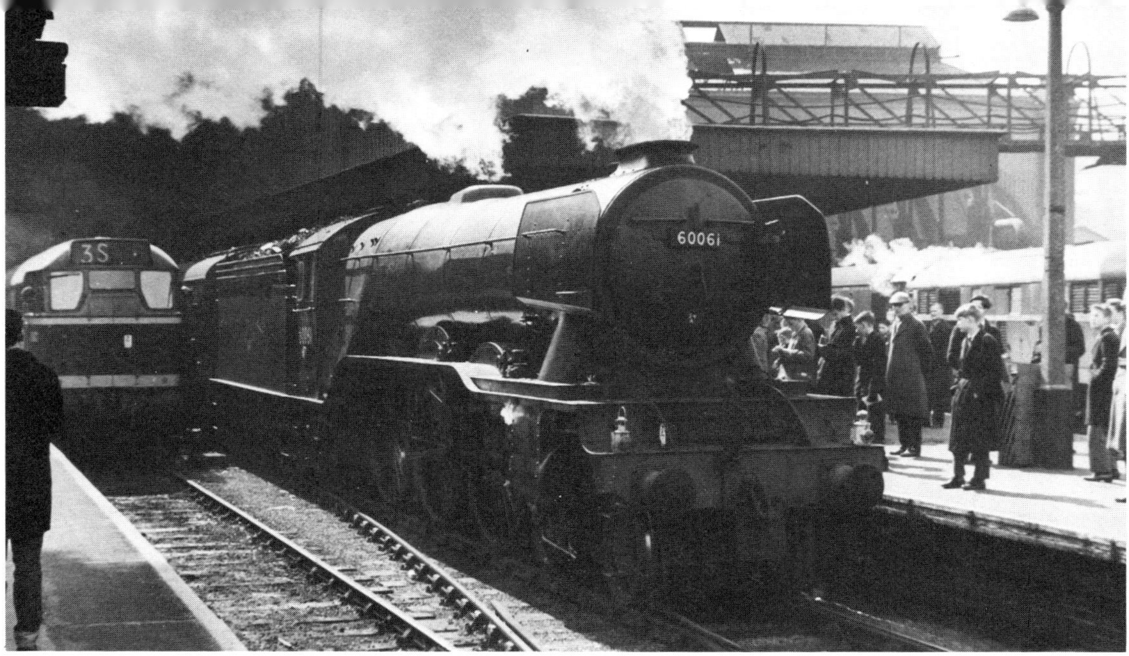
3S
60061

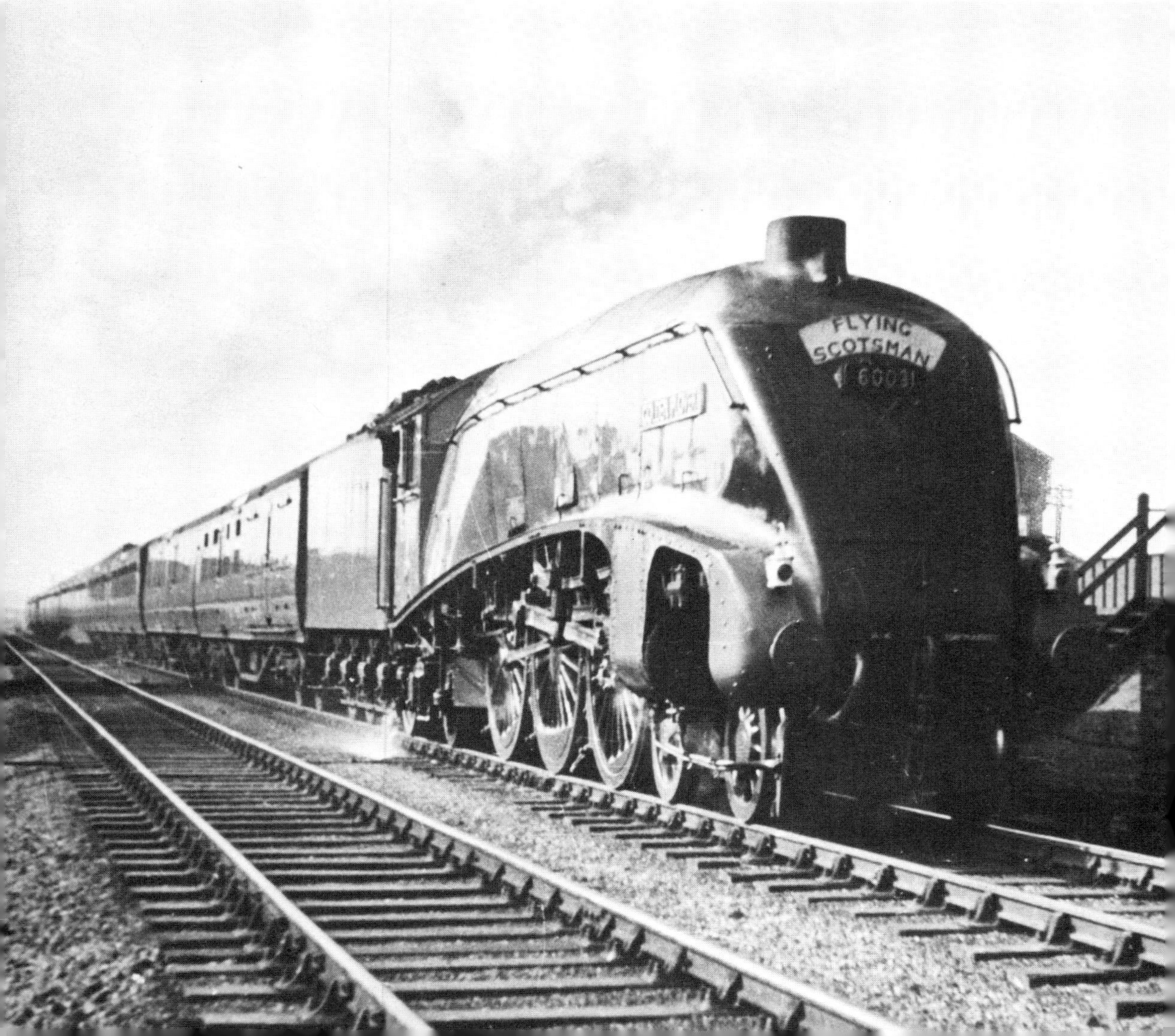
FLYING
SCOTSMAN
60031

Top left: The 220lb pressure 'A3s' were the traditional Gresley Pacifics. Fitted with double-chimney and smoke deflectors, No 60061 *Pretty Polly* pulls away from King's Cross with the 'Heart of Midlothian' on 31 March 1962. *IAL*

Bottom left: The 'A4s' were majestic to the last, and removal of the valances over the motion made them more interesting to look at. With a whirl of exposed Walschaerts motion No 60031 *Golden Plover* sweeps past Finsbury Park with the down 'Flying Scotsman' on 28 August 1948. *G. R. Mortimer*

Top: 'Deltic' No 9020 *Nimbus* carries a new style headboard specially designed for the 'Flying Scotsman' on 12 March 1964. The crest in the form of a winged Scottish thistle symbolises the name of the train. *BR*

Above: Now an HST, the 'Flying Scotsman' still lives up to its name and is accelerating away from King's Cross on 13 June 1978. *I. J. Hodson*

On the Kyle Line

Although the 'Lewisman' and 'Hebridean' names have gone, corresponding services on the line from Dingwall to Kyle of Lochalsh have attracted a tourist traffic which has kept the route open to passengers through a period when its future seemed in doubt.

Above: The 07.05 from Dingwall to Kyle of Lochalsh skirts Loch Carron near Plockton, piloted by Class 26 No 26.035. *G. A. Watt*

Centre right: The 17.52 Kyle of Lochalsh to Inverness hugs the coast as it leaves Kyle headed by No 26.027. *John Chalfcraft*

Bottom right: Passengers in the observation saloon of the 10.30 Inverness to Kyle watch the 11.04 Kyle to Inverness passing them at Achnasheen on 20 August 1979. *R. E. Ruffell*

The Car-Carriers

The 'tail' of open flat wagons carrying passengers' cars is no longer a characteristic of Motorail services. An earlier period is recalled in these pictures.

Above: A Class 47 locomotive heads the 12.40 St Austell-Crewe Motorail service out of Bristol on 30 July 1977. *Les Bertram*

Centre left: The Newton-le-Willows to Stirling Car Carrier is taken past the site of Dillicar troughs on 15 June 1968 by Class 47 No D1849. *D. Wharton*

Bottom left: The London-Fishguard Car-Carrier, seen at Fishguard with D1733, was part of a drive by British Railways to attract traffic to its four car-carrying routes to Ireland in a period when motoring holidays in the country were becoming popular. *BR*

Fliers to the North-West

Above left: Rebuilt 'Scot' No 46124 *London Scottish* heads a Euston-Liverpool express, past Sudbury Junction box. *C. R. L. Coles*

Above right: The 'Mancunian' to Manchester was one of a trio familiar to commuters returning from Euston to their suburbs. Three headboards, 'Mancunian', 'Midlander' and 'Merseyside Express' could be seen at the same time in the departure platforms. Drifting to the terminus in this picture is rebuilt 'Scot' No 46116 on the 'Mancunian'. *E. R. Wethersett*

Below: A St Pancras-Manchester service was named the 'Palatine' by British Rail. The up train is about to leave Manchester Central in the charge of No 46131 *The Royal Warwickshire Regiment*. *Eric Oldham*

The Fenman

It could hardly be said until the improved timetable of 1953 that the 'star turn' of Eastern Region train services was to be found on the Cambridge main line out of Liverpool Street. After the halcyon days preceding World War 2, when five-coach buffet car trains were making the run of $55\frac{3}{4}$ miles between Liverpool Street and Cambridge three times daily in 65min each way — the fastest service ever offered — the train service over this line steadily worsened. Up to 1953 the fastest train on the service, the 'Fenman', subject of this chapter, needed 80min to make the non-stop run in the down direction, and 75min for the return run to London.

There were, of course, extenuating circumstances. The 5-mile exit from Liverpool Street to Coppermill Junction is the most tortuous and difficult used by any main line trains out of London. Between Hackney Downs and Clapton Junction it is double-line only, and the Cambridge trains have to be dovetailed in with the dense Walthamstow and Chingford suburban service. In the 1950s and 60s, the Lea Valley became highly industrialised, making it necessary to superimpose on a double-track main line (with a fair length of goods loops) already carrying a very heavy freight traffic and a number of main line passenger trains, a busy outer suburban passenger service, with frequent stops between Tottenham and Cheshunt. At rush hour periods, it is extremely difficult to arrange a clear path for express passenger trains, and the whole line between Tottenham and Broxbourne Junction is in urgent need of doubling.

Possibly rather more use could have been made of the section between Broxbourne and Cambridge for higher speeds, the only serious obstacles being the severe speed restriction over Bishops Stortford station curve, and the modest climb (more long-drawn-out from the north side) up to Elsenham summit in both directions. The extraordinary layout of Cambridge station, with its one enormously long platform for both up and down main line trains, also is the reverse of helpful to down trains in making a punctual arrival at the university town.

The name 'Fenman' was given to a Hunstanton-Liverpool Street service in the summer of 1949. In the early 1950s the main portion of the 'Fenman', with buffet car, began its journey at Hunstanton each morning at 6.45am, calling at all stations over the $15\frac{1}{4}$ miles to King's Lynn, reached at 7.21am. In the terminal station here the train was reversed, and left for London at 7.30am; with stops at Downham and Ely, it strolled across the flat Fenland to make its appearance in Cambridge at 8.31am. Meantime a through portion had left Bury St Edmunds at 7.57am, making westwards through Newmarket to run into Cambridge 10min later. The train was assembled at Cambridge in similarly unhurried fashion, and left for Liverpool Street at 8.48am, arriving at 10.03am, the journey of $112\frac{1}{4}$ miles from Hunstanton having taken no less than 3hr 18min.

Similar leisurely progress characterised the return journey. Going north, the 'Fenman' was the lineal descendant of the 4.30pm from Liverpool Street to York, a Great Eastern express of days before the first world war which also was non-stop to Cambridge, but in 72min rather than the 80min of 1953. The 'Fenman' reached Cambridge at 5.50pm, and the Bury section was the first to leave, at 5.58pm; it reached Bury St Edmunds at 6.45pm. The Hunstanton train followed at 6.04pm, running into Ely at 6.24pm (17min later than the GER 4.30pm down 50 years earlier!), King's Lynn at 7.14pm, and Hunstanton at 7.55pm, having taken 3hr 25min giving an overall average of 33mph!

The locomotive in the 1950s was usually one of the ubiquitous B1 4-6-0s, but this might be replaced by a B17 4-6-0 of the 'Sandringham' class, or an ex-Great Eastern B12/3 4-6-0, as a reminder of earlier and happier days.

Improvements, however, were not far distant, and the first of them took effect in the summer of 1953. After having recast their Colchester main line service, the Great Eastern operating authorities turned their attention to the Cambridge line, over which some substantial accelerations, in which the 'Fenman' shared, took place. The down train was speeded up by 12min to Cambridge, this section now taking 68min, and the gain to Hunstanton, reached at 7.35pm, was 20min. From now on the Bury St Edmunds portion was run separately from London, and in its place was a through portion for March and Wisbech, detached at Ely. For the attachment of the latter on the morning up run extra time had to be allowed at Ely, so that the cut in the southbound time, 15min, was not quite so great. The start from Hunstanton now was at 6.50am, and from Cambridge at 8.45am, with a Liverpool Street arrival at 9.53am. Eventually the 'B1' 4-6-0s were displaced by diesels, at first by Class 31, but later Class 37.

Finally there came another recasting of the service. As with the limitation of the through Colchester line workings from Liverpool Street to Norwich, so from now on, to secure better rolling stock utilisation, the Cambridge line workings were to King's Lynn and back only, connection to and from Hunstanton, even with the 'Fenman', being by diesel multiple-unit. Eight-coach trains became standard, one four-coach section, including restaurant car, working between Liverpool Street and Ely and the other four coaches to and from King's Lynn; also the 'Fenman' lost its through Wisbech coaches. The 'Fenman' left King's Lynn at 7.48am, and with calls at Magdalen Road, Downham and Littleport was not into Ely till 8.26am. The stop there now was 2min only, and at Cambridge 3min; away from the University city at 8.48am the 'Fenman' ran into Liverpool Street at 9.58am. In the down direction the start of the 'Fenman' was at 4.36pm, and by reason of an additional stop, at Audley End, Cambridge was not reached until 5.43pm. From there, with the same halts as in the up direction, it took 57min to run into King's Lynn by 6.43pm, in 2hr 7min from London. The 'Fenman' title was abolished in the 1968 timetable, although the train continued. Connections with Hunstanton were severed by closure of the King's Lynn-Hunstanton line on 5 May 1969.

When the Cambridge line service was improved in 1979, 36min past the hour at alternate hours became the off-peak pattern for Liverpool Street-King's Lynn trains. There was still, therefore a 4.36pm departure for King's Lynn and this 'ex-Fenman' continued to stop at Audley End, and was only 1min faster to Cambridge. Three years later the standard off-peak departures were at 35min past alternate hours both from Liverpool Street and King's Lynn, and the overall time of the 4.35pm down was again 2hr 7min from London. The up train was outside the standard pattern, keeping close to its traditional time with departure from King's Lynn at 7.46am. From Cambridge to Liverpool Street it conformed to the standard 63min non-stop schedule of 1969, giving an arrival in London at 9.48am.

The Flying Scotsman

Probably the distinction of being the first Anglo-Scottish express to receive a title belongs to the train which, almost without interruption from June 1862 until 1982, moved out of King's Cross terminus in London at 10 o'clock every weekday morning on its journey of 392.9 miles to Edinburgh Waverley. For a brief period during World War 1, in 1917 and 1918, the train left London at 9.30am, but the 10am departure was soon restored, and there was no such interruption during World War 2 period.

Precisely when the name 'Flying Scotsman' came into use it is difficult to say; it has certainly been in vogue for well over half a century. But it was not until after the formation of the LNER had brought into one company the three partners in the East Coast route — the Great Northern, North Eastern and North British that the title was officially adopted, and began to be shown on the headboards of the carriages, and in timetables and other public announcements.

When it first appeared, the 10am from King's Cross was known as a 'Special Scotch Express'. As far as Retford it carried a through portion for Sheffield and Manchester; at York there was a halt from 2.25 to 2.55pm to enable passengers to obtain lunch; and Edinburgh was reached at 8.30pm, in 10½hr from London. The corresponding up train, however, took an hour longer. In January 1871 the NER line was opened from Shaftholme Junction, north of Doncaster, to York through Selby (the previous route was through Knottingley and Church Fenton), and in 1872 the same company completed the direct Team Valley line from Durham to Newcastle; with these and other aids to faster running the journey in both directions had come down to 9hr by 1876.

In November 1887 the decision was reached to admit third class passengers to the 'Flying Scotsman'; and this momentous announcement helped to precipitate the 'Race to Edinburgh' of the following year. Schedule times were slashed by both the East Coast and West Coast companies; in the 17 days from 27 July 1888 to 13 August, the East Coast accelerated the 'Flying Scotsman' from 9 to 7¾hr, and on 14 August the famous train made its appearance in Edinburgh Waverley at 5.32pm, 13min early, in 7hr 32min from London. Matters then quietened down until the last day of the month, when this time was bettered with one of 7hr 26¾min, notwithstanding 26½min spent at York for lunch.

The final schedule of August 1888 allowed 117min for the 105.5 miles from King's Cross to Grantham, 88min for the 82.7 miles on to York (reached in 3½hr), and 20min at York; next came 93min for the 80.6 miles on to Newcastle, by way of the old High Level Bridge, and, after reversal there, 137min for the 124.5 miles from Newcastle to Edinburgh. Water-troughs were not yet in use, and the North Eastern 4-4-0 locomotives had to carry enough water in their tenders for this lengthy run. Between London and York the famous Stirling '8-footers' of the Great Northern were used. Engines were changed at Grantham, York and Newcastle.

After the 1888 'Race' had collapsed by agreement between the competitors, the schedule of the 'Flying Scotsman' settled down to 8½hr each way and, apart from the 15min curtailment of the York 'lunch' stop after the introduction of restaurant cars in 1900, it was destined to remain unchanged for many years. This was the result of an agreement reached between the East and West Coast companies, after the 'Race to Aberdeen' in 1895, that the overall times of the day trains between London and both Edinburgh and Glasgow should not be cut below 8¼hr.

It is astonishing that the 'Flying Scotsman' should have had to wait 21 years from the introduction by the Great Northern Railway of the first British dining cars before being provided with cars of its own; but the development, when it came, was one of great thoroughness. On 1 August 1900, two new trains appeared on the 10am services from King's Cross and Edinburgh Waverley. Each consisted of eight 12-wheel cars, 65ft 6in long with bow ends, buckeye automatic couplers, Pullman vestibules and clerestory roofs — a revolutionary advance on the stock previously in use. The trains weighed 265 tons, and seated 50 first class and 211 third class passengers. Locomotive power had increased to suit, for on the Great Northern the Stirling 4-2-2 engines had given place in turn to the Ivatt 4-4-0s, and then to the first of the Ivatt Atlantics. The North Eastern Railway in 1900 was just bringing into use the efficient 'R' class 4-4-0s of Wilson Worsdell's design.

For reasons already given, the next stage of 'Flying Scotsman' history was dull. Trains of new rolling stock appeared in 1914, including a set of three restaurant cars in which, for the first time, an entirely separate kitchen and pantry car was included. Three years later, in the middle of the first world war, the restaurant cars were withdrawn, and the 'Flying Scotsman' was slowed ultimately to 9hr 50min in each direction. But the end of the war saw a rapid return to normal, with restaurant cars early in 1919, and the old 8¼hr schedule restored by 1923. Another pair of new trains came into service in 1924, and the 'Flying Scotsman' for the first time acquired a set of three restaurant cars articulated on the Gresley system, and also equipped for cooking by electricity.

While the schedule time agreement between the East Coast and West Coast Companies continued in force, it was necessary for the rivals to find other outlets for their competitive energy. One form taken by this rivalry was non-stop running over great distances, which finally resulted, from May 1928 in the 'Flying Scotsman' being scheduled to make the longest non-stop run in the world, over the 392.9 miles between King's Cross and Edinburgh.

A new train was put into service, including a coach, marshalled next the restaurant cars, which contained a cocktail bar, a retiring room for ladies and a hair-dressing room with barber complete — all novelties in British practice, and designed to beguile, in various ways, the hours of this lengthy journey.

To make possible a change of crew *en route* without stopping the train, corridor tenders were built which could be vestibuled to the leading coach, so providing a through passage from the train corridor on to the footplate. The ludicrous aspect of the new non-stop schedule, however, was that, despite the availability of the powerful Gresley Pacific locomotives which had been first introduced in 1922, the LNE and LMS train time agreement compelled the 'Flying Scotsman' to spin out the full 8¼hr on the journey, and so to maintain an average speed of no more than 47.6mph. The much heavier main train that followed the non-stop daily made all the usual stops and took exactly the same time!

At last, in 1932, when trains in all parts of the country were being speeded up, the minimum time agreement could be maintained no longer. In May of that year came the first acceleration of the 'Flying Scotsman' that had taken place for 32 years; 25min were cut from the schedule in each direction, reducing the time to 7hr 50min between King's Cross and Edinburgh. When the non-stop first portion, which always operated during the summer only, began to run in July, a more enterprising cut of 45min on the previous summer's schedule brought the overall time down to 7½hr, and the speed up to 52.3mph; in 1936 this became 7¼hr, and in 1937 7hr, with an average speed now raised to 56.1mph. Corresponding reductions were made in the winter schedule, until in 1938 and 1939, up to the outbreak of World War 2, the 'Flying Scotsman', with all the stops included, was running between London and Edinburgh in 7hr 20min each way.

This winter schedule provided one of the hardest locomotive tasks in the country. For in 1938 yet another new pair of trains had been introduced, and this time with electrically-driven pressure ventilation plant on each coach, which increased the weight of the stock considerably. Going north, the formation from the engine was a brake third and composite coach for Glasgow; a composite with luggage compartment for Perth; three thirds, a buffet car, a triplet articulated restaurant car set and a first for Edinburgh; and a composite, third, and brake third for Aberdeen, 14 vehicles in all, weighing no less than 504 tons. Occasionally one of the Edinburgh thirds might be cut out; but more often, especially at weekends and in the up direction, the load would be added to, and the hard-worked locomotive might then have behind the tender 15 or 16 bogies of this heavy stock, with a total load behind the tender of fully 600 tons. The use of a full-length buffet car for light refreshments, in addition to the restaurant cars proper, was an innovation derived from American practice.

By some curious tradition, for many years past, the work demanded of the engines of south of York, relatively to the gradients, had always been harder than north of that point. So it was with the 'Flying Scotsman'. From King's Cross northwards, the 10am was required to run the 105.5 miles to Grantham, notwithstanding the 1 in 105 start, the 8-mile pull at 1 in 200 to Potters Bar, the severe slack through Peterborough and the lengthy grind at 1 in 200 and 1 in 178 to Stoke Summit, in 110min. A stop of 2min there was followed by a mile-a-minute sprint to York — 82.7 miles in 83min — and that city was reached at 1.15pm. After 4min at York, there was a relatively easy allowance of 90min for the 80.2 miles to Newcastle, almost dead level to Darlington, and with no severe handicaps beyond, other than the slowing through Durham. For the 67 miles from Newcastle to Berwick the train had 77min, and for the 57.5 miles on to Edinburgh 67min; neither of these lengths had any grades more severe, in the northbound direction, than those between London and Grantham.

Southbound, the 'Flying Scotsman' had to tackle the formidable Cockburnspath bank, south of Dunbar — 4 miles at 1 in 96 up — in the course of a 65min schedule to Berwick; from Berwick to Newcastle in 75min was relatively easy, as also the 48min allowed for the 36 miles from Newcastle to Darlington, where the only severe obstacle was the recovery up a short 1 in 101 gradient from the bad slack through Durham. But it was after leaving Darlington, at 1.18pm, that the hard work began, and it got progressively harder as the journey proceeded. The straight and level 44.1 miles from Darlington to York had to be run in 45min (58.8mph); the 82.7 miles from York to Grantham in 85½min (58.4mph); and then, to crown all, the engine was left 105½min in which to run the 105½ miles on to King's Cross at exactly 60mph. With a load of 550 to 600 tons, the schedule of this train south of York had no superior in the country for difficulty, and probably, indeed, no rival. Engines were changed in each direction at Newcastle only. A precision of timing to which we have become accustomed in later years was seen in the fact that the stop at Grantham was booked to half-minutes — from 3.32½pm to 3.34½pm.

As to the sections of the northbound 'Flying Scotsman', the Aberdeen portion, on the rear, was drawn back on arrival at Edinburgh, and attached to the 5.40pm restaurant car express, calling at Kirkcaldy, Cupar, Leuchars Junction, Dundee, Broughty Ferry, Arbroath, Montrose and Stonehaven; it reached Aberdeen at 9pm. In summer, however, when the non-stop service was being run between London and Edinburgh, a much faster connection was arranged; passengers then left Edinburgh at 5.15pm, and were in Aberdeen at 8.15pm, in 10¼hr from London. The Glasgow coaches were taken off the front of the 'Flying Scotsman' and transferred to the 5.43pm restaurant car expresss, which brought them into Queen Street at 6.45pm, and the Perth coach was worked forward similarly by the 5.55pm train, reaching Perth at 7.13pm.

In the reverse direction, the first section to start was that from Aberdeen, in a breakfast car train at the early hour of 6.40am; the Perth coach left at 8.25am, and the Glasgow vehicles at 8.35am, all being marshalled in order before departure of the main train from Waverley at 10am.

During World War 2 there were numerous changes in the schedule of the 'Flying Scotsman'; the through service was confined to London-Edinburgh, and for most of the war period two trains in each direction daily. Preceded by a relief train at 9.40am, the 'Flying Scotsman' proper, at 10am from King's Cross, settled down to a call at Peterborough only (11.38am-11.45am) between London and York, reached at 2.02pm; then, after a stop of 13min, at Newcastle (3.55pm-4.05pm) and Berwick (5.29pm-5.34pm), with an arrival in Waverley at 6.55pm. Coming south, the train called at Berwick and Newcastle, and then at Darlington from 1.41pm to 1.46pm, after which York was missed, and the next stop was at Grantham from 4.25pm to 4.35pm. The up 'Flying Scotsman' reached London at 6.45pm, in 8¾hr.

From 1 October 1945, however, there was a very substantial speed-up. The down 'Flying Scotsman', complete once again with its restaurant cars, but with stops unchanged, was accelerated by no less than 50min, to reach Edinburgh at 6.05pm. The up express now had an 8hr schedule, arriving in London at 6pm, and the relief services in each direction received equally drastic treatment. In October 1946 further new timings came into force; the old Grantham stop replaced that at Peterborough, and then followed a non-stop run to Newcastle, 162.9 miles; with a third stop, at Berwick, the 'Scotsman' was due into Edinburgh at 6.10pm. Coming south the 8hr schedule and the stops remained unaltered.

Vast loads were run during the earlier part of the war. The train was seldom made up of less than 20 bogie vehicles, with a loaded weight of 680 tons or more, but on many occasions this increased, in the up direction especially, to 21, 22, and even 23 bogies, which with packed complements of passengers and their luggage brought the total weight behind the engine tenders to little short of 800 tons. These trains were worked single-headed for the most part by the highly competent streamlined Pacifics of the A4 class. In the late stages of the war, however, with indifferent coal and lower than normal standards of maintenance it became necessary to lay down a limit of 18 bogies, bringing the gross load down to about 635 tons, and later 15 bogies became the maximum.

In the summer of 1949, as it became more convenient to run the non-stop service between London and Edinburgh as a relief to the 'Flying Scotsman' proper, and as it was not desired to alter the time-honoured 10am start of the latter, a new train called the 'Capitals Limited' took over the non-stop working. It is of interest to recall that during September 1948, while the then non-stop 'Flying Scotsman' was being diverted between Tweedmouth and Edinburgh by way of Kelso and Galashiels (because of the branches in the main line north of Berwick), there were several occasions on which the journey of 408½ miles was actually completed without stopping — the longest non-stop runs ever made in British history. The 'Flying Scotsman' itself had settled down to a schedule with stops at Grantham and Newcastle only, involving non-stop runs in succession of 105.5, 162.9 and 124.5 miles. The 1952-1953 winter timetable allowed 7hr 50min each way between King's Cross and Edinburgh, and that of the previous summer 12min less.

By now the Glasgow section of the 'Flying Scotsman' had become a complete restaurant car train, which acted as a relief to the 'Flying Scotsman'. The former left King's Cross at 10.05am, and, calling at Peterborough, York, Darlington, Durham, Newcastle and Berwick, reached Edinburgh at 6.26pm and Glasgow at 7.53pm. In the southbound direction the corresponding train, with the same stops, started from Glasgow at 8.35am and Edinburgh at 10.10am, and was due in London at 6.27pm. The down Glasgow train carried the prewar Aberdeen coaches of the 'Flying Scotsman', but in the up direction these once more were attached to the 'Flying Scotsman' itself.

Steady acceleration had now begun. In 1955 it was decided to run the train non-stop in each direction daily over the 268.4 miles between King's Cross and Newcastle, and to cut the London-Edinburgh time to 7hr. The next development of note, after more acceleration, occurred in 1962, and it was a startling one. By now 3,300hp 'Deltic' diesels had taken over from A4 Pacifics the working of the East Coast trains, and so made it possible to speed up the 'Flying Scotsman' in each direction between King's Cross and Edinburgh Waverley to the time of the prewar 'Coronation' streamliner — 6hr, including the Newcastle stop. This was with a tare load up to 385 tons — 11 coaches — as compared with the 'Coronation' 278 tons (or 312 tons when the observation car was attached).

By 1967 the overall time had come down still further, to 5hr 50min each way (actually 5hr 49min working time on the southbound run). For the 268.4 miles from King's Cross to Newcastle the allowance was 3hr 52min (69.4mph), and for the 124.5 miles from there to Edinburgh 114min (65.05mph). Coming up the times were 113min from Edinburgh to Newcastle and 3hr 53min on to London. The normal formation of the 'Flying Scotsman' northbound was composite brake and second corridor for Aberdeen (not a very attractive service for through passengers, as they had to wait 70min at Waverley before the start of their Aberdeen connection); compartment second, compartment second with miniature buffet, open second and compartment second; kitchen restaurant car with 33 seats and 48-seat open restaurant car; two compartment firsts and another composite brake. This 11-coach set weighed 394 tons, or about 420 tons with a normal complement of passengers and luggage. At this period the 'Flying Scotsman' was making the journey between London and Edinburgh in 2hr 25min less than its schedule up to 1932, and 1½hr less than in 1939.

The 1970s saw the train formed of air-conditioned Mk 2 stock. Essential engineering works between Newcastle and Edinburgh brought some deceleration but in 1977 high speeds could be resumed and the 'Flying Scotsman' schedule was cut to 5hr 27min from King's Cross to Edinburgh. At the same time the departure of the up train from Edinburgh was moved to 9.50am, surrendering the traditional 10am to an Edinburgh-Plymouth train which was thereby able to make important connections for South Wales at Birmingham. The up 'Flying Scotsman' time to King's Cross was 5hr 28min.

By this time HSTs for the East Coast Route were on the horizon. When the first HST schedules went into operation in May 1978 the 'Flying Scotsman' was among the services converted to the new rolling stock. At once the down journey to Edinburgh, still at 10am from King's Cross, was shortened to 4hr 52min, stopping only at Newcastle and averaging 87.5mph to that point. The up departure from Edinburgh was changed again, this time to 10.10am, and the overall time to London was 4hr 50min. These were the fastest times of the day, and that distinction was retained for the

'Flying Scotsman' in 1982 when its London-Edinburgh journeys were shortened to 4hr 35min down and 4hr 38min up. But the 'Flying Scotsman' was no longer the 10am from King's Cross. Its departure was put forward to 10.35 and the famous 10am 'slot' was occupied by an HST to Aberdeen.

The Golden Arrow

For many years the South Eastern & Chatham Railway and its successor, the Southern Railway, had maintained a service to Paris leaving Victoria at 11am, but the title 'Golden Arrow' was not bestowed on the train until 1929, when, in the palmy pre-depression and pre-airline days, it was decided to inaugurate a service exclusively for first class Pullman passengers between the two capitals. A special steamer, the *Canterbury*, was built to provide for the Channel crossing between Dover and Calais, and the trains on both sides — the 'Golden Arrow' in England and the 'Flèche d'Or' in France — were composed exclusively of Pullman cars, with the necessary vans added for luggage. An independent service of trains on both sides, with a separate steamer, was provided for ordinary first and second class passengers who desired to travel at a cheaper fare than the inclusive £5 rate for the 'Golden Arrow' journey.

Leaving Victoria at 11am, the 'Golden Arrow' was due at Dover Marine station at 12.38pm. For transfer to the *Canterbury* the time allowed was 17min, and for the crossing from Dover to Calais 75min. On what was then the Northern Railway of France, the 'Flèche d'Or' was waiting on the quayside, headed by one of the famous four-cylinder compound Nord Pacifics, and was booked to cover the 184 miles from Calais to Paris in 190min, bringing passengers into the French capital at 5.35pm. On the English side, a train of 10 Pullmans and two brakes was needed to accommodate the traffic.

As the first class traffic began to fall off in the depression years, however, and with the increasing tendency of this class of passenger to save time by making use of air travel, before many years had passed it was found impossible any longer to justify a service confined to first class passengers alone. Most of the hitherto exclusive *trains-de-luxe* on the Continent were beginning to admit second class passengers, and second class sleeping cars were appearing on the 'Blue Train', the 'Rome Express', and many other famous services. The 'Golden Arrow' then followed suit; on the English side the first class Pullmans were supplemented by first and second class corridor coaches, and on the French side, where two trains were necessary, a second class Pullman joined the first class cars, as well as the through sleepers for the 'Blue Train' and other long-distance services. This change took place in May 1931.

For many years the 'Lord Nelson' four-cylinder 4-6-0s monopolised the 'Golden Arrow' workings, though 'King Arthurs' took their turn from time to time. The maximum load that the 4-6-0s of either type were permitted to take over this difficult route was 425 tons. Before the outbreak of World War 2 a train of four Pullmans, six corridor coaches, and two 6-wheel brakes normally sufficed for the 'Golden Arrow', and as the tare weight of such a formation was about 375 tons it could be expanded by two coaches if necessary.

The route between Victoria and Dover is anything but easy from the locomotive point of view. The principal difficulty is concentrated in the $30\frac{1}{2}$ miles between London and Tonbridge, with its lengthy ascents in both directions to Knockholt summit. The down journey begins with the 1 in 62 climb out of the terminus on to the Grosvenor Bridge, and subsequent adverse gradients include $1\frac{1}{2}$ miles at 1 in 102 to Penge tunnel, and 2 miles at 1 in 95 to Bickley Junction, with reduced speed round the curve at Orpington. But the worst continuous climb is on the up run, where the 'Golden Arrow', after slowing down for the Tonbridge curve, is faced with 4 miles up at 1 in 122, and 2 miles at 1 in 144, the latter through Sevenoaks tunnel. Over the well-aligned and fairly level stretch east of Tonbridge, however, high speeds are possible.

The down 'Golden Arrow' had always left Victoria at 11am, and latterly was booked to reach Dover Marine at 12.35pm, so covering the 78 miles in 95min, at an average of 49.3mph. But the allowance of $41\frac{1}{2}$min for the 41.4 miles from Tonbridge to Folkestone Junction demanded a mile-a-minute average.

Whereas the boat on the outward service worked from Dover to Calais, for some years up to the war the return service was routed via Boulogne-Folkestone, and the inward 'Golden Arrow' therefore started from Folkestone Harbour. Alternative paths were provided in the working timetable, including one 10min later, but if the boat was punctual, the normal scheduled departure was 3.44pm. The first stage of the journey was up the steepest gradient on the entire Southern Railway system, at 1 in 30 for $\frac{3}{4}$mile, from the Harbour to the sidings at the Junction station, for which at least two and sometimes three 0-6-0 tanks were needed; the allowance for the 1.2 miles was 5min.

At Folkestone Junction, the 'Lord Nelson' 4-6-0 was waiting and backed on to the opposite end of the train, leaving for London at 3.54pm. The start of the run was fast, for the 'Golden Arrow' was booked to pass Tonbridge, 41.4 miles, in 42$\frac{1}{2}$min; of this distance the 35.9 miles from Sandling Junction to Tonbridge were allowed 33min only, a scheduled average of 65.3mph. Then followed the stiff climb to Knockholt and the cautious running required through the London suburbs, so that 43$\frac{1}{2}$min were conceded for the 30.6 miles from Tonbridge into Victoria, where the arrival was 5.20pm.

The 'Golden Arrow' disappeared, of course, with the outbreak of war, but was reinstated on 15 April 1946, leaving Victoria at 10am, and with 100min (later accelerated to 95min and in 1952 to 92min) allowed to Dover Marine. The formation from now on was 10 Pullmans and two vans, and the locomotive, latterly a 'Merchant Navy' or 'West Country' Pacific and later still the 'Britannia' Pacific *William Shakespeare*, carried large gilt arrows on its side and on the smokebox door.

In the 1952-1953 winter timetable a radical alteration was made in the outward journey, for the 'Golden Arrow', for the first time in its history, was transferred to the afternoon service leaving Victoria at 2pm (and, for the change of time in October, at 1pm). This meant a diversion from Dover to Folkestone and, owing to the longer Fokestone-Calais crossing a deceleration from 6hr 52min to 7hr 34min in the running time from London to Paris. The return working via Calais-Dover remained unchanged, however, at 12.30pm from Paris, and 7.30pm (6.30pm from the change of time) into Victoria. Thus the prewar arrangement, outward via Dover and inward via Folkestone, had been exactly reversed.

The quick transit of the 'Golden Arrow' service in its first years was not maintained. The only part of the journey that was faster in the 1960s was between Victoria and Dover, where in 1962 the substitution of 2,550hp electric locomotives for the former steam power permitted a cut to 80min in the time for the 78 miles — a very smart timing in view of the gradients and slacks between Victoria and Tonbridge. But port formalities increased the time between train arrival and boat departure at Dover Marine from the original 17 to 35min; the Channel crossing, at 80min, was 5min longer; Calais Maritime needed 30 instead of 15min; and despite the high-speed electric run between Amiens and Paris, the French National Railways, in contrast to the British 18min acceleration from Victoria to Dover, still took their 3hr 10min from Calais to the French captial. So the overall London-Paris journey required 6hr 55min as compared with 6hr 35min in 1929. In the reverse direction the journey was 10min longer still. It is a matter of great surprise that the French National Railways, so speed-conscious in all other directions, seemed to take so little interest in the 'Golden Arrow' and its companions.

In the later years of the service departure from Victoria was at 10.30am; the 'Golden Arrow' proper by this time included no more than four first class Pullmans; and the remaining accommodation was second-class ordinary coaches only. The train was relieved during the summer by a multiple-unit electric train at 10am. Throughout British winter time the start has to be an hour earlier in order to conform to Continental time. In the reverse direction the 'Golden Arrow' left Paris Nord at 12.30pm, reaching Calais Maritime at 3.42pm; the boat crossing was from 4.10 to 5.30pm; and with a 6.10pm departure from Dover Marine the Southern 'Golden Arrow' was into Victoria by 7.35pm.

The new times and longer journeys did little for the 'Golden Arrow's' image, and across the Channel the Wagon-Lits company decided to withdraw its Pullmans, now some 40 years old, from the connecting 'Fleche d'Or'. It was becoming increasingly difficult to justify allocating a special set of coaches to perform one return trip daily between London and the Channel coast. The Southern's other boat train services, apart from the 'Night Ferry', were now worked by emus. Withdrawal of the 'Golden Arrow' was seen to be inevitable and it occurred at end of the summer service of 1972.

The Golden Hind

A development of the 1960s which steadily gained momentum was the provision of fast early morning trains from provincial cities to London, and return workings in the evening, designed to promote business travel by giving executives and others ample time to attend to their affairs in the capital without the necessity for staying away overnight. So it was that the summer of 1964 saw the introduction by the Western Region of a new express from Plymouth to Paddington and back — the 'Golden Hind'. The name, like that of the 'Mayflower', which ran for a time in the postwar years, was derived from Plymouth's maritime history. But whereas the 'Mayflower' was an existing train of no great distinction, the 'Golden Hind' was an entirely new service, and, moreover, in faster time than any previously scheduled between Paddington and Plymouth. This was 3hr 50min up and 3hr 55min down; the extra 5min were because of the difficulty of finding a suitable high-speed path out of Paddington in the early evening.

It was decided to start the morning 'Golden Hind' from Plymouth at 7.05am, to call at Newton Abbot for the benefit of passengers from the Torbay branch (with a record 3hr 20min time from Torquay to London), and after that at Exeter and Taunton; the final timing was 127min for the 142.7 miles from Taunton to the Paddington arrival at 10.55am. Going down, the start was fixed at 5.20pm, and with 131min to Taunton and 2hr 42min to Exeter and the Newton Abbot stop, Plymouth passengers were back in their home town by 9.15pm. Later, to come into line with the even-interval departures at 30min past the hour from Paddington to the West of England, the down 'Golden Hind' was altered to start at 5.30pm, and with a better path to Reading reached Taunton in 123min (69.6mph), and Exeter in the record time of 2hr 34min. Arrival at Plymouth was at 9.20pm. The up working was unchanged. Among very smart intermediate times were 29min down and 30min up for the 30.8 miles over Whiteball summit between Taunton and Exeter. In 1968 the London-Plymouth time was further reduced to 3hr 45min.

At the start a maximum formation of 7 coaches, including restaurant car, was laid down, but the working timetable later permitted a 2,700hp 'Western' diesel to take 290 tare tons on this timing, which covered up to 8 coaches of the heaviest stock. Seat reservation was compulsory.

The train has proved a great success and has well justified its introduction. In 1970 air-braked Mk 2 stock was introduced, with considerable improvement to the 'Golden Hind's' image of modernity and comfort, and in 1971 the train was accelerated by 5min in each direction, the up service leaving Plymouth 5min later, at 7.10am, and the down train arriving 5min earlier. In 1972 the 'Golden Hind' was extended to Penzance. An early departure from Penzance — 5.10am — brought the train into Paddington at 10.38am, in time for the stock to form the down 'Cornish Riviera', then leaving at 11.30am. Similiary, the stock of the up 'Cornish Riviera', arriving at 4.30pm, formed the 5.30pm 'Golden Hind' departure from Paddington.

As an HST the 'Golden Hind' was starting the day in 1982 with an even earlier departure, leaving Penzance at 5.07am and arriving Paddington at 10am. The down train left Paddington at 5.25pm and was due into Penzance exactly 5hr later. The London-Plymouth time was 3hr 15min up and 3hr 13min down.

The Heart of Midlothian

The afternoon services between King's Cross and Edinburgh, by the East Coast route, which were provided with new standard stock and named the 'Heart of Midlothian' on the occasion of the 1951 Festival of Britain, had a very lengthy history. Before World War 1 departures from both King's Cross and Edinburgh were at 2.20pm, and with stops at Grantham, York, Darlington, Newcastle and Berwick — and Doncaster and Peterborough in addition coming south — the journey was a leisurely one, taking 8hr 25min in each direction. In the first decade of the present century, the down express was one of the last Great Northern trains to carry a slip coach, which it detached at Doncaster.

In the period between the wars the times of starting were considerably altered, and gradually settled down to 1.20pm from London and 2.05pm from Edinburgh, while the post-1932 accelerations eventually produced the very fast timings (in view of the number of intermediate stops) of 7hr 25min down and 7hr 30min up. One notable booking of the down express was over the 124.5 miles from Newcastle to Edinburgh in 130min; this was made possible by shedding at Newcastle a through portion for stations between there and Edinburgh, while the main train ran non-stop.

During World War 2 starting times varied considerably; after the war the King's Cross start, at first 1pm, was changed to 1.15pm, and then, in accordance with the systematic departure plan, it became 2pm. From Edinburgh the departure for the south for a long time was at 1.30pm, but for the same reason this became 2pm also. The stops going north were at Peterborough, York, Darlington, Newcastle, Alnmouth, Berwick and Dunbar; coming south, they were at Berwick, Newcastle, Darlington, York and Grantham. The southbound express carried a through portion from Aberdeen, which left the Granite City at 10.20am.

In the autumn of 1957 an interesting experiment was tried of running the 'Heart of Midlothian' through to Perth, and, moreover, not by the direct Forth Bridge route, but using the former London Midland & Scottish line through Falkirk and Stirling, in order to give the last-mentioned town a through service. Reverting temporarily to a 1pm departure from King's Cross, the 'Heart of Midlothian' was due in Edinburgh at 8.30pm and Perth at 10.24pm, exactly 2hr ahead of the leisurely 1.35pm from Euston. Southbound, departure from Perth was at 11.25am, in time for departure from Edinburgh at 1.30pm, and arrival in King's Cross by 9.05pm. The only disadvantage of this arrangement was that it severed the connection at Perth with the 8.20am from Inverness, which had enabled passengers via the Forth Bridge to catch the 'Heart of Midlothian' at Edinburgh. But the through Perth workings of this express and the 'Fair Maid' did not attract public patronage, and both soon after were withdrawn.

Very substantial accelerations of the 'Heart of Midlothian' followed the introduction of 'Deltic' diesel power. In the final years to 1968, despite the 12-coach formation on the down journey, of 432 tare tons, the train had to cover the 76.4 miles from King's Cross to Peterborough in 67½min, and the 111.8 miles on to York in 101½min; from York to Darlington, 44.1 miles in 40min, was another fast timing. Thus the time over the 392.9 miles from London to Edinburgh, with seven stops totalling in duration 25min, had been cut to 6¾hr. Coming south, with a heavier 13-coach load of 466 tare tons, the diesel had a still harder task, for with one stop less the run had to be completed in 6½hr. From Edinburgh to Newcastle 124.5 miles in 122min, including a Berwick stop, left nothing to spare; nor did 39min for the 44.1 miles from Darlington to York, 79½min for the 82.7 miles on to Grantham, and 96½min for the 105.5 miles from Grantham to London.

The Hebridean and the Lewisman

By contrast with the train last described, the 'Hebridean' had nothing to offer in the realm of either weight haulage or high speed, but this is understandable when its route is considered. This was through the heart of the almost uninhabited Highlands of Scotland, over a line of the most formidable gradients, single track throughout and with a severe overall speed restriction as well as many additional restrictions for curves. The name originated in the late 1930s, in LMSR days, because the 'Hebridean' and its companion the 'Lewisman', crossing Scotland by means of the 63½-mile Dingwall & Skye branch of the former Highland Railway, provided connection at the Kyle not merely with the ferry to Kyleakin, in the Isle of Skye, but also with the mail steamers to Stornoway.

It was from Kyle, in the very small hours, at 5.05am on a summer morning in peacetime, that the 'Lewisman' started its journey. On this trip, singularly enough, when the sleepy traveller was the most in need of the comfort of refreshments, a restaurant car was absent. A through coach for Glasgow was attached, and after arrival of the 'Lewisman' in Inverness at 8.10am, was transferred to the 8.35am express for the south, on which the passenger from Kyle was able to obtain his belated meal. This through coach reached Glasgow (Buchanan Street), 263 miles from Kyle, at 1.44pm. The 'Lewisman' itself, after a wait of two hours at Inverness, and now having acquired its restaurant car, started back at 10.15am, and finished its day at Kyle of Lochalsh at 1.40pm.

It had been preceded in this direction by the 'Hebridean'. The latter was booked to leave Inverness, as a breakfast car train, at 7.25am, complete with a through coach for Kyle which had left Glasgow on the sleeping car train for Inverness at 10.45pm on the previous evening. The 'Hebridean' reached Kyle of Lochalsh at 10.31am, and the eastbound 'Hebridean' was due to start 14min later, at 10.45am, for Inverness, arriving back at 2pm.

During the winter months two of these four workings were withdrawn. The westbound 'Lewisman', at 10.15am from Inverness, ran with its timing unchanged, and the eastbound 'Hebridean', apart from starting five minutes earlier, at 10.40am, and reaching Inverness 18min later, continued on its way throughout the year. But so far as the timetable was concerned, neither of these trains ever returned to its starting-point! For some years one restaurant car was used for both workings, and this meant transferring it from the 'Lewisman' to the 'Hebridean' at the passing loop at Achnasheen, where the two trains were scheduled to meet. Passengers on the 'Lewisman' who had not finished their lunch by 12.13pm were liable to lose the last course or two, as the car was due to be on the way back to Inverness six minutes later!

After the war the name 'Lewisman' did not reappear, but the 'Hebridean' name was retained for the 10.40am from Inverness. After a non-stop run over the $18\frac{1}{4}$ miles to Dingwall (all intermediate stations having been closed) the train stopped at all stations on the Kyle branch and was into Kyle of Lochalsh at 1.40pm. The scenery, especially at the western end of the run, from Loch Carron past the finely situated village of Plockton, is magnificent, and from May to September inclusive justified the running of an observation car on the tail of the train, with attendant; this also supplied refreshments, for the restaurant car had long since ceased to run. The observation car did not return on the eastbound 'Hebridean', however, as this train now left the Kyle at 11.10am and met the westbound train at Achnasheen. The eastbound 'Hebridean' was the faster of the two, for it completed the $82\frac{1}{4}$-mile run to Inverness in 2hr 50min.

Up to the general introduction of diesel power in Scotland, Stanier Class 5 4-6-0s worked the Kyle traffic, having taken over from the ex-Highland 4-6-0s of Cumming's design. After dieselisation Type 2 1,250hp diesels reigned supreme until the more powerful (1,750hp) Class 37 locomotives began to work on the line in 1982. Although the trains are relatively light, they can prove a tough proposition to handle in bad weather over the fearsome gradients of this line, as steep in places as 1 in 50. The service has now become second class only. A 10.40am departure from Inverness conveys a 'vintage observation car', which returns from Kyle at 5.10pm but the trains are unnamed.

It may be added that up to the war the 10.10am and 3.30pm from Wick to Inverness both carried restaurant cars and names — the 'John o'Groat' and 'Orcadian' respectively — as also their return workings at 4.10pm and 10.25am, but the names were not perpetuated and the restaurant cars gave place to miniature buffets. Inverness-Wick trains today are second class only but buffet service continues. Class 37 locomotives have been introduced on these services as well.

The Hull Pullman

Seven years after the 'Yorkshire Pullman' had begun to run, it was decided in 1935 to extend Pullman facilities to Hull, and at the same time to give the citizens of Hull the fastest service — $3\frac{1}{2}$hr — that they had ever enjoyed to and from London. So the train was stopped at Doncaster in both directions to allow cars for Hull to be attached and detached. On the reinstatement of the 'Yorkshire Pullman' after the war, the four Hull cars were still attached, though up to February 1966, despite the accelerations that had taken place on the main line, there had been no reduction in the London-Hull time. Indeed, the up run now took 3hr 40min, or 10min longer.

But from March, 1967, there was a notable change, for Kingston-upon-Hull now had its own 'Hull Pullman'. This was a train of six cars with a bogie brake, which left King's Cross in charge of a Class 47 diesel at 5.30pm on a timing of 136min over the 156 miles to Doncaster (68.8mph), and with calls after that to set down at Goole and Brough was into Hull by 8.45pm in $3\frac{1}{4}$hr from London. In the up direction a start from Hull at 10.35am, with the same stops and a run up from Doncaster in 134min, secured an arrival in London by 1.44pm. This up journey in 3hr 9min was, by a margin of 21min, the fastest tabled between Hull and London up to that time.

In October 1968 the up 'Hull Pullman' departure was put forward to 6.45am, a stop at Retford was added, and the train was into King's Cross at 10am. The down train now left at 5.35pm. At the same time the second class Pullmans were withdrawn and the formation became first class Pullmans and second class ordinary stock. It was a popular train and in the mid-1970s increased loadings required 'Deltic' power, but with planning for HSTs going ahead the end of all the Eastern Region Pullmans was near and at the end of the 1977-78 timetable the service was withdrawn. In its final phase the down 'Hull Pullman' reached Hull in 2hr 58min with stops at Doncaster, Goole and Brough. The up train called additionally at Retford and made the journey to London in 3hr 5min.

The Irish Mails

For many years past, save in wartime, the principal Irish mail trains left Euston at times between 8 and 9 in the morning and at a corresponding hour in the evening, and were due back in London round about 6 o'clock morning and evening. In London & North Western days, 8.30am and 8.45pm were the departures for the Holyhead-Kingstown service; two boat trains were run from Euston in connection with the North Wall boats, first at 11am and later at 1.20pm, and also at 10.15pm; and yet a fifth for the Holyhead-Greenore route to Northern Ireland, at 7.30 in the evening. But the Greenore services were not revived after World War 1.

The day 'Irish Mails' between Euston and Holyhead carried restaurant cars of which the service was renowned as something quite superlative, even by LMS standards. The night trains included first and third class sleeping cars, out of which their patrons had to turn at the most uncomfortable hour of 2.20am on the down journey, though coming up the passenger who had endured the unpleasantness of the Irish Sea was off the boat and into his cosy berth by midnight, and could remain in it until 8am, if he so desired. Both day and night services incorporated in their formations two Post Office sorting coaches for handling the mails, and so were 'Irish Mails' in every sense of the term.

The mail services between Euston and Holyhead, though at one time known unofficially as the 'Wild Irishmen', have always been distinguished more for weight than for speed. Indeed, between Chester and Holyhead particularly, the loads handled on these trains were often greater than permitted anywhere else on the LMSR system without pilot assistance. Even in the piping times of peace, it was nothing unusual for a 'Royal Scot' 4-6-0 to be expected to handle trains up to 16 or 17 bogies, with a full weight of 510 to 540 tons, over the North Wales main line.

By 1939 the down morning 'Irish Mail' from Euston had strayed by 15min from its earlier 8.30am departure, which was now given over to a Liverpool and Manchester train, and had become 8.45am. A one-minute stop was made at Watford to pick up passengers, and the next 65.1 miles to Rugby were run in 60min. The Rugby times were 10.18 to 10.21am; then came a run over the 75.5 miles to Crewe in 83min, and a stop of 9min there. Away from Crewe at 11.53am, the 'Irishman' made its last stop at Chester from 12.19 to 12.27, and then ran the 84.4 miles on to Holyhead in the easy time of 98min. On the journey the postal apparatus was in use at Nuneaton, Llandudno Junction, and finally at Menai Bridge, just before crossing the Britannia Tubular Bridge into Anglesey.

The evening 'Irish Mail' was also publicly advertised to leave Euston at 8.45, but the actual working departure was 8.50pm. Running times were easier — 93min to Rugby (with no Watford stop), 90min on to Crewe, 26min from there to Chester, and 97min from Chester to Holyhead — and with longer station stops the Holyhead arrival was not till 2.20am. Every Friday night during the summer, and nightly during the height of the season, this train was relieved by an 8.45pm express which ran the entire 263.6 miles from Euston to Holyhead without a stop in 5hr 10min. The morning 'Irish Mail' was similarly relieved on Fridays by a non-stop at 8.30am, which completed the journey in 5¼hr.

Of the up 'Irish Mails', the night train was the slower. At 13min after midnight it drew out of Holyhead, and was allowed 97min to Chester, 27min on to Crewe, 83min from Crewe to Rugby, and 84min over the 82.6 miles from Rugby to Euston, where the arrival was at 5.30am. The postal apparatus on this train had a busy time, and was in action at Bangor, Rhyl, Stafford, Tamworth, Nuneaton, Bletchley, Hemel Hempstead and Harrow.

As for the up day 'Irish Mail', it was booked out of Holyhead at 12.40pm, and allowed only 94min for the 84.4 miles to Chester, where there was a 10min stop, followed by a booking of 27min to Crewe. Here there was an allowance of 11min — chiefly to deal with mails — and then an 82min run to Rugby was followed by a fast 82min for the final 82.6 miles to Euston (just over 60mph), bringing the train into London at 5.50pm, in 5hr 10min from Holyhead. With the invariably heavy load, this timing meant very hard work for a 'Royal Scot'. At summer weekends this train also was relieved by a non-stop to Euston in

5hr 3min, at 52.2mph.

For some years the regular 'Irish Mails' in addition to the summer non-stops were through engine workings between Euston and Holyhead, manned exclusively by Holyhead engine-crews in both directions. Pacifics were used for a short time, but later the 'Irish Mail' was turned over to the capable rebuilt 'Royal Scots'.

During most of the war, the day 'Irish Mail' was run in each direction, but not the night service: from London the former left at 8.15am, with a portion for Manchester on the rear, and with additional stops at Colwyn Bay and Bangor reached Holyhead at 2.34pm. In the reverse direction the start from Holyhead was at 1.45pm, and the only stops were at Chester, Crewe and Watford, bringing the train into Euston at 7.40pm — a slowing down of no more than 45min on the prewar schedule.

After the war it was not until October 1946 that the night service was restored; but the competition of air travel had become such that the day service operated during the summer months only. By the winter of 1952-1953 the 'Irish Mail' was being booked out of Euston at 8.45pm (8.50pm in the working timetable), and was due in Holyhead at 2.25pm, so taking exactly the same time for the journey as before the war. Customs formalities by now had come in to delay the journey, so that the up 'Irish Mail' was not able to leave Holyhead until 1.10am instead of the prewar 12.13am; the Euston arrival had become 6.30am, after a journey 3min longer than the prewar 5hr 17min.

Electrification between Euston and Crewe revolutionised the working of the 'Irish Mails'. Though there were still nominally non-stop runs between Euston and Holyhead, a stop was of course necessary at Crewe to change from electric to diesel power. The relief night train was an all-the-year-round working. It left Euston at 8.55pm, and just short of Crewe was diverted to the Basford Hall sorting sidings, where there was a booked stop from 11.16 to 11.26pm for the locomotive change. The Holyhead line was then joined at Crewe Steelworks at 11.23½pm, and with a non-stop run from there Holyhead was reached at 1.30am, a journey of 4hr 35min from London. This was the train known officially as the 'Irish Mail', which included in its formation the sleeping cars; what was formerly the main train started at 9.20pm, called at Rugby, Crewe and Chester, and was not into Holyhead until 2.16am, still with an hour in hand before the Dun Laoghaire steamer left. It was the 9.20pm down which carried the mails, though no use was now made of the exchange apparatus during the journey.

The day 'Irish Mail' was operated from the beginning of July until mid-September, and also had a daily relief, which started at 8.25am and was allowed the standard 121min for 158.1 miles to Crewe. After a wait of 11min here there was a non-stop run to Holyhead, in 113½min for the 105.7 miles, with an arrival — such was the precision of the working timetables — at half-a-minute after 12.30pm. This train was provided with a miniature buffet only; the main train, with restaurant cars and mails, started at 8.45am, stopped at Watford Junction to pick up and thereafter at Rugby and Crewe, but not as formerly at Chester. Arrival at Holyhead was at 1.04pm. Such was the change that took place with electric and diesel haulage that these trains might be made up to 600 tare tons between Euston and Crewe and 550 tons between there and Holyhead.

The up workings were similar, except that the night relief, at 12.55am, stopped in Crewe station instead of Basford Hall sidings for its engine exchange. The up night 'Irish Mail', at 1.10am from Holyhead, called at Chester, as well as at Crewe and Rugby. The former was into London by 5.30am and the latter by 6.02am. The day 'Irish Mails' were faster: the relief got away from Holyhead at 3.32pm, and with stops at Crewe and Rugby reached Euston at 8pm, but the day 'Irish Mail' did not start until 4.20pm, and stopping at Crewe and Watford followed the relief into Euston at 8.33pm.

'Irish Mail' is one of the names that has lived on for what the LMR describes as 'merely historical reasons' but it now appears in the timetable only for the year-round overnight services.

The Irish Mail via Fishguard

It was in 1906, after immense expenditure in blasting away a rocky hillside to make the necessary shelf on which to lay out the station, that the Great Western Railway brought into use its new port of Fishguard, in West Wales. The aim was to operate direct services between England and Southern Ireland, and GWR steamers began to run both by day and night between Fishguard and another new port which had been created at Rosslare, just across the St George's Channel. Connecting restaurant car trains were put in service between Rosslare, Waterford and Cork, and another connecting service was introduced between Rosslare and Wexford. Direct steamers ran also from Fishguard to Cork and Waterford.

The prospects of Fishguard grew still brighter when the Cunard Steamship Company decided to make this a port of call for its steamers coming across the Atlantic from New York to Liverpool. Disembarkation at Fishguard, with fast rail travel over the GWR from there to Paddington, made possible a far earlier arrival in London than was possible after the normal steaming up the Irish Sea into the Mersey. The possibilities of this traffic were so great that the GWR bestirred itself into making a costly new line to avoid the traffic handicaps in the vicinity of Swansea; the 'Swansea District Lines', as they were called, left the South Wales main line at Court Sart, east of Neath, crossed the Neath River south of that place, then tunnelled under the main line and struck due west through Felin Fran to Morlais East Junction, where a turn was made due south to rejoin the main line near Llanelli. Actually this route saved only $\frac{1}{2}$-mile, but it avoided some severe gradients and congestion on the old main line. It is now confined to freight traffic except between Morlais Junction and the main line.

Originally the plan was to continue westwards from Morlais to Pembrey, on the main line beyond Llanelli, which would have made a wonderfully direct route to Fishguard. But meantime the claims of the great port of Southampton on all the leading Transatlantic services had become so strong — partly because the use of Southampton made possible also a call at Cherbourg, across the English Channel, for the traffic to and from the mainland of Europe — that Cunard decided to transfer its liners from Liverpool to Southampton. This transfer put Fishguard completely out of the picture, and as a result the remainder of the Swansea District Lines scheme was never completed. So Fishguard was left with its Irish services; these never grew beyond relatively moderate passenger dimensions, though freight traffic, chiefly agricultural, was on a large scale.

At first the boat trains left Paddington at 8.45 both morning and evening, and each was allowed $5\frac{1}{2}$hr to make the journey of 261.4 miles from Paddington to Fishguard Harbour. With various special trains, at different times, the GWR has run the entire distance non-stop, but in ordinary daily working the largest intermediate towns were of too great importance to be missed out in this way. So both trains called at Newport and Cardiff; in order to obtain a direct run past Swansea without reversal, the stop here was made at Landore, $1\frac{1}{4}$ miles away. In addition, the morning boat train called at Reading and the evening one at Swindon. Engines were changed only once, at Cardiff. Restaurant cars were run on both services, and the evening train in addition carried a first-class sleeping car, from the warmth and comfort of which its occupants were required to turn at the uninviting hour of 2.15am, on arrival at Fishguard.

During World War 1 the night boat service between Fishguard and Rosslare survived, but not the day service, and the latter was never reinstated until 1965, so that the morning express from Paddington became a train to Pembroke Dock and Neyland, and no longer an 'Irish Mail via Fishguard'. In the recovery period after World War 1 the Great Western Railway decided to standardise its main line departures out of Paddington, and as the South Wales starting times were fixed at 5min to the hour, the exit of the evening boat train was advanced to 7.55pm. The original stop at Swindon was exchanged for one at Didcot, and eventually the latter gave place to a stop at Reading instead. By now Swansea had become too important to bypass, and the train was running into Swansea and out again, instead of taking the direct spur from Landore; a further nightly stop had been added at Llanelli, and the train was prepared also to stop at both Severn Tunnel Junction and Neath if passengers wished to alight.

Up to 1939, therefore, the 'Irish Mail via Fishguard', leaving Paddington at 7.55pm, ran the 36 miles to Reading in the then standard allowance of 40min, and was booked to stand there 6min, dealing with a considerable volume of luggage, parcels and mails. Away again at 8.41pm, it continued through Didcot and Swindon to Wootton Bassett, where the finely engineered junction made it possible to take the diverging line to Badminton at a speed of 50mph. For most of the distance between here and the summit at Badminton the line rises at 1 in 300, and it then passes through the $2\frac{1}{2}$ miles of Sodbury Tunnel before descending at the same inclination to the junction with the Bristol-South Wales main line at Patchway.

At Stoke Gifford East Box, just before Patchway, two slip coaches were detached, to be worked by a waiting tank engine into Bristol, and so providing a late evening service from London to that city. From Patchway the descent steepens to 1 in 68, and then, after a level strip, to the 3 miles at 1 in 100 which lead to the middle of the Severn Tunnel. In the opposite direction this is the worst bank on the route, for although the 1 in 68 is flattened on the up line to 1 in 100, up trains are faced with 6 miles at 1 in 100 between the middle of the tunnel and Pilning, and with a further 12 miles at 1 in 300 before the summit is breasted at Badminton — an arduous task.

Including the conditional stop at Severn Tunnel Junction, the down 'Irish Mail *via* Fishguard' was allowed 106min to run the 97.4 miles from Reading to

Newport. Here a stop of 4min was scheduled, and a short run of 16min brought the train into Cardiff at 10.47pm, for a wait of 8min and a change of engine. There are awkward grades between Cardiff and Swansea, and this length of 45.8 miles was allowed exactly one hour, bringing the train into Swansea at 11.55pm. Here reversal took place, and on the stroke of midnight the train, after a second change of engine, was due out westwards. From Swansea for 1¾ miles the line climbs at 1 in 60 and 1 in 52 to Cockett tunnel, so that an assistant engine was provided either to the summit or to Llanelli, where a stop of one minute was made from 12.22 to 12.23am. Then came a schedule of 77min over the remaining 60.3 miles, including some heavy grades, to Fishguard Harbour, reached at 1.40am.

In the reverse direction the start on the up journey of the 'Irish Mail *via* Fishguard' was made 2¼hr later, at 3.55am. Banking assistance was needed from the start, for the single-track line out of Fishguard climbs at 1 in 50 for 1¾ miles past Manorowen halt. The first scheduled stop was at Gowerton, 67 miles from Fishguard, at 5.18am, to take on another assisting engine for the 2¼-mile climb at 1 in 50 to Cockett. Fifteen minutes later the train was in Swansea. Leaving Swansea at 5.37am, as in the reverse direction there was an allowance of exactly an hour to Cardiff, and the start from there was at 6.45am, and from Newport at 7.05am. An easy allowance followed of 113min to Reading, and after a 5min stop there, the schedule was as long as 44min to Paddington, for the boat train had to be fitted in between other morning arrivals. Into London at 9.47am, the up 'Irish Mail' had thus taken 5hr 52min for the 263.6 miles from Fishguard *via* Swansea, as compared with 5¾hr in the opposite direction.

The make-up of the train included composite sleeping car, composite restaurant car, corridor first, about three corridor thirds and a third brake, two or three long brake-vans, and the Bristol slip coaches in the down direction — 11 or 12 bogies in all out of Paddington, and two less in the reverse direction. Between London and Cardiff a 'Castle' 4-6-0 was the invariable rule; west of Cardiff either 4-cylinder or 2-cylinder 4-6-0s might be used. The Fishguard-Rosslare service did not long survive the outbreak of World War 2, and with its withdrawal the boat trains in each direction were cancelled also, though the 8.55am from Paddington continued to run to Pembroke Dock.

From 1 October 1945, however, the 7.55pm down was restored as far as Swansea, and the 8.55am down had a through portion for Fishguard reinstated on Tuesdays, Thursdays and Saturdays. For a time the latter was relieved as far as Swansea by an 8.50am breakfast-car train, which called only at Newport and Cardiff, and reached Swansea at 1pm, but this was withdrawn in the coal crisis, and after its reinstatement ran only on Saturdays and during the summer season. Irish boat passengers *via* Fishguard from then on left Paddington on the 6.55pm express, but the boat portion was provided on Mondays, Wednesdays and Fridays only; on other days the express terminated its journey at Swansea at 11.25pm, after having called at Reading, Newport and Cardiff. The time to Swansea thus exceeded that of prewar days by 30min.

When the boat portion was run, it left Swansea at 11.30pm, and with one intermediate halt, at Llanelli, made its way into Fishguard Harbour at 1.15am, as compared with the prewar 1.40am. At Fishguard, the train had a turn-around time of 3¾hr, and then was away on Tuesdays, Thursdays and Saturdays, back to Paddington at 4.55am. In this direction, after leaving Llanelli, the train avoided Swansea altogether by taking the direct line through Morlais and Felin Fran, already mentioned. Cardiff was reached at 8.07am, in time for attachment to the daily 8.15am for Paddington, but this made so many stops that the boat passengers were not into London until 11.40am — a run slower by 53min than in prewar days.

In 1964 the day service between Fishguard and Rosslare was reinstated during the summer months, and in the following years diesel traction has greatly accelerated the boat trains, but no train now carries the title 'Irish Mail', and several different expresses have provided the connecting services from and to Paddington either as through trains or through portions.

In the 1950s, when as previously mentioned the then General Manager of the Western Region was seeking to find an excuse for painting set trains in the former Great Western Railway chocolate-and-cream colours, three other trains on the South Wales service received names. One was the 5.55pm from Paddington, which in 1950 acquired the title 'Red Dragon', a distinctly lethargic beast, for in the down direction, with numerous stops, it was not until ten minutes before midnight that the last of its tail dragged its weary way into Carmarthen. The up journey was rather better; although the Carmarthen section had to be away by 7.30am, the main train did not leave Swansea until 8.45am, and was a very popular service from Cardiff and Newport, running up non-stop from the latter in 165min and reaching Paddington at 1.05pm.

Another named train was the 'Capitals United' — the capitals, of course, being London and Cardiff — which had a good deal of fun poked at it as representing a mythical Western Region football team. This was the 3.55pm from Paddington to Cardiff the 8am return train, which received their titles in 1956. But of considerably more distinction was the 'Pembroke Coast Express', so named in 1953, when it was an entirely new service leaving Paddington at

10.55am. Within a year it had been accelerated to cover the 133.4 miles from London to Newport in 128min — the fastest South Wales service ever worked by steam power — and to reach Swansea in $3\frac{3}{4}$hr; it had a through portion for Pembroke Dock. In the opposite direction the return at first was from Pembroke Dock at 7.45am, Swansea at 10.35am and Cardiff at 11.56am, with a Paddington arrival at 3.10pm, but later this became an evening train up, with a timing of 3hr 55min from Swansea to London. All these titles disappeared on or before the WR timetable reorganisations of the 1960s.

The Irishman

It would be difficult to find a more remarkable route, from the gradient point of view, than that by which the 'Irishman' and the 'Fast Belfast' made their way from Glasgow to the port of Stranraer, in south-west Scotland. For the first $41\frac{1}{4}$ miles, to Ayr, it is nearly level; over the final 37 miles, from Girvan to Stranraer, it is the exact opposite, and the $3\frac{3}{4}$ mile climb at 1 in 54 and 1 in 56 from Girvan up to Pinmore tunnel is a fitting introduction to the fearsome switchback that follows. The objective at Stranraer, of course, was the steamer service to and from Larne, in Northern Ireland, which explains the names 'Irishman' and 'Fast Belfast'.

Of the two trains, only the 'Irishman' ran throughout the year. But while the Glasgow-bound passenger in peacetime, with its help, could leave Belfast as late as 6.25pm, and be in Glasgow just before midnight, it was a different proposition going south. For the 'Irishman', leaving Glasgow St Enoch at 8.05pm, deposited him at Stranraer by 10.57pm, with all night to wait before the Larne steamer started at about 6.30 on the following morning, though he could console himself with a comfortable cabin on board. Thus the southbound journey between Glasgow and Belfast took nearly 13hr, as compared with $5\frac{1}{2}$hr going north.

In peacetime summers the boat service was duplicated, and it then became possible to make a much faster trip from Glasgow to Belfast. The 'Fast Belfast' came into operation, leaving St Enoch at 3.50pm, and its passengers crossed to Larne the same evening and reached Belfast by 10pm. In the reverse direction, departure from Belfast was at 9.28am, and the 'Fast Belfast' ran into St Enoch precisely 6hr later. Both the 'Irishman' and the 'Fast Belfast' were restaurant car trains of corridor stock, and normally were limited to about six bogie vehicles south of Girvan, as the difficulty of the route is so great that piloting was essential between Girvan and Stranraer if this load was exceeded. From the Glasgow & South Western 4-4-0 classes originally used, locomotive power changed by degrees to the Midland 4-4-0 compounds, then to 2-6-0s, Class 5 4-6-0s, and finally to 'Jubilee' 4-6-0s until diesel traction took over.

The 'Irishman', southbound, got away from St Enoch station in Glasgow at 8.05pm, and with stops at Paisley, Troon and Prestwick, reached Ayr, 41.3 miles away, in 56min. From Ayr to Girvan there are some severe ups-and-downs, at gradients between 1 in 63 and 1 in 72, and five separate summits, of which the highest is Maybole, where the train stopped. Including this stop, the 'Irishman' ran the 21.4 miles from Ayr to Girvan in 34min.

At Girvan the real tug-of-war begins, with the terrific 1 in 54-56 climb already mentioned, and over single track, which entails reduced speed through every passing loop, for tablet-exchange purposes. From Pinmore tunnel there is a sharp descent to Pinwherry; then follows a still longer climb, $8\frac{1}{2}$ miles of it, and mostly at about 1 in 70, through Barrhill to the highest summit, at milepost $16\frac{1}{2}$. Through wild country the train now swings downwards, slowing for Glenwhilly, and then for the S-shaped 'Swan's Neck', which is the terror of northbound drivers when making their way up a long 1 in 57 grade to the summit. More slacks at Challoch Junction, Dunragit, Castle Kennedy, and a final one at Stranraer Junction, and the 'Irishman' was into Stranraer Harbour at 10.57pm, having taken 74min for the final 37.9 miles from Girvan.

Of the 74min, 6min were allowed at Pinwherry, where the two 'Irishmen' were booked to meet. The northbound train had the right-of-way here, and needed it, with an allowance of only 63min to get through from Stranraer Harbour to Girvan — a tough task indeed through such exposed country on a wild winter's night. After a 5min wait at Girvan to take water — and breath! — the 'Irishman' had a smart booking of 28min for the 21.4 miles over Maybole summit into Ayr, and finished with a 56min run over the 41.3 miles into St Enoch, arriving at 11.50pm. This last timing was fairly easy, for certain conditional stops were permitted between Stranraer and Ayr for passengers through from Ireland who wished to alight, and the final timing allowed the 'Irishman' to recover some at least of any minutes so lost. If no additional stops were called, it was due in St Enoch at 11.45pm. To railwaymen this train was known as 'The Paddy'.

The 'Fast Belfast' had somewhat similar peacetime schedules. There were intermediate halts at Paisley, Irvine, Ayr, Girvan and Dunragit, and Stranraer was reached at 6.45pm, after a 66min run from Girvan. Northbound, the 'Fast Belfast', getting away from Stranraer Harbour at 12.50pm, had the same Dunragit stop and 66min timing to Girvan, then halts at Maybole, Ayr and Paisley were scheduled, with an arrival in St Enoch at 3.28pm.

Of these expresses the only recognisable example left after the war was the northbound 'Irishman', but its departure from Stranraer Harbour was put back to 10.15pm, and with many conditional stops added to the regular ones, its weary passengers were not due to make their appearance in Glasgow until the distressingly 'small hours' — actually at 1.05 the following morning. In the summer of 1945 the southbound 'Irishman' returned to the timetable, leaving St Enoch as before at 8.05pm, but not due in Stranraer Harbour until 5min before midnight. In the later steam days it was considerably accelerated, and though not leaving Glasgow till 8.45pm, it reached Stranraer Harbour by 11.57pm. Conversely, the northbound 'Irishman' was made much earlier, and getting away from Stranraer Harbour by 9.15pm, and with all conditional stops between Ayr and Paisley cut out, it came to rest in St Enoch only 5min later than in pre-war days, at 11.50pm. The name 'Irishman' was restored to both these trains but by now the restaurant cars had been withdrawn.

During the war years this route had become of considerable importance, and a good deal of work was done on lengthening the single-line passing loops between Girvan and Stranraer, and in easing the curves at the entry to and exit from each loop, so greatly speeding up the working. With the growing 'roll-on-roll-off' motorcar traffic, the sailings between Stranraer and Larne increased, as did the number of through trains between Glasgow and Stranraer Harbour. Diesel multiple-units took the place of steam-hauled trains, and refreshments were no longer provided on them. 'Irishman' was regularly a dmu from the summer of 1958. At the end of the 1966-67 timetable the name was dropped.

The Lakes Express

In earlier years the train which ultimately became the 'Lakes Express' ran during the summer season only, but eventually its popularity was such as to call for weekend running throughout the year, and by 1939 it was a permanent service down on Fridays and Saturdays, so far as concerned the main Euston-Windermere section, and up on Saturdays and Mondays. In summer, when the daily working began, a through portion was added for the Keswick line. This express shared in the general LMSR acceleration which began in 1932, and ultimately had some smart timings.

Leaving Euston at 12 noon, it stopped first at Rugby, 82.6 miles, in 88min, and spent 8min there. Missing Stafford, Crewe and Warrington, it called next at Wigan, and was allowed 117min for the 111.4 miles from Rugby to this point. The Wigan stop was made both to give a connection to Southport, which here is only 17 miles away, and to detach a through portion for Preston and Blackpool. Departure from Wigan was at 3.37pm and the next stop, 4.20pm at Lancaster, was to get rid of a through section for Barrow-in-Furness and the coast line up to Whitehaven, Workington and Maryport.

Next came a halt at Oxenholme, at 4.48pm, and from here the Keswick portion was first away, at 4.53pm, running on to Shap and Penrith, and there reversing (5.40 to 5.47pm). Curiously enough, this part of the train crossed Cumberland via Keswick to reach Workington at 7.26pm, 38min in front of the coaches which had meandered round the coast via Barrow, on their way to come finally to rest at Maryport at 8.17pm.

However, any passenger in a hurry to reach Maryport would hardly make the 8¼hr journey offered by the 'Lakes Express', for he could leave Euston luxuriously on the 'Coronation Scot' streamliner at 1.30pm, make a 'snap' 5min connection at Carlisle with the 6.18pm, and be in the Cumberland port at 7.19pm, a shorter journey by 2½hr! Long before this the main portion of the 'Lakes Express' had left Oxenholme, called at Kendal and run into Windermere at 5.25pm.

Coming up, the first part of the 'Lakes Express' to

start was that from Workington, at 9.05am. Getting away from Keswick at 9.59 and Penrith at 10.47am, it ran into Oxenholme at 11.35am, there to await the main train from Windermere, which started at 11.15am. The complete train, restarting at 11.53am, called at Lancaster and next at Preston (12.43 to 12.51pm), attaching the through Blackpool section there. A non-stop run followed to Crewe, where a stop was made from 1.49 to 1.56pm.

On the way from Crewe to Euston the only halt was at Bletchley; the express was allowed exactly 2hr to run the 111.4 miles from Crewe to this point, and 51min for the final 46.7 miles to Euston, so arriving at 4.50pm. There were thus several differences in the stops going down and coming up; on the latter, Bletchley, Preston and Tebay replaced Rugby, Wigan and Shap on the former. The journey over the whole 259½ miles from Euston to Windermere took 5hr 25min, and 10min longer was needed for the return.

The 'Lakes Express' included a set of three restaurant cars — open first, kitchen, and open third — in the Windermere portion, with first class brake, two third corridors, and third brake; but this might be expanded somewhat in the summer season. The Keswick and Workington section (the only part of the train which actually saw one of the English Lakes at close quarters, for it skirted the whole length of Bassenthwaite Lake) was normally three coaches, composite corridor and two third brakes. Then there were the two-coach Blackpool portion, and on the down journey a further two coaches for the Furness line.

Between Oxenholme and Windermere a 4-4-2 or 4-6-2 ex-LNWR tank often provided the motive power, followed later by a standard 2-6-4 tank, but between Keswick and Workington, with severe weight restrictions over the bridges of the one-time Cockermouth, Keswick & Penrith Railway, a veteran in the shape of a Webb 'Cauliflower' 0-6-0 had to suffice, notwithstanding such gradients as the 4 miles of 1 in 62 from Threlkeld up to Troutbeck, to be negotiated by the up train. In later years new lightweight 2-6-0 locomotives became available.

During the war, through midday service was provided between Euston and Windermere and vice versa, and in the later war summers to and from the Keswick line also, but as a part of other trains; in the down direction the service was on the 10.25am from Euston, taking 7hr 20min to Windermere and about an hour less at summer weekends. In the up direction the wartime version of the 'Lakes Express' left Windermere at 11.10am, and during the earlier years was detained for 48min at Crewe to await the North Wales express due in Euston at 6.42pm; but, first at weekends and then daily, in the last war years, the Windermere and Blackpool train assumed sufficient importance to be worked up independently from Crewe and to reach London at 5.55pm.

After the war the 'Lakes Express' returned to service, leaving Euston at 11.50am (working time 11.52), and appearing in the public timetable as though still non-stop to Wigan. But this was not the case, as a stop was made at Crewe from 2.54 to 3.02pm to drop the Barrow and Whitehaven section, complete with its own restaurant car. This was a curious arrangement, for both portions then stopped on each other's tails at Wigan, Preston and Lancaster. The 'Lakes Express' proper reached Windermere at 6.05pm, and the Workington portion was into Keswick at 7.03pm and Workington at 8.09pm. In the reverse direction the earliest departures were from Workington at 8.35am and Keswick at 9.38am; while the main train made its way out of Windermere at 10.50am. In this direction, as in earlier years, there was no Barrow portion, but a Blackpool section was attached at Preston; Euston was reached at 5.15pm, except on Saturdays, when the Wigan and Warrington stops were omitted and the arrival was 10min earlier.

Something like the 'Lakes Express', though nameless, survived in summer until 1965, including the Keswick portion, but from the introduction of the electric service between Euston and Crewe the only through service from Euston to Windermere became the 9.05am down, making numerous intermediate stops and reaching its lakeside destination at 1.51pm; this train conveyed also a through portion for Blackpool. The return journey was begun at 4.08pm and in this direction without any other through portion the arrival in Euston was at 9pm. Windermere had a second through train to Euston at 11am, and on Saturdays through coaches for Windermere were attached to the 11.55am from Euston, but Keswick no longer enjoyed any through communication with London. Today Keswick is no longer rail-connected and Windermere has no through trains to or from London.

The Lancastrian and The Mancunian

Most popular of all the trains on the express service between London and Manchester, with little doubt, was the 6pm from Euston, which assumed the title 'Lancastrian' in January 1928. In London & North Western days, for many years the 5.30pm from Euston provided the evening business service from London to Manchester and Liverpool, but growth in traffic compelled division into various independent sections, of which the 6pm to Manchester, later 6.05pm, was one. From that time onwards the Manchester train was booked non-stop over the 183 miles to Stockport, where the rear portion, with through coaches for Colne and Rochdale, was detached. The 6.05pm was due in Manchester at 9.35pm, and was one of the first trains to bring this Lancashire city within 3½hr of London.

On the opening in 1909 of the new line from Wilmslow to Levenshulme, avoiding Stockport, the 6.05pm down was transferred to it and the first stop then became Wilmslow, 176.9 miles from Euston, where the train divided.

When the 1932 accelerations took place, it was decided to cut the time allowance to 3¼hr from Euston to London Road, and this made necessary a mile-a-minute schedule to Wilmslow, 176.9 miles in 176 minutes. In order to ensure a clear road for the 'Lancastrian', it was made to change places with the Liverpool train, which had become the 'Merseyside Express'; instead of 6.05 and 5.55pm, the departure times became 6 and 6.05pm respectively. Also, in order to keep the 'Lancastrian's' load within the 'XL Limit' of the working timetables, the East Lancashire section was cut off this express, and transferred to the Heysham boat train at 6.10pm from Euston. The 'Lancastrian' continued to call at Wilmslow, but no division of the train took place there. It was booked to pass Crewe at 8.36pm, call at Wilmslow from 8.56 to 8.59pm, and reach Manchester London Road, 188.5 miles from Euston, at 9.15pm.

The down 'Lancastrian' was usually made up to about twelve bogie vehicles. From the rear end were first class brake, first, open first, first class restaurant car, kitchen car, third restaurant car, and the remainder third class, partly open and partly compartment stock. This made up a total tare weight of approximately 360 tons, well within the compass of 'Royal Scot' haulage. The maximum load permitted was 415 tare tons. After 4-6-0 No 6170 *British Legion* had been rebuilt with taper boiler, forerunner of the highly successful 'Royal Scot' rebuildings of later years, it was used frequently on this train. In the years immediately preceding World War 2 engines of the first Pacific series began to make their appearance on the 'Lancastrian'.

On the southbound journey, the stock of the 6pm from Euston returned from Manchester on the noon service, and when the former train became the 'Lancastrian', the 12.05pm from London Road assumed the same title. This meant that the train followed a different route when travelling south from that used in the northbound direction; and the different route meant a different type of engine, for nothing heavier than a 'Patriot' or 'Jubilee' 4-6-0 was permitted to work over the Stoke-on-Trent route. The southbound 'Lancastrian' called first at Stockport, arriving at 12.15pm, and here 6min were allowed for the attaching in front of the East Lancashire portion from Colne, Burnley, Blackburn, Bolton and Manchester Victoria.

Leaving Stockport at 12.21pm, and diverging from the Crewe line at Cheadle Hulme, 2¼ miles to the south, the 'Lancastrian' then climbed to Macclesfield, where a stop was made at Hibel Road station from 12.40 to 12.43pm. An even steeper climb follows, from the Central station at Macclesfield up to Macclesfield Moss box, which for 1¼ miles is at 1 in 102, and up this banking assistance was invariably provided. The only remaining stop was at Stoke-on-Trent, reached at 1.10 and left at 1.15pm, and from here to London once again a mile-a-minute run was scheduled — 145.9 miles in 145min — for an arrival in Euston at 3.40pm. The up train regained at Colwich, 6.4 miles south of Stafford, the main route followed by the down 'Lancastrian'. For an engine of the type used this was no easy task with a load that was usually between 400 and 440 tons, but excellent time was kept by the Longsight drivers, and the spotless condition of the engines turned out by this shed for the run was always a pleasure to see.

It is of interest to recall that in earlier days, when the train, then unamed, left Manchester London Road at 12.10pm, and was due in Euston at 4pm, motive power was provided by the then North Staffordshire Railway between Manchester and Stoke. The NSR had some fine superheated 4-4-2 tanks, similar in appearance to the Brighton I3 class, and although the load was less in those days than it became later, these tanks, and their 0-6-4 successors, did some magnificent work on this first stage, to Stoke, where the tank would be replaced by a 'George the Fifth' 4-4-0 of the London & North Western for the non-stop run of 140.4 miles to Willesden Junction in 148min.

The full load from Stockport, immediately before the outbreak of war, was usually about 14 bogies. From the engine there were first the four East Lancashire coaches — a composite brake, composite, and two thirds — then first class brake, two firsts, first restaurant, kitchen, third restaurant, three thirds, third brake, and a bogie van on the rear for mails.

The 'Mancunian' workings were the precise opposite of those of the 'Lancastrian', for the up 'Mancunian' was a 3¼hr train between Manchester and Euston, non-stop from Wilmslow, and the down 'Mancunian' took the Stoke-on-Trent route, with the same stops as the up 'Lancastrian', and four others in addition. Out of Manchester the up 'Mancunian', starting from London Road at 9.45am, was usually worked to Wilmslow by a 2-6-4 tank locomotive, arriving at 10.02am. The express engine, which had picked up at Stockport through coaches from Colne, Huddersfield and Rochdale, was waiting at Wilmslow, and there transferred them to the front of the Manchester portion. The combined train then left at 10.08am and was due to make the run of 176.9 miles to Euston in 172min, at an average of 61.7mph. As with the down 'Lancastrian', a 'Royal Scot' 4-6-0 was normally used on this service, though latterly Pacifics had begun to appear on the train.

Going north, the down 'Mancunian', like the up 'Lancastrian', had to be content with a 'Patriot' or 'Jubilee' 4-6-0, on account of travelling via Stoke-on-Trent. But this was a lighter train, as although it carried a through portion for Northampton, this came off early in the journey, at Bletchley, and there were no through coaches for the East Lancashire towns. Departure from Euston was at 4.10pm, and Bletchley was reached at 5.02pm and left at 5.05pm. After this some smart running was needed, for the allowances were but 38 and 36min respectively for the 35.9-mile and 33.7-mile Bletchley-Rugby and Rugby-Lichfield stages. Only 2min were allowed at each of these stops. Stone-on-trent was reached at 7pm, and with halts at Congleton, Macclesfield and Stockport, the 'Mancunian' was due in Manchester London Road at 8.05pm.

After the outbreak of World War 2, recognisable versions of two of these four trains, though much slower than in peacetime, and without their distinctive names, remained. A train resembling the down 'Lancastrian' was split off from what at first was a combined express from Euston to Liverpool and Manchester at 5.30pm. Except on Saturdays, the Manchester section left Euston at 5.38pm calling at Stafford, Wilmslow and Stockport, and reaching London Road at 9.47pm, and with its journey of 4hr 9min was 54min slower than in peacetime. Then, from 7 October 1946 the down express resumed its prewar 6.00pm departure and its non-stop run to Wilmslow; continuing via Styal, it was due in Manchester at 9.45pm, in 3¾hr from Euston. The Colne portion was detached at Wilmslow, as in former days, and continued via Stockport. From mid-September 1952 however, the down express once again lost its Colne section, was put on to a 'Special Limit' timing, and with the Euston-Wilmslow timing cut to 187min, it was brought into Manchester by 9.30pm, in 3½hr from London. This change reduced its load to 12 coaches.

In the morning, the traffic from Manchester had become heavy enough to require two trains. The 9.45am from London Road travelled via Styal, and, running non-stop over the 188.5 miles to Euston, was due in London at 1.20pm; the 9.52am, later 10.00am, and later still 10.05am, worked up via Stoke, attaching through Colne coaches at Stockport; and stopping after that at Macclesfield and Stoke-on-Trent it was due in London at 2pm. Loads up to 15 and 16 bogies were worked by rebuilt 'Royal Scot' 4-6-0s. By 1949 the 6pm from Euston and the 9.45am from Manchester had resumed the name 'Mancunian', but as yet the name 'Lancastrian' had not been revived.

The latter reappeared, however, when, under pressure from the Associated Chambers of Commerce, a new morning express was put on in the middle 1950s from Euston at 7.45am to Liverpool and Manchester, calling at Watford Junction to pick up passengers and next at Crewe, though the title was not conferred until 1957, by which time the start out of Euston had become 7.55am. By 1958 this express had been accelerated to make a mile-a-minute run from Watford to Crewe, 140.6 miles in 136min. The Manchester portion of this train, starting back at 4pm, became the up 'Lancastrian'. There were many fluctuations in the timing of both the 'Lancastrian' and the 'Mancunian' during the earlier years of the Euston-Crewe electrification work, and then, when in the autumn of 1962 almost all the Euston — Manchester passenger traffic was transferred to the Midland route, only the 9.40am up and 6.00pm down 'Mancunian' remained. Finally, in April 1966 with the introduction of the full electric timetable, and the intensive use of the new train sets, many of them making two double journeys daily, all train titles on this route other than the 'Manchester Pullman' disappeared.

The Manchester Club Trains

Just as the South Coast has always been a popular place of residence for London businessmen who could afford the cost of a season ticket and the time for travelling to and from London daily, so the nearest part of the West Coast has attracted the business fraternity of Manchester and Salford. In this case, Blackpool, Lytham, St Annes and Southport have been the most favoured resorts, and the late Lancashire & Yorkshire Railway did its utmost to encourage and develop this traffic.

In the year 1895, before corridor trains had come into general use, a number of first class season ticket holders in the Blackpool area, thinking that it would be pleasant to enjoy a wider range of each other's company en route than was possible in the compartment stock of that time, approached the L&Y management with a novel request. It was that, in return for a guarantee that a specified number of first class season tickets would be taken out annually between Blackpool and Manchester at higher than the ordinary rate, they should be provided with saloon accommodation.

The request was agreed to, and two (later three) comfortable saloons, provided with an attendant and facilities for serving light refreshments, were marshalled in one of the morning expresses from Blackpool, and a return express from Manchester shortly after 5pm. Although in the course of time centre corridor stock was introduced by the L&YR throughout the trains concerned, and later was replaced by LMSR standard vestibuled cars of the latest and most luxurious type, the club cars never lost their popularity, and continued to run up to the outbreak of the second world war. By then, too, the club saloons had become two palatial LMSR vehicles specially adapted for the purpose. In later years, club saloons were attached to other evening Blackpool trains also.

Participation in the travelling club was always subject to very strict rules, so that all undesirable travelling companions might be excluded, and the regular members had their own recognised seats. Even any undesired opening of windows en route was strictly forbidden! In later years a third class section of the club was established also, and had its own third class reserved car adjacent to the two first class saloons.

The 'Blackpool Club Train' — an unofficial though fairly widely known title — left Manchester Victoria station at 5.14pm, and up to the outbreak of World War 2 was due to make its first stop at Lytham at 6.14pm. This time of 60min required far harder running than the distance of 41.9 miles might suggest. The older and more level main line through Bolton was not followed, but like most of the non-stopping expresses, the 'Club Train' followed the Liverpool line as far as Dobbs Brow Junction, and from there took the spur line through Hilton House to join the Bolton line at Horwich Fork Junction, near Chorley.

Thus it was necessary to climb the $2\frac{1}{4}$ miles at 1 in 72 — 99 from Pendleton up to Pendlebury, and to follow on over sharp undulations, with the complication of slacks over colliery workings, to Dobbs Brow. Here a reduction of speed made an unfortunate prelude to an even steeper climb of $2\frac{1}{2}$ miles, partly at 1 in 69, to Hilton House, with a shorter drop from there to Horwich Fork. Finally, there was a slack at Euxton Junction, where the main line from Euston to Carlisle was joined, and another very severe one through the great station at Preston.

After that the hard-worked locomotive had practically level track on through the junctions at Kirkham and Wesham and round the coastline to Lytham and Blackpool. The usual four stops were made between these two points, and the arrival at Blackpool Central, 52.3 miles from Manchester Victoria, was at 6.36pm. In the reverse direction departure from Blackpool Central was at 8.10am, and after stopping at the coast stations, the 'Club Train' left Lytham at 8.31am, and ran non-stop to Salford, arriving at 9.36am, and Manchester Victoria at 9.40am. The Salford stop was generally made by Manchester-bound trains, in order to enable those with business in that part of the city to alight there.

As to locomotive power, the Lancashire & Yorkshire 7ft 3in inside cylinder Atlantics designed by Aspinall held sway for many years, to be followed from 1906 by the Hughes 4-cylinder 4-6-0s — a much more suitable type of engine, after its efficiency had been improved by superheating, for such heavy grade work. Some years after the grouping, standard LMS types began to filter into these Lancashire & Yorkshire services; first the Class 5 4-6-0s appeared, and then the 'Jubilee' 3-cylinder 4-6-0s, which in later years were the engines principally used. The load grew eventually to between 9 and 11 bogie vehicles, according to season, centre corridor stock throughout and more than two-thirds first class.

After the war this popular express, still made up of the same stock, though without the club saloons, left Manchester Victoria at 5.16pm, and had its timing to Lytham eased to 67min. Stopping as previously at Andsell, St Annes, Squires Gate and Blackpool South, it was due in Blackpool Central at 6.46pm. On the inward journey it left Blackpool at 7.40am, made the same stops to Lytham and additional halts at Kirkham and Salford, and reached Manchester at 9.14am.

Commuter traffic on this route is no longer on its one-time scale, and is accommodated in diesel multiple-unit sets, with no 'club' characteristics. A departure from Manchester Victoria at 5.20pm continued, however; for a time the trains ran with additional stops at Preston and Kirkham, and Blackpool Central having been closed the journey came to an end at 6.36pm at Blackpool South.

The 'Llandudno Club Train' made the longest journey of any of the Manchester club services. The club saloons appeared before World War 2, and eventually this particular 'club' became the proud possessor of two of the magnificent 12-wheel first class saloons built originally by the LNWR for the American boat services between London and Liverpool. These were marshalled in a train of standard LMS corridor stock.

In its heyday, this train had some fast timings in relation to the difficult route covered. Up to 1914 it left Manchester Exchange at 4.55pm, ran non-stop over the 40 miles to Chester in 48min, including severe slowings through Earlestown Junction and Warrington, and the climb to Halton tunnel, and was allowed 34min for the 30 miles on to Rhyl, reached in 85min from Manchester. After making further stops at Abergele, Colwyn Bay and Llandudno Junction, the express made its way into Llandudno at 7.03pm, in 2hr 8min from Manchester, 87¾ miles distant. A portion for Bangor was detached at Llandudno Junction and reached its destination at 7.30pm.

Before the outbreak of World War 1, with eleven 8-wheelers of some 320 tons loaded weight, the 'George the Fifth' 4-4-0 or 'Prince of Wales' 4-6-0 rostered for this duty had no easy task to keep time. The return morning service had an even smarter schedule, and made the Llandudno-Manchester run in precisely 2hr, leaving at 8.10am and arriving in Manchester Exchange at 10.10am.

By 1939 the Manchester businessmen residing on the North Wales Coast were evidently taking life more easily, and found that they could get away from their offices earlier in the afternoon. The 'Llandudno Club Train', therefore, was now leaving Exchange 25min earlier, at 4.30pm, and the benefits of the service were extended to Warrington, where a stop was made to pick up passengers. The overall time, however, was still 2hr 8min, and Llandudno was reached at 6.38pm. An additional service, with more intermediate stops, was leaving Manchester Exchange for Llandudno at the old starting time of 4.55pm. What the businessmen had gained in the afternoons they lost in the mornings, however, for the start from Llandudno was at 7.48 instead of 8.10am, and the journey was 9min longer.

Through the war period the service still continued, but without any club saloons, and badly slowed down. The 4.30pm from Exchange, though with only one additional stop at Frodsham, was not now due in Llandudno till 7.20pm; and it needed a start from Llandudno as early as 7.15 in the morning to be in Manchester by 10.00am. But in May 1946, there came a speed-up, bringing the 4.30pm into Llandudno at 6.50pm, while a morning start at 7.40 instead of 7.15am got the businessman into Manchester by 10.00am. Later, further acceleration brought the Llandudno arrival forward to 6.48pm, and the Manchester arrival of the 7.40am eastbound became 9.57am.

By the late 1960s, as with the successor to the former 'Blackpool Club Train', diesel multiple-units had taken over the Llandudno service. The start was still at 4.30pm from Manchester Exchange; the stops were unchanged; and Llandudno was reached at 6.40pm, 2min earlier than in 1939, though after a run 8min longer than in 1914. Inwards, the express got away from Llandudno at 7.45am, and with Flint added to the other stops deposited its passengers in Manchester at 10.00am. Today Manchester Exchange is closed and the North Wales trains run to and from Victoria, calling at most stations and generally requiring Llandudno passengers to change at Llandudno Junction.

The third of the 'Manchester Club Trains', which assumed this role at a date rather later than those to Blackpool and Llandudno, operated between Manchester and Windermere. It left Manchester Exchange at 5.10pm, and used a route which except in the height of the summer had ceased to be followed by any other regular passenger train. Of this route another singular feature was that part of it belonged to the London & North Eastern Railway; it was originally the Wigan branch of the Great Central Railway, and later became LNER property.

From Exchange the 5.10pm took the LNWR Liverpool main line to Eccles, and there branched northwards towards Wigan. But 2¼ miles short of Wigan it diverged again to the north, at Bickershaw Junction, in order to bypass Wigan on the east side. The LNER Wigan branch was reached at Hindley & Platt Bridge station, and LNER metals were followed for 50ch to Amberswood East Junction, after which the Whelley line was taken, bringing the 5.10pm up to join the LNWR London-Carlisle main line at Standish, 3¼ miles north of Wigan. The first stop was at Preston, and for this distance of 32.3 miles, 50min were allowed.

After an LMS interlude by way of Chorley, however, another curious route was devised for the down 'Windermere Club Train'. Leaving Exchange at 5.10pm as before, it transferred immediately to the adjacent Lancashire & Yorkshire tracks, and ran over the L&Y Liverpool line as far as Hindley, near Wigan. Here it ran round a short spur to join the Whelley line, at a point which cut out the previous running over the LNER. From Manchester to Preston the time allowed was still 50min. After Preston the express called at Lancaster and Carnforth, but was content to slow severely through Oxenholme, where it left the main line, instead of calling there. Kendal was the only remaining stop, and after the steep climb of Staveley bank. Windermere was reached at 7.20pm, 2hr 10min in all from Manchester.

In the southbound direction, the 'Windermere Club Train' was due out of Windermere at 8.30am, and stopped at Kendal and Lancaster (but not Carnforth) to Preston. South of Preston, the main line was taken as far as Wigan, and a stop was made there, before divergence eastwards through Tyldesely and Eccles into Manchester. This journey took exactly 2hr, and Exchange was reached at 10.30am.

A formation of about seven bogies sufficed for this service, including a single club saloon. For most of the years of the train's existence, non-corridor lavatory stock was provided for the ordinary passengers, but had given place to a corridor set before the outbreak of World War 2. For locomotive power it was customary to use an ex-LNWR 'Prince' 4-6-0 from Windermere to Manchester and a Midland compound in the reverse direction.

After the war the train still ran with corridor stock which included an open vestibule first class car as some substitute for the club saloon, but there were more stops and the running was slower. Still leaving Manchester Exchange at 5.10pm, the express called at Preston, Lancaster, Carnforth, Oxenholme, Kendal, Burneside and Staveley, and reached Windermere at 7.32pm. In the reverse direction the start was 20min earlier, at 8.10am; the stops were as on the north-bound journey, with the addition of Wigan and Eccles, and Manchester was reached at 10.30am. There was a lively sprint over the 19.1 miles from Oxenholme to Lancaster in 20min, which at 57.3mph at that time was one of the fastest post-war schedules from start to stop on the LMR. The locomotive used was generally a Class 5 6ft 4-6-0.

A train of this description, of course, was by no means of use alone to Lakeside residents who wished to travel to and from Manchester. At Lancaster there was by far the largest influx, including passengers brought from both the Carlisle main line and the Furness line by connecting trains. Between Lancaster and Preston the 'Windermere Club Train' thus was usually filled to capacity.

Today there are no through trains between Manchester and Windermere. The 7.52am from Windermere runs through to Lancaster and connects with a train reaching Manchester Victoria at 10.05am. On the return journey passengers can leave Manchester at 6.12pm on a Nottingham-Glasgow service and by changing at Oxenholme reach Windermere at 8.36pm.

The Manchester Pullman and Liverpool Pullman

It was doubtless as some compensation to Manchester businessmen for the deceleration of their service to and from Euston during the work of electrification, and for its eventual almost complete transfer to the Midland route until the work was complete, that the London Midland Region authorities drew up plans for a Pullman service between the two cities. Moreover, this was not to be a locomotive-hauled train of standard cars, but an entirely new self-contained Pullman train set, with incorporated diesel-electric power, carrying first-class passengers only. When the train appeared, in the summer of 1960, it was seen to have abandoned the standard Pullman livery of chocolate and cream for an eye-arresting blue shade, while the six cars set new standards both of external lines and internal furnishing and décor including full air-conditioning.

The only intermediate stop was at Cheadle Heath, to pick up on the morning journey and to set down on the return. At first the departure from Manchester Central was at 8.50am, and the St Pancras arrival at 12.03pm, but as many passengers on what soon became a very popular service wanted to start their business in the capital earlier than midday, the starting time was soon altered to 7.45am and the St Pancras arrival to 10.55am, so reducing the overall time to 3hr 10min — the shortest scheduled up to that date between Manchester and London. In the down direction the 'Midland Pullman' left St Pancras at 6.10pm, and including the Cheadle Heath stop was into Manchester by 9.20pm. The non-stop run between Cheadle Heath and St Pancras was one of 181.3 miles, covered in 177min, including the climb to the 981ft summit at Peak Forest, and the slow running required round the Chaddesden avoiding line at Derby.

When the 'Midland Pullman' was first put on, its usefulness was extended by a midday run to Leicester and back, but when it was proposed to extend this midday trip to Nottingham the opposition of the railway men's union to catering by what they regarded as an outside company was so great that for a time the midday working was taken off. The trouble was resolved in the summer of 1961, however, and after that there was an 11.20am start from St Pancras to Leicester, Loughborough and Nottingham, reached at 1.20pm, and a return from Nottingham at 3.45pm, with a St Pancras arrival at 5.45pm. The 85min run from St Pancras to Leicester, 99.1 miles (70mph average) was the fastest that had ever been scheduled over Midland metals up to that time.

With the completion of the LMR electrification between Manchester, Liverpool and Euston in April 1966, two new 'Manchester Pullmans' between Euston and Manchester Piccadilly replaced the 'Midland Pullman'. The new cars were designed for haulage by standard electric locomotives; each train comprised eight of them, still carrying first class passengers only. At one stroke the 3hr 10min time by the Midland route came down to between 2hr 35 and 37min, according to train, and from March 1967 onwards the times were pared sufficiently to bring Manchester within 2½hr of London twice daily in each direction. The morning down 'Manchester Pullman' was at 7.50am from Euston and called at Watford Junction to pick up and Wilmslow to set down; it was into Manchester Piccadilly by 10.20am. The evening service left London at the old 'Lancastrian' time of 6pm, stopped only at Wilmslow and Stockport and arrived at 8.30pm.

Of the up trains, the morning 7.35am called at Stockport and Wilmslow and the evening 5pm at Wilmslow and Watford, with Euston arrivals at 10.05am and 7.30pm respectively. Needless to say, these schedules required some extremely fast running, from Wilmslow to Watford at 80.4mph and Watford to Wilmslow at 80mph start-to-stop. From April 1967 there were two additional 'Manchester Pullman' workings, down at 10.50am (after arrival of the 7.50am from Manchester), calling at Stafford, Stoke-on-Trent, Macclesfield and Stockport and reaching Manchester by 1.40pm; this train returned at 2.15pm and with the same stops was into Euston by 5.05pm, in good time for the 6pm run back to Manchester. On Fridays, when first-class custom was usually reduced, four second class corridor coaches replaced four of the Pullmans on all six workings; on Saturdays, in common with most British Pullman services, the trains did not run.

'Liverpool Pullmans' were also introduced but on this route the patronage was not sufficient to justify all-Pullman sets. So these trains were made up daily of four first class Pullmans and four ordinary second class coaches. They also were slightly accelerated from March 1967 onwards, though with 193.8 miles to cover did not quite get down to the even 2½hr. The down morning service preceded the 'Manchester Pullman' by 5min at 7.45am, called at Watford and Runcorn and was due in Liverpool Lime Street at 10.20am; the evening 'Pullman' ran 10min behind the Manchester train, at 6.10pm, and with a stop at Runcorn only was at its destination by 8.43pm. Coming up, the departures from Lime Street were at 7.55am and 5.40pm, both calling at Runcorn and the evening train also at Watford, with Euston arrivals at 10.27am and 8.15pm respectively. The down morning 'Liverpool Pullman' made the then fastest scheduled run in the British Commonwealth, over the 163.1 miles from Watford to Runcorn in 119½min at 81.9mph start-to-stop. The evening run up over the same course was only ½min slower, at 81.9mph; also the 6.10pm down was booked at 81.5mph from Euston to Runcorn, 180.6 miles in 135min.

The Pullmans on the Liverpool trains were taken off at the end of the 1974/5 timetable but fast services with ordinary first and second class stock continued at similar times, but unnamed. The 'Manchester Pullman', however, has survived, becoming the last Pullman service on British Railways. In 1982 the trains were normally all-Pullman throughout the week but the number of cars available was shrinking and on occasions a Mk 1 first class restaurant car was included in the formation. Stops at Crewe were added to the 7.35am from Manchester and the 5pm from Euston. Apart from variations in departure times the schedules were unchanged, although the 10.50am down and 2.15pm up workings had been withdrawn at the end of the March 1967 to 6 May 1968 timetable.

The Master Cutler

It would need no very profound thought to decide that the title 'Master Cutler' has a connection with Sheffield. Such indeed is the case. Between the two wars a popular LNER breakfast car express left Sheffield for Marylebone at 7.30am, and with stops only at Nottingham and Leicester was into London by 10.40am. For the final 103.1 miles from Leicester to Marylebone the time allowed was no more than 109min; this included the by no means easy gradients of the Great Central line proper, and also the much more difficult Metropolitan line grades, such as the tremendous climb from Aylesbury up past Wendover, and then the entry to London through the dense Metropolitan electric service between Rickmansworth and Harrow. Nevertheless this train, at first usually with G. C. 'Director' 4-4-0s or Atlantics, and later with the LNER B17 4-6-0s and loads of eight or nine coaches, kept very good time.

After World War 2 a morning express from Sheffield to Marylebone reappeared, and with the introduction of the 1947 winter timetable received the name of 'Master Cutler'. It was a popular and heavily-patronised service, as it was faster than the corresponding London Midland Region train, and so had grown to a formation of ten or eleven bogie vehicles of the latest stock. The only additional stop was Rugby, but the speed had declined sadly from prewar days. On its first restoration, departure from Sheffield was at 7.35am and Marylebone was not reached until 11.25am; but concurrently with the name 'Master Cutler' being conferred there was a 15min acceleration. Sheffield now was left at 7.40am, and Marylebone was reached at 11.15am, and although the time was still 25min slower than prewar, the up 'Master Cutler' had become the fastest train operating between London and Sheffield by either competing route. But to ensure better timekeeping it became necessary by 1953 to decelerate the journey by 12min, and the Marylebone arrival then became 11.27am.

The return 'Master Cutler' was at 6.15pm from Marylebone. Before the war this was an express to Bradford, which left London at 6.20pm, and was one of the hardest of all Great Central trains to work. Because of the congestion of the Metropolitan line during the evening rush hour, the 6.20 took the longer loop route through High Wycombe and Princes Risborough, but even so was allowed only 113min for the 107.6 miles from Marylebone to Leicester. In Great Central Atlantic days, the haulage of a 9-coach load out of Marylebone was an exceedingly tough proposition, but the Leicester drivers kept wonderful time with this train. The load was reduced progressively by the detaching of two slip coaches, one at Finmere and the other at Woodford. Later, the 'slips' were withdrawn and stops at both stations were substituted, and this made the working harder still, for the extra time conceded to Leicester was no more than 6min, and the 34 mile run from Woodford to Leicester had to be made in 34min, start-to-stop. But by now the 3-cylinder B17 4-6-0s had arrived, and with speeds of from 80 to 90mph where conditions permitted, time was still kept.

On its postwar restoration, the starting time of this express from Marylebone was altered from 6.20 to 6.15pm; the Wycombe route once again was followed, and as on the up journey a Rugby stop was introduced. But Sheffield was not reached until 10.14pm, as compared with the 9.38pm of prewar days. With the conferring of the name 'Master Cutler' in October 1947 there was an improvement, and the Sheffield arrival was advanced to 10.02pm; by September 1949, this had been further improved to 9.58pm. By this time the restaurant cars on this train had been replaced by new combined restaurant and tavern cars of Southern design, which aroused such stormy protests, however, that they were later withdrawn. The ubiquitous B1 4-6-0s handled the train for some time, but Gresley Pacifics then returned to the Great Central Section for these and other of the harder workings. Later, as with the up 'Master Cutler', the down working also was decelerated, and the Sheffield arrival went back to 10.08pm.

The 'Master Cutler' was one of the only two officially titled trains that ever ran on Great Central metals, and it continued to run while the Great Central was in decline, though the name was destined eventually to be transferred to another route altogether. This was in the year 1958, when it was decided that Sheffield should have its own Pullman service, and what better title for it than 'Master Cutler'? But instead of operating the train over the

Great Central route, the Eastern Region authorities settled on the much faster Great Northern route, to and from King's Cross. The new train was a six-car formation, and with what was now becoming a standard practice of getting business executives into London as early in the morning as possible, it was decided to start from Sheffield Victoria at 7.20am, call only at Retford, and cover the 138.6 miles from there to London, with diesel power of course, in 131min, arriving at 10.05am. Return was at 7.20pm, with one minute less allowed to Retford than on the up run, and a 10.05pm arrival in Sheffield. It was also arranged that the Pullman set of cars should not be idle during the day, but between the morning and evening runs should make another trip to Sheffield and back, calling en route at Peterborough, Grantham and Reford. Some smart point-to-point timings made it possible to complete these midday runs in 2hr 55min each way.

Later there were several changes in the schedules. In 1966 the evening departure from King's Cross was put forward to 6.15pm, and the mid-morning start to 10.45am; departures from Sheffield became 7.25am and 2.45pm. Moreover, in 1965 the Sheffield terminus had become the Midland station and not the former Great Central Victoria, a spur having been brought into use between the GC line east of Victoria station and the MR line at Nunnery Junction. In the 1967-1968 timetable the evening departure from King's Cross had gone back to 7.20pm, and the time for the 138.6 miles to Retford had come down to 114½min (72.6mph); Sheffield was reached at 9.53pm, in only just over 2½hr. Up in the morning, with the 7.25am departure unchanged, arrival in London at 10am made the overall time 2hr 35min. The midday workings on which the Pullman did not carry a title, were at 10.50am down and 3.35pm up, in 2hr 42min down and 2¾hr up. This was easily the quickest communication that Sheffield had ever had with London.

The 'Master Cutler' was taken off in October 1968 and had not grown in size to anything more than the original six Pullman cars plus a bogie brake. In 1971 the 'Master Cutler' title was revived, this time in the St Pancras service. Footnotes in the timetables to the 7.20am from Sheffield and the 5.50pm return train described them as the 'Master Cutler'. The up train was accelerated by 5min to reach St Pancras in 2hr 35min, and the down train by 6min to make the journey in 2hr 31min, the gain in both cases being achieved by faster running between Sheffield and Leicester. The train was formed of ordinary stock. Air-conditioned stock was introduced in 1975 and at that time the locomotive carried a headboard with the Company of Cutlers' crest, which also appeared on restaurant car menus, window labels etc. In the timetables the name had been promoted meanwhile from the footnotes to the columns themselves, where it has remained. In the last timetable before the 'Master Cutler' became an HST the up train left Sheffield at 7.20am and was into St Pancras at 9.50am. The 4.55pm down 'Cutler' had a similar 2½hr timing. Both trains called at Chesterfield, Alfreton & Mansfield Parkway, and Leicester.

With three different main lines and London terminals in its history, the 'Master Cutler' is exceptional among British titled trains. It underwent yet another change on 4 October 1982 when the working to and from St Pancras was taken over by an HST. The up journey, leaving Sheffield at 7.23am, was scheduled in 2hr 15min. The down departure was changed to 5.30pm and the train ran into Sheffield at 7.45pm.

The other named train over the Great Central main line which was referred to earlier was the 'South Yorkshireman', which first appeared in the timetable in 1948. As a through train from Marylebone to Bradford, it took over the function of the prewar 6.20pm down Bradford express; in the up direction, leaving Bradford (Exchange) at 10am, it was the post-war counterpart of the prewar 10am from Bradford to Marylebone, though with fewer stops. But whereas the latter train returned from Marylebone to Bradford at 6.20pm, the 'South Yorkshireman' started north at 4.50pm, and as far as Sheffield was a postwar substitute for the 4.55pm down Manchester express of prewar days. This used to run the 103.1 miles from Marylebone to Leicester in no more than 108min, and had the very lively timing of 24min for the 23.5 miles from Leicester to Nottingham, so getting to Sheffield at 8.01pm in no more than 3hr 6min from London.

The 'South Yorkshireman' had an extra stop at Aylesbury, and from there, with its 10 coaches instead of the six of prewar days, for a time it had a smart postwar booking of 69min over the 65.2 miles from Aylesbury to Leicester, and 26min for the 23.5 miles thence to Nottingham, later increased to 73 and 29min respectively. At first the 'South Yorkshireman' was taken round the loop from Heath in order to call at Chesterfield, but the patronage was not sufficient to justify the continuance of this halt, and when it was taken out of the schedule, and the train was given a straight run from Heath to Staveley Town, the Sheffield arrival was brought forward from 8.42pm to 8.26pm, in 3hr 36min from Marylebone. This was subsequently altered to 8.40pm, and the journey then became longer by 44min than that of the pre-war 4.55pm down.

At Sheffield three of the 10 coaches, with the two restaurant cars, were dropped, and the Eastern Region B1 4-6-0 was replaced by a London Midland Region Class 5 for the continuation with the five remaining vehicles to Bradford, a task performed in Great Central days by one of the massive Hughes 4-cylinder 4-6-0s of the Lancashire & Yorkshire Railway.

Incidentally, the LMR engine carried an ER headboard for this part of the run. Then followed the stiff climb from Sheffield to Penistone, where a halt was made, and over the moors to Huddersfield; conditional stops were allowed for at Heckmondwike, Liversedge and Cleckheaton, and with one remaining regular stop, at Low Moor, the 'South Yorkshireman' wended its way into Bradford Exchange station at 10.20pm, having taken 5½hr for the journey from Marylebone.

Southbound, the Class 5 4-6-0 was ready for the steep pull out of Bradford at 10am; in this direction the Penistone stop was omitted, but the 'South Yorkshireman' would call at Brockholes and Shepley, between Huddersfield and Penistone, if there were through passengers to pick up. The train was into Sheffield at 11.20am; here the Class 5 made way for a B1 4-6-0. Leaving Sheffield at 11.27am, and calling in this direction at Loughborough and Rugby in addition to Nottingham, Leicester and Aylesbury, the 'South Yorkshireman' was due in Marylebone at 3.30pm, a total journey time of 5½hr from Bradford. For some time no stop was made at Aylesbury, and the London arrival was at 3.10pm, but timekeeping was not good, and a 20min deceleration followed, partly through the difficulty of finding a later path through the dense electric service after Rickmansworth. The Aylesbury stop was then added, in part to justify this considerable increase in running time. But the speed was a sad decline from the smart running of Great Central days. Not long afterwards the train was withdrawn.

The Merseyside Express

In earlier London & North Western days a single express from Euston at 5.30pm was sufficient to carry the evening traffic from London to Liverpool and Manchester, and to various other parts of Lancashire as well. But as the extent of the patronage and the luxury of the accommodation grew, and especially as more and more passengers demanded to be fed en route the 5.30pm by degrees split into various independent trains. First of all, the Manchester passengers were given a separate 6pm express, and the 5.30pm became a train for Liverpool and Fleetwood. Then, in 1905, an express at 5.55pm down was allocated exclusively to Liverpool, making a non-stop run to Edge Hill. Later a stop was added at Mossley Hill, a more convenient alighting point for many residents in the southern suburbs of Liverpool.

The name 'London-Merseyside Express' was conferred on this train in 1927, a year later to be abbreviated to the simpler 'Merseyside Express'. In 1932, when the 6.05pm down 'Lancastrian' was accelerated to make a 3¼hr run to Manchester, the two trains changed places, and the 5.55pm 'Merseyside' start was altered to 6.05pm. The latter train was booked to run the 189.7 miles to Mossley Hill in 200min, at 56.9mph, and so continued to the outbreak of World War 2; then, after calling at Edge Hill, Lime Street was reached at 9.40pm. The Edge Hill stop was to detach the two rear Southport coaches, which were worked round through Walton to Bootle, on the electric Liverpool-Southport line, and reached Southport, after making certain intermediate stops, at 10.30pm.

In the up direction the 'Merseyside Express', which for some years left Liverpool Lime Street at 10am, and was due into Euston at 1.30pm, was also accelerated to start 10min later, and to make the journey to London in 3hr 20min. In this direction the Southport coaches, leaving Chapel Street station at 8.50am, were worked through into Lime Street, and attached to the front of the London express there. This arrangement enabled the 'Merseyside' to dispense with an Edge Hill stop, and to call only at Mossley Hill, from which the run of 189.7 miles to Euston was booked non-stop in 189min at 60.2mph. Often between Crewe and Stafford the up 'Merseyside', running on the fast road, would overtake the 'Pines Express' from Manchester to Bournemouth, on the slow road, and at times a lively race would develop, especially over the falling gradients south of Whitmore. This is a reminder that the down 'Merseyside' often had a similar race with the 6.06pm from Euston to Northampton, which ran non-stop to King's Langley.

Latterly the 'Merseyside' became a very heavy train for its fast schedule; it was seldom less than 14 or 15 coaches and, if the latter, weighed about 490 tons empty and 525 tons with passengers and luggage. Two complete sets of dining cars were provided — a kitchen car flanked by two open first class cars, and a twelve-wheeled third and kitchen with an open third, five vehicles in all. The first class accommodation included one of the lounge brake cars, furnished with armchairs, that were built originally for the 'Royal Scot'.

During the war the 5.30pm departure from Euston

of much earlier history was resumed; for some time the Liverpool and Manchester trains were worked as one combined formation again, but eventually, except on Saturdays, this became too heavy a single-engine load, and the Manchester train thereafter was run separately. With stops at Crewe and Mossley Hill, the 5.30pm down reached liverpool Lime Street at 9.46pm; coming up, the start was at 10am, and with stops at Mossley Hill, Crewe and Watford, London was reached at 2.22pm — a slowing-down by one hour of the peacetime schedule. After the war, on 7 October 1946, the Euston departure was altered to 5.45pm, and the journey time was cut to 3hr 55min: in September 1949 the historic 6.05pm (working time 6.07pm) departure was reverted to, following instead of preceding the 'Lancastrian', an Edge Hill stop was introduced to detach the Southport coaches, and Lime Street from then on was reached at 9.50pm. The up express, starting at 10.10am, came down to a public timing of 3hr 40min (3hr 37min working time).

The morning express from Euston to Liverpool, at 10.40am, also in earlier years used to run combined with a Manchester train, and started at 10.30am, but latterly it became a separate departure at 10.40am. In summer it carried the name of 'Manxman', by reason of connecting at Liverpool with the Isle of Man boats. Through sections were run to Southport, like that of the evening train, and also — an oddity for a train travelling north-westward out of London — to Swansea; the latter coaches, attached in rear, were taken off at Stafford and worked to Shrewsbury, whence they made the lengthy cross-country journey by way of the Central Wales spas to reach Swansea Victoria at 6.35pm. The 'Manxman', calling only at Stafford and missing Crewe, was due in Liverpool Lime Street at 2.18pm.

The up 'Manxman' was the express leaving Lime Street at 2.10pm, calling at Mossley Hill and Crewe, and then making a fast run over the 156 miles from Crewe to Euston, in 152min, and so reaching London at 5.30pm. During the war period, the 2pm from Liverpool did not reach London until 6.15pm, but by 1953 this popular express, which called at Rugby only, had been speeded up to a run of 3hr 45min, reaching Euston at 5.45pm. The morning train from Euston, by now leaving at 10.30am, had had all its intermediate stops cut out, and was taking the same 3¾hr for a non-stop journey of 193.7 miles, but its running was confined to the summer only.

The Festival of Britain in 1951 was made the occasion of naming a third train of the Euston-Liverpool service, and equipping it with new standard stock throughout. This was the 12.05pm from Euston to Liverpool and the 5.25pm back. In years gone by the up express had a distinguished record, as for some years it was one of the fastest trains on the LMSR. It was timed over the 152.7 miles from Crewe to Willesden Junction in 142min (64.5mph) from 1932 onwards, and when later the Willesden stop was taken out, the timing became 148min for the 158.1 miles from Crewe to Euston (64.1mph). Up to the outbreak of war, this express was running from Liverpool to Euston in 3¼hr — the fastest time on record to that date.

The new name given this train was 'Red Rose', Lancashire counterpart of the Yorkshire 'White Rose' between Leeds and King's Cross. At that time the former was reaching Euston at 9.10pm, but in September 1952 the arrival was advanced to 9pm, with a 165min run up from Crewe, bringing the overall time down to 2hr 35min. As already mentioned, the down 'Red Rose' at first was the 12.05pm from Euston to Liverpool, but with some timetable rearrangement in 1951, the departure was altered to 12.30pm, and the train was made non-stop from Euston to Liverpool (Lime Street) in 3¾hr.

Yet another train over this route which in 1954 received a name was the then 4.30pm from Euston to Liverpool, which was altered to start at 4.55pm, and by omitting its Rugby and Crewe stops became non-stop to Lime Street in 3hr 27min; it received the title 'Shamrock'. The return was the 8.10am from Liverpool to Euston, stopping only at Bletchley, south of Crewe, and accelerated at the same time by 15min to be into London by 11.45am. There were many fluctuations in the timings of these four trains during the electrification period, and when electric working finally began in April 1966, with the new even-interval service and intensive stock working, all the names disappeared.

The Midday Scot

Among the titled trains of Great Britain the 'Midday Scot' had a comparatively short reign, for although it began to run in 1889, it did not receive an official name until 1927. For many years it was known to the railway staff as 'The Corridor', from the time when, in July 1893, it became one of the first London & North

Western expresses to be formed of corridor stock throughout. It had been provided with a first class dining car from 1891; in 1893 second class was withdrawn, and both first and third class passengers were provided with restaurant car accommodation. It is remarkable that when, from its first journey in 1889, the up train left Glasgow Central at 2pm and reached London Euston at 10.50pm, the time was not varied by more than 5min in the next 25 years.

A great day in the history of the 'Corridor' was 11 July 1908, when there was introduced to the service one of the finest sets of passenger stock that the country had seen up to that time, or, indeed, for years afterwards. This was a magnificent train of 12-wheel cars, marred only by the inclusion of two considerably older West Coast Joint Stock dining cars. The formation going north at that time, from the engine, was brake third, composite restaurant car, composite coach, and brake third for Glasgow; composite restaurant car, composite and third brake for Edinburgh; and composite brake for Aberdeen; to which were added a composite brake for Whitehaven, and a composite for Altrincham.

The last-mentioned vehicle — a most curious working — came off at Crewe, and was worked from there via Sandbach and over the Cheshire Lines Committee's route. The Whitehaven and Aberdeen coaches were detached at Preston and continued from there on the back of a following express from Liverpool and Manchester to Glasgow.

Leaving Euston at 2pm, the main train had called already at Willesden Junction, Rugby and Crewe; from Preston it was run non-stop to Carlisle, where it had now become the regular procedure to attach the McIntosh inside-cylinder 4-6-0 No 903 *Cardean*. In her light blue livery, the famous Caledonian engine with her train of chocolate-and-white 12-wheelers, made an ensemble quite unmatched at that time. The Scottish stops were at Beattock, for banking assistance to Summit, and in the open country at Strawfrank Junction, outside Carstairs, to detach the section for Edinburgh. The Glasgow section was into Central station by 10.20pm, and the Edinburgh portion reached Princes Street 10min later.

Coming south, both parts of the train started simultaneously at 2pm from Glasgow and Edinburgh, and both included, on the rear, sections for Liverpool and Manchester. The Edinburgh train, notwithstanding a stop at Symington to pick up the Aberdeen coach, kept ahead of the Glasgow all the way to Preston. From Glasgow the main part of the 'Corridor', headed by *Cardean*, ran the 102.3 miles to Carlisle without a stop — the only 100-mile run made by the train in either direction — and then called at Penrith as the only halt between Carlisle and Preston. At Preston the Edinburgh, Aberdeen and Glasgow coaches, having shed their Liverpool and Manchester 'tails', were joined up, and proceeded to call at Crewe, Rugby and Willesden Junction before reaching Euston at 10.45pm. At this period, the 'Corridor' dropped a slip-coach (attached at Crewe) at Nuneaton, to replace a previous Nuneaton stop.

As to London & North Western motive power, in the earliest phase of its history the 'Corridor' was associated with the famous Webb 3-cylinder compound *Jeanie Deans*, which used to work it daily from Euston to Crewe and back — a tough task for a 2-2-2-0 locomotive of such modest dimensions. By 1908 the Webb 4-4-0 compounds had given place to the 'Precursor' 4-4-0s and the 'Experiment' 4-6-0s, followed by their superheated 'George the Fifth' and 'Prince of Wales' variants; and before the outbreak of World War 1 the 4-cylinder 4-6-0 'Claughtons' were available for the working of a train which was now a minimum formation of 400 tons between London and Preston.

During the latter part of World War 1 the 'Corridor', shorn of its dining cars, was the only LNWR day service between London and Glasgow; the starting time had changed from 2 to 1pm, and with slower running and additional stops, the down train did not reach Central till 11.10pm, while the up train ran into Euston 10min later. Recovering in the post-war period, by 1923, the year the LMSR came into being, the 'Corridor' was leaving Euston at 1.30pm, and reaching Glasgow at 10pm, while the up train had precisely the same times. The stops going north were now Rugby, Crewe, Lancaster, Carlisle and Carstairs; on the southbound run the Glasgow train was stopping at Symington to collect the Edinburgh portion, and calling only at Carlisle and Crewe between there and London. The Aberdeen section followed from Law Junction as a separate train, and made the calls that in earlier years had been made by the up 'Corridor'.

So matters continued until 1932, when the LMSR and LNER at length broke loose from the bonds of the agreement which for 32 years had restricted the overall times of their Anglo-Scottish day trains to a minimum of $8\frac{1}{4}$hr. The 'Midday Scot' — as the 'Corridor' had become five years earlier — shared in the acceleration. At first the times came down to 8hr 5min northbound and 8hr southbound; later the up train was accelerated to 7hr 55min, despite an additional stop at Lancaster from 1933 onwards. The Stanier Pacifics had now appeared on the scene, and not only ousted the 'Royal Scot' 4-6-0s, which had been changed en route at Crewe only, but worked the 'Midday Scot' through in each direction unchanged over the $401\frac{1}{2}$ miles bertween Euston and Glasgow. In the northbound direction, also, the trains acquired at Crewe a Great Western composite brake running through from Penzance to Glasgow, attached next the engine.

In the fourteen months from May 1936 to June 1937 inclusive, the 'Midday Scot' reached the height of its fame. In the down direction it reverted to its historic departure hour of 2pm from Euston, and was relieved by a new express from London at 1.30pm, so that it could run non-stop over the 158 miles to Crewe in 163min. A new stop was made at Penrith, and the timing of 59min for the 51.2 miles over Shap Summit from Lancaster to Penrith, with a minimum trainload of 14 bogies (about 445 tons) and often more, was the hardest, from the locomotive point of view, that had ever been included in the train's schedule. At Carlisle, reached at 7.35pm, the train divided, and the Glasgow section was run non-stop from there to Central in 116min, arriving at 9.35pm. The Edinburgh and Aberdeen portions continued together to Lockerbie, and there they also parted company; Lockerbie to Edinburgh non-stop brought that section in at 9.55pm, and Perth passengers enjoyed a total acceleration of 72min by getting into that city at 11.28pm. The up 'Midday Scot' but little altered, reached Euston at 9.20pm.

Then came the upheaval caused by the introduction of the 'Coronation Scot' streamliner in July, 1937. For the first time in its history the 'Midday Scot' ceased — officially — any longer to provide an advertised service between London and Glasgow, although it was provided with Glasgow coaches in order to accommodate passengers to and from intermediate stations. Still leaving Euston at 2pm, the train shrunk to no more than six coaches — third brake, third restaurant and kitchen, semi-open first and third brake for Edinburgh, and composite and third brake for Glasgow — which nevertheless boasted the services of a Pacific for its haulage. To Crewe there was now a booking of over a mile-a-minute — 158 miles in 156min — and here the GWR coach was picked up. After leaving Crewe at 4.45pm, the next stop was at Wigan, where through coaches from Manchester to Glasgow and Edinburgh were marshalled in the centre of the train; this took from 5.23 to 5.32pm. Passing Preston, the 'Midday Scot' proceeded to Lancaster, where a stop from 6.19 to 6.24pm was needed to add a portion from Liverpool to Glasgow, bringing the load up to 14 vehicles.

At Carlisle, reached at 7.44pm, the express split up into its Edinburgh and Glasgow sections. The Pacific came off, and was replaced by a 'Jubilee' 4-6-0, which took the six-coach Edinburgh portion — four from London and two from Manchester — out at 7.49pm, and was due to run into Princes Street at 9.45pm, in 7¾hr from Euston. Then the Pacific backed down at Carlisle on to the remaining eight — which might be nine or ten if more through Glasgow coaches had been run from London — and leaving at 7.56pm, made Glasgow Central at 9.55pm. Glasgow passengers had to be careful to get their dinners betimes, as they had no restaurant car service from Carlisle onwards.

In the reverse direction, the locomotive task was distinctly harder. The Pacific locomotive moved out of Glasgow Central at 1.35pm, 5min behind the 'Coronation Scot', with a load of from four to six bogies. At Law Junction, 18.3 miles away, there was waiting the London portion of the 10.05am express from Aberdeen, a four-coach restaurant car set similar to that from Edinburgh, and hungry Glasgow passengers could then get their lunch. Meantime the 'Midday Scot' proper had left Edinburgh at 1.40pm, and awaited the Glasgow and Aberdeen portions at Symington.

The full train of 12 to 14 vehicles, including two pairs of restaurant cars, leaving Symington after a 4min stop at 2.36pm, was next booked to make a 72min run over the 66.9 miles from Symington to Carlisle, including the climb to Beattock summit, and in the summer months added further to its load at the Border city by acquiring two through coaches from Stranraer, which made it possible to get through from Northern Ireland to London in the compass of a single day. The load might now be anything up to 16 coaches, with a tare weight of 500 tons or more, and this had to be worked over the 141 miles from Carlisle to Crewe, including the Lancaster stop, in 176min, and finally over the 158 miles from Crewe to Euston in the smart time of 160min. The up 'Midday Scot' was thus brought into London at 9.30pm.

Through most of World War 2, though suspended for several lengthy periods, the 'Midday Scot' continued to run. Once again it became a London-Glasgow train, and with no Edinburgh or other portions. It was also a very heavily-patronised service; and in the northbound direction almost daily it needed formations of 15 or more coaches, crowded to capacity. Leaving Euston at 1pm, it stopped only at Rugby and Crewe to Carlisle, and then at Carstairs (to give connections to Edinburgh, Perth and the North) and at Motherwell; Glasgow was reached at 9.58pm. In the other direction, also leaving Glasgow at 1pm, the wartime version of the 'Midday Scot' called at Motherwell, Carstairs, Carlisle and Crewe, and then made a call unknown in peacetime, at Watford, to set down passengers — a convenience for residents in the north-west suburbs introduced at the time of the London Blitz. Arrival in London was at 9.56pm, 2min before the Glasgow arrival of the northbound train. The through Pacific workings continued unchanged. Restaurant cars were restored to the train both ways on 1 October 1945, and the up Watford stop was excised in May 1946. From 7 October 1946 the down train was altered to leave at 1.15pm, but the Glasgow arrival was put back to 10.05pm; the up express, however, was accelerated to reach Euston at 9.50pm.

By 1953 the up 'Midday Scot' had had its Glasgow start altered to 1.30pm, to bring it into Carstairs behind instead of in front of the through Perth portion, and from there the train made a spirited dash over the 73.5 miles to Carlisle, including Beattock summit, in 75min. South of the Border a stop was now regular at Preston as well as Lancaster, and the Watford stop had been reinstated, Euston being reached at 10pm, after $8\frac{1}{2}$ hours en route. The northbound 'Midday Scot', with stops unchanged, now allowed 8hr 20min, was into Glasgow by 9.35pm. During the winter the latter acquired, as far as Crewe, a through Blackpool portion which in summer left Euston as an independent restaurant car train at 1.30pm.

The next change of note was an extraordinary one. With the introduction of the 1959-1960 winter service, the authorities decided to put the 'Royal Scot', 'Midday Scot' and 'Caledonian' on to identical schedules, calling only at Carlisle in each direction, and with loads rigidly restricted to eight bogies completing the London-Glasgow journey in $7\frac{3}{4}$hr. Second class passengers were seated uncomfortably in four abreast open stock; booking of seats was compulsory; no standing was permitted; and in the case particularly of the well-patronised 'Midday Scot' this meant inevitably that some passengers got left behind. By the omission of the Crewe stops important connections with the 'Midday Scot' were severed, and the change in the southbound start out of Glasgow from 1.30 to 3pm was another cause of considerable dissatisfaction. Thus as soon as the summer of 1960 it had become necessary to reinstate the Crewe stop of the up train and the 1.30pm Glasgow start, also to relax the severe restriction of load, even at the cost of deceleration, while by 1962 a stop at Wigan had been added. At this period speed restrictions due to the electrification work had become so numerous that no less than 48min recovery time was being allowed in the schedules between Euston and Carlisle.

With the introduction of the full electric timetable in April 1966 the 'Midday Scot' losts its name but the Euston start got as close to the original as 2.05pm (the even hour being for Liverpool and Manchester departures). In addition to radical acceleration south of Crewe, considerable changes took place north of that point; a later development in 1966 was the diversion of the down train north of Carlisle from the former Caledonian to the Glasgow & South Western line, in order to give a direct service to Dumfries and Kilmarnock. Southbound, however, the Caledonian route was followed.

In later years 45min past the hour became the standard departure time from Euston to Glasgow but there was a variation at midday to give a Glasgow train at 2pm as recently as 1981. With electrification to Glasgow already seven years old, the journey then took 5hr 54min with stops at Rugby, Crewe, Preston, Lancaster, Oxenholme, Penrith, Carlisle, Carstairs and Motherwell. In the 1982 timetable there was a gap from 12.45 to 2.45pm in Glasgow departures from Euston and the lingering echoes of the 'Corridor' died away.

The Night Ferry

In the past there have been a number of proposals for providing transport for passengers and freight between Great Britain and the mainland of Europe without change of carriage or wagon. The first such scheme was abortive; it was the Channel Tunnel, work on which was actually begun between Folkestone and Dover, at the English end, but which was later abandoned, though the project later became a live issue again. Then followed the train ferry idea, already well developed in Scandinavia for providing communication between the mainland and islands of Denmark and both Germany and Sweden. Across the English Channel this first took shape during World War 1, when train ferries were established between Richborough in East Kent and Dunkerque, and also between Southampton and Le Havre, greatly facilitating the movement of war material.

After the war, the two initial cross-Channel train ferries went out of use, but were succeeded by a permanent train ferry between Harwich and Zeebrugge in Belgium, which came into operation in April 1924. Once again this ferry was for freight only, except that it was used to transport to Europe dining, sleeping and Pullman cars that had been built in Britain for Continental use. At last, in 1936, the dream of years took shape by the completion of a train ferry terminal at Dover which, with the remodelled Dunkerque terminal of earlier years, made it possible to establish the first passenger service between London and Paris without change of carriage. The first through train ran on the night of 4 October in that year.

The aim was to provide, not faster transport than the day services via Dover-Calais and Folkestone-Boulgone, but a comfortable night route which permitted the passenger to go to bed on leaving London, and to wake up on the French side in time to dress, breakfast on the train, and reach Paris at the beginning of the business day. The same facilities were provided in the reverse direction. As a result, for the first time in history the blue sleeping cars of the International Sleeping Car Company were seen in a London terminus every day. The sleeping cars and two brake vans alone ran through; passengers in ordinary first and second class compartments had to change at Dover and Dunkerque on and off the ferry steamers, on which comfortable passenger accommodation was provided, in the same way as they did on the day service. After World War 2 through sleeping cars were worked to Brussels as well as to Paris, and the 1967-1968 winter saw a through sleeper to Basle also.

The first journey in the day of the 'Night Ferry' train was up from Dover to Victoria, which was reached between 8 and 9pm all the year round. In the reverse direction the start from Victoria was between 9 and 9.30pm in winter and an hour later in summer. For the 78 miles between Victoria and Dover Marine the time allowed at first was 89min down and 110min up. From 1936 until the war two 4-4-0 locomotives were used to work the train; from its postwar revival 'West Country' Pacifics took charge, but the increase in accommodation eventually made it necessary for these locomotives to be piloted also. Later on several of the larger 'Merchant Navy' Pacifics were drafted to Dover shed to handle the 'Night Ferry' and other Continental trains, and the former also was handled by standard Class 7 'Britannia' Pacifics.

The formation of the train from Dover to Victoria from the engine backwards had been known at peak periods to rise to as much as two French vans and 10 sleeping cars, all of International Sleeping Car Company's stock working through from Paris to London; then, attached at Dover, a restaurant and kitchen car, buffet car, corridor first, two corridor seconds, another restaurant and kitchen car, and a first class brake — twelve Continental and seven SR vehicles, making this about the heaviest passenger train in Great Britain. The sleeping cars were of the usual Continental type although shortened from the Wagons-Lits standard length and reduced in width to conform to SR loading gauge restrictions.

The 'Night Ferry' took the Chatham route to Dover, and when the line was electrified the outward service on 8 June 1959 was the first public electric train to use it. Haulage on that occasion was by the Class 71 2,552hp Bo-Bo locomotive No E5003. From that time the 71 class, unassisted, became the regular motive power until the locomotives were withdrawn in 1976, when Class 73 electro-diesels took over.

Air and car ferry traffic severely dented patronage of the 'Night Ferry' although businessmen appreciated the service in winter when aircraft were liable to diversions because of weather. By the 1970s, however, the Wagons-Lits stock was ageing. There had been some postwar replacements of wartime losses — a few cars passed into Mitropa service on the Continent — but originals of 1936 were still in use. There was little justification commercially for costly replacements. Proposals to re-equip the train with BR sleeping cars were considered and seemed to offer a reprieve but were not put into effect. Notice of withdrawal was given, and the last 'Night Ferry' train left Victoria on 31 October 1980. It was headed uncharacteristically by Class 33 No 33.043 but the locomotive carried the headboard of former years resurrected for the occasion. By this time the 'Night Ferry' had shrunk dramatically. The catering vehicles which ran between Victoria and Dover had been withdrawn, and a typical formation in the last months was three or four sleeping cars, a BR Mk 1 brake van, and two or three luggage vans.

The Night Limited

At one time the train which later became the 'Night Scot' provided the fastest daily service between London and Glasgow. In the days when the East and West Coast companies were still bound by their agreement not to cut the times of the day trains below a minimum of 8¼hr from London to either Glasgow or Edinburgh, there was no such restriction on the night services. While the Great Northern, North Eastern and North British companies were timing their down night express to Aberdeen to reach Edinburgh in 7¾hr from London, therefore, the London and North Western scheduled their principal night Scottish service, at 11.50pm from Euston, to reach Glasgow Central at 7.50am, 8hr later, calling at Crewe, Carlisle and Carstairs.

In the years after World War 1, however, the train by degrees grew considerably heavier, and the speed was much reduced. Departure time finally became 11.45pm from London Euston, and arrival in Glasgow was 9.35am. But the traveller was compensated for this later arrival by the insertion at Carlisle, in the centre of the train, of a couple of restaurant cars, which enabled him to have breakfast in comfort before alighting. The formation of the train from Carlisle might include six or more 12-wheel first class sleeping cars, two third class sleepers, a composite coach, two corridor thirds, and two brakes, with a 12-wheel dining car and an adjacent open car for meal service, making an empty weight of at least 530 tons.

The stops on the down journey were now at Rugby, Crewe, Preston and Carlisle, where the 'Night Scot' was due at 6.28am, and had a booked stop of 22min to give time for the marshalling of the restaurant cars in the centre of the train. A curious feature of the working was that this express, while waiting at Carlisle, was overtaken by another train which had left Euston at 12.20am, 35min later, and was due in Carlisle at 6.35am. From Carlisle, leaving at 6.50am, the 'Night Scot' had a most leisurely allowance of 2¾hr for the 102.3 miles on to Glasgow. Any gain on schedule was impossible, for the train was due to pass Lockerbie 8min after the Glasgow-bound 'Tinto', which called at all stations to Carstairs before beginning to run 'express passenger', had left. So if the northbound 'Night Scot' was on time, constant signal checks were almost inevitable over a considerable part of its journey in Scotland, though the timing certainly had the merit of making a late arrival in Glasgow extremely unlikely. A scheduled stop was made at Symington, where a supply of morning newspapers was put on board the train; the timetable also showed a conditional stop at Lockerbie to set down passengers, and a stop at Beattock was necessary for banking assistance.

In the up direction the 'Night Scot', before the war, had become a train of distinction by being booked to make the run of 243.3 miles from Glasgow to Crewe without any intermediate stop. This meant that a load often equal to that of the down journey — for, although no restaurant cars were run on the southbound working, their place might be taken by more sleeping accommodation, which frequently reached a total of eight first class 12-wheelers and two third class cars — had to be worked by the one engine, first over the 1,015ft altitude of Beattock summit, then down virtually to sea level north of Carlisle, and after that up on to Shap, 915ft above the sea, in the compass of this one-stop break.

Departure from Glasgow was at 10.45pm, and 5hr 5min was allowed for the run to Crewe; in all the circumstances, the scheduled average of 47.9mph was not to be despised, especially in rough winter weather. There was an allowance of 10min at Crewe, and whereas the public timetable booked the 'Night Scot' into Euston at 7.15am, in 8¾hr from Glasgow, the working time of arrival was 10min earlier, at 7.05am.

As to locomotives, the 'Royal Scots' had a fairly lengthy reign on the 'Night Scot', until the advent of the Pacifics; with the latter, through workings from Crewe to Glasgow and back to Crewe were first arranged, but with the introduction of through locomotive workings between Euston and Glasgow, the 'Night Scot' became one of the trains to be rostered regularly for a Pacific throughout in each direction.

Wartime witnessed some striking developments in the working of the 'Night Scot'. The name went, but the train remained, and was one of the most popular on the service. The main portion left Euston 2½hr earlier than in peacetime, at 9.15pm, with an average load of 15 bogies, a number of them sleeping cars. Stopping at Crewe from 12.27 to 12.37am, it was booked to make its next halt at Beattock at 4.39am, for assistance up the famous 10-mile bank to Beattock summit. From Beattock, left at 4.46am, to Glasgow was a non-stop run of 62.6 miles, and Glasgow Central was reached at 6.15am, in 9hr from London. The wartime 'Night Scot' was thus 50min quicker than the peacetime service — a most unusual inversion of the normal wartime order.

During most of the war the traffic was so heavy that three trains in all were necessary in each direction, at about the same departure hour, to handle all the passengers, and each of them usually a 15-coach formation. The first down service, at 8.40, later 8.50pm, was reserved exclusively for Service passengers. This was of considerable note in being booked nightly to make the longest wartime non-stop run in the world, over the 301.1 miles from Euston to Kingmoor, 2 miles north of Carlisle, where there was a stop to change enginemen and examine the train. The time allowed was 6hr 25min, so that no more than moderate speed was called for.

Following the 9.15pm there was also the 9.20pm for Glasgow; this train, without sleeping car accommodation, called at Crewe from 12.40 to 12.50am, and next at Kingmoor, like the 8.40pm down, from 4.02 to 4.09am; from there it travelled by the Glasgow & South Western line, non-stop over the 115.5 miles to St Enoch, which was reached at 6.50am in 9½hr from London. In the public timetable both the 9.15 and 9.20pm were advertised as non-stop from Euston to Glasgow, their intermediate stops being for operational purposes only.

In the reverse direction the arrangements were

somewhat similar, except that the wartime version of the southbound 'Night Scot' at 9.30pm from Glasgow Central, was unique in Great Britain at that time in being composed only of first class and third class sleeping cars. It was preceded at 9.05pm (9.08pm working time) by a relief train without sleeping accommodation. The latter ran through Carlisle, but stopped at No 12 box, south of the station, to change enginemen, from 11.37 to 11.42pm; after that the only stop was at Crewe, from 3.04 to 3.07am, and Euston was reached at 6.25am. Ten minutes later the 'Night Scot' arrived, after having run non-stop from Glasgow to Crewe, and halted there from 3.13 to 3.24am.

The strangest of these schedules, however, were those of the southbound Services sleeping car special and a third section of the 'Night Scot', which performed some odd feats of passing and repassing one another on the way to London. The former left Glasgow St Enoch at 9.27pm, and called at Kilmarnock and Dumfries on the way down to Carlisle, only to find, on passing Gretna Junction, that the 9.38pm from Central, stopping at Motherwell to pick up passengers, had preceded it by 6min. Both trains ran through Carlisle, and changed engine-crews at Carlisle No 12 box, from which the train from Central got away at 12.14am, and the Services sleeper at 12.25am.

But while the 9.38pm from Central was making a leisurely stop at Crewe from 3.27 to 3.50am, the sleeping car train slipped by at 3.38am, and got ahead, and notwithstanding a 'set down' stop at Watford which was inserted in the schedule in the later months of the war, reached Euston at 6.55am. The 9.38am from Central made a call at Rugby and was into Euston 13min later. It is a fitting commentary on the amazing extent of long-distance traffic in wartime that four expresses, composed of a total of at least 60 coaches and filled to capacity, should have been required to leave Glasgow every night between 9.08 and 9.38pm, and to reach Euston between 6.25 and 7.08am, doing little else than to convey through traffic. All the express trains mentioned in this chapter normally were through Pacific workings between London and Glasgow.

After the war, from May 1946, there was a complete revision of the night service between Euston and Glasgow. The principal down 'sleeper' reverted to its prewar 11.35pm departure, now acquired a couple of breakfast cars at Carlisle, and reached Glasgow Central at 9.45am — a journey of 10hr 10min. The up run took 80min less — 10.35pm from Glasgow and 7.25am into Euston; it was still an all-sleeping car train.

In the 1950s the 'Night Scot', no longer named, had settled down to a departure from Euston at 11.40pm. The first stop was made at Carlisle, at 6.10am. From here, after a 20min wait, during which the two breakfast cars were marshalled into the train, departure was at 6.30am, now by the Glasgow & South Western route, with stops at Dumfries and Kilmarnock to set down sleeping car passengers. At Kilmarnock a pilot was attached to help this heavy train up Stewarton bank, and there was a special stop at Lugton to detach it; beyond Strathbungo the sleeper was switched back to the Caledonian line, and ended its journey in Glasgow Central at 9.30am, an overall journey of 9hr 50min. In the reverse direction the all-sleeping car train left Glasgow Central at 10.20pm, via Carstairs, and the only stop was at Carlisle No 12 box, south of the station, to change enginemen; the express was booked into Euston in the working timetable at 7.03am and in the public book 12min later. It was followed by a 10.30pm sleeper from Glasgow Central, which took the G&SW route, called at Kilmarnock to pick up passengers, and then, like its immediate predecessor, at Carlisle No 12 only to London, which it reached 20min after the 10.20pm sleeper.

In the middle 1960s the train once again acquired a name — no longer 'Night Scot' but now 'Night Limited'. With the inauguration of electric working between Euston and Crewe a stop at Crewe in both directions of course became necessary, though the public timetable showed the express as making no stops between London and Glasgow Central other than that at Motherwell to set down; from Crewe to Motherwell was actually non-stop, no banker being needed from Beattock despite the weight of the train. Departure from Euston was at 11pm, and Crewe was reached at 1.17am; 8min were allowed here for the locomotive change, after which the train had no stop until it set passengers down at Motherwell at 5.57am. Glasgow Central was reached at 6.20am. With so early an arrival breakfast cars were no longer needed, but passengers could remain in their berths until 7.30am. Southbound, the 'Night Limited' left Glasgow Central also at 11pm, and Motherwell at 11.16pm; in this direction there was a stop at Carlisle from 1.05 to 1.07am to change the locomotive crew, and after the locomotive-changing stop from 3.57 to 4.07am at Crewe, the 'Night Limited' was into Euston by 6.35am. The train formation in both directions comprised eight first class sleeping cars, three second class cars, a converted Pullman refreshment car called the 'Nightcap Bar', and two brakevans, the 14-coach formation having the formidable tare weight of 584 tons, which meant a total nightly load of over 600 tons — the second heaviest regular passenger working in Great Britain.

The 'Night Limited' title continued after electrification throughout to Glasgow in 1974. In 1982 the down train was leaving Euston at 11.30pm and with stops at Carlisle and Motherwell to set down was into Glasgow in $6\frac{3}{4}$hr at 6.15am. The up train was at

11.10pm from Glasgow, arriving Euston at 5.23am, with a stop to set down at Preston on Sunday mornings in summer at the unholy hour of 2.11am. there were various changes at weekends, including a sleeping car from Fort Wiliam.

The Night Scotsman

Like its rival, the 'Night Scot' from Euston to Glasgow, the 'Night Scotsman' was a considerably faster train in earlier years than it became in the period before World War 2. In 1914 it was leaving King's Cross at 11.30pm, and taking a level 8hr to Edinburgh; by 1939 the departure time had come forward to 10.25pm and the arrival in Edinburgh Waverley had been retarded to 7.15am, making a journey of 8hr 50min. Moreover, by 1939 the business done by the 'Night Scotsman' to and from Scottish cities north and west of Edinburgh had grown to such dimensions that Edinburgh passengers from London were no longer welcome on it, but had to take the following 10.35pm sleeping car train from King's Cross.

Stops were made by the 'Night Scotsman' at Grantham, York and Newcastle, to pick up passengers only. On arrival at Waverley at 7.15am, like the 'Aberdonian' the 'Night Scotsman' split into three component parts — Glasgow, Perth and Aberdeen. Each of the three sections formed part of a breakfast car train; two of these trains started simultaneously at 7.35am — to Aberdeen, due at 11.12am, and to Glasgow, due in Queen street at 8.49am; the third portion left at 7.30am for Perth, due at 8.55am. The last-named had a Pullman restaurant car, of which several were at work on the LNER in Scotland before World War 2.

In the reverse direction, curiously enough, no train up to 1939 officially carried the title 'Night Scotsman', though the 11pm from Edinburgh Waverley, running just ahead of the 'Aberdonian', and conveying through coaches and sleeping cars from Dundee (9pm), Inverness (4.15pm) and Perth (8.10pm) would qualify for the description. This train had stops at Berwick, Newcastle, York and Grantham, and was due in King's Cross at 7.15am. In both directions the 'Night Scotsman', like all the LNER night expresses, was a train of great weight, usually made up to 13 or 14 vehicles, with six to eight of them first or third class sleeping cars.

Over the whole length of the East Coast main line the worst bank is Cockburnspath, which faces southbound trains, and begins at Innerwick, 4½ miles south of Dunbar. It is introduced by 1¾ miles at 1 in 210, and then steepens to 4¼ miles continuously at 1 in 96. The steepest incline on the route is 1¼ miles at 1 in 78 up into Edinburgh Waverley, but this can be taken by northbound trains 'at the double', and causes little difficulty. Much worse in its effect is the start out of King's Cross, averaging 1 in 107 for 1½ miles through two tunnels in which the rails are invariably slippery.

But there are also long and gruelling stretches of more moderate gradient, such as 8 miles at 1 in 200 up to Potters Bar, 9 miles mostly at 1 in 200 and 178 up to Stoke Summit (5½ miles south of Grantham), 4½ miles at 1 in 190 northwards from Berwick, and another 6 miles at 1 in 200 a little further north to Grantshouse, at the summit of Cockburnspath bank. Coming south, apart from the last-mentioned, the worst pulls are from Newark past Grantham to Stoke Summit, finishing in 5 miles at 1 in 200, and from Arlesey past Hitchin to Stevenage, concluding with 5 miles at the same inclination.

During World War 2 this train retained its title. It was a through train between King's Cross and Edinburgh only, leaving London at 10.15pm and due in Waverley at 7.42am, and this was no more than 37min slower than in peacetime. Also it was preceded nightly, in the last year of the war, by a relief express at 10pm, calling only at Grantham and Newcastle (except a momentary stop at York to change engine crews), and reaching Edinburgh at 6.57am. This timing was only 7min slower than in peacetime. In October 1946 the Edinburgh arrival was altered to 7.05am, so restoring the prewar timing of 8hr 50min.

Curiously enough, in the up direction the train which in the peacetime timetable was distinguished by no name was now officially titled the 'Night Scotsman', and carried the roof-boards of that train. Leaving Edinburgh Waverley at 9.40pm, it called at Dunbar, Berwick, Newcastle and Darlington to pick up passengers only, then at Grantham and Peterborough, running into King's Cross at 7.10am — a much slower journey of 9½hr. But by October 1946 the start from Waverley had been altered to 10pm, and the journey time to King's Cross cut to 8½hr.

By 1954 the 'Night Scotsman' had become a train of considerable distinction. All stops between King's

Cross and Newcastle had been cut out, and this non-stop run of 268.3 miles was the longest made throughout the year on Eastern and North Eastern Region metals up to that date, though beaten in summer, of course, by the London-Edinburgh run of the 'Capitals Limited'. Moreover, it had become far faster than the prewar 'Night Sctosman', for with departure from King's Cross at 10.15pm and arrival in Edinburgh at 6.21am, the overall time had come down to 8hr 6min. Southbound, with departure from Edinburgh at 10.40pm and arrival in London at 6.57am, additional stops at York and Grantham made the overall time 8hr 17min; in this direction it was a relief 'sleeper' at 10.20pm from Edinburgh that made the Newcastle-London non-stop run and completed the journey in 8hr.

Not until the summer of 1963 did a radical change come about in the working of the 'Night Scotsman', and this was when sufficient 3,300hp 'Deltic' diesels had become available to work practically all the through East Coast expresses. The down 'Night Scotsman' was altered to leave King's Cross at 11.35pm, to cover the 268.4 miles to Newcastle non-stop in 4hr 40min and the 124.5 miles on to Edinburgh in 124min, so achieving a time of no more than 6hr 52min between the English and Scottish capitals — something completely unprecedented for a night service. The up working was made nearly as fast. In the event, however, threading these and other extremely fast trains through the night freight traffic proved a little too difficult, and eventually they settled down to slower timings. The start of the down 'Night Scotsman' was still at 11.35pm, but the allowance to Newcastle was 4hr 9min; after a stop there for 11min (operational only and not for passengers) the time allowed on to Edinburgh was 135min, Waverley being reached at 6.50am, 23min later than in 1963. Southbound, departure from Waverley was at 11.20pm; the Newcastle stop was from 1.38 to 1.48am; and the King's Cross arrival was at 6.44am, a journey 9min longer than in the reverse direction. The normal load was seven first class sleeping cars with 70 berths, and three second class cars with 66 berths, plus two brake vans, the tare weight of the train being 464 tons, though it might be made up to a maximum of 530 tons at times of pressure.

The 'Night Scotsman' is still named at the time of writing and is one of the few remaining locomotive-hauled trains at King's Cross. The 11.35pm departure from King's Cross and 11.20pm from Edinburgh have been maintained but the down train stops at Peterborough to pick up at 12.57am and sets down at Berwick, Dunbar and Drem before running into Waverley at 6.58am. On the up run the 'Night Scotsman' picks up at Dunbar and Berwick, and sets down at Peterborough, reaching King's Cross at 6.04am. In 1982 the 'Night Scotsman' and 'Night Aberdonian' were among the Anglo-Scottish overnight services to which the new Mk 3 sleeping cars were allocated. They are 10-car trains plus a guard's brake, weighing some 400 tons. The sleeping cars work in pairs — one car with 13 compartments and the other with 12 compartments and an attendant's pantry, the attendant serving both vehicles. On the northbound 'Night Scotsman' there is a 'tail' of three Motorail vans. Concurrently with the introduction of the new sleeping cars the departure of the 'Night Aberdonian' from Aberdeen was put back from 9.25pm to the more convenient time of 10pm but the King's Cross arrival at 7.34pm was only 13min later than previously. Timings of the sleeping car trains are based on haulage by Class 47 locomotives and a maximum speed of 95mph.

The Norfolk Coast Express

Actually the title of 'Norfolk Coast Express' did not appear after the London & North Eastern Railway absorbed the Great Eastern Railway, on which it was originated, in 1907. In fact, the title went out with the first world war. In later years, too, the train retained but a pale shadow of its glory in Great Eastern days; from a daily service it was restricted to Mondays, Fridays and Saturdays only, and its running times were eased out. But when the set of corridor stock, with restaurant cars, was first brought into service by the GER, the problem set the locomotives of that day, in relation to their dimensions, was one of the most exacting that this country has ever known.

It was after the GER had installed two sets of water troughs on its Colchester main line, at Halifax Junction, south of Ipswich, and at Tivetshall, that the idea was conceived of running a special express from London to the Norfolk Coast during the currency of the summer timetables. In 1897 the service was first brought into operation, with a non-stop run over the

130.2 miles between Liverpool Street and North Walsham. In the following year the 4-2-2 locomotives of Class 10 came into service, and were used on a train of mixed six-wheel and bogie stock, but without corridors. The year 1900 saw the introduction of the first Holden 4-4-0 locomotives — the famous 'Claud Hamilton' series — and the earliest of these, like the single-drivers, were fired with oil fuel.

The corridor restaurant car train came into being in 1907, and was given the title of 'Norfolk Coast Express'; and from then on the haulage of the train became a task requiring the highest degree of locomotive performance, and the utmost skill in handling. Engine crews from the top links at Stratford, Ipswich and Norwich sheds alternated in the working of the train, and there was keen competition between all three sheds as to which could maintain the best timekeeping record. A representative of Stratford Works always accompanied the crew on the footplate, and took notes of the running; this was a pleasant species of summer outing that usually fell to works pupils. The train ran only during the months of July, August and September.

The minimum formation of the 'Norfolk Coast Express' was twelve bogie vehicles. Of these the first eight, including three restaurant cars, were for Cromer; the next two were for Sheringham, by the connection between the Great Eastern and Midland & Great Northern Joint Line from Cromer Junction, opened in the previous year; and the rear two, detached at North Walsham, were for Mundesley-on-Sea, and continued round the joint coast line to Overstrand. The total empty weight of this formation was 317 tons. But at busy summer weekends the make-up might rise to 13, 14 and even 15 bogies; and even then, with a tare weight of all but 400 tons, and a full weight of 430 to 440 tons, time was seldom lost. Yet the locomotives employed, at that date innocent of superheating or other modern refinements of design, weighed no more than 50 tons without their tenders.

In these circumstances, as will be realised by all who know the difficulties of this route, the maintenance of schedule was a miracle of competence. Shortly after leaving Liverpool Street the engines had to face the 1 in 70 rise to Bethnal Green Junction. Just as they were getting away nicely with their train there came the slowing through Stratford, 4 miles out, nominally to 25mph. Then, after continuously rising grades, there came the formidable climb up Brentwood bank, $3\frac{1}{4}$ miles long, and with $2\frac{1}{2}$ miles at 1 in 85-103, to Ingrave summit. From here to Colchester, though continuously undulating, the line had no difficult gradients; there were the complications of 30 and 40mph speed restrictions through Chelmsford and Colchester respectively, though of these the drivers often took some very liberal views. Swinging ups and downs between Colchester and Ipswich ended with a bad slowing through Ipswich, usually observed with more strictness than those previously mentioned.

Between Ipswich and Norwich there were more heavy grades, but the worst obstacle of the entire journey was the running through Norwich, entailing two miles of reduced speed, and a 15mph slack over Trowse swing-bridge. Immediately after this, from Whitlingham, came a climb of a mile at 1 in 80 on to some of the high ground of Norfolk. Thus there was little respite anywhere on the journey, and the schedule of 158min for the 130.2 miles from Liverpool Street to North Walsham meant far more than its apparently moderate average of 49.4mph might indicate. From Shenfield to Trowse, including the Chelmsford, Colchester and Ipswich slacks, the distance of 93.8 miles had to be run in 105min, at an average speed of 53.6mph throughout.

At different periods of Great Eastern history the down 'Norfolk Coast Express' left Liverpool Street at 1 and 1.30pm, but the time allowed to Cromer was unvaried at 2hr 55min in each direction for the 138.1 miles. In the up direction the start from Cromer was always at 1pm, and Liverpool Street was reached at 3.55pm.

The advent of the 4-6-0s of the '1500' class in 1912 was shortly followed by their introduction to the 'Norfolk Coast Express', and from then on the task set the locomotives became less exacting. Under London & North Eastern auspices, as previously mentioned, the name disappeared, the operation was cut down to three times weekly, the start from Liverpool Street was altered to 12.25pm, and the allowance to North Walsham increased to 159min. Cromer was then reached in 2hr 57min. On the up journey departure from Cromer was at 12.50pm, and from North Walsham at 1.08pm, and the arrival at Liverpool Street was at 3.49pm, in under three hours.

Since World War 2 there has been no more non-stop running between Liverpool Street and North Walsham, and since the introduction of the hourly express service between London and Norwich through running between London and the Cromer branch has ceased also, passengers for Cromer and Sheringham being now required to change into diesel multiple-units at Norwich Thorpe. But with schedules of just under 2hr from Liverpool Street to Norwich the fastest time from London to Cromer has come down to 2hr 49min, 6min faster than the 'Norfolk Coast Express' despite eight intermediate stops and a change as compared with the former Great Eastern train's one stop only.

Executive Style Travel

The 'Master Cutler' (steam-hauled between Marylebone and Sheffield) appeared while the popular stereotypes were still Pilot-Officer Prune and Flying-Officer Kite rather than steelmen, oilmen and executives in general. The train has had a varied history, becoming a diesel-hauled Pullman from King's Cross in 1958 (above) and later switching to St Pancras as a train of ordinary stock. The next change was to HST in 1982 (left). *BR*

Among the Eastern Region trains with 'Executive' titles the 'Hull Executive' was distinguished by being the fastest locomotive-hauled train on British Railways. Adorned with headboard and laurel wreath 'Deltic' No 55.015 *Tulyar* waits to leave King's Cross on 2 January 1981 (above), the day before HSTs took over on the service.

Headboards are now the exception, appearing only on special occasions, but the Eastern Region gives its 'Executive' trains an identity by motifs derived from civic coats of arms on coach labels, menu cards, and lapel badges (right). *BR, Keith Grafton*

Take a Train to Catch a Ship

Today the slogan is 'Take a train to catch a plane'. Air travel and car ferries have reduced the role of the boat train while electrification of the routes to the Channel Ports has turned many of the breed into emus barely distinguishable from the longer-distance commuter services.

Above: Embellishment of the 'Golden Arrow' London-Dover Pullman when restored in 1946. Bulleid's first streamlined Pacific, *Channel Packet*, still carries its 'alphanumeric' number 21C1. The train is leaving Victoria. *BR*

Centre left: Although most boat train services became emus when both routes to the Kent Coast had been electrified, locomotive haulage was necessary for trains of special stock'. The Class 71 electric locomotive heading the 'Golden Arrow' in this picture belonged to a versatile series equally at home on fast passenger and freight workings. *IAL*

Bottom left: Stewarts Lane in steam days. The locomotives of the 'Golden Arrow' and the 'Night Ferry' meet. *R. C. Riley*

Above: Class 71 electric No E5008 arrives at Victoria with the 'Night Ferry' on 30 September 1971. The vans and sleeping cars have crossed the Channel by train ferry. *J. H. Cooper-Smith*

Centre left: A longer sea crossing and consequently lower London-Paris fares gave a utilitarian image to the Newhaven route. Ex-LBSC Atlantic No 41 (named *Peveril Point* by the Southern Railway) is near Lewes with a Newhaven Continental boat train on 3 September 1928. *E. R. Wethersett*

Bottom left: Channel Islands boat trains between Waterloo and Weymouth were the last BR trains to carry roof boards regularly. This photograph was taken in 1978. *David Maxey*

Above right: A Channel Islands boat train passes Vauxhall on its way out of Waterloo on 21 June 1977. The locomotive is Class 74 electro-diesel No 74.005, one of the conversions from Class 71 electrics. *B. Denton*

Above, far right: 'Britannia' class Pacific No 70003 *John Bunyan* has steam up at Liverpool Street for the run to Harwich Parkeston Quay with the 'Hook Continental'. *C. B. Wilkin*

Bottom right: Harwich-Esbjerg sailings connect with train services to Copenhagen. The up 'Scandinavian' boat train from Parkeston Quay is shepherded past Wrabness on 8 July 1950, by 'B1' 4-6-0 No 61192. *G. R. Mortimer*

90

THE
HOOK
CONTINENTAL
70003

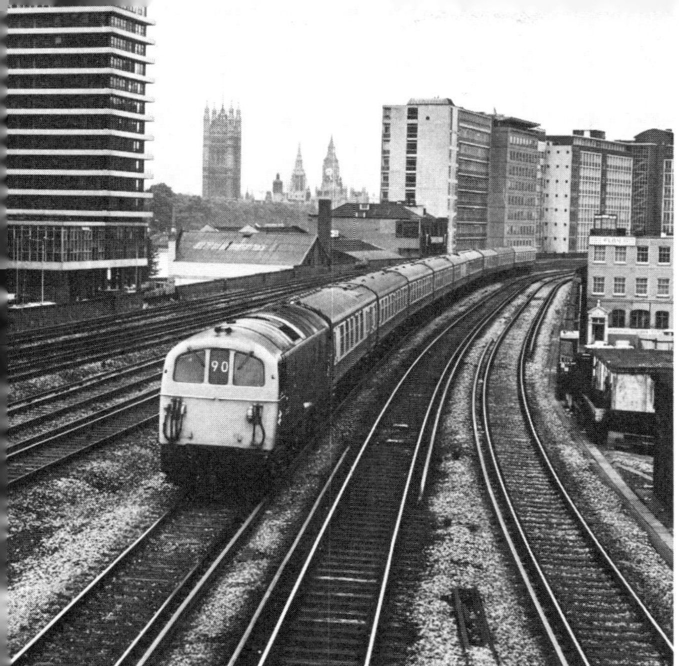

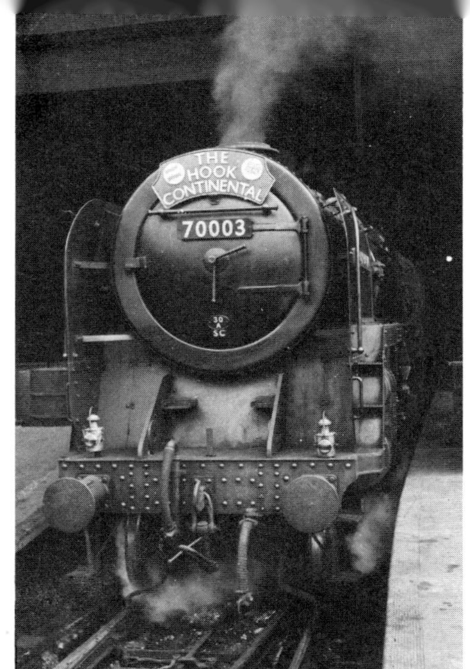

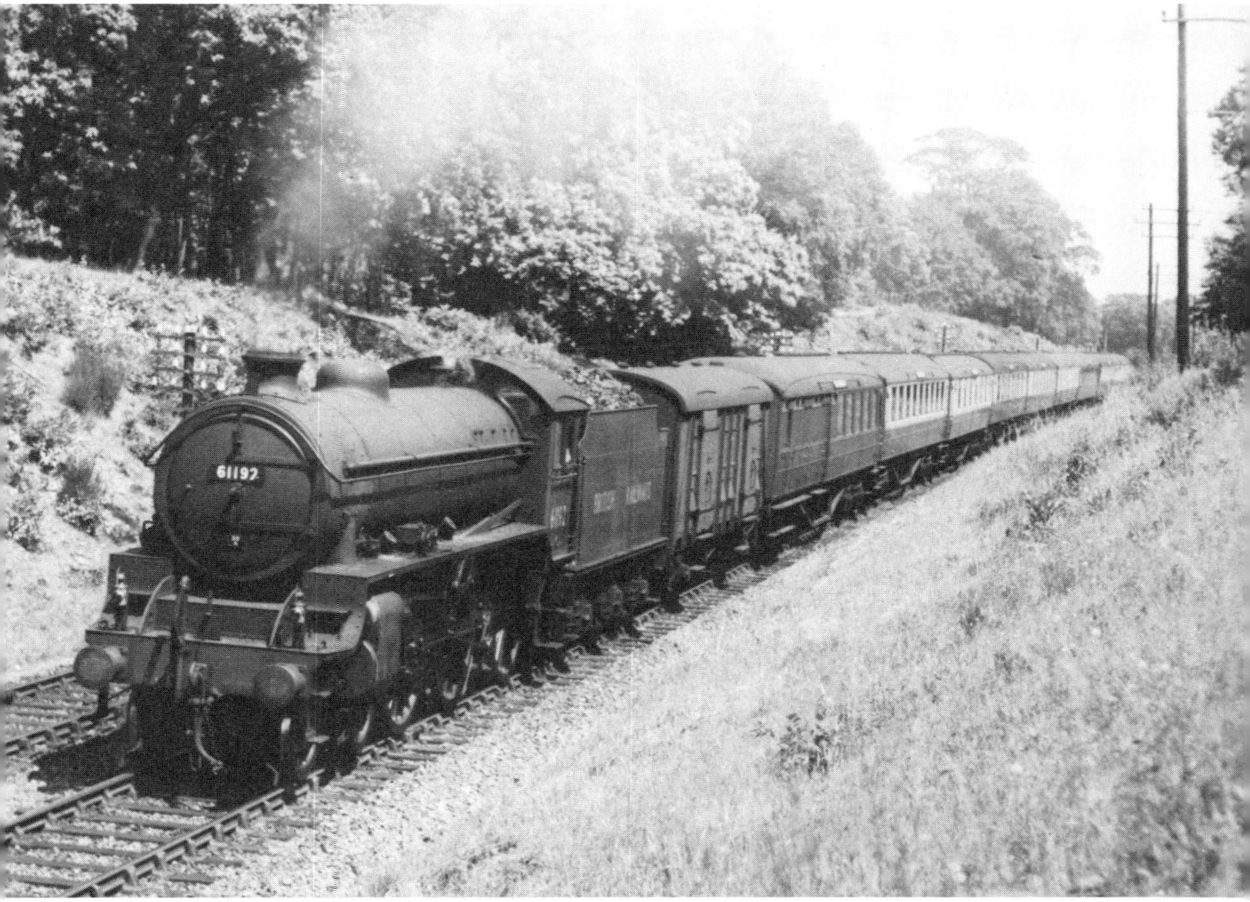
61192

61265

1E
78

NEW MILLS SOUTH JUNCTION

Top left: The through service between Harwich Parkeston Quay and the North was not officially named until 1983, when it became the 'European', but was long known as the 'North country Continental'. In this illustration the electric locomotive that has brought the train from Sheffield via the Woodhead Tunnel has handed it over at Guide Bridge to 'B1' No 61265, and the train is on its way again to Manchester Central and Liverpool. *G. Richard Parkes*

Centre left: By 1966 the 'North Country Continental' had been curtailed to run between Manchester and Harwich, with diesel power throughout although still taking the electrified Woodhead route between Manchester and Sheffield. Class 37 No D6701 heads the eastbound service through Godley Junction on 3 June 1966. *F. Wilde*

Bottom left: Now diverted to the Midland route between Manchester and Sheffield, the 'North Country Continental' is eased over the points at New Mills South Junction by Class 40 No 40.019 on 9 June 1976. There will be a locomotive change at Sheffield. The line on the left from Cheadle is now freight only. *B. Watkins*

Top right: The 'Norseman' leaves York in August 1961 behind 'A4' Pacific No 60015 *Quicksilver*, bringing passengers who have crossed the North Sea to Tyne Commission Quay, Newcastle. *L. Metcalfe*

Centre right: The up 'Irish Mail' arrives at Chester on 20 August 1951 in the care of rebuilt 'Scot' No 46161 *Kings Own*. *P. M. Alexander*

Bottom right: No 46159 *The Royal Air Force* approaches No 2 platform at Euston with the up 'Ulster Express'. *F. Spencer Yeates*

Memories of the Great Central Section

From a point near the former Calvert station to Rothley on the section preserved by the present Great Central Railway the old GC main line has disappeared from the map. This was the route of the 'Sheffield Special', ancestor of the long-lived 3.20 down Manchester from Marylebone.

Above: In the mid-1930s 'Sandringham' 4-6-0s from the GE Section began to take turns with the ex-GC 'Director' class 4-4-0s on Marylebone-Manchester expresses, a foretaste of the 'Football' engines of the 'Sandringham' class built specifically for the GC route. No 2840 *Somerleyton Hall* heads the 3.20pm from Marylebone alongside the electrified Metropolitan Line tracks near Harrow-on-the-hill. *LPC*

Centre right: In BR days 'B1' class 4-6-0 No 1188 storms out of Marylebone with the 3.20pm.

Bottom right: Under BR auspices the GC Section had its first officially named trains. The 'South Yorkshireman' was a Marylebone-Bradford service here seen leaving Aylesbury on 7 August 1959 with 'Black Five' 4-6-0 No 45260. *M. Mitchell*

Scottish Inter-City

Several of the fast trains between Aberdeen and Glasgow by the ex-Caledonian main line received names. This is still an Inter-City service but after Perth the trains turn eastwards to join the East Coast Main Line, the Caledonian route through Forfar to Kinnaber Junction being closed.

Above: Standard 4-6-0 No 73006 heads the southbound 'Granite City' near Forteviot in May 1955. *W. J. V. Anderson*

Below: The 'Saint Mungo' passes the closed station at Robroyston on 23 February 1961 with 'A2' Pacific No 60528 *Tudor Minstrel* at the head. *S. Rickard*

New Power for LM 'Scots'

Steam still had several years to run when the first main line diesels made their debut. The changeover accelerated with completion of the first designs built under the modernisation plan of 1955.

Above: The famous LMS 'twins', Nos 10000 and 10001, pass Tring with the up 'Royal Scot' in 1950. *BR*

Centre left: Class 40s were still known as 'English Electric Type 4s' when they fulfilled the promise of Nos 10000 and 10001 by taking over principal LMR main line duties. One of the class passes Bushey Troughs with the down 'Royal Scot' in May 1962. *M. Pope*

Bottom left: Class 40 No D336 approaches Harrow & Wealdstone station with the northbound 'Caledonian' on 11 April 1961. *M. Edwards*

Above right: The northbound 'Mid-Day Scot' climbs towards Shap on 15 April 1965, lifted easily up the bank by D312. *Gerald T. Robinson*

Bottom right: A few weeks after electrification, Class 87 No 87.006 races southwards down Shap with the up 'Royal Scot', still named in the timetable but now one of the family of 'Electric Scots'. *Brian Morrison*

D312
87 006

Below: A new Anglo-Scottish service was introduced with electrification to Glasgow in 1974. Routed from Euston via Birmingham and giving a day-time journey to Inverness, the train was named the 'Clansman' although by that time the practice of naming on the LMR was virtually confined to keeping a few of the traditional names in being. In this view No 47.211 winds the 'Clansman' through the wooded slopes between Dunkeld and Pitlochry on 24 July 1979, having taken over from electric power in Mossend Yard on the outskirts of Glasgow. *Stephen Mason*

The North Briton

In the first decade of the present century competition between railways to secure passenger traffic was keen. It developed between individual railways and groups of railways working in association, because the more progressive companies were awakening to a realisation of their capacity to run fast — stirred up in the first place, no doubt, by the amazing exploits of the 1895 'Race to Aberdeen' — and were determined to develop this capacity in full measure.

This competitive idea, no doubt, was behind the decision of the North Eastern Railway, in conjunction with the North British, to put on a new train in the morning from Leeds to York, Newcastle and Edinburgh, with connections to Glasgow, Perth and Aberdeen; after five hours' turn-around time in the Scottish capital, it would return by the way it had come, and be back into Leeds the same night. The actual extension of the train's run to Glasgow came about in the year 1910. Such was the genesis of the train which in the spate of new train names was dubbed the 'North Briton'.

The competitor against which this train was to operate, needless to say, was the Midland, and the traffic angled for was that between the West Riding of Yorkshire and Edinburgh. From Leeds to Edinburgh via Newcastle is 230¼ miles, whereas the Midland and North British route via Carlisle was 211¼ miles; but the North Eastern had a great advantage over the rival in the matter of gradients. In addition the new train had a valuable function in getting West Riding businessmen and people from York into Newcastle by mid-morning, and in providing a fine fast mid-morning service from Newcastle to Edinburgh and beyond. Coming south, however, the new train ran too late to perform quite the same useful functions, and through its history it was never so heavily patronised from Newcastle to York and Leeds.

A timetable of 1904 shows the then 'North Briton' — at that time unnamed — as leaving Leeds New station at 8.50am, and running the 25½ miles to York in 35min. After an unaccountably long wait of 13min under the curved roof of the great station, the express then set out on a run which, all conditions considered, I am inclined to think must have required the fastest running in the whole of Great Britain at that period. For to cover the 80¾ miles from York to Newcastle Central (which, be it remembered, at that time required the use of the tortuous Gateshead connections and over the old High Level Bridge, for the King Edward Bridge was not yet open) the timetable allowed no more than 82min.

True, the line is beautifully straight and level from York to Darlington. But after that come the sharp ups-and-downs of North Durham, the severe slowing over Durham viaduct, the slow travelling at the end of the run as already mentioned, and possibly even then the first permanent way slowings due to pitfalls had begun to appear. It was not long before this 82min schedule began to be eased out, first to 84min and then by a wider margin, and it is significant that nothing so fast reappeared in North Eastern timetables until the coming of the first streamliner in 1935. But think of the difference — the seven-coach 'Silver Jubilee' with a big 4-6-2 capable of doing 90mph on the level with the greatest ease, and the NER R class 4-4-0 of 1904 with its five-coach load! Time in these early days was certainly kept, and it needed a most creditable performance.

At Newcastle Central the train was reversed and provided with a composite restaurant car and composite corridor brake for the remainder of the journey. The non-stop timing of 142min for the 124½ miles from Newcastle to Edinburgh was easily the fastest of the day, and brought the train into Waverley by 1.30pm. Here it remained until 6.25pm, when it started south again. After stopping in this direction at Berwick also, it reached Newcastle at 9.05pm, and dropped the dining car and its companion vehicles. Another additional stop in the southbound direction was Darlington; York was reached at 10.55pm, and Leeds, after a lengthy York wait of 15min, at the late hour of 11.45pm.

While the times of the 'North Briton' on its northbound journey changed relatively little throughout most of its history — except during the war periods and after, of course — on reinstatement after the first world war, to make the southbound service more attractive by doing away with excessively late arrivals, the starting time from Edinburgh was put forward by more than an hour. By 1910 the train was working through to and fro between Leeds and Glasgow, 277½ miles each way, or 555 miles over the double journey.

Moreover it had become a corridor restaurant car train throughout, and so far as I can trace, the restaurant cars and their staffs made a longer continuous journey in a single day than any other cars in Great Britain, serving breakfast, luncheon, tea and dinner.

By 1914 the 'North Briton' left Leeds at 9am, was in Edinburgh by 1.32pm (with 84min from York to Newcastle and 138min from there to Edinburgh); at 1.52pm, in charge of the North British, the train was continuing to Glasgow, where, after a wait from 3.08 to 5pm at Queen Street, it began its long return journey, in readiness to leave Edinburgh for the south at 6.25pm. Little improvement had been made in this direction, and the arrivals at York and Leeds, 11 and 11.58pm, were later than ever. From Leeds to Newcastle, northbound, the engine now was usually one of the large Worsdell R1 4-4-0s, with Atlantic haulage between Newcastle and Edinburgh.

By 1939 the 'North Briton' had increased considerably in weight, with additional coaches and modern stock. For a number of years a Neville Hill 'Shire' or 'Hunt' 4-4-0 would make a gallant effort with it to Newcastle, where a Pacific would take over; coming south, it was normally Pacific haulage from Edinburgh to York. This working had been transformed; Glasgow now was left at 4pm, not 5pm, and Edinburgh at 5.10pm, not 6.25pm; an additional stop was slipped in at Dunbar; Newcastle was reached at 7.41 and left at 7.48pm, and the train hurried on to York by running the 44.1 miles from Darlington in 43min start to stop. So York was reached at 9.22 instead of 11pm, and Leeds at 10pm instead of midnight — a vast improvement involving a total acceleration of 50min.

After the war the 'North Briton' (officially named in the 1949/50 timetable) earned the condsiderable distinction of being the first post-war train in Britain to get back to a mile-a-minute schedule — 44.1 miles from Darlington to York in 44min — while the October 1950 timetable showed a further cut to 43min, which demanded a start-to-stop average of 61.7mph. In the summer of 1952 the time was pared again to 42min, putting the average up to 63mph. This was done with a train of ten or eleven bogie vehicles, the normal formation in both directions.

The 1952-1953 winter timetable showed the 'North Briton' as leaving Leeds at its 1939 time of 9.05am, and York at 9.41am, with a fast run from there to Darlington, against the rising tendency of the road, in 46min. Newcastle was reached at 11.14am and left at 11.20am for a non-stop run to Edinburgh in 132min — 13min less than in 1939 and 6min less than 1914. Edinburgh thus was made by 1.32pm, and the train then was detained 18min at Waverley station. Arriving in Glasgow at 2.57pm, the 'North Briton' had a turnaround time of 63min before setting out on the return journey to Leeds at 4pm. Leaving Edinburgh at 5.14pm, and still with calls at Dunbar and Berwick, the express ran into Newcastle at 7.40pm, York at 9.20pm, and Leeds at 10.02pm, only 2min later than in 1939.

In the 1960s diesel haulage, usually by a Class 47 unit, made a considerable acceleration possible; also, in conformity with the principle of giving business executives the maximum time possible for the transaction of their affairs, the northbound run was earlier than in former years. The 'North Briton' now left Leeds City at 8.40am and York at 9.14am, with a fast run from there to Darlington, where a stop was still made, in 42min. A new stop was at Durham, and Newcastle was reached at 10.43am. After 4min here, the third stop additional to those of former days was at Dunbar (the 95.3 miles from Newcastle to Dunbar were covered in 92min), but the arrival at Edinburgh was at 12.51pm, so that even with five intermediate stops instead of two, the express was 34min faster from Leeds to Edinburgh than when it first ran. But the through running to and from Glasgow which continued for so many years had been abandoned; a diesel connection brought passengers into that city by 1.56pm, in 5hr 11min from Leeds. The southbound journey was not quite so fast; the 'North Briton', with a connection from Glasgow at 4pm, was away from Edinburgh at 5.08pm, and with the same stops as in the opposite direction reached Newcastle by 7.25pm, York by 9.05pm and Leeds by 9.45pm. The fastest sprint was over the 44.1 miles from Darlington to York in 39min, at 67.8mph.

In 1968 the 'North Briton' lost its name, along with several other trains, but the name was restored in 1972 and lasted until 1975 when the working was recast as a Leeds-Edinburgh-Dundee service. Later this service was extended to and from Aberdeen but in 1978 the last echo of the 'North Briton' disappeared when, with the rebuilding of East Coast services based on HST workings, the Leeds-Aberdeen train was cut back to run only between Leeds and York, with connections for Scotland at York.

The North Country Continental

A typical example of the enterprise of the one-time Great Eastern Railway, linked with its Continental services based on Parkeston Quay, was the connecting express to and from the Midlands and the North, inaugurated in 1885, which soon acquired the unofficial name of 'North Country Continental'. It was one of the first long-distance cross-country trains to be put into service in Great Britain, and one of the first British trains, also, to be provided with restaurant car accommodation. Indeed it is believed to have been the very first train in the country on which, from July 1891, third class passengers were admitted to the exclusive precincts of a 'dining saloon'. The dining cars in question were six-wheelers, for at that early date the GER had done little or nothing towards the construction of bogie stock.

In 1906 a modern corridor train was completed at Stratford Works for this service. It consisted of a set of six cars (including composite kitchen car, and adjacent open third and semi-open first) with a six-wheel brake for the Harwich-York section, which was the main part of the train; two bogie vehicles for Manchester and two more for Liverpool; and two at the rear end for Birmingham. Going north, the 'North Country Continental' left Parkeston Quay just after 7am, and took the northern spur at Manningtree to reach Ipswich. From here the Norwich main line was followed to Haughley, where the train diverged westwards to Bury St Edmunds, and then followed a single line from a point just east of Newmarket to Ely. A short run across the Fens brought the train into March, where the first division took place. The two rear cars were detached, to continue to Peterborough, and from there over the LNWR through Market Harborough to Rugby and Birmingham.

From March the 'North Country Continental' had an almost dead level spin for many miles through Lincolnshire, through Spalding and Sleaford to Lincoln, where a second division took place. The Liverpool and Manchester coaches were worked forward from Lincoln by the then Great Central Railway, travelling on separate trains from Sheffield. The main section of the train went on through Gainsborough to Doncaster, where it joined the Great Northern main line, and from there to York. Great Eastern locomotives were used throughout; by the time the new train came into use in 1906, 'Claud Hamilton' 4-4-0 engines were available for its haulage. For a short time, about 1903 and 1904, a connecting express ran from Lincoln over the Lancashire, Derbyshire & East Coast Railway via Langwith, Clowne, and the Sheffield District Railway, into the Midland station at Sheffield. This carried also a through coach for Manchester Central, which continued from Sheffield over the Midland Dore & Chinley line.

As far as Black Carr Junction, Doncaster, the GER engines were working over their own right-of-way, for this far-seeing company was responsible with the GNR for building the Great Northern & Great Eastern Joint Line between Huntingdon, March, Lincoln and Doncaster; north of that point, running powers were exercised over the Great Northern and North Eastern Railways to reach York. Actually, GER locomotives made four daily appearances in York, as at that time there were three express trains daily in each direction between Liverpool Street, London and York via Cambridge and the so-called 'Cathedral Route'.

Now leaving Parkeston Quay at 7.02am, the 'North Country Continental' deposited its passengers in Birmingham at 12.11pm, Manchester at 1.38pm, Liverpool at 2.45pm and York at 12.32pm, in nice time to connect with the northbound 'Flying Scotsman'. In the southbound direction, the train left York at 4pm, picked up at Lincoln the coaches which had left Liverpool at 2.30pm and Manchester at 3.20pm, and at March those which had worked out of Birmingham at 4pm, and arrived at Parkeston Quay at 9.35pm, just ahead of the boat trains from London. One set of stock thus sufficed for the double journey each day (except for the Manchester and Liverpool coaches), and made by far the longest daily run of any Great Eastern train.

On the revival of the Great Eastern Continental services after the 1914-1919 war, the working of the 'North Country Continental' was somewhat modified. The restaurant cars were transferred to the Manchester and Liverpool sections, which in both directions were amalgamated and altered to travel via Manchester Central. A through York section of the train was worked between Lincoln and York in each direction, and the through Birmingham coaches were still detached and attached at March.

In the course of years there was little change in the running times of this train. From its earlier 7.02am departure, the 'North Country Continental' was later altered to start at 7.25am. With identical stops — at Ipswich, Bury St Edmunds, March and Spalding, and a new one at Sleaford — Lincoln was reached at 11.20am as compared with the 10.56am of the earlier years. The York section left at 11.27am, called at Doncaster from 12.16 to 12.20pm, and then had the singular distinction of travelling to York by way of Knottingley — the original main line from London to York before the direct line through Selby had been built — including the use of LMSR metals between Shaftholme Junction and Knottingley.

This was done to keep the 'Continental', when running late, out of the way of the accelerated 'Flying Scotsman', which latterly was due in York as early as 1.15pm, only 9min after the former train. But the 'North Country Continental' was 11min slower from Parkeston Quay to York in 1939 than it had been in 1914, 25 years earlier. Actually a through composite brake for Glasgow was run in the York portion, but as its passengers could save hours by changing into the 'Flying Scotsman' at York, it worked north as ordinary stock, ready for return as a through Glasgow-Harwich coach on the following morning.

Meantime, the Liverpool restaurant car portion got away from Lincoln at 11.32am, stopped at Worksop, Sheffield and Guide Bridge, and reached Manchester Central at 1.55pm, and Liverpool Central at 2.43pm — an acceleration of 25min over the 1914 times to Liverpool. One of the most remarkable through cross-country locomotive workings in the country was made by this train, for a 3-cylinder 4-6-0 of the B17 ('Sandringham') class took it over at Ipswich and worked it right through, for 216 miles, to Manchester — a continuous journey of 5¾hr with unchanged engine-crew, varying in characteristics from the extraordinary flatness of the Fen country to an altitude of all but 1,000ft above the sea on entering Woodhead tunnel; and from the quietude of a single-line country branch to the teeming manufacturing areas of Sheffield and Manchester.

Although the train set and the restaurant car staff ran on into Liverpool, they did not remain there for the night. For in order to utilise the stock to the best advantage, each afternoon the train was used to form the 4pm express from Liverpool to Hull, via Sheffield and Doncaster, reaching Hull Paragon at 7.34pm. And it was from Hull, at 8.55 in the morning, that the stock of the 'North Country Continental' set out as a breakfast car train to Liverpool, this time avoiding Manchester by taking the direct line from Godley to Glazebrook, and reaching Liverpool at 12.30pm, before taking up its real Continental duties at 2.20 in the afternoon. The first constituent of the southbound 'North Country Continental' to get on the move, however, was the through Glasgow coach, coming out of Queen Street terminus at 8.35am. On reaching Edinburgh, this was attached to the 10.15am train, following the 'Flying Scotsman', and brought into York at 2.18pm, where it had a 72min wait before the York section of the 'Continental' started.

From Manchester Central at 3.10pm and York at 3.30pm, the two main portions of the train converged at Lincoln, arriving at 5.20pm and 5.15pm respectively. An ample stop for marshalling was made here, with a departure at 5.32pm and a non-stop run to Spalding, for there was no halt at Sleaford in this direction. At March the two coaches from Birmingham were attached, and the complete train then pursued its sedate cross-country course to Ipswich, where the locomotive, which had been in continuous steaming from leaving Manchester at 3.10 until 8.37pm, was detached, and replaced by another of the same type for the short final stage. Parkeston Quay was reached at 9.12pm, and Harwich at 9.25pm. Between Harwich and Hull, via Liverpool, the main restaurant car train travelled 406 miles daily. In summer months the 'North Country Continental' frequently loaded to 13 or 14 bogie vehicles between Harwich and March, and at weekends required duplication.

Many changes have befallen the 'North Country Continental' since the 1939-1945 war. In the matter of route, there was no longer a direct line from Lincoln to Retford; the train therefore took the former Great Northern & General Eastern line as far as the crossing of the Trent at Gainsborough, joining there the one-time Great Central main line from Grimsby to Sheffield. At Retford it was soon no longer necessary to traverse the sharp curves through the station, as the flyunder opened in 1966 could be taken at speed. At Sheffield there was a change from diesel to electric power for the climb to Woodhead Tunnel and the descent to Manchester where the train ran into Piccadilly Station instead of as formerly into Central. This meant that there was no longer any through working to Liverpool, although during the summer season a connecting diesel multiple-unit was run between Manchester Piccadilly and Liverpool Lime Street. Also York no longer had a through service; during the summer season passengers for York and Newcastle could change at Lincoln into the following 8am Colchester-Newcastle train, and during the rest of the year into a train run specially from Lincoln to Newcastle at 11.42am.

Departure of the 'North Country Continental', still a restaurant car train, became 7.20am from Harwich Town and 7.40am from Parkeston Quay, 10min ahead of the 'Hook Continental'. Stops were still made at

Ipswich, Stowmarket, Bury St Edmunds, Ely, March, Spalding and Sleaford to Lincoln, reached at 11.19am, where there was a halt of 5min. After calling at Worksop the train was into Sheffield by 12.38pm, where 4min sufficed to change from diesel to electric power on the 1,500V dc Woodhead route. The running on to Manchester was far faster than in steam days, and with both Penistone and Guide Bridge stops Piccadilly was reached by 1.43pm. The Liverpool passengers then had to wait no less than 37min for their summer connection, which did not get them into Lime Street until 3.10pm; but that was because the same diesel unit was used to make the eastbound connection also, leaving Liverpool at 1.15pm and getting into Manchester Piccadilly at 2.15pm. Here a wait of 27min was needed before the departure of the 'North Country Continental' at 2.42pm.

The same stops were made on the southbound as on the northbound run; the former was a little the faster of the two, and got its passengers to Parkeston Quay at 8.41pm, 39min ahead of the 'Hook Continental', and into Harwich Town at 8.55pm. Thus almost exactly six hours were spent between Parkeston Quay and Manchester. At the expense of crossing London between Liverpool Street and Euston it was possible to reach Manchester by the 'Hook Continental' and one of the fast London Midland electrics in 4hr 50min, and to return as late as 5pm by the 'Manchester Pullman' and the 'Hook Continental' in 4hr 20min.

Late in the 1960s it was decided that the changeover to electric traction at Sheffield cost more than any saving in energy costs and the train was worked throughout between Harwich and Manchester by a Class 37 diesel. For a time the 'North Country Continental' was the only regular passenger service running the whole length of the Woodhead route. On 5 January 1970 Sheffield Victoria was closed to all traffic and the train was re-routed via Sheffield Midland and the Hope Valley line to Manchester Piccadilly. In the 1973-74 timetable the train was diverted from the GN&GE Joint route it had followed from its earliest days and from March was sent to Peterborough, then by the East Coast main line to Grantham, across to Nottingham, and into Sheffield from the south. This change involved reversal at Sheffield. The time came down to 5hr 39min northbound but the southbound train was allowed 6hr 2min.

There was yet another change in the eventful history of the 'North Country Continental' in May 1983. The train was extended to serve Glasgow and Edinburgh, being switched from Manchester Piccadilly to Manchester Victoria and continuing via Bolton to the West Coast main line at Preston. It now consisted of a six-coach portion, including buffet car, for Glasgow, and five coaches for Edinburgh. The train was formed throughout of Mk 2 air-conditioned stock.

The North Eastern

Not until the autumn of 1904 did the Great Northern and North Eastern Railways decide that the time had come for passengers from London to York, Tees-side and Newcastle to have at their disposal a later afternoon departure than the 2.20pm Edinburgh train. True, the 6.15pm down Bradford express had a connection from Doncaster which reached York by 10.15pm, but not until 24min after midnight did any wearied passengers for Newcastle find themselves in the Tyneside city. So the announcement of a new express from King's Cross at 5.30pm, to be into York by 9.05pm and Newcastle by 10.42pm, completing the journey in 5hr 12min as compared with 6hr 9min, not surprisingly received a warm welcome in North Eastern England. It was the beginning of a long history, although the train did not receive its name until 60 years later and then carried it only for a few years.

The new service did not require completely new mileage. For many years past the Great Northern and Midland Railways had been competing for the traffic between London, Nottingham and Sheffield; there was still some competition also between the Great Northern and London & North Western for the patronage of London-Manchester passengers, the GNR exercising running powers for this purpose over the Manchester, Sheffield & Lincolnshire line from Retford to Manchester. Then, with the opening in 1899 of its London Extension, the MS&LR became the Great Central Railway, the GNR opposition to the extension having been withdrawn on condition that the two companies jointly built Nottingham Victoria station, and that the GCR granted the GNR running powers over its line from Nottingham to Sheffield. From then on, certain GNR Manchester trains that had been routed via Retford transferred to the Nottingham route, and among them the 5.30pm down. So it was that to this express there was attached, as far as Grantham, a portion for Newcastle.

By now the Manchester train had shrunk to no more than three coaches, including a restaurant car, and at first the Newcastle portion was of no more than four coaches, the whole making up a train of about 250 tons. Passengers in the Newcastle portion desiring dinner thus had to obtain their meal before Grantham. But the Newcastle section of the train soon became by far the more popular of the two, and by 1905 had acquired its own dining facilities; for a time both sections of the train had their own restaurant cars, but in the summer of 1905 the GNR put on a new Sheffield and Manchester express at 6.10pm, travelling via Retford and running the 161½ miles from King's Cross to Sheffield non-stop in 170min. From that time onwards the Manchester portion of the 5.30pm down was terminated at Nottingham; as its restaurant car was required for an up morning working it continued to run in the formation for a year or so, but later the Nottingham portion shrunk to a single 12-wheel composite coach, and finally disappeared altogether.

The first restaurant car set working in the 5.30pm from King's Cross from 1905 onwards was a six-coach formation of some rather ugly straight-sided stock which the North Eastern Railway was turning out of York Carriage Works at that time; ten coaches in all were built for joint Great Northern and North Eastern use. At first the 5.30pm had the fastest timings of all the East Coast expresses — 117min for the 105.5 miles from King's Cross to Grantham and 94min for the 82.7 miles thence to York, with GN motive power; then followed one of the two North Eastern Railway mile-a-minute schedules — extremely rare in those days — 44min for the 44.1 miles from York to Darlington, followed by 42min for the 36 miles from Darlington to Newcastle. An additional stop, at Durham, was soon introduced, and the time from London to Newcastle then became 5¼hr. At that time the 8.15 and 11.30pm down sleeping car expresses were both allowed only 5hr 12min from King's Cross to Newcastle, but these were non-stop between York and the Tyneside city.

By 1904 the large-boilered Ivatt Atlantics were in service, and one of these usually headed the 5.30pm from King's Cross to Grantham. But from Grantham to York a variety of motive power was used — occasionally an Atlantic, but more often one of the 1330 class Ivatt 4-4-0s, or a 266 class 4-2-2; and on one unforgettable occasion I rode behind one of Patrick Stirling's 8ft single-drivers, which ran the 82.7 miles from Grantham to York in 93min 25sec touching just over 70mph before Newark. Later the Ivatt superheated 4-4-0s of the 51-65 series appeared on the scene, and often worked the train over this section.

At York it was a striking contrast to be taken over by one of Wilson Worsdell's V class Atlantics for the run on to Newcastle, though these massive machines never showed themselves capable of any better performances than one of the same designer's R class 4-4-0s which also appeared on the train from time to time. In the up direction at first the running was nothing like as fast; the train left Newcastle at 7.40am and with many more intermediate stops was not into King's Cross until 2.20pm — a journey of 6hr 40min. But shortly afterwards the starting time was altered to 8am, all stops were cut out other than those made in the down direction, and London was reached by 1.30pm, an acceleration of 70min.

So matters continued until World War 1 laid its heavy hand on all train services. By the time of the Armistice the 5.30pm down was being allowed 133min to reach Grantham, 102min from there to York, 57min on to Darlington (including a stop at Northallerton), and, with the Durham stop, 50min from Darlington to Newcastle, with an arrival at 11.25pm. Coming up with the same stops to York and after that at Doncaster and Peterborough, a 7.50am start and 2.15pm arrival had the overall time roughly at its 1904 level. Restaurant cars of course had been withdrawn; their first reappearance was in 1919, when a North Eastern dining car was attached to the down train at Doncaster, and provided breakfast in the up train as far as that point; but full restaurant car service was soon restored, and by 1923 the express was practically back to its prewar schedule.

These times remained with but little alteration until 1921, when H. A. Watson, the then General Superintendent of the North Eastern Railway, had the curious hunch that too many of the East Coast trains were stopping at York, and decided that the 2.20 and 5.30pm from King's Cross should both cease to call at the passenger station, but should stop instead at Clifton Junction, just north of it, to change engines. The same applied to the 8am from Newcastle to London. By 1923 both the GNR and the NER had become swallowed up in the London & North Eastern Railway, and it was ruled accordingly that the run of 126.8 miles in each direction between Grantham and Darlington should be made non-stop. This meant that Gateshead engine-crews had to work south as far as Grantham with the up train, and from Grantham to Newcastle with the down — a distinctly uneconomic arrangement which meant the engine remaining idle at Grantham for 8hr, while engine crews had to travel as passengers from Grantham after the up run, and to travel south as passengers to Grantham to take over the down run.

By now the 5.30pm down had grown to a 9-coach

formation of 265 tare tons. It was clear that the North Eastern drivers liked the Great Northern main line, and proceedings on the northbound run got steadily faster until one evening when I was on the train, with NER Z class 4-4-2 No 721 at the head, we passed Selby, 68.85 miles from the Grantham start, in 65min 5sec, no less than 12min early! True, the allowance of 142min for the 126.8 miles from Grantham to Darlington was ridiculously easy, but on this particular night the driver of No 721 had overdone things to such an extent that his engine had to come off the train at York with a hot bearing.

By 1928 there came a modest acceleration, despite the considerable weight to which the train had now grown — a minimum of 11 and often 12 or 13 coaches, of from 335 to 405 tons tare and 355 to 430 tons gross. The allowance for the 105.5 miles from King's Cross to Grantham came down to 114min, and from Grantham to Darlington to 138min; by now, of course, Pacific haulage was standard throughout. In 1931 the decision was reached to reinstate the York stop, but not until 1932 did there come about a real improvement in the schedule. This brought the time from King's Cross to Grantham down to 112min, the 82.7 miles from Grantham to York had to be covered in 89min, and with a smaller speed-up north of York, Newcastle was reached at 10.37pm, the earliest yet.

But the year 1935 was to see the most revolutionary of all changes in the working of the 5.30pm down, and to demote it from its proud position. For on 30 September of that year its starting time in the down direction was taken by the new streamlined 'Silver Jubilee', which at one stroke cut the London-Newcastle time down to 4hr, and had to reach its only stop, Darlington, at 70.4mph average in 198min for the 232.3 miles from King's Cross. Up till then there had been a 5.45pm from King's Cross to Hull, and with this the former 5.30pm was amalgamated, which made necessary a Doncaster stop; the Grantham-Doncaster run came into the mile-a-minute category, 50.5 miles in 50min start-to-stop. But until now the North Eastern Area had not got the York-Darlington run down again to its former 44min; this still took 47min, and Newcastle was not reached until 10.55pm, in an overall time of 5hr 10min, only 5min faster than that of 1904. The up schedule, however, was better; the train was now leaving Newcastle at 8.15am, and with stops at Durham, Darlington, York and Grantham was into London by 1.15pm, in 5hr exactly, including a 43min sprint over the 44.1 miles from Darlington to York.

Once again, in 1939, war intervened. At first evening passengers to the North East Coast had to be content with a 4pm from King's Cross, serving a number of destinations and taking 7hr to Newcastle; then, in January 1940 a separate 5pm to Newcastle reappeared, making the normal stops of the former 5.30 and reaching its destination at 10.50pm; a corresponding 8am from Newcastle was into King's Cross by 1.55pm. By the end of the war, however, the service had degenerated badly; although the express, once again at 5.30pm from King's Cross, reached York by 9.50pm, it was not until 2½hr later, after numerous intermediate stops, that it made its weary way into Newcastle Central. The up journey was somewhat less tedious; the 8.05am from Newcastle called only at Durham, York and Grantham, and was into King's Cross by 2.05pm, while it was relieved by an 8.50am from Darlington, stopping at York and Peterborough and due in London 15min earlier.

Recovery after World War 2 was much slower than after the first. Rumours in 1948 that the 'Silver Jubilee' was to take the rails once again proved to be unfounded; 13 years to the day after the inaugural run of the 'Silver Jubilee' it was the 'Tees-Tyne Pullman' that started out of King's Cross at 5.30pm, again non-stop to Darlington, but taking 5hr 20min to Newcastle as compared with the 4hr of the 'Jubilee'. The former 5.30pm down was therefore altered to start at 5.35pm.

Various changes now succeeded one another, chiefly in the realm of acceleration. In 1959, during the short-lived reign of the 'Tees-Thames' restaurant car train from Saltburn to King's Cross, the 8am from Newcastle omitted its York stop, and called instead at Doncaster to pick up a through portion from Hull to London; later came a non-stop 60mph run from Darlington to Peterborough. In 1962 there was an acceleration by 23min of the 5.35pm down, from now on booked into Newcastle by 10.40pm. In the autumn of the same year the through Middlesborough and Saltburn portion of the 5.35pm down was withdrawn. One of the biggest changes was reserved for 1963, when 'Deltic' diesels had become available for the haulage of this popular express. In the up direction it was altered to leave Newcastle at 7.50am, to call only at Durham and Darlington and to be into King's Cross by 12.05pm. Northbound, the starting time was changed from 5.35pm to 6.05pm, the Peterborough stop was cut out, and a 3hr timing was laid down for the 188.2 mile run from King's Cross to York, Newcastle being reached by 10.38pm, an acceleration of 32min. By 1964 the Newcastle arrival was even earlier, at 10.31pm, and in that year the decision was reached to confer the name 'North Eastern' on this express and its opposite number.

One might have thought that the ultimate in speed had been reached by 1966, with the down 'North Eastern', at 6.10pm from King's Cross, taking no more than 163min to York — 69.3mph — and a time of 4¼hr to Newcastle with three stops, but not so. Also by now the two-stop up 'North Eastern' was completing the journey in 4hr 5min; and both trains were permitted to load up to 400 tons. But 1967 saw a climax, for the 'North Eastern' was promoted to the ranks of the new eight-coach 'Deltic'-hauled flyers. So, northbound, it now left King's Cross at 6pm for a run timed at 73.4mph to Darlington — 232.3 miles in 190min — and with the Durham stop still continued was into the Tyneside city by 9.55pm. In the reverse direction there was an even faster (3hr 50min) journey to London, now starting from Newcastle as early as 7.25am, with no Durham stop and also with a time of 190min from Darlington, so bringing its passengers into London as early as 11.15 in the morning.

In 1968 the 6pm down was distinguished in the timetable by a laconic 'High Speed' instead of the more descriptive 'North Eastern' title, which was not revived. Instead the service has continued into the HST era as the 'Newcastle Executive'.

The Northern Irishman

While the boat service between Stranraer and Larne has always provided the quickest and most direct route between Scotland and Ireland, and also between Tyneside and Northern Ireland, it has also been a considerable attraction to passengers between other parts of England and Northern Ireland because of the shortness of the sea passage across what often can be the very turbulent waters separating the two countries. Of the two-hour voyage between Stranraer and Larne Harbours, almost half is made in the sheltered waters of Loch Ryan, leaving little more than an hour of the open sea, though truth to tell a high north-westerly or south-easterly wind can make this short crossing exceedingly rough.

Access from Carlisle and the south to Stranraer at first was over the metals of the Glasgow & South Western Railway to Dumfries and Castle Douglas, and from there by the independent Portpatrick & Wigtownshire Railway, opened in 1862. In the following year, the Caledonian, which had just opened a branch from its main line at Lockerbie into Dumfries, took over the working of the PP&W, and so matters continued until 1885, when the Glasgow & South Western Railway, which in 1877 had completed its own line from Girvan to Stranraer, and all the time had been restless at the invasion of its territory by the Caledonian, came into part ownership of the PP&W, or, as it has always been known colloquially, the 'Port Road'. The Caledonian and the G&SW had a quarter share each, and the other owners were their English partners, the London & North Western and the Midland Railways.

At first the London & North Western showed no particular interest in the Stranraer route, as it had its own Belfast service via Holyhead and Greenore, and was directly interested also in the services via Liverpool and via Fleetwood. The Midland, however, soon was running a sleeping car express between St Pancras and Stranraer Harbour, which in the years up to World War 1 left St Pancras either at 8 or 8.15pm, with a restaurant car over the first stage of its journey, and provided a good late evening express to Leicester, Nottingham, Sheffield and Leeds as well as for Irish boat passengers.

With the Grouping, just as the Midland Heysham boat train eventually was transferred from St Pancras to Euston, so the same happened to the Stranraer boat train. Up to the second world war this went out of Euston at 7.40pm, as a second part of the 7.30pm Highland sleeper. During the war, the Stranraer route became an extremely important means of communication with Ireland, and for a time two sleeping car trains were run from Euston every evening, the first carrying through boat passengers only, and the second making the same intermediate stops as the old 7.40pm; but the time of departure from Euston had now become as early as 4.50pm, to allow a margin for delays en route.

After the war, as train services began to recover, it became possible to retard the start from London to 6.30pm; the stops were at Crewe, to detach the restaurant cars, Wigan, Preston, Carlisle and Dumfries, and Stranraer Harbour was reached at 4.25am. In the summer of 1951 the departure was made even later, at 7.55pm, and Stranraer Harbour was now reached at 5.45am. The following summer the name 'Northern Irishman' was given to this train. For the winter of 1952-1953 it was decided to combine the 'Northern Irishman' with the second, or Perth, portion of the 7.20pm Highland sleeper, starting at 7.30pm, so that the Stranraer service was back in time almost exactly where it was before World War 2. Arrival at Stranraer Harbour was still at 5.45am. After their introduction, the standard Class 6 light Pacifics were used to work this train over the extremely hard gradients of the 'Port Road'.

The year 1965 brought about a remarkable change in the routing of the 'Northern Irishman', and this resulted from the closing down of the Portpatrick & Wigtownshire line. The only alternative route possible was by way of the former Glasgow & South Western main line as far as Mauchline, from there by a little used branch from Mauchline down to Ayr via Newtown-on-Ayr, and from Ayr over the coast line through Girvan to join the former route at Challoch Junction, not far short of Stranraer. This increased the distance between Dumfries and Stranraer from 73¾ to 133¼ miles; moreover, although there were formidable gradients on the PP&W line, including lengthy stretches of 1 in 80, they fell considerably short in steepness of the inclines that the 'Northern Irishman' now faced, such as the 1 in 54 up to Pinmore Tunnel, or the long 1 in 57 and 1 in 67 grades between Pinwherry and New Luce. In these circumstances it was quite creditable, when the change was made, that the Stranraer Harbour arrival of the train was no more than 35min later than before, and that with a departure from the Harbour at 10pm Carlisle was reached only 23min later, at 1.42am, though the Euston arrival at 8.30am was 40min later.

But the Euston-Crewe electrification changed all that from April 1966, onwards, though at the same time the boat train lost its name. Departure from Euston was at 8.40pm, and stops were made at Rugby, Nuneaton, Crewe and Wigan before Carlisle was reached at 2.18am. After calling at Dumfries, the train was then non-stop to Ayr (4.17-4.23am); there was also a stop at Girvan, and a final 70min run over the formidably-graded 37¾ miles between there and Stranraer Harbour. Returning at 10.10pm, the boat train was scheduled to Girvan in 62min, and the Ayr stop (11.43-11.49pm) provided Ayr residents with their first-ever sleeping car service to London, though an exit from the train soon after four in the morning was hardly much attraction in the opposite direction! Other stops were the same as in the down direction, with the addition of Bletchley, and what formerly was the 'Northern Irishman' came to rest at Euston at 7.42am, a journey almost exactly an hour shorter than when the diversion via Ayr was first made.

There was another drastic extension of the London-Stranraer boat train route in 1976 when the Mauchline-Newtown line was closed and the trains had to travel as far north as Kilmarnock before branching westward to join the line through Ayr. The overnight service corresponding to the 'Northern Irishman' was allowed 9hr 16min in 1982 but a day train was then running in summer and reached Stranraer Harbour in 8hr 18min from Euston.

The Peak Express and The Palatine

Before the Midland and London & North Western Railways came into the LMSR group in 1923, the competition between the two companies for the passenger traffic between London and Manchester was the subject of keen rivalry. There was little difference in length between the principal LNWR route via Crewe and the Midland via Derby — 189 and 190 miles respectively — but there was no comparison between the respective gradients.

Apart from the 1 in 75 climb out of Euston, the LNWR had hardly an inclination worth mention; whereas the Midland, save for the 44 level miles from Wigston to Ambergate, was severely graded throughout its length, and finally compelled its hard-worked locomotives to climb to an altitude of 980ft above sea level at Peak Forest, in the heart of the Peak area of Derbyshire. But the ride through the superb Derbyshire scenery, from Ambergate past Millers Dale to Chinley and beyond, together with the characteristic excellence of Midland rolling stock and catering, were factors that influenced many regular travellers in favour of the Midland route.

The dignified and deliberate LNWR had managed to get its best trains down to a run of 3½hr between Euston and Manchester, though for the most part its times ranged between 3hr 40 and 50min. Nevertheless the Midland, even if the lightness of its trainloads be admitted, by 1904 was nearly tying with the 'Premier Line' with overall schedules of 3hr 35 to 40min, despite the formidable difficulties of its route. The best Midland trains could not afford the time to stop at Derby, and avoided that town by the Chaddesden curve, stopping only at Leicester on the northbound journey; coming south, in different years there were non-stop runs over the 175.1 miles from Chinley, and even the 186.9 miles from Cheadle Heath to St Pancras, in both cases via the Dore and Chinley line and Chesterfield. Indeed, in the summer of 1914, after the opening of the Midland Adelphi Hotel at Liverpool, on Friday evenings the Midland ran a non-stop express at 6.10pm from St Pancras to Liverpool, using the Cheshire Lines system from Cheadle Heath, and taking only 4hr 10min for the 217¾ miles.

After the Grouping, the competitive urge between the two routes no longer existed, but in the years before World War 2, the LMSR began to realise the advantage of the Midland route as helping to relieve the busy Western Division main line, and accelerated the trains between St Pancras and Manchester to an extent that restored the best times of competitive days. Derby had now become too important an industrial centre to miss, and halts at Leicester and Derby were both a 'must' on every run, while stops at Chinley were added in the case of certain trains carrying through portions to and from Liverpool.

In the further outbreak of LMSR train naming which took place in 1938, two trains between St Pancras and Manchester Central received appropriate titles. In the down direction the 10.30am from St Pancras became the 'Peak Express' and the 4.30pm the 'Palatine'. In later Midland days the principal down Manchester expresses had all been arranged to leave London at 25min past the hour — in fact, they had become known unofficially as the 'Twenty-Fives' — but in the accelerations of October 1937 the starting times were altered to the even half-hour in each case. In the reverse direction the 'Palatine' was a morning express from Manchester Central, at 10am, and the 'Peak Express' provided the principal afternoon departure at 4.25pm.

The down 'Peak Express' was the fastest train of the day between St Pancras and Manchester, and despite an additional Derby stop restored the 'crack' 3hr 35min time of Midland days. It began its journey with a mile-a-minute run to Leicester — 99.1 miles in 99min. Practically the same speed was required on to Derby — 29.4 miles in 30min. With 4min at Leicester and 5min at Derby, the train had 77min left for the exceedingly difficult 61.5 miles from Derby over the Peak Forest summit to Manchester. In 1939, however, this train was slowed down 21min by the addition of four stops between Derby and Manchester. The down 'Palatine' stopped at Bedford, and had an easier timing. To Leicester the allowance was 105min and from there to Derby 33min. Between Derby and Manchester there were stops at Matlock, Chinley and Cheadle Heath, and Manchester Central was not reached till 8.26pm, in 3hr 56min from St Pancras.

Coming up, the 10am 'Palatine', with a Cheadle Heath stop, reached Derby at 11.26am, and left 7min later on a 31min run to Leicester. From Leicester to St Pancras the standard 60mph 90min time was allowed, and London was reached at 1.48pm, in 3hr 48min from Manchester. The southbound 'Peak Express' at 4.25pm ran non-stop to Derby in 78min, called at Loughborough, Leicester and Luton, and was due in St Pancras at 8.12pm, a journey of 3hr 47min.

For the Manchester workings generally, a standard set of cars would be third class brake, two corridor thirds, third restaurant and kitchen, open first restaurant, and first brake, six coaches in all, with an additional two attached for part of the journey, such as the Manchester Victoria portion of the down 'Peak Express', the Liverpool portion on the up and down 'Palatines', and the Manchester-Leicester additional accommodation on the up 'Peak Express'. The down 'Palatine' was usually a 7-coach train as far as Chinley and six from there to Manchester. Locomotive power over the Midland had been transformed by the coming of the Stanier 4-6-0s, and without their help it would not have been possible to work such loads over such a route in these times. It was customary to use a 'Jubilee' 4-6-0 between St Pancras and Derby, and a Class 5 4-6-0 between there and Manchester, until certain bridges at Chapel-en-le-Frith had been rebuilt, after which the 'Jubilees' could work through.

World War 2 made havoc of the Midland Manchester services, and lengthened the overall times between St Pancras and Manchester Central to between 5¼ and 5¾hr. No recognisable trace of either the 'Peak Express' or the 'Palatine' remained until the new timetable of October 1946, when three of the workings reappeared, but nameless. They were at 10.15am and 4.15pm from St Pancras, and 4pm from Manchester Central. Journey times ranged from 4hr 18 to 38min. There were no longer any through portions to and from Liverpool.

In subsequent years times over this route gradually improved, but it was not until the 2,500hp 'Peak' diesels had taken over from steam, and in particular after the bulk of the London Midland London-Manchester traffic had been turned over from the North Western to the Midland line, while the electrification of the former was proceeding, that the latter really came into its own. Over the Peak Forest summit, between Derby and Manchester, the loads of the fastest trains were limited to nine coaches (320 tons), but other expresses were allowed to take up to 11 coaches north of Derby, and south of that point considerably greater loads than this. By 1957 the name 'Peak Express' had disappeared, but in that year the name 'Palatine' was revived, and conferred on the 7.55am from St Pancras to Manchester (later 8.05pm). The train returned from Manchester at 2.25pm, and for some time followed the ordinary route via Leicester, reaching St Pancras at 6.10pm.

But in 1962 this train was diverted via Nottingham, and this was such a popular service that when the full load had been made up at Derby the 'Peak' diesel had to handle 13 coaches, or on a Friday evening no fewer than 14, with a tare weight of 470 tons and a gross load of over 500 tons, on an allowance of no more than 126min for the 123.5 miles from Nottingham with a 3min stop at Kettering included. I once timed the express in these conditions, when our net time for the 72 miles up from Kettering was no more than 62min — an astonishing performance. With the diversion, the start from Nottingham was at 4.24pm; St Pancras was reached at 6.30pm. During this period several Manchester expresses once again by-passed Derby by the Chaddesden Curve, and the fastest St Pancras-Manchester time (excluding the 'Midland Pullman'), with far heavier train loadings than in former years, came down to 3hr 35min in the case of the 9.25am from St Pancras — the temporary Midland replacement of Euston's 'Comet'.

The glory of the Midland route lasted until April 1966 when the inauguration of the Euston electrification reduced the once famous Midland Manchester main line to no more than secondary route status. Only three trains were left in each direction between St Pancras and Manchester, each with 11 or 12 intermediate stops, and though their point-to-point timings were extremely sharp, especially between London and Derby, their overall times were 4hr or slightly over. In 1968 all services from Derby were diverted to Manchester Piccadilly. The old main line through the Peak District became a branch from Derby to Matlock only and such St Pancras-Manchester through workings as survived travelled via Sheffield. By 1981 there was no more than one down and two up through trains on Sundays only calling at all principal stations. In the following year even these disappeared.

The Pines Express

From 1904 onwards, when the first through coaches were arranged by the London & North Western and London, Brighton & South Coast Railways to run between Liverpool, Manchester and Brighton, a keen competition began between a number of railways and continued for years with numerous new developments, to provide through service between the great cities of Merseyside and the Midlands and the South, South-East and South-West coasts. Thus the Great Western and London & South Western inaugurated a new restaurant car express between Birkenhead and Bournemouth, and the GWR, by virtue of its right of access to Manchester either via Crewe or via Warrington, in 1910 began to run a through section of this train to and from Manchester London Road, by the Crewe route, connecting with the main train at Wellington.

This was too much for the London & North Western, and as a result of negotiations with the Midland, the precursor of the 'Pines Express' came into service in October 1910. It was arranged to use LNWR metals between Manchester and Birmingham, and between these cities it provided a useful new express, with a time of 1¾hr from Birmingham to Manchester — the fastest that had been known up to that time. From New Street in Birmingham it was worked by the Midland Railway to Bath — and, incidentally, to avoid reversal travelled out of the east end of New Street and via Camp Hill to King's Norton — while at Bath the Somerset & Dorset Joint Railway (Midland and London & South Western) took charge for the final stage of the journey.

After suspension during World War 1, the train was reinstated much in its old times, and received the title of 'Pines Express' in 1927. It became even more exclusively LMSR in 1930, when this company took over the provision of motive power on the Somerset & Dorset Joint Line, which previously had its own independent locomotives. The only stretch of purely 'foreign' territory traversed was 7¾ miles of Southern metals from Broadstone through Poole into Bournemouth.

By 1939 the main restaurant car section of the southbound 'Pines Express' was leaving Manchester London Road at 10.10am, and at Crewe was picking up a four-coach set for Birmingham, and through coaches for both Bournemouth and Southampton, which had left Liverpool Lime Street at 9.40am. The combined train was due away from Crewe at 10.49am, and — most unusually for an express — was booked to take the slow road to Stafford, through which it passed on the west side of the station. This was to avoid fouling the path of the up 'Merseyside Express', due through Crewe at 10.57am, and the result often was a race from Whitmore down to Stafford, if the 'Pines' was behind time. The latter stopped next at Wolverhampton, and then ran across into the Midland Division side at Birmingham New Street, arriving at 12.02 noon. Here the four-coach set from Liverpool was detached, and a Midland Division locomotive took charge of the remainder, usually about six for Bournemouth, one of which was a through coach from Bradford, and the Southampton coach on the rear.

Departure from Birmingham was at 12.13pm, and

by 1.10pm the express was in Cheltenham, where the Southampton coach was detached; the latter was handed over to the Great Western Railway, to be worked over the one-time Midland & South Western Junction line through Swindon to Andover, and thence over the Southern to Southampton Terminus, arriving at 5.05pm. The main train stopped next at Gloucester, and then had 48min for the $41\frac{3}{4}$ miles to Bath. In the Queen Square station at Bath reversal was necessary.

After Bath came the locomotive tug-of-war, for the tremendous gradients through the Mendips had to be tackled. One result of the LMSR assumption of locomotive responsibility was the introduction between Bath and Bournemouth of the ubiquitous and capable Class 5 4-6-0s, which greatly eased the power problem. Beginning at Bath Junction, there was first a 2-mile climb at 1 in 50 to the north portal of Combe Down tunnel; again from beyond Radstock there were 3 miles up at 1 in 50, followed by another 4 miles almost as steeply inclined to the summit at Masbury, and then by a descent to Evercreech Junction which for 7 miles also was largely at 1 in 50. From Templecombe to Blandford the line was single-track, which, though equipped for automatic tablet-changing, involved slacks through the station loops. In the circumstances, 2hr 17min for the $71\frac{1}{2}$ miles from Bath to Bournemouth West, with four intermediate stops, was not bad going. The total time for the run of 252 miles from Manchester to Bournemouth, reached at 4.37pm, was 6hr 27min.

Northbound, the 'Pines Express' left Bournemouth West at 10.35am, and with six intermediate stops made the better time of 2hr 5min to Bath. Departure from Bath was at 12.44pm, from Gloucester at 1.37pm, and from Cheltenham (where the 'Pines' picked up from the GWR the through coach which had made its way out of Southampton Terminus at 10.10am) at 1.51pm. From here a fast run was made to Bromsgrove, 31.1 miles in 31min, at just over a mile a minute. The Bromsgrove stop was necessary for taking banking assistance up the formidable Lickey incline, which climbs two miles at 1 in $37\frac{3}{4}$ up to Blackwell. From King's Norton the direct line was taken into Birmingham, via Selly Oak, and this meant that the train passed through New Street in the same direction — from west to east — on both southbound and northbound journeys, and even used the same platform at that station.

To avoid reversal in this direction, the Western Division locomotive thus had to take its train out of New Street from the eastern end, and in consequence the train left Birmingham via Aston and Bescot. In this direction Wolverhampton was avoided by taking the straight line northwards from Willenhall to Bushbury. With the 4-coach Liverpool section added, and now a formation of about 11 bogies, the 'Pines Express' ran the 54 miles to Crewe non-stop in 70min, arriving at 4.02pm. Here the severance of Liverpool and Manchester sections took place; the Liverpool section reached Lime Street at 5.21pm and the 'Pines Express' proper was into Manchester London Road at 4.51pm, in a minute over $6\frac{1}{4}$ hours from Bournemouth.

At summer weekends, on Mondays, Fridays and Saturdays, the express was divided, and the principal section of the train then followed a very curious route, used by no other regular express train, and avoiding both Wolverhampton and Birmingham. From Bushbury it continued direct to Darlaston and there turned leftwards into Walsall, where the change from Western to Midland Division engine took place. From Walsall the old Midland branch through Sutton Coldfield was used down to Castle Bromwich, on the Derby-Birmingham main line, from which it was a straight run to Saltley and then on through Camp Hill by the train's normal route. The same course was followed in the opposite direction.

The 'Pines Express' was withdrawn on the outbreak of World War 2, but it was restored between Manchester and Bournemouth on 7 October 1946, with a timing of 7hr southbound and $7\frac{1}{4}$hr northbound. It was soon accelerated to 6hr 56min southbound and 6hr 51min northbound, but the southbound schedule was later eased to 7hr 12min. Restaurant cars reappeared, and through coaches to and from Sheffield were added to those between Liverpool and Bournemouth. Departure from Manchester was at 10.20am, and from Bournemouth West at 9.45am; rather unusually, the latter train finished its journey not in London Road, but at Manchester Mayfield. The Southern Region had now taken over the responsibility for the locomotive power between Bath and Bournemouth, and used its light Pacifics over this section.

From then up to the time of its disappearance the 'Pines Express' suffered further changes of route. The first and most revolutionary change followed the closure of the Somerset & Dorset Joint Line; this resulted in a transfer of the 'Pines Express' from the former route through Stafford, Birmingham New Street, Cheltenham and Bath to the former Great Western line via Market Drayton, Wellington, Birmingham Snow Hill, Oxford, Reading West, Basingstoke and the Southern line from there, so that the 'Pines' entered Bournemouth from the east instead of the west, and incidentally could now serve Southampton. The final change was when in 1963 closure of the line from Nantwich through Market Drayton to Wellington compelled a further diversion via Shrewsbury, with a stop there; but the increased speed with diesel power made this possible without any increase in overall journey time.

In its final form the southbound 'Pines Express' left Liverpool at 9.45am and Manchester at 10am; it reached Southampton at 3.54pm, Bournemouth at 4.44pm and Poole at 5.10pm. Northbound, at 9.38am from Poole, 10.02am from Bournemouth and 10.43am from Southampton it was due in Manchester by 5.06pm and Liverpool at 5.11pm. But in March 1967 with the opening of the electrification through Birmingham, the 'Pines Express' ceased to run. Current through services between Manchester, Liverpool and Bournemouth follow the final 'Pines' route except that they again travel to and from Birmingham via Stafford and Wolverhampton.

The Ports-to-Ports Express

In 1897 what until then had been the Manchester, Sheffield & Lincolnshire Railway changed its name to Great Central Railway, and greatly enhanced its importance and its range by the new main line opened in 1899 from north of Nottingham to London. The next business was to attract traffic to the new route, and the possibilities were further increased when in 1900 a short spur line was opened from Woodford & Hinton, 34 miles south of Leicester, to Banbury on the Great Western. In course of time various through passenger services were established over this connection between the North-East of England and the West and South.

With one exception, all these through trains continued southwards over the GWR to Oxford and beyond. This exception was the unofficially-named 'Ports-to-Ports Express', for which a more direct route had to be found in order to link Banbury with South Wales. It was planned by making use of a sleepy country branch, single-track throughout, which never previously had seen an express train. This was the line from King's Sutton, just south of Banbury, through the old-world towns of Chipping Norton, Stow-on-the-Wold and Bourton-on-the-Water to Cheltenham, from which town main line running could be resumed through Gloucester to Newport, Cardiff and beyond.

Originally the 'Ports-to-Ports Express', which began its career in May 1906, was designed to run between Newcastle-on-Tyne and the port of Barry. In later years it was extended westwards to Swansea, though still running between Cardiff and Bridgend by way of Barry instead of by the direct main line. In addition to connecting the ports of Tyneside and Teesside with those of South Wales, in LNER days two further ports were linked with the service by the running of a through coach to and from Hull and Goole, detached and attached at Sheffield.

In 1939 the express was leaving Newcastle at 9.30 in the morning, and with stops at Durham, Darlington and Northallerton reached York at 11.32am. On the way it suffered the indignity of being put on to the slow loop south of Eryholme to let the 'Silver Jubilee' streamliner get by. The next stage, from York at 11.42am, was a non-stop run to Sheffield, by way of the Swinton & Knottingley Joint Line through Pontefract, with an arrival in Sheffield at 12.51pm. Here reversal was necessary, and with the through coach from Hull — which had left there at 10.35am and had travelled to Sheffield via Doncaster — at the head end, the train left for the south at 1pm. A fast run was made over the Great Central metals to Banbury, with calls at Nottingham, Loughborough, Leicester and Rugby, and the GWR station was reached at 3.30pm.

To this point the locomotive power had been similar to that of the 'Aberdeen-Penzance' service, but something much lighter was needed for the Banbury-Cheltenham line, and for years, until the advent of the 4-6-0 'Manors', the GWR used Moguls over this section, through between Banbury and Cardiff. After the fast LNER running, the allowance of 82min for the 44¾ miles from Banbury to Cheltenham South came somewhat as an anticlimax, even if the lethargy, in the circumstances, was unavoidable. Stopping at Gloucester and at Chepstow, the 'Ports-to-Ports Express' skirted the Severn estuary to reach Newport at 6.30 and Cardiff at 6.51pm.

Up to 1922, the Great Western Railway relinquished its charge of the train at Cardiff and handed over to the Barry Railway for the short run between Cardiff and Barry, but from the Grouping this line, with its extension through Aberthaw to Bridgend, became part of the GWR. It was considerably more circuitous, of course, than the direct main line from Cardiff to Bridgend, and the 54 miles from Cardiff to Swansea, with stops at Barry Docks, Barry, Bridgend, Pyle, Port Talbot and Neath, took just over 1¾hr. Swansea was reached at 8.45pm, after a 397 mile journey taking 11¼hr.

In the northbound direction, the GWR in later years cut out the journey by the Barry loop, and leaving Swansea at 8.15am, ran the 'Ports-to-Ports Express' direct to Cardiff, with stops at Neath, Briton Ferry, Port Talbot, Bridgend and Llantrisant. Cardiff was left at 9.40am and Newport at 10am, and with the same stops on Great Western territory beyond Newport as in the reverse direction, the express found its way into Banbury at 12.40pm. Four minutes later the LNER were away on the journey to Sheffield, and with halts at Rugby, Leicester and Nottingham this stretch of $107\frac{1}{4}$ miles was completed in 2hr 19min. The Hull coach, detached at Sheffield, found its way into that port at 4.45pm; the main train, reversing in Sheffield, got to York by 4.19pm. A stop of 11min sufficed here, and again with the same stops as coming south the end of the journey, at Newcastle, was attained by 6.15pm. This was a considerably faster effort than that of the southbound train, and cut the through journey to 10hr precisely.

For most of the year a 6-coach corridor set, including restaurant car, and the through composite corridor coach to and from Hull, provided comfortably adequate accommodation, though the formation was added to as required during the summer. London & North-Eastern and Great Western coaches were used on alternate days. The train was withdrawn on the outbreak of war. The only through passenger trains in wartime continuing to use the Woodford-Banbury link between the LNER and the GWR were the York-Swindon service, and the through train between Newcastle and Ashford, later diverted to Southampton.

The 'Ports-to-Ports Express' reappeared in October 1946, but modified at the GWR end by being run between Banbury and Newport via Oxford, Swindon and the Severn Tunnel, a considerably longer route than the previous one via Cheltenham. Except on summer Saturdays, at the northern end of the route the terminal point was York and not Newcastle. Leaving York at 12.20pm, the 'Ports-to-Ports Express' was in Swansea by 9.08pm, and coming north, with a departure from Swansea at 8.15am, York was reached at 5.12pm.

In the winter of 1952-1953 the working of the train was cut short at Banbury, and to Fridays and Saturdays only; thus it ceased to touch any ports at all. But this was largely because of the establishment of a new and far more direct through service between Cardiff and Newcastle by way of Gloucester and the LMR line through Birmingham and Derby to York; this cut the Cardiff-Newcastle time to 8hr 32min, and that in the reverse direction to $8\frac{1}{4}$hr, both far faster than ever previously.

The Queen of Scots

It is curious to reflect that the one-time Great Eastern Railway, serving a comparatively limited area of agricultural country in the Eastern Counties, should have been the means — indirectly, perhaps, but none the less effectively — of introducing Pullman car trains between London and the cities of the West Riding of Yorkshire, the famous Spa at Harrogate, and as far afield as Newcastle, Edinburgh and Glasgow. The reason was that in 1914 the GER acquired an American General Manager, Mr — later Sir — Henry Thornton. Accustomed as he was to Pullman travel in the United States, Thornton not unnaturally thought that Pullman service, already established south of the Thames, ought to be popular on the railway which had now come under his control. So an agreement was made with the Pullman Car Company, and a number of new Pullman cars found their way on to the Great Eastern main line.

But while the cars prospered on the Continental boat trains between Liverpool Street and Parkeston Quay, they were less of a success elsewhere, and when the GER came into the London & North Eastern group in 1923, with a considerable period of the Pullman agreement still to run, it was an urgent question whether a more profitable use for these Pullmans might not be found. Except for the Continental boat trains, therefore, the cars were withdrawn from the Great Eastern, and a set of them was formed into an all-Pullman express, called the 'Harrogate Pullman', to run between King's Cross, Leeds, Harrogate and Newcastle, in the summer of 1923. The time of 3hr 25min in each direction between King's Cross and Leeds equalled the best that had ever operated between London and Leeds, and this was the longest non-stop run on the LNER at that time.

The down 'Harrogate Pullman', as the train was called, consisted of six cars, two first class and four third class. It left King's Cross at exactly the same time — 11.15am — as the up train left Harrogate, and the journey between London and Harrogate took four hours each way. The down train reached Leeds at 2.40pm; reversing at the Central station, it joined the NER line and continued up the long 1 in 100 climb past Headingley and Horsforth to Bramhope tunnel.

From Pannal it climbed round an extremely sharp curve on to Crimple viaduct, and up a short 1 in 91 stretch into Harrogate. Leaving here at 3.20pm, the train dropped sharply downhill — 1 in 66 at first, to Bilton Road Junction — to Ripon, and after making calls there and at Darlington, reached Newcastle at 5pm.

Coming south, the 'Harrogate Pullman' started from Newcastle at 9.20am, called at Darlington, left the London main line at Northallerton for the Harrogate and Leeds detour, and stopped at Ripon and Harrogate to Leeds. Pulling out of Leeds at 11.50am, and rejoining the Newcastle-London main line at Doncaster, the train reached King's Cross at 3.15pm. Two years later the working of the Pullman was extended to Edinburgh, with a stop at Berwick, and the entire journey took 8hr 35min; going north the 11.15am start was unaltered, but on the southbound journey a departure from Edinburgh at 8.30am retarded the exit from Harrogate to 1.05pm, and from Leeds to 1.40pm; King's Cross was now reached at 5.05pm.

In September 1925 another change was made. A second all-Pullman train, which later became the 'West Riding Pullman', had been trying a variety of routes in order to establish itself in public favour, and it was decided to make this into a special Leeds and Bradford service at 11.10am from King's Cross. It was thus possible to schedule the 'Harrogate Pullman' as a non-stop express over the 198.8 miles from King's Cross to Harrogate; the start was changed to 11.20am, and the Pullman was booked into Harrogate at 3.03pm. This run covered an interesting route, including the use of LMSR metals from Shaftholme Junction, 4½ miles north of Doncaster, to Knottingley, then by a spur line to the LNER line at Ferrybridge, and on through Church Fenton and Tadcaster up to Crimple Viaduct and Harrogate. Edinburgh was now reached at 7.35pm, in 8¼hr. On the southbound run, the 'Harrogate Pullman', leaving Edinburgh at 8.30am and Harrogate at 1.05pm as before, followed the same non-stop course to London and was due at 4.45pm.

So matters continued until May 1928, when a new and very handsome train of seven all-steel Pullmans, all eight-wheelers, appeared on the service, bearing the attractive title of the 'Queen of Scots'. As the 'West Riding Pullman' from the same date was moved to an afternoon departure from London, the 'Queen of Scots' reverted to the Leeds route, and left King's Cross at 11.15am. Further, it was extended from Edinbirgh to Glasgow, and reached Queen Street at 8.45 in the evening, after completing a route 450.8 miles in length. Coming south, it started from Glasgow at 10.05am, and Edinburgh at 11.15am, and was booked to reach King's Cross at 7.35pm. The timing for the non-stop runs between London and Leeds in each direction was still 3hr 25min as in 1923.

From that time onwards there were no changes other than the speeding-up that began with the general acceleration of all the Anglo-Scottish services in May 1932. When the 'Queen of Scots' was withdrawn on the outbreak of war in September 1939, the starting time from London was 11.20am, and no more than 191min was allowed for the 185.7 miles from King's Cross to Leeds — an average of 58.3mph. The up run was a minute quicker (58.5mph). Harrogate was reached in 3¾hr, Edinburgh in 7¾hr, and Glasgow in 8hr 53min. In the reverse direction the 'Queen of Scots' was due away from Glasgow at 10.15am and Edinburgh at 11.20am; departure from Harrogate was at 3.23pm and from Leeds (Central) at 3.55pm, and King's Cross was reached at 7.05pm. An additional stop was made in this direction at Holbeck, ½ mile after leaving Leeds Central, at 3.57pm.

Between London and Leeds various types of locomotive were tried on the Pullman workings, including the Great Central 4-cylinder 4-6-0s, which could not maintain their steam pressure on these lengthy runs, and the Great Central 'Director' 4-4-0s, which did well, though without adequate reserve. It was the Ivatt Atlantics of the one-time Great Northern, however, which will always be associated with the Pullmans. Some of the most famous LNER main line drivers first made their reputations in the Pullman link, and as for the engines, to quote from an historic phrase used in another connection, this was their 'finest hour'. Timekeeping with the 290-ton load was exemplary, and on many of the runs a considerable amount of time lost by permanent way and signal checks was recovered to achieve a punctual arrival. Later the all-conquering Pacifics appeared on the train, and from Leeds northwards it was generally a Pacific working.

After the war the 'Queen of Scots' was reinstated, and by the winter of 1952-1953 the 'Queen of Scots', now a ten-car formation of about 400 tons, was reaching Leeds in 3½hr from London, at 3.30pm. Here two cars were detached, and the eight-car remainder was into Newcastle by 5.44pm. Between Newcastle and Edinburgh the timing in both directions was the fastest yet scheduled for one of the Pullmans — 124.4 miles in 132min — and Waverley was reached at 8.02pm; the Glasgow arrival was at 9.14pm. Coming south, the 'Queen of Scots' was leaving Glasgow at 10.50am, Edinburgh at 12 noon — in both directions the London and Edinburgh starts were in conformity with the systematic departure plan of the Eastern and North Eastern Regions — Newcastle at 2.18pm, and Leeds at 4.36pm, with a King's Cross arrival at 8.05pm. As in the opposite direction, eight cars were run from Glasgow and ten from Leeds. By now the engines used were almost invariably Peppercorn Class A1 Pacifics.

The 'Queen of Scots' shared in the subsequent accelerations, but eventually, when under the Beeching régime the necessity for economies in all directions was becoming increasingly necessary, it was realised that patronage of the train north of Harrogate was insufficient to justify its continuance, and that if it were run between King's Cross and Harrogate only, with a through Bradford portion, one set of cars could make the return journey daily. In the summer of 1964, therefore, this change took place, and as Scotland was no longer being served, the attractive title 'Queen of Scots' had to be dropped; in its place the name 'White Rose' was transferred from its previous owner to the Pullman train. But not for long, however. On the introduction in March 1967 of the new Eastern and North Eastern Region high speed service with 'Deltic'-hauled eight-coach trains, this Pullman service disappeared. In its last year the 'White Rose' left King's Cross at 11.25am, and covered the 175.8 miles to Wakefield in 154min, reaching Leeds at 2.21pm and Harrogate at 3.04pm; it returned at 4pm, from Leeds at 4.40pm and Wakefield at 4.57pm, running into King's Cross by 7.35pm — in both directions, of course, far faster with 'Deltic' power than in steam days.

The Royal Highlander

Lineal descendant of the flyer which as far back as 1895 made the fastest time ever known between London and Aberdeen, the 'Royal Highlander' received its title in the year 1927. This record was achieved during the historic 'Race to Aberdeen' between the West Coast and East Coast Companies. The genesis of the contest was an announcement by the West Coast companies — the London & North Western and Caledonian Railways — that from 1 July 1895 their 8pm express from Euston would reach Aberdeen at 7.40am, 15min earlier than before. The race had begun.

Night after night the competing trains made faster times, and finally the timetables were scrapped altogether. The West Coast, running an additional train behind their racing express to make the ordinary intermediate stops, reduced their load to three coaches of 70 tons weight, and omitted all halts except those at Crewe, Carlisle and Perth. On the morning of 23 August 1895 their train, which had left Euston at 8pm the previous evening, rolled into Aberdeen Joint Station at 4.32, having cut more than *three hours* from the schedule that precipitated the race! The distance of 540 miles had been covered in 8hr 32min, at an average of 63.3mph throughout, including stops.

From Euston to Crewe the engine was *Adriatic*, one of the Webb 2-2-2-0 three-cylinder compounds, which covered the 158.1 miles in 147½min. At Crewe, *Hardwicke*, a 'Jumbo' 2-4-0, took over, and achieved the astonishing feat of running the 141 miles to Carlisle, including the 915ft altitude of Shap, in 126min, at 67.2mph. From Carlisle the Caledonian Railway provided a 4-4-0 locomotive, which covered the 150.8 miles over Beattock and Kinbuck summits to Perth in 149½min; and finally another Caledonian 4-4-0 ran the 98.7 miles from Perth to Aberdeen in 80½min, at an average of 66.9mph. With this epoch-making performance, by common consent the railways concerned regarded the race as finished.

By the time the 'Royal Highlander' received its name, in 1927, it had become a much more leisurely train, but its weight had vastly increased. In winter it left Euston at 7.30pm, and made calls at Bletchley, Rugby, Crewe, Wigan, Carlisle and Stirling, being due into Perth at 5.24 in the morning. Here the Inverness and Aberdeen sections parted company. The latter got away at 5.40am, and with stops at Forfar, Bridge of Dun, Laurencekirk and Stonehaven was into Aberdeen at 7.40am. But the Inverness section, which had to collect the through sleeping cars and coaches off the rival 'Aberdonian' from King's Cross, and to attach a breakfast car for the sustenance of its hungry passengers, was not due to leave Perth until a whole hour after arrival, at 6.25am, and with various regular and conditional stops reached its northerly destination, 568¾ miles from London, at 9.50am.

On its winter working the 'Royal Highlander' took out of Euston three pairs of sleeping cars, first class and third class, for Inverness, Aberdeen and Perth respectively, together with composite coaches for each destination and third class brakes or long luggage brakes. On the back of the train was a restaurant car, provided to enable the long-distance travellers comfortably to take dinner before reaching Crewe. The whole train might amount to 12 or 13 vehicles from London.

In the height of the summer season, however, such a formation as this was nothing like enough to accommodate the traffic, and three independent trains were run nightly. The normal 7.30pm was put back to 7.40, and was preceded by a 7.25 to Inverness and Oban, and a 7.20 — the 'Royal Highlander' proper — to Inverness and Aberdeen. This express was booked to call first at Crewe from 10.22 to 10.32pm, where engines were changed. From here the next publicly-booked stop was at Perth, but in the working timetable a stop was shown at Motherwell to detach parcels vans for Glasgow; the run of 230.4 miles from Crewe to Motherwell at that time was among the longest scheduled regularly on LMSR metals. With such a load as that conveyed on this train, however, unless two engines were in use, a stop also at Beattock, 180.7 miles from Crewe, was necessary for assistance up the famous bank.

Arriving at Perth at 4.46am, the Aberdeen section was away 5min later, and with one intermediate stop only, at Coupar Angus, was due in Aberdeen at 7am, 40min earlier than in winter. The main train, too, waited only 23min instead of an hour at Perth, and so was into Inverness at 8.45am, 65min earlier than on the winter working. It was, of course, the difficulty of the 118 miles between Perth and Inverness that accounted for the lengthy allowance of 3hr 36min over this stretch. There were 28 miles of single track from Stanley Junction to Blair Atholl, and another 48½ miles from Dalwhinnie to Daviot (this section now extends to Culloden Moor); and to add to many other formidable gradients, the engines had to face the terrific climb from Blair Atholl to Druimuachdar summit, 1,484ft above sea level, which includes 14 miles at 1 in 70-80; together with another climb from Aviemore to Slochd summit, 1,350ft above the sea, with 6 miles at 1 in 60-75. In the opposite direction, too, there is a fearsome start out of Inverness, including 12 miles almost continuously at 1 in 60 up to beyond Daviot.

In later years the Highland workings were greatly eased by the advent of the Stanier Class 5 6ft 4-6-0s, which in double-harness could handle loads up to about 500 tons. In the summer season the up night workings from the Highlands to Euston were very complicated, and no train was described officially as the 'Royal Highlander'; nor was there a winter train with the title coming south, though actually the counterpart of the down working was the 4.15pm from Inverness, leaving Perth at 8.30pm, and due in Euston at 6.55 the following morning. The Aberdeen train, leaving the Granite City at 7.50pm, was 95min later from Perth and due in London at 8am.

During World War 2 this service was of such importance, for naval and military reasons, as to require two trains nightly, at 7.20pm from Euston to Inverness and at 7.30pm to Perth, though neither carried a name. The 7.20pm resembled its peacetime counterpart, for it made stops at Crewe, Beattock (for the banker), and Motherwell (to drop the Glasgow vans), to Perth, reached at 5.26am, or 40min later than before the war. A wait of 49min was enjoined at Perth, and at 6.15am the sleeper set out on a run of just over 4hr to Inverness, arriving at 10.18am. The heavy train formation from London, save for the Glasgow vans, was run through over the whole journey, and with various accretions at Perth, provided a considerable problem of haulage on the Highland line.

On 1 October 1945 this train had the distinction of being one of the first LMSR trains to have a postwar acceleration, and its time was cut to less than the prewar allowance. For the first part of the 'Royal Highlander', still leaving Euston at 7.20pm, was booked into Inverness 1¾hr earlier, at 8.37am. This was done in part by cutting the Perth stop from 49 to 19min (4.46 to 5.05am), but chiefly by paring the running times. The timing proved too tight, however; the wait at Perth later was expanded to 45min, and by 1954 Inverness was not being reached till 9.34am.

Since then there have been many changes in the working of this important service. In 1957 the name was restored in both directions, and there have been very substantial accelerations due first to electric working between Euston and Crewe, with diesel power from there northwards and then to electrification through to Motherwell. The start of the 'Royal Highlander' out of Euston was put back to 8.20pm. It was a very heavy train, beginning with two restaurant cars, which came off at Crewe, and continuing with five passenger coaches and five sleeping cars (six on Fridays) with a brake van on the rear — 493 tare tons or 538 tons on Friday nights. This load was worked over the 158.1 miles to Crewe in 137min. Here a 2,750hp diesel took over, and after a 13min wait had a non-stop run in 166½min to Carlisle, where a brief halt (1.36½/1.39am) was made to change engine crews. There was no longer a Stirling stop, and the next stage was the 150.8-mile run over Beattock summit to Perth in 177min. Perth thus was reached by 4.30am. Despite the early hour, a breakfast car was attached here, and after a wait of 15min the 'Royal Highlander', now probably in charge of a couple of 1,160 or 1,250hp diesels, set out at 4.51am for the tremendous climbs to Druimuachdar and Slochd Mhuic summits, calling at all the nine stations still open between Perth and Inverness.

But even with these stops the Perth-Inverness time could be cut to 3hr 24min. So with an arrival at 8.15am, the journey from London was shortened to 5min under 12hr, or 2hr 25min less than when the 'Royal Highlander' first received its title in 1927, and 3 hours less than during World War 2.

In the up direction the principal change was in the progressively later starts from Inverness; the 4.40pm of 1939 and the wartime 3.30pm became 7pm; while the Euston arrival, 7.45am in 1939, and 8.20am during the war, was stabilised at 7.28am. So the former journey times of 15hr 5min and all but 16hr during the war were reduced to 12hr 28min — a very substantial gain for 'Royal Highlander' travellers.

Electrification throughout the West Coast Main Line brought further improvements. In 1962 the down train did not leave Euston until 9.55pm and completed the journey to Inverness in 10hr 58min. A section for Fort William was worked into Glasgow Queen Street and attached to the 6am train to Mallaig. The up train, at 8.20pm from Inverness, was slower, Euston arrival being at 7.42am. In this direction the Fort William sleepers were worked south by other overnight trains except on Saturdays, when they joined the 'Royal Highlander'. The name and the northbound departure time were still current in 1983. Southbound, the 'Royal Highlander' left Inverness at 8.30pm.

The Royal Scot

West Coast rival to the East Coast 'Flying Scotsman', the 'Royal Scot' has had an even longer, though not unbroken, history; and it was not until 1927 that the title of 'Royal Scot' was conferred. One break in the sequence of departures from Euston at the familiar hour of 10am occurred in the latter part of World War 1 when it was decided to concentrate the morning London to Glasgow traffic on the 8.50am train from St Pancras, and the Edinburgh passengers on the corresponding train from King's Cross. For the sake of intermediate stations from Rugby onwards, a Perth portion was run on the 9.10am down Liverpool train, but no through travellers were supposed to use it from London to Glasgow or Edinburgh.

Up to 1914, the 10am from Euston, tied down by the East and West Coast agreement to a minimum journey time of 8¼hr to Glasgow, was a train with through sections for Glasgow and Edinburgh, each with its own restaurant car, and a through portion on the rear for Aberdeen. As with a number of other London & North Western expresses, except in summer it continued to call at Willesden Junction to pick up passengers, and then at Rugby and Crewe, where it divided. From here the Glasgow and Edinburgh portions ran independently, both having acquired through coaches from Birmingham, and both non-stop to Carlisle. The only remaining stop of the Glasgow train was at Symington, and Glasgow Central was reached at 6.15pm. The Edinburgh train followed close behind, slipped a carriage at Lockerbie, dropped its Aberdeen portion at Symington, and was into Princes Street also by 6.15pm.

Coming south, the two trains, 10am from Glasgow and 10.05am from Edinburgh, in the same way ran independently of one another as far as Crewe; the Glasgow train could be 'flagged' to stop at Motherwell by anyone wanting to join it; both called at Carlisle, and the Edinburgh train had an additional stop at Preston before Crewe was reached. At Crewe the through Birmingham coaches were detached, and the Glasgow and Edinburgh sections were joined for the run to London, calling only at Rugby and terminating at 6.20pm.

In the recovery period from 1919 onwards, the down and up trains reappeared in much their previous form, but from 1927 onwards developments began to take place. As the terms of the agreement forbade competition in time, a kind of race in non-stop running began instead. In the summer of 1927 the LMSR made the 'Royal Scot' a train for through passengers between London, Edinburgh and Glasgow only. A 'Claughton' 4-6-0, piloted by a 'George the Fifth' 4-4-0, hauled the train non-stop to Carnforth, 236 miles from Euston; here a stop was made at Carnforth No 2 box, south of the station, to examine the train, and a couple of 4-4-0 compounds took over for the run over Shap and Beattock summits to Symington, 130 miles distant, where the Edinburgh portion was detached before the final run into Glasgow.

That summer the LNER tried non-stop running from London to Newcastle, 268.3 miles, so the LMSR, now in possession of its new 'Royal Scot' 4-6-0 engines, cut out the Carnforth stop, and on the northbound journey ran through over the 301 miles from Euston to Kingmoor, 2 miles north of Carlisle. When the LNER decided to go a step further, in May 1928, by making the entire journey of 392¾ miles from King's Cross to Edinburgh without a stop, the LMSR was no longer in a position to retaliate owing to the necessity of calling at Symington for the division of their train. But with sly humour, and entirely without warning, on the Friday before the 'Flying Scotsman' started its daily world record run the LMSR stole the LNER thunder by dividing the down 'Royal Scot', and running *both* sections without a stop from starting-point to destination. 'Royal Scot' 4-6-0 No 6113, *Cameronian*, took the Glasgow train on its non-stop break of 401.4 miles, and compound 4-4-0 No 1054 handled the 6-coach Edinburgh portion. The latter's run of 399.7 miles was the longest without a stop ever made by a 4-4-0 locomotive in Great Britain, while the former was a British record for any type of locomotive to that date.

All this time the 8¼hr overall schedule still persisted, and it was not until 1932 that acceleration began. By 1939 the 'Royal Scot' had become a far faster train. In summer it was booked to reach the Citadel station at Carlisle at one minute before 3pm, so covering the 299.1 miles from Euston in 299 minutes, at precisely 60mph. For the whole journey to Glasgow the time had come down to 7hr, and with this load the work required of the locomotive was considerably harder than that of the 'Coronation Scot' streamliner on its 6½hr run.

On the winter schedule of the 'Royal Scot' the allowance was eased by 20min to allow for additional stops at Rugby and Crewe. The train was booked to run the 82.6 miles from Euston to Rugby in 80min, and the 75.5 miles on to Crewe in 75min — two runs in succession at over 60mph. Leaving the Aberdeen section at Crewe, to be attached to a following express from Birmingham to Glasgow, the 'Royal Scot' then covered the 141 miles from Crewe to Carlisle in 154min, and had a minute over 2hr in which to complete the run of 102.3 miles to Glasgow, Symington stop included — a rather easier task than that required in summer.

On the up journey, the 'Royal Scot' by 1939 was maintaining a non-stop run from Carlisle throughout the year. In summer, there were two up non-stops daily. The Glasgow train carried Glasgow to London passengers only, and its sole intermediate stop was at Carlisle No 12 box, south of the station, to change the engine-crew. The Edinburgh portion stopped at Symington to attach a through section which had left Aberdeen at 6.50am and Perth at 8.55am; the next stop was Carlisle Citadel station, and then Euston.

Including the 'Coronation Scot', therefore, there were five daily non-stop runs between London and various points and Carlisle from 297.9 to 299.1 miles away. In winter the Glasgow and Edinburgh sections were joined at Symington, and then made the non-stop run from Carlisle Citadel to Euston. While the summer 'Royal Scot' reached Euston in 7hr, the winter train, though with only one additional stop, required 7hr 25min — 5min more than the down run, even though the down 'Royal Scot' stopped also at Rugby and Crewe — to travel up from Glasgow.

The year after the accelerations began, the first Stanier Pacifics became available for the haulage of the train. The load was substantial; in summer the down train, from the engine backwards, usually comprised third brake, two compartment thirds, two open thirds, kitchen car, open first, corridor first, and brake for Glasgow; and first brake, open first, kitchen car, open third, compartment third, and third brake for Edinburgh, total 15 vehicles of about 450 tons. In winter, from Euston, the train usually had about eight coaches in the Glasgow portion, four for Edinburgh, and two for Aberdeen.

A wartime version of the 'Royal Scot' ran in both directions throughout World War 2. Load was generally limited to 17 bogies, including brake, first brake, two open firsts, open composite, and the remainder third class. It soon became necessary to split off the Perth section, and this ran as a second train at 10.05am, the first portion of which, familiarly known as the 'Jellicoe' from 1914-1918 war associations, was reserved for Service personnel travelling to the Highlands. The through journey of the latter to Thurso, 721½ miles in all, was the longest regular through passenger run ever known in Great Britain, and lasted until 7.20 on the following morning, 21¼hr after leaving London.

On the down journey, the wartime 10am from Euston called at Rugby, Crewe, Carlisle and Symington, but had no through coaches for Edinburgh; latterly it was due in Glasgow at 6.55pm. Coming up, a feature of the working was the daily queue of passengers at Glasgow Central, often extending from the barrier out to the front of the station, and at times well round the corner and 100yd or so down Union Street. For most of the war period the non-stop run from Carlisle to Euston was maintained, and the arrival in Euston was scheduled at 6.56pm.

After the war, restaurant cars were restored in both directions on 1 October 1945. A fortnight later the trains ceased to call at Carlisle passenger station; the 10am from Euston stopped at Kingmoor for examination and change of engine-crew, and the 10am from Glasgow at Carlisle No 12 box for the same purpose. From 7 October 1946 the up express was accelerated to reach Euston at 6.15pm, 41min earlier, but the down train required 8½hr to reach Glasgow. With the introduction of the 1950-1951 winter service, the stops in both directions at Carlisle passenger station were reinstated; the time from Euston to Glasgow became 8hr 25min, and that from Glasgow to Euston 8hr 13min. The first sign of the diesel invasion came in the early part of 1950, when the up 'Royal Scot' was frequently worked through by the twin diesel-electric units Nos 10000 and 10001.

In the summer of 1952 a complete set of new standard stock displaced that previously in use on the

'Royal Scot', and the times in both directions between Euston and Glasgow were reduced to 8hr. The up 8hr timing remained in the 1952-1953 winter timetables, but with the reintroduction of the usual winter stops on the down run, the Euston-Glasgow time became 8hr 10min. In summer the train loaded to 14 bogies each way; in winter the down train, with both Glasgow and Perth sections and restaurant cars in each, was frequently made up to 16 bogies, whereas 12 bogies sufficied on the up run.

The next change of note came with the 1959-1960 winter timetable, when, as noted already, the authorities decided on the extraordinary procedure of putting the 'Royal Scot', 'Midday Scot' and 'Caledonian' on to identical schedules, with an intermediate stop in each case at Carlisle only and loads strictly limited to eight coaches. So far as concerned the 'Royal Scot', the one-stop schedule involved no change, but the limited load did, as also did the alteration in the starting time out of Euston from 10 to 9.05am. With the reduced train weight, there was certainly a substantial acceleration; the time of 7¼hr between London and Glasgow represented a cut of 40min. To such an extent did the 9.05am start of the down train reduce its patronage, however, that a year later an unprecedented stop at Preston was introduced and continued for some years afterwards; the up train also resumed its passenger stop at Carlisle Citadel. By now the work of electrification was interfering with the running so much that by the 1960-1961 winter the total recovery allowance in the down schedule south of Preston had mounted to no less than 48min, whereas north of that point the train was booked to cover the 90.1 miles over Shap Summit from Preston to Carlisle in the fast time of 89min.

Limited space forbids any detailed description of the many variations in the schedule of the 'Royal Scot' until the electrification between London and Crewe became accomplished fact, and 2,700hp diesels had assumed responsibility for the working north of Crewe. By 1966 the train had largely regained its former popularity, and soon a 13-coach load of 450 tons tare was required in both directions. So also was a stop at Crewe coming up as well as going down for change of locomotive. Most astonishing of all the developments, however, was the speed-up between Euston and Crewe, which reduced the northbound time to 121min, and the southbound to 119min, the latter requiring a start-to-stop average of 79.8mph.

Between Crewe and Glasgow extra time was allowed in 1967 because of continuous rail-welding work, but even so the 141 miles between Crewe and Carlisle were covered in 150min down and 153min up, and the 102.3 miles between Carlisle and Glasgow in 115min down and 111min up. The former 10am departures from both terminals, however, had receded into the past; all even-hour starts out of Euston being monopolised by Liverpool and Manchester trains, so that the down 'Royal Scot' got away at 10.05am, while the up express left Glasgow Central at 10.10am. This at first was 10.15am, but from March 1967 all the West Coast timings had 5min added, making the down and up Euston-Glasgow timings 6hr 40min and 6hr 35min respectively.

In late 1967 the first Class 50 2,700hp diesels came into service and worked the 'Royal Scot' north of Crewe. From the 1970-71 timetable these locomotives were used on the train in pairs, enabling the schedule to be brought down to 5hr 55min northbound and 6hr southbound. Soon electrification work north of Crewe imposed restrictions, and in the 1971-72 timetable the train was routed by the Glasgow & South Western line through Dumfries between Carlisle and Glasgow. With electrification to Glasgow complete, the 'Royal Scot' became a 5hr train in each direction from 6 May 1974, leaving Euston at 10.45am and Glasgow at 10.10am. At this time the whole of the Euston-Glasgow service was advertised as the 'Electric Scots'. In the later 1970s arrears of track work caused schedules to be eased and at the time of writing the 'Royal Scot' is allowed 5hr 26min northbound and 5hr 28min coming south. Other trains on the service are faster but with its fiftieth anniversary well behind it the 'Royal Scot' title seems secure. On the anniversary date itself, 11 July 1977, Class 87 No 87001 at the head of the train was formally named *Royal Scot* before leaving Euston, the nameplates being unveiled by Mrs Jill Parker, wife of the Chairman of the British Railways Board.

The Royal Wessex

Back in London & South Western days, in 1899, the first non-stop train came into operation between London and Bournemouth. It left Waterloo at 4.10pm, and at first was due in Bournemouth Central at 6.16pm, but in 1911 the time was cut to the even two hours. A corresponding service left Bournemouth for

Waterloo in the morning. These were the forerunners of the 'Bournemouth Limited', a title which was conferred on the train on its revival in July, 1929. In this reappearance, corridor stock, with restaurant cars, replaced the compartment stock of the earlier days.

The non-stop run of 107.9 miles between Waterloo and Bournemouth Central is one of the longest that has been operated regularly in Britain without the aid of track water-troughs. Such runs as these, and even the non-stop runs of 88.1 miles between Salisbury and Exeter, 83.7 miles between Waterloo and Salisbury, and 79.2 miles between Waterloo and Southampton, were the justification for the eight-wheel tenders, with 4,500gal capacity, which the LSWR attached to all its larger express locomotives. Even with this provision, water supply could be a considerable problem at times to drivers on the London-Bournemouth run.

Between Waterloo and Bournemouth there are no very severe gradients, but the locomotives have to face some lengthy banks which, though of moderate inclination, can be very trying when loads are heavy. Out of Waterloo the work is mainly 'against the collar' for the first 50 miles; there is the long pull up to milepost 31 between Brookwood and Farnborough, though this is no steeper than 1 in 300 at any point, and then the line rises at 1 in 249 for five miles past Basingstoke to milepost 51, where the Southampton and Salisbury lines diverge. But the worst task is in the up direction, where trains have to negotiate an incline that averages 1 in 252 for 16½ miles continuously past Winchester to the summit at Litchfield tunnel. The only really severe slack is at Northam Junction, Southampton, where the line to Southampton Central diverges on a very sharp curve from the old line to Southampton Docks, although the limit here was raised from 15mph to 25mph in 1980; more moderate slacks are enforced round the curve between Redbridge and Totton, and through Christchurch station, which is at the foot of steep gradients in both directions.

The Drummond 4-cylinder 4-6-0s with 6ft 7in driving wheels, LSWR Nos 443-447 and 458-462 (which later from their wide splashers, became widely known as the 'Paddlebox' class), were introduced chiefly for use on the Waterloo-Bournemouth service, and took their share on the non-stops. Then followed the more efficient 'King Arthurs', but the last stage in the prewar history of the 'Bournemouth Limited' was unique, for with the introduction of the 'Schools' there came a reversion from the 4-6-0 to the 4-4-0 wheel arrangement. As the timetable allowance had now contracted to 116min for the down and 118min for the up journey, the task set the 'Schools' was one of the most exacting entrusted to any 4-4-0 locomotive class in recent times.

In the years immediately preceding World War 2, the formation of the 'Bournemouth Limited' was one of 11 bogies, weighing empty about 360 tons; the working book limit was 365 tons. In the summer and at weekends the limit might be exceeded by a twelfth vehicle, in which even the 'Schools' 4-4-0 was faced with a gross load of fully 415 tons, and work of a most exceptional description was then required. I have records, however, which show that *King's Wimbledon* worked a 10-coach train of 345 gross tons over the 107.9 miles from Bournemouth Central to Waterloo in a net time of 108min; while *Malvern* brought a 12-coach load of 415 tons up in 114½min net — a wonderful performance.

On the down journey the 'Bournemouth Limited' left Waterloo at 4.30pm, passed Southampton Central in 83min, and was due in Bournemouth Central at 6.26pm. Here the Weymouth and Swanage coaches in the front of the train, were detached, and headed usually by an ex-LSWR 4-4-0 locomotive, continued at 6.31pm to Poole and Wareham, where the Swanage coaches came off. The Weymouth portion had a working arrival at Wareham at 6.51½pm, and a departure at 6.54pm for Dorchester and Weymouth, reached at 7.24pm, in 2hr 54min for the 142.8 miles from Waterloo. Meantime the Swanage coaches had reached that Purbeck resort 3min earlier, and the main section of the 'Limited', including the restaurant cars, restarting from Bournemouth Central at 6.35pm, and with the 'Schools' 4-4-0 at the head, was into Bournemouth West by 6.43pm.

In the morning, the earliest start for users of the up 'Bournemouth Limited' was from Weymouth at 7.42am, for a journey of 2hr 56min to Waterloo. On the Weymouth-Bournemouth stretch one very fast booking was over the distance of exactly 15 miles from Dorchester to Wareham in 16min (begun at 7.57½ and finished at 8.13½) from start to stop, but this is mainly downhill. Stopping after that at Poole, the train from Weymouth found the Bournemouth West section, which had started at 8.20am, awaiting at Central, and ran through and back on to it at 8.35am. The combined train started for London at 8.40am, and reached Waterloo at 10.38am. The 'Bournemouth Limited' was withdrawn on the outbreak of war, and since then there has been no daily non-stop running between Waterloo and Bournemouth.

From 1 October 1945, however, an express from Weymouth at 7.38am (later altered to 7.34) and Bournemouth Central at 8.40am to Waterloo was reinstated, and in 1951, in honour of the Festival of Britain, it received the title 'Royal Wessex'. With additional stops at Southampton and Winchester, the 'Royal Wessex' was into Waterloo 12min later than in 1939, at 10.50am and in consideration of its much heavier loading (13 coaches weighing 445 tons tare), the effort required of the Bulleid Pacifics became greater than with the 'Schools' before the war. In the reverse direction the name was borne by the 4.35pm train, which made the same stops (and Brockenhurst in addition) reaching Bournemouth Central at 6.55pm, West at 7.13pm, and Weymouth at 7.55pm — 26min slower than the prewar 'Bournemouth Limied'.

In the final years of its life the 'Royal Wessex', as with all the other trains on the Waterloo-Bournemouth route, had extra time allowed because of the electrification work; the Weymouth portion now was starting at 7.30am; stops were made at Dorchester, Wool, Wareham and Poole before Bournemouth Central, but there were no longer any through portions from Swanage or Bournemouth West; indeed, the latter station had now been closed. At Central the train was made up to a 12-coach load, and after stopping at Southampton and Winchester the Waterloo arrival had been retarded to 11.02am, a journey 20min longer than that of 1945. Going down, the Waterloo start was still at 4.35pm, but with the same stops as coming up, it was not until 7.10pm that the 'Royal Wessex' reached Bournemouth Central, while the Weymouth portion was not due there until 8.16pm, 21mins later than in 1945, and after a journey 47min longer than that of the 'Bournemouth Limited'.

The name 'Royal Wessex' has disappeared, but with the electrification the fastest service on record over this main line came into operation, the standard time between Waterloo and Bournemouth, including the Southampton stop, being cut to 1hr 40min. The 79.2 miles from Waterloo to Southampton were covered in 70min, with speeds up to 90mph. Even these schedules were improved as the service settled down and by 1982 the time to Southampton was 67min and to Bournemouth 1hr 36min. With diesel traction beyond Bournemouth, calling at all stations to Dorchester except Holton Heath, the Waterloo-Weymouth time was 2hr 42min.

The Scarborough Flyer

In the years before World War 1, the attractions of Scarborough and other resorts on the North East Coast were thought to appeal mainly to the citizens of the West Riding of Yorkshire and the Midlands; facilties for travel to and from London were not of the best. But after the Grouping the London & North Eastern Railway lost no time in attempting to popularise Scarborough with Londoners also, who by now were not put off by long journeys in taking their holidays. In 1923, the first year of Grouping, a through summer express was put on from King's Cross at 11.50am to Scarborough, with a non-stop run in $3\frac{1}{2}$hr over the 188.2 miles between King's Cross and York, the longest regular break that had been scheduled over Great Northern and North Eastern metals to that date. Scarborough was reached at 4.20pm, in $4\frac{1}{2}$hr from London; and a corresponding up express left Scarborough at 3pm, running non-stop from York and reaching London at 7.30pm.

In 1933 the London-York allowance was brought down to $3\frac{1}{4}$hr, and Scarborough was reached in 4hr 10min from London; then, in 1935, by a bold stroke the schedule over the 188.2 miles between King's Cross and York was cut to the even 3hr, and the start-to-stop speed rose to 62.7mph, making the 'Scarborough Flyer' one of the fastest trains on the LNER, apart from the streamliners subsequently introduced. The 42 miles between York and Scarborough were allowed 50min, and with 5min spent at York, the overall time between London and Scarborough had now come down to 3hr 55min for a journey of 230.2 miles.

In its earlier days the down 'Scarborough Flyer' had been combined with a portion for Glasgow, and later for Newcastle, but this had now disappeared, and had been replaced by a through composite brake for Whitby, attached next to the engine going north. This was transferred to a train leaving York at 2.15pm, calling only at Pickering, Goathland and Grosmont, and reaching Whitby at 3.55pm. The normal formation of the 'Scarborough Flyer', including the Whitby coach and two restaurant cars, was about 11 bogies, 365 tons tare and 385 or 390 tons gross, though the make-up varied somewhat according to traffic demand.

On the up journey the 'Scarborough Flyer' left Scarborough at 10.40am, reached York at 11.30 and there picked up the Whitby coach (which had started at 9.40am); departing from York at 11.35am, it was due in King's Cross at 2.35pm according to the public timetables, though the working book allowed 2min more. In both directions between King's Cross and York Pacifics were used, and the North Eastern Area handled the train between York and Scarborough with D49 class 'Shire' or 'Hunt' 4-4-0s, or perhaps a C7 class Atlantic.

On Saturdays considerable expansion was needed to accommodate the traffic. During the height of the season, the 'Scarborough Flyer', at 11am, was preceded by a restaurant car train to Scarborough at 10.50am, which called at York to change engines, though not publicly booked to do so; this was due in Scarborough at 3.07pm, and the 'Scarborough Flyer' proper, with its timing to York eased to 3hr 20min at 3.15pm. To Whitby a special restaurant car train was run at 11.25am, with two stops en route, it called first at Selby to detach a through portion for Bridlington, and then at York to change engines, though neither of these stops appeared in the public timetables; Whitby was reached at 4.39pm. There were similar up Saturday arrangements, with trains from Scarborough at 10.20 and 10.40am, due in King's Cross at 2.25 and 2.45pm, and, sandwiched between them, the 9.40am from Whitby, due in London at 2.35pm.

World War 2, of course, brought this service to an end, and when the war was over it was not until the summer of 1950 that a so-called 'Scarborough Flyer' reappeared in the timetable, on Fridays, Saturdays and Sundays only in the down direction and Saturdays, Sundays and Mondays in the up, but with nothing in its speed to justify such a title as 'Flyer'. Leaving King's Cross at 11.05am, and calling at Grantham, York and Malton (where a through section for Whitby was detached) the train was due in Scarborough at 3.52pm; in the reverse direction the departure from Scarborough was at 11.30am and the arrival in King's Cross 4.16pm. By the summer of 1952 matters had improved, though the running of the train was now confined to Fridays and Saturdays down, and Saturdays and Sundays up. Leaving King's Cross at 11.20am, and still calling at Grantham, the 'Flyer' reached York at 2.50pm, and Scarborough at 3.48pm, in just under $4\frac{1}{2}$hr; the up journey was slower, with departure from Scarborough at 10.07am, and arrival in London at 2.55pm.

Today, like so many other well-known seaside expresses of the past, the 'Scarborough Flyer' is but a memory. In summer during the 1960s one remaining through service of the week between London and Scarborough, without name or refreshment facilities and on Saturdays only, left King's Cross at 11.30am, and so far from being non-stop to York, called at Peterborough, Grantham, Retford and Doncaster; yet such was the speed over the East Coast main line by that time that the time taken over the 188.2 miles to York, four stops included, was no more than 3hr 13min. Return from Scarborough, also on Saturdays, was at 10.55am, and in this direction the only intermediate stop south of York was at Grantham; King's Cross was reached at 3.12pm. A miniature buffet coach which had worked down to York on a relief Friday night express to Aberdeen provided passengers returning from Scarborough with refreshments. There was no longer a through service to and from Whitby for the line from Malton to Grosmont had been closed, neither did the successor of the 'Scarborough Flyer' call at Malton any more.

A similar through London-Scarborough service continued into the 1980s. The down train in 1982 left King's Cross at 11.22am and called additionally at Stevenage and Newark but took only 2min longer to York. In the reverse direction departure from Scarborough was at 9.15am and the stops were the same as on the down journey. There was no refreshment service in either direction.

The Sheffield Special

After the Great Central Railway had opened its London Extension in 1899, many ambitious moves were made in the hope of attracting the travelling public to the new route from Marylebone to the Midlands and the North. But well-established travel habits are difficult to alter, and the GCR was additionally hampered in that its new London terminus was not connected with any London underground line, though it did later acquire a station on the Bakerloo tube, when the latter was opened.

One Great Central slogan was 'Every Express Vestibuled with Buffet Car Attached', and an attractive service of meals and light refreshments on all long-distance trains was a feature of the GCR arrangements. Another feature was speed. Although the entry to London, over the Metropolitan line from Quainton Road to Harrow, with its difficult grades, was not conducive to speed, the new GCR line between Quainton Road and Annesley, north of Nottingham, was laid out expressly to permit fast running, and only through Leicester and Nottingham, and through the mining area further north, were any service slacks in force.

In 1903 a new afternoon express for Sheffield appeared in the GCR timetable. The starting time was fixed at 3.25pm, and with the help of the water-troughs at Charwelton and Killamarsh the train was booked to make the run of 164.7 miles non-stop in 3hr 8min. By 1904 this was cut to 2hr 57min, and in 1905 to as little as 2hr 50min. This was the fastest schedule ever in force between Marylebone and Sheffield, and equalled the best bookings over the competing Midland and Great Northern routes until the advent of the 'Master Cutler's Pullman from King's Cross. The GCR train became known as the 'Sheffield Special', though this name did not appear in the timetables or official literature. There was an up non-stop also, at 8.50am from Sheffield to Marylebone.

At first a formation of three coaches, headed by a Robinson 4-4-0 locomotive, sufficed to carry the traffic. Later, when the Robinson Atlantics had come into use, the normal formation was four bogies, with an additional non-corridor coach which was slipped at Leicester, and worked from there through to Grimsby and Cleethorpes. In the course of time the allowance to Sheffield was eased to 2hr 57min, at which it remained up to World War 1, and the Marylebone departure was altered to 3.15pm. The main train continued from Sheffield to Manchester, slipping at Penistone a portion for Bradford, which consisted of a composite slip brake, and a through coach from Bournemouth which had been brought to Sheffield immediately ahead on the Bournemouth-Newcastle through train. The only other stop was Guide Bridge, after which the 'Sheffield Special' was worked round the southern outskirts of Manchester into the Central Station, where it was due at 7.25pm, in time to connect with the 7.30pm to Liverpool. In earlier years it had a very tight timing of 50min from Sheffield to Manchester London Road, a distance of 41¼ miles over Dunford summit, and including a Guide Bridge stop.

During World War 1 the 'Sheffield Special' continued to run, complete with its restaurant car, and at speeds but little inferior to those of peace (like most of the GCR services), but with stops at Leicester and Penistone replacing the slip portions, and an additional stop at Nottingham. Sheffield was reached at 6.37pm and Manchester at 8pm. After the war this arrangement continued, and the express, still without any official name, settled down to a departure from Marylebone at 3.20pm. The 103.1 miles to Leicester were run in 109min; in the compass of this run came the 6-mile climb at 1 in 105 from Rickmansworth up to Amersham, a gruelling task for the engine. After a two-minute stop at Leicester, from 5.09 to 5.11pm, the 23.4 miles on to Nottingham had to be run in the smart time of 25min. The stop at Nottingham Victoria was from 5.36 to 5.38pm, and in view of the gradients between there and Sheffield, with 7 miles at 1 in 130 up to Kirkby South Junction, the continued rise on easier inclinations to Pilsley, and the not infrequent slowings for colliery subsidences, the allowance of 48min for the 38.2 miles from Nottingham to Sheffield was by no means easy.

But the hardest task of all was reserved for the conclusion, in the tremendous pull from Sheffield up to the eastern portal of Woodhead tunnel, nearly 1,000ft above sea level, by grades which for 18½ miles continuously were at 1 in 120 to 1 in 132. In the middle of the ascent came the stop at Penistone, where a through coach for Bradford was detached; leaving Sheffield at 6.30pm the 'Sheffield Special' ran the 12.9 miles to Penistone in 23min; the next 23.4 miles, over Dunford summit and down to Guide Bridge, took 32min, and after a 2min stop there, the last stage of 11.1 miles into Manchester Central occupied 16min. Arrival in Manchester was at 7.45pm, and the 4hr 10min which the 'Sheffield Special' was allowed in its heyday had thus expanded to 4hr 25min overall.

For many years the working of this express was entrusted to the highly efficient 'Director' class 4-4-0s of Robinson's design, and it was on such workings that they were seen at their best. It is doubtful if any other 4-4-0 locomotives have been expected to handle so onerous a continuous locomotive working as this, nearly 4½hr in length without respite and including speeds up to and exceeding 80mph on the well-laid-out line south of Nottingham, as well as climbing the long and arduous gradients through most of the journey. It has been calculated that on this journey of 212 miles a locomotive required to lift its train through an aggregrate difference in altitude of no less than 2,900ft before Manchester was reached.

In LNER years standard stock appeared on the train, and its normal formation was seven coaches, including a through LMSR composite brake for Halifax on the rear. The rest of the train, from the engine backwards, was usually third class brake, third corridor, third restaurant car, first class restaurant and kitchen car, composite and third brake; this made a tare weight of 243 tons, and a gross weight of about 260 tons. By now the B17 or 'Sandringham' 3-cylinder 4-6-0s had replaced the 'Directors' to be succeeded by Pacifics and 'Green Arrows'. No up working ever ranked with the down train as the 'Sheffield Special'; the nearest approach was probably the 2.15pm from Manchester London Road, making the same stops from Guide Bridge, and due in Marylebone at 6.38pm. Both trains were withdrawn on the outbreak of war in 1939. After the war no recognisable successor to the 3.20pm down ever reappeared in the timetable and the Great Central route from London to Manchester is itself now a thing of the past.

Trains for Summer Holidays

Holiday traffic between the great centres of population and the coastal resorts was particularly heavy before it was eroded by the private car, and the services were prolific in named trains.

Above: 'Battle of Britain' Pacific No 34109 *Sir Trafford Leigh-Mallory* leaves Waterloo for the Hardy country in June 1951. *Brian Morrison*

Left: West of Exeter that many-portioned train, the 'Atlantic Coast Express' split into a number of short sections. No 34080 *74 Squadron* has only two coaches in tow at Launceston on 15 August 1960 as it heads for the Far West at Padstow. *A. Tyson*

Top left: For many years the 'Sunny South Express' was the best known of the cross-countries between the north-west and the South Coast because of its evocative name. In this photograph LBSC 'B4' class 4-4-0 No 42 *His Majesty* stands with the train in Addison Road (now Kensington Olympia) station en route between the LNWR at Willesden Junction and the LBSCR at Clapham Junction. *L. E. Brailsford*

Centre left: A short-lived through service between Paddington and Brighton also used the West London line. In this 1906 view at Addison Road it is formed of LBSC Marsh rolling stock headed by the Billinton 'B4' 4-4-0 *Siemens*. *L. E. Brailsford*

Bottom left: The Southern Region's up 'Man of Kent' (Charing Cross-Ramsgate) with 'Schools' 4-4-0 No 30924 takes the curve at Minster Junction in 1960. *P. Ransome-Wallis*

Top right: Blackpool is not usually thought of as a top resort for Londoners but it has been served by some fast trains, including the one-time 'Blackpool and Fylde Coast Express'. Rebuilt 'Scot' No 46150 *The Life Guardsman* has brought a down Blackpool express to the top of Camden Bank in July 1958. *Brian Morrison*

Bottom right: An up express from Carlisle with through coaches from Windermere for visitors returning from the Lake District approaches Tring on 19 May 1952 behind No 46161 *King's Own*, a rebuilt 'Royal Scot'.

46150

Above right: Class V2 'Green Arrow' 2-6-2 No 60893 passes York Holgate with the up 'Scarborough Flier' on 15 August 1953.
H. Gordon Tidey/Real Photos

Centre right: The down 'Torbay Express' blasts out of Parson's Tunnel, Dawlish, on 5 April 1952, powered by 'Castle' No 5086 *Viscount Horne*. *C. H. S. Owen*

Below: Line closures brought several changes of route for the cross-country 'Pines Express' from the North to Bournemouth. Here it is passing Hinksey Yard, Oxford, on 20 July 1963, with 'Battle of Britain' No 34085 *501 Squadron* heading for its home territory on the Southern via Reading and Basingstoke.
Gerald T. Robinson

'Limited' Motive Power

Above: 'Manor' class 4-6-0 No 7814 pilots 'King' No 6009 *King Charles II* (in an experimental blue livery) on the 'Cornish Riviera' descending Hemerdon bank on 16 June 1948. *W. J. Alcock*

No longer 'Limited' and no longer leaving Paddington at 10.30, the 'Cornish Riviera' name lives on among a whole family of fast HST services to the West. In its time the train has been entrusted to a varied selection of Great Western and Western Region motive power.

Below: 'Hall' No 6940 *Didlington Hall* takes the 'Riviera' out of Penzance on 17 April 1954. *B. K. B. Green*

Above: Pacific power for the 'Riviera'. 'Britannia' standard 4-6-2 No 70021 *Morning Star* leaves St Erth with the down train on 19 April 1952. *B. A. Butt*

Right: Diesel-hydraulic B-B No D800 *Sir Brian Robertson* crosses Hayle Causeway with the down 'Limited' on 2 October 1958. *B. A. Butt*

Below right: D600, one of the original A1A-A1A 'Warships', stands on the up train in Penzance station on 5 June 1958. *P. Thatcher*

Far right, top: Diesel-hydraulic C-C No 1009 *Western Invader* is signalled out of Truro on 28 November 1974. *Brian Morrison*

Far right, bottom: Class 253 HST unit No 253.015 forming the down 'Cornish Riviera' on 11 January 1980 makes light work of Dainton bank. *Mark S. Wilkins*

1A19

The 'Trans-Pennines'

The name 'Trans-Pennine' originated with the six-car dmus built at Swindon for the North Eastern Region and put to work on cross-country services between the North-East, Yorkshire and Lancashire by the Standedge Tunnel route. It denoted a train service with its own distinctive rolling stock rather than an individual train.

Top: Before the diesels came: Unrebuilt 'Scot' 4-6-0 No 46156 *The South Wales Borderer* heads a Newcastle-Liverpool express at Linthwaite on the ex-LNW Manchester-Huddersfield line. *IAL*

Above: A 'Trans-Pennine' dmu forms a Hull-Liverpool service on the first day of working with these units in January 1961. *Ken Smith*

Above left: Locomotive haulage returns to the Trans-Pennine route, and 'Deltic' No 55.013 *The Black Watch* finds employment after being displaced from the East Coast Main Line by HSTs. The train is the 13.05 Liverpool-York, sweeping round the curves between Mossley and Greenfield as it speeds towards Standedge Tunnel on 6 July 1979. *B. Watkins*

Above: The 11.10 Liverpool-Hull begins the descent from Marsden, at the eastern end of Standedge Tunnel, to Huddersfield on 8 July 1976. *David A. Flitcroft*

Left: A 'Trans-Pennine' unit leaves the western end of Standedge Tunnel, passing the site of the former Diggle station. The original bore of 1849 is on the right. *Larry Goddard*

The Midland Route to Scotland

Above: The daytime St Pancras-Edinburgh service was named the 'Waverley' by BR. It travelled between Carlisle and Edinburgh by the Waverley Route of the former North British Railway, now closed. Rebuilt 'Scot' No 46145 *The Duke of Wellington's Regiment (West Riding)* takes the northbound train past Long Preston on 16 May 1959. *M. R. Galley*

Left: The St Pancras-Scotland service is no more, although Settle-Carlisle which the Midland built to be free of partial dependence on the LNWR struggles on for local needs. The up 'Thames-Clyde Express' (St Pancras-Glasgow) is headed by No 6133 near Bell Busk. *W. Hubert Foster*

Below left: Diesel power brought important accelerations to St Pancras services. Class 45 No D34 heads the up 'Waverley' out of Skipton on 21 August 1967. *L. A. Nixon*

Right: The 'Thames-Clyde Express' shared in the 'shot in the arm' of diesel power. A Class 46 shows its paces at Ais Gill on the up 'Thames-Clyde' on 10 September 1972. *J. H. Cooper-Smith*

1M86

Full Fare — Cheap Fare

When BR's enthusiasm for naming trains was at its height the Eastern and North Eastern Regions put on a Newcastle-King's Cross service called the 'Northumbrian'. Some years later, in an effort to stimulate rail travel between the north-east and the London area the Eastern Region launched its 'Highwayman' cheap fare special between Newcastle and Finsbury Park, travelling by the coast line through Sunderland and Hartlepool.

Above: Class 46 No D174 approaches Knebworth on 5 July 1963 with the up 'Northumbrian'. The locomotive carries the express headlamp code. Train descriptions displayed in the describer panel were sometimes-difficult to read if cleaning had been perfunctory. *Brian Stephenson*

Below: The down 'Highwayman' slows to pick up at Stevenage on 16 May 1970. This was a buffet car service in both directions. In the formation shown behind Class 40 No D254 the buffet car is No E1706E, a Thompson vehicle. *D. L. Percival*

Steam Specials

The tradition of nameboards and named trains has been kept alive by specials worked by preserved steam locomotives.

Above: Enthusiasts' societies were organising special trips before the final withdrawal of steam on BR in 1968. 'Jubilee' 4-6-0 No 45562 *Alberta* struggles past Linthwaite (between Huddersfield and Manchester) with a Jubilee Preservation Society special from Leeds to Carlisle via Manchester. *L. A. Nixon*

Left: 'West Country' Pacific No 34092 *City of Wells* travels northward on the Settle & Carlisle line with the 'Cumbrian Mountain Pullman' formed of former Pullman vehicles purchased in 1981 by the Steam Locomotive Operators Association. *L. A. Nixon*

Below left: The 'Scarborough Spa Express' was launched in 1981 as a York-Scarborough steam service. In 1982 the itinerary was extended to a York-Leeds-Scarborough round trip. Veteran preserved Pacific No 4472 *Flying Scotsman* heads the 1982 train near Strensall Common on the York-Scarborough leg. *BR*

The Silver Jubilee

History was made in Great Britain on 27 September 1935 when, at 2.25 in the afternoon, the first British streamlined train with fully streamlined locomotive slipped out of King's Cross terminus in London for a test run to Grantham and back. It was 110 years to the day after George Stephenson had driven *Locomotion No 1* over the Stockton & Darlington Railway at the opening of the first public railway to come into existence. The new 'Silver Jubilee', so named in honour of the Silver Jubilee of the reign of King George V, which was celebrated in 1935, was a striking testimony to the tremendous advance in the luxury and speed of transport that had taken place in little over a century.

Few who participated in the 'Silver Jubilee' trial are likely to forget the experience. For certain reasons it was desired to ascertain how much time the new A4 Pacific locomotive, No 2509 *Silver Link*, might be expected to have in hand on the schedule to which the train was to run from the following Monday. From the start therefore the special began to gain time; up the 1 in 200 ascent to Potters Bar speed was increased steadily to 75mph; after the summit of the 'Northern Heights' had been breasted near Knebworth the 100mph mark was crossed at milepost 25; and for the next 30 miles the speed was continuously above that figure, and might have remained so but for the need of caution round the curves at Offord.

Twice in succession a maximum speed of 112½mph was reached, the highest on record in Great Britain up to that time. For 43 miles continuously an average of 100mph was maintained, and the 70 miles from Wood Green to Fletton Junction, where the driver began to reduce speed for the severe curve through Peterborough, were covered at an average speed of 91.8mph, notwithstanding the inclusion in this length of the long 1 in 200 climbs from Wood Green to Potters Bar and from Hatfield to Woolmer Green. From King's Cross *Silver Link* passed Peterborough, 76.4 miles, in the unprecedented time of 55min 2sec, or 8½min less than the time fixed for the train's regular running.

The 'Silver Jubilee' went into service on 30 September 1935. Its daily journey began at Newcastle Central at 10am; the 36 miles to Darlington, with heavy gradients and the severe slack over Durham viaduct, were allowed 40min, and from there, after a stop of 2min, the 232.3 miles to King's Cross were run non-stop in 3hr 18min, at a scheduled average of 70.4mph, bringing the train into London at 2pm. Three and a half hours later, at 5.30pm, the return journey was begun, with exactly the same time allowance; Darlington was reached at 8.48pm and left at 8.50pm, and the arrival in Newcastle was at 9.30pm.

From the first day the 'Silver Jubilee' was highly popular — so much so, indeed, that intending passengers who had neglected the precaution of booking their seats well in advance stood the risk of being left behind. A supplement of 5s (25p) first class and 3s (15p) third class was charged for a seat, and it was rarely that the train ran with a single seat vacant. Despite the fact that the 'Silver Jubilee' did not run on Saturdays or Sundays, in two years the supplementary fares alone accumulated a sum sufficient to pay the entire cost of building the train. It had proved that the British public wanted speed, and was prepared to pay for it.

The schedule of the train was such as to demand speeds of 90mph over considerable stretches of favourable track in order to maintain time. The fastest point-to-point timing was over the 27 miles from Hitchin to Huntingdon, in the northbound direction, allowed only 19min; moreover, this booked average of 85.3mph included a 70mph slowing round the curves at Offord. Severe reductions of speed were necessary through Peterborough, Selby and York in both directions. For the first time, also, in view of the high average speed of the train, it became necessary to impose limits of 70 to 80mph at various points where speed restrictions had never operated previously.

In order to check the drivers' observance of these restrictions, the engines were fitted with self-recording speed indicators, which not only gave them a visible indication of their speeds, on a dial in the cab, but also recorded the speed automatically on a paper tape moved by clockwork, and so made it possible at the end of each journey for the speed throughout to be checked. Another precaution connected with the speed was that of keeping two block signalling sections clear ahead of the 'Silver Jubilee' instead of the normal one.

The original formation of the train was three

articulated sets of coaches, making seven vehicles in all, carried on ten bogies. At the north end was a 'twin', consisting of brake third and third class, both compartment coaches. Next came the restaurant car 'triplet', with open third class car, kitchen and pantry car, and open first class car. At the south end there was a second 'twin', one vehicle of which was a first class car, half open and the other half divided into three compartments, and a four-compartment first class brake behind that. The demand for accommodation was such that at a later date an additional coach body was built into the leading 'twin', making it into a 'triplet', third class throughout. This addition increased the empty weight of the train from 200 to 248 tons, and the number of vehicles to eight.

In conformity with its name, the 'Silver Jubilee' had an exterior finish of silver-grey throughout, with stainless steel fittings, and the four locomotives specially built for the service — Nos 2509 *Silver Link*, 2510 *Quicksilver*, 2511 *Silver King* and 2512 *Silver Fox* — were painted in the same grey shade. Later, as more of the A4 streamlined Pacifics were built, and the Garter blue colour was adopted, Nos 2509 and 2512 were painted blue also, and from that time onwards any of the A4 class engines might be rostered to work the train. In the four years up to World War 2 the 'Silver Jubilee' train ran about 540,000 miles without mishap, and was reckoned to have earned for its owners a revenue of some 12s 6d (63p) a mile. The train was withdrawn on the outbreak of war, and was never reinstated; after that the restaurant car triplet was used between King's Cross and Newcastle, and the five passenger coaches for some time led a humdrum life on the 'Fife Coast Express' between Glasgow and St Andrews.

The 'Fife Coast Express' had a long but fragmented history. The North British Railway put on a summer train between Glasgow and Crail in 1910, naming it the 'Fifeshire Coast Express'. In 1939 the name was still in the timetable, but now borne by two trains to Dundee, one from Edinburgh and one from Glasgow. There was a reminder of the original service, however, in that the Glasgow train had a Crail portion which was transferred to the one from Edinburgh at Dalmeny, where both trains made an unadvertised stop for the purpose. After the war the name returned, slightly modified, as the 'Fife Coast Express', being given to the 7.15am from St Andrews to Glasgow and the 4.07pm back. The name did not last many years but the ex-streamliner coaches were working in Fife until the early 1960s.

The Sunny South Express

It was in 1904 that the 'Sunny South' idea first took shape. In the cities of the Midlands and the North there had been some agitation for through facilities for holiday travellers to the South Coast, avoiding the complication of crossing London. The first experiment was a service of through coaches between Manchester and Brighton in 1904; but the popularity of the service was so great that in the following year it had blossomed out into a complete restaurant car express, organised jointly by the London & North Western and London, Brighton & South Coast Railways and formed of the former company's stock, between Liverpool and Manchester, Brighton and Eastbourne.

The idea was infectious, and before long the Kent Coast was sharing in the same facilities, while through coaches were being run from the Midland and Great Northern systems also, by way of the Metropolitan line through Snow Hill, Herne Hill and the Bickley junctions to Folkestone, Dover and Deal. One daily service, running in 1914, comprised coaching stock of the North Western, Midland and Great Northern Railways, marshalled at Herne Hill into one curious composite assemblage for its journey over the South Eastern & Chatham line to Ramsgate. For a short period one could travel through also from Paddington to Brighton.

A remarkable episode in the pre-1914 history of the 'Sunny South Express' was the through working of locomotives between Brighton and Rugby arranged jointly by the London, Brighton & South Coast and London & North Western Companies in the latter part of 1909. The LNWR engine was one of the 'Precursor' 4-4-0s, No 7, *Titan*; but the LBSCR placed reliance on one of the new 4-4-2 tanks of Earle Marsh's design, No 13 of Class I3. The round trip was one of 264 miles, which the tank locomotives used to complete on the one heaped-up bunker full of coal, about $3\frac{1}{4}$ tons.

Most amazing of all was the fact that the Brighton engine, with a tank capacity no greater than 2,100 gallons, could daily run the 90 miles between East Croydon and Rugby without taking water, though this meant working a 7-coach 235-ton train non-stop over the 77.2 miles between Willesden and Rugby at 53mph. Consumption averaged no more than 27lb of fuel and 22gal of water per mile. One essential factor of this success was that the Marsh tank had been fitted with a Schmidt superheater; and this exchange with little doubt marked an important turning point in LNWR locomotive history, for it resulted in the building of the 'George the Fifth' class, one of the most competent 4-4-0 designs in British annals.

After World War 1, during which these through services were suspended, the 'Sunny South Express' duly reappeared. But like many other pre-1914 through services to and from holiday resorts eventually it became a weekend service only over a large part of the year. Through the summer season it reverted to daily service once more, and at weekends expanded to several independent trains.

In summer the main southbound train, with the restaurant cars attached, left Manchester London Road at 10.40am, and was joined at Crewe by the 10.35am from Liverpool Lime Street. The combined train, leaving Crewe at 11.46am, then called at Nuneaton, Rugby and Northampton to Willesden, which was reached at 3.11pm. At Rugby the express acquired some through coaches from Birmingham, which had left New Street at 12.30pm. At Willesden Junction the Southern Railway took over, and starting at 3.24pm worked the 'Sunny South Express' round the West London Line, skirting the Metropolis through Kensington Addison Road, and Clapham Junction to East Croydon. From Clapham Junction onwards the express had to be fitted into the dense electric service, and was due into Brighton at 4.55pm. This was 15min slower from Liverpool to Brighton than in 1904. Away again at 5.04pm, with an engine on the opposite end of the train, a non-stop run was made to Eastbourne in 41min, and here a second reversal took place. The final stage of the journey, completing a total of 278½ miles from Manchester, was to Bexhill, St Leonards and Hastings, reached at 6.25pm, after a journey lasting 7¾hr.

Going north, a start was made from Hastings at 11.10am, Eastbourne at 11.49am, and Brighton at 12.35pm, reaching East Croydon at 1.27pm, Kensington at 1.53pm, and Willesden at 2.02pm. Here the LMSR took charge, and the next stop was Northampton, where the Birmingham coaches were detached, instead of at Rugby. The 'Sunny South Express' then made a non-stop run over the 94.6 miles to Crewe (where the Liverpool and Manchester sections separated) in 106min, reaching Crewe at 5.15pm. By arrivals in Manchester at 6.19pm and Liverpool at 6.24pm, the northbound 'Sunny South' improved on its southbound times by 36min.

On summer Saturdays the workings were very complicated. Additional through restaurant car trains ran in each direction between Birmingham and Hastings, by the 'Sunny South' route, and also between Birmingham and the Kent Coast resorts. The latter were diverted beyond Addison Road through the Latchmere and Longhedge junctions on to the Eastern Division main line from Victoria, continuing to Chatham, Herne Bay, Margate and Ramsgate. Through coaches were run on the latter train from Liverpool and Manchester, and the Midland Division of the LMSR contributed a through section from Sheffield and Leicester to Hastings, which was attached at Northampton. World War 2 brought these 'Sunny South' activities to an abrupt end, but they were later restored between Birmingham, Leicester, Brighton, Eastbourne and Hastings on Saturdays only during the summer. The attractive name 'Sunny South Express', however, did not reappear. Daily through trains throughout the year between Manchester and Brighton were introduced by BR in 1979, but the motive was to serve Gatwick Airport as much as to renew a facility for the South Coast resort. The trains are not routed via Willesden but use the connection between the West London line and the Western Region at North Pole Junction, travelling to and from Birmingham via Oxford and Banbury.

The Talisman

In the summer of 1956 the welcome news became public that after 17 years the prewar 'Coronation' was to have a postwar successor — as yet not so fast for arrears of track maintenance were still being dealt with, but with plenty of promise for the future. This proved to be a new train called the 'Talisman', which went into service in September of that year. It left Kings Cross at the same 4pm departure time as its distinguished predecessor, with a mile-a-minute run over the 268.4 miles to Newcastle in 268min. Edinburgh was reached in 6hr 40min from London, at 10.40pm. The starting time coming up was also at 4pm, half an hour earlier than the 'Coronation's', and after an easy 129min allowance to Newcastle, the non-stop run from there to King's Cross was allowed 265min, for an arrival, as in the down direction, at 10.40pm. In the early years the eight-coach formations of this express included the beautiful twin first class sets from the 'Coronation', with their armchair seating, which were greatly appreciated by the patrons of the new service; the haulage was by A4 Pacifics.

Such was the success of the 'Talisman' that in the following year, 1957, the East Coast authorities decided to double the service by adding two-way morning 'Talisman' workings. In the down direction the recently-installed 7.50am express from King's Cross to Leeds had been including in its formation a portion for Newcastle; this the new 7.45am 'Morning Talisman' took over, getting its passengers to Newcastle in 25min less time by 12.19pm, and into Edinburgh by 2.30pm, an earlier arrival from London in the Scottish capital than had ever been possible previously with a day train. For the southbound journey a start from Edinburgh Waverley as early as 7.30am was fixed; Newcastle was left at 9.45am, no more than 25min behind the 'Tees-Tyne' Pullman', which the 'Talisman' followed into Kings Cross at an interval of 13min only, at 2.15pm, thus offering some rather serious competition with the former. One operating advantage of the twin 'Talisman' services, morning and evening, was that it now became possible, with roller-bearing stock, to use the same train sets for a double working in the day, covering no less than 786 miles, the greatest daily mileage of any British coaching stock up to that date.

In the autumn of 1957 there was an interesting development in the working of the 'Morning Talisman' in each direction; it was decided to extend the train to Perth, and in celebration of the fact to rechristen it the 'Fair Maid'. Now leaving King's Cross at 7.50am, and with additional stops at Darlington and Berwick, the 'Fair Maid' reached Edinburgh at 2.36pm, and after a 14min wait proceeded over the Forth Bridge to Dunfermline and Perth, where it was due at 4.18pm. In the up direction Perth passengers had a very early start, for even with the exit from Edinburgh deferred for an hour to 8.30am, Perth needed to be left at 6.40am; London was now reached at 3.30pm. But the title 'Fair Maid' lasted no more than a year; in the autumn of 1958 the through running to Perth and back came to an end; the 8.30am southbound start from Edinburgh, however, now became permanent.

During the subsequent years acceleration went on steadily until in the summer of 1962, now with 3,300hp 'Deltic' diesels available, the afternoon 'Talisman' trains in both directions came down to the six-hour timings between King's Cross and Edinburgh of their prewar 'Coronation' predecessors. This involved covering the 268.3 miles between London and Newcastle in 4hr 1min down and a minute more up. In the same summer timetable the down morning 'Talisman' acquired a Grantham stop in addition to those at Darlington, Newcastle and Berwick; coming up the stops were the same as in the opposite direction, Grantham excepted, and the London arrival was at 2.15pm. In 1963, to conform to the pattern of departures from Edinburgh at the even hours, the 'Morning Talisman' was altered to leave Waverley at 8am. Next, in accordance with the increasing popularity of stops outside London, for the benefit of suburban residents, it was arranged in 1964 for the down 'Morning Talisman' to stop at Hitchin to pick up, and the up 'Afternoon Talisman' to call at the same station to set down.

In the following year, because of the withdrawal of the West Coast 'Caledonian' between Euston and Glasgow, it was arranged that the down 'Afternoon Talisman' should continue from Edinburgh to Glasgow Queen Street, for the first time in history bringing Glasgow within 7hr of King's Cross. This involved starting the up 'Morning Talisman' from Glasgow as early as 7am in order to maintain the 8am departure from Edinburgh, and this did not appeal sufficiently for the through Glasgow running to be continued for more than a year. Another odd experiment tried at about this time with both 'Talisman' train sets was to substitute four Pullman cars for the first class accommodation, which made the Pullman supplement compulsory for first class passengers. This arrangement certainly did not appeal to many thrifty Scots travellers; and in addition it was found that the older Pullmans which were the only cars available at the time did not take kindly to such high speed travel, and frequently had to be taken out of service for repairs. It was little surprise that this rather ill-advised experiment had no more than a very short life. A stop at Darlington introduced towards the end of 1964 into the schedules of both afternoon trains, however, was considerably more popular and became permanent.

With the introduction in March 1967 of the new 7.55am down Newcastle flyer from King's Cross, calling only at Darlington and completing the journey in 3hr 50min, the down 'Morning Talisman' was retimed to make no fewer than eight intermediate stops — at Hitchin, Peterborough, Grantham, Doncaster, York, Darlington, Newcastle and Berwick — yet such were the powers of the 'Deltics' that even with an eleven-coach load of all but 400 tons tare the journey of 392.9 miles was completed in 6hr 19min. The 'Afternoon Talisman', with the same load and two stops only, was in Edinburgh by 9.55pm, in 5hr 55min from London. The up 'Morning Talisman', still at 8am from Edinburgh and with Berwick, Newcastle and Darlington stops, had a 6hr run; and the up afternoon train, calling at Newcastle, Darlington and Hitchin, took 2min less.

The 'Talisman' was withdrawn in 1968 but restored in 1971 for one King's Cross-Edinburgh service in each direction. The name was carried by the 4pm departures from King's Cross and from Waverley, the down train making the journey in 4hr 45min and the up in 4hr 57min. The down 'Talisman' was worked by an HST from April 1978, as the return working of a set which had travelled up to London on the 8am from Edinburgh. In May 1979 the full East Coast HST service was introduced and the up and down trains both had the 'Inter-City 125' image.

The Tees-Tyne Pullman

Early in 1948 strong rumours began to go the rounds that the 'Silver Jubilee' was to go into service once again, and the hopes of ex-LNER enthusiasts began to rise accordingly, though it was obvious that nothing approaching the prewar standard of speed was to be anticipated as yet. But when the new train materialised, on 27 September 1948, it turned out to be another addition to the British Pullman fleet, with the name of 'Tees-Tyne Pullman'. It reproduced the 'Silver Jubilee' to the extent of leaving London at 5.30pm, and having no publicly-booked stop over the 232.2 miles between King's Cross and Darlington; but whereas the 'Silver Bullet', as its regular patrons often called it, bridged this distance in 3hr 18min, at 70.4mph, the new train was found to have been given no less than 4hr 27min (52.2mph), and the Pullman was to reach Newcastle at 10.50pm as compared with the 'Jubilee's' 9.30pm. The up journey was to be similar; leaving Newcastle one hour earlier than the 'Jubilee', at 9am, the 'Tees-Tyne Pullman' would be into London at 2.16pm, 16min later.

In May 1949 however, the first welcome acceleration of the 'Tees-Tyne' took place, bringing the London-Newcastle time in each direction down to the even five hours, and in September 1949 a year after the train's inauguration, there was a second speed-up. In the winter of 1949-1950, therefore, the 'Tees-Tyne Pullman' was reaching Newcastle in 4hr 55min from King's Cross, and the southbound train was making the run in 4hr 52min, a cut of 25min northbound and 24min southbound on its timings of a year earlier. The original schedules included an unadvertised stop at Grantham to change engine crews, but as soon as it could be arranged for the men to work through between Newcastle and King's Cross, it became possible to make a cut in the King's Cross-Darlington times to 251min northbound and 247min southbound, both non-stop, the latter requiring a more respectable overall average speed of 56.5mph.

From May 1949 the up 'Tees-Tyne Pullman' left Newcastle at 9.15am. Also, from the same date, the down 'Tees-Tyne' changed places with the 'Yorkshire Pullman', and gained a much earlier departure from London, at 4.45pm; the arrival at Darlington then became 8.56pm, and at Newcastle 9.40pm, not far removed from the prewar 'Silver Jubilee' times. Later adjustments in timing made the arrivals of the down train 8.50pm at Darlington and 9.37pm at Newcastle, while the up 'Tees-Tyne' was due in King's Cross at 2.08pm; between Darlington and King's Cross the non-stop times were 248min up and 245min down. The train soon became very popular, especially with Tees-side and Tyneside business men, and ran well filled in both directions, even though the supplementary fares (12s (60p) first class and 6s 6d (33p) third class) were more than double the 5s (25p) and 3s (15p) supplements of the 'Jubilee'. In view of the all-round increase in prices that was taking place the later rise in 'Tees-Tyne' supplements to 15s (75p) first class and 8s 6d (43p) second class was modest, and patrons also had the enjoyment of the much finer cars that were introduced in recent years.

When it first ran, the 'Tees-Tyne Pullman' comprised eight cars, two of them Pullman brakes. Such was the popularity of the service that in the 1960s, notwithstanding the competition of other fast morning and evening services, such as the eight-coach flyers in 3hr 50min and the 'Talisman' trains, the Pullman required nine full length cars, including the 'Hadrian Bar', and a separate bogie brake (the old Pullman brakes having disappeared), making a total weight of 395 tons. 'Deltic'-hauled, speed was far higher than when the train began to run, especially as an additional stop was made at York in each direction. In 1965 its timing of 33min only for the 44.1 miles from Darlington to York — 80.2mph start-to-stop — introduced the first 80mph run to a British timetable, but this record was soon to be handsomely beaten by a number of London Midland electric schedules and a half-minute added later to the Darlington-York time reduced its average speed to 79mph.

In 1969 the second class Pullmans in the 'Tees-Tyne' were replaced by ordinary stock and the 'Hadrian Bar' was withdrawn, all passengers sharing the restaurant-buffet car on the non-Pullman section. The train had been running to Newcastle in 4hr 2min and its average speed from King's Cross to York was 70.5mph. The up service, at 9.15am from Newcastle, was 1min faster. In 1975 the 5pm departure from King's Cross was taken over by an Edinburgh train, and the 'Tees-Tyne' came back to 4.30pm. This was the final change in the schedule and saw the Pullman into Newcastle in $3\frac{3}{4}$hr. The acceleration was short-lived for the train was eliminated in the 1976-77 timetable, victim of the deepening business recession and its effect on business travel from Tees-side and Tyneside.

The Thames-Clyde Express

Among the titles bestowed by the LMSR on various trains in 1927, the morning services in each direction between St Pancras and Glasgow, linking the Thames with the Clyde, received the appropriate name of 'Thames-Clyde Express'. Under LMSR auspices, after the 1932 accelerations, the trains which figure in this chapter had settled down to a 10am departure from St Pancras and 9.30am from Glasgow (St Enoch).

The Midland and Glasgow & South Western route was not merely longer than that of the one-time London & North Western and Caledonian Railways — $424\frac{1}{2}$ miles (or $426\frac{1}{4}$ miles via Sheffield) as compared with $401\frac{1}{2}$ miles — but it was much more heavily graded, so that it could never compete effectively in time. It was, however, the scenic attraction of the former, especially through the Pennines from Hellifield and down the Eden Valley to Carlisle, that caused it to be preferred by many even as a route between London and Glasgow, apart from its value to the intermediate cities of Leicester, Nottingham, Sheffield and Leeds.

By 1939 the 'Thames-Clyde Express' had participated in the general acceleration, and began its day by running the 72 miles from St Pancras to Kettering, the first stop, in 71min, notwithstanding the hard uphill start, to just beyond St Albans, and such banks as the 3 miles at 1 in 119 to Sharnbrook summit. Leicester, 99.1 miles, was reached at 11.44am, in 32min from Kettering. From Leicester the next stop was at Chesterfield, and the 47.2 miles from Leicester were allowed 57min, with a fine level start to Trent, a very severe slack through that junction, and a moderate climb up the Erewash valley. After 3min wait at Chesterfield, the express avoided Sheffield and the stiff grind up to Bradway tunnel by taking the old main line direct to Rotherham; the Chesterfield-Leeds stretch of 49.7 miles was run in exactly one hour. At Leeds the engine which had worked through from London, almost invariably a 'Jubilee' 4-6-0, was left in the platform, where the usual reversal of the train took place.

In later years a through engine working became customary on this train between Leeds and Glasgow, $228\frac{1}{2}$ miles, and until World War 2 this was generally assigned to a 'Jubilee' 4-6-0; but during the war the rebuilt 'Royal Scots' appeared on the scene, and did great execution with loads mounting at times to 14 and even 15 bogies without pilot assistance, though of course on a much slower schedule.

The prewar 'Thames-Clyde', after making the 36-mile run from Leeds to Hellifield in 45min, then had the sharp booking of 51min for the 46 miles from Hellifield to Appleby, including the 15-mile climb from Settle Junction to Blea Moor tunnel, almost entirely at 1 in 100. The downhill 30.8 miles from Appleby to Carlisle had an easy 35min, and the Border city was reached at 4.09pm.

Over the Glasgow & South Western line also there were latterly some smart timings. Stops were made at Annan, Dumfries, Mauchline (to give a quick connection to Ayr), and Kilmarnock, but notwithstanding the long climb from Dumfries over the high ground near New Cumnock, 616ft above sea level, with its 13 miles of almost continuous 1 in 200-150 grade to Drumlanrig tunnel, beyond Carronbridge, and the even steeper ascent out of Kilmarnock, at about 1 in 80 for 3 miles of its $4\frac{1}{2}$ miles of length, the train was due in St Enoch at 6.38pm, in 2hr 23min from Carlisle and 8hr 38min from London.

Coming south, the running to Carlisle was similar to that in the reverse direction, except that there was no stop at Mauchline; the 115.5 miles required 2hr 20min and Carlisle was reached at 11.50am. Here passengers who wanted to make a fast run to London could change into the 'Royal Scot' and save a clear hour. Five minutes only were allowed at Carlisle, and at 11.55am the 'Thames-Clyde' was away on a non-stop run of 113 miles to Leeds, reached at 2.20pm.

From Leeds the stops were at Sheffield, Trent (where until 1937 a Nottingham coach was detached) and Leicester, and the journey concluded in St Pancras after a 60mph run over the final 99.1 miles from Leicester in 99min, at 6.25pm. Like the 'Royal Scot', the 'Thames-Clyde' was thus slower coming south than going north, needing 8hr 55min — 17min more — though with six intermediate stops as compared with eight. The diversion through Sheffield added $1\frac{3}{4}$ miles of distance and an entirely disproportionate amount of very hard work, for the start out of Sheffield to the south end of Bradway tunnel is $5\frac{1}{2}$ miles at 1 in 100.

Through much of the year a set of eight coaches sufficed for the through working — third class brake, compartment third, open third, third restaurant, kitchen, composite restaurant, composite and first class brake. An extra composite or third might be attached from St Pancras to Leeds. At Carlisle the composite from Nottingham, which had been brought thus far by the down 'Thames-Forth Express', was added. In the reverse direction, the head of the train included through composite brakes for Bristol, detached at Leeds, and for Nottingham, which ran through as far as Trent

World War 2 had a remarkable effect on this train. Though still leaving St Pancras at 10am, it was not due in St Enoch until all but 3hr later than before, at 9.32pm. On the southbound journey it started 30min later at 10am, and was due to reach St Pancras at 9.40pm, $3\frac{1}{4}$hr after its previous arrival — a journey not far short of 12hr, and often considerably more than that by reason of late running.

The northbound run was increased in length to 444 miles by a circuitous course from Kettering to Chesterfield by way of Nottingham and Derby. Through some years of war this had the extraordinary result that both the 10am from St Pancras to Glasgow and the 10am from Glasgow to St Pancras stopped at the same platform at Trent, travelling in the same direction — the latter coming direct down the Erewash valley from Chesterfield to Leicester, and the northbound train momentarily running due south through Trent on its way from Nottingham to Derby. Another curious characteristic of the northbound run was that the 10am from St Pancras passed daily through more tunnels than any other train in Great Britain. There were nine, for example, between Kettering and Nottingham and 14 between Hellifield and Carlisle alone, helping to make up a total of 40 on the run. Of these no fewer than six — Belsize, Corby, Glaston, Clay Cross, Bradway and Blea Moor — were tunnels over a mile long; the 40 tunnels totalled about 15 miles in length.

Heavy wartime loads were invariable on this run; from London at least nine in the Glasgow portion and four through coaches for Edinburgh, with an additional coach attached to go as far as Nottingham or Leeds, replaced at Leeds by an additional brake-van, composed the train. The motive power between St Pancras and Leeds was a 'Jubilee' 4-6-0, sometimes assisted by a 4-4-0 for all or part of the journey; and latterly, as previously mentioned, one of the rebuilt 'Royal Scots' between Leeds and Glasgow.

After the war ended, from 1 October 1945, both trains regained their restaurant cars, and lost their through Edinburgh coaches. The southbound express was greatly accelerated, and calling after Carlisle only at Leeds, Sheffield, Nottingham and Kettering, was due in St Pancras 80min earlier, at 8.20pm. October 1946 witnessed a complete timetable recasting, in which the 10am down, altered to start at 9.55am, returned to the Leicester route, became non-stop from Leeds to Carlisle, and was into Glasgow St Enoch by 7.23pm. Coming south, also via Leicester, the 9.50am from St Enoch, as it then became, was due in St Pancras at 7.24pm. In subsequent years the 'Thames-Clyde Express', which recovered its name in 1949, was slowed down lamentably, deceleration being due in part to the reduced speed enforced over much of the route between Trent and Leeds because of pitfall subsidences in the mining area. In the 1952-1953 winter timetable the down train was leaving St Pancras at 9.50am, and taking no less than 10hr 5min to Glasgow; the up train, starting from St Enoch at 9.15am, required 10hr 13min to St Pancras.

Later, the 'Thames-Clyde Express' underwent some very remarkable changes. With changes in Regional boundaries, it passed out of what formerly was Midland and later London Midland & Scottish territory at a point just south of Chesterfield into the Eastern Region, in which it continued as far as Cudworth. From here through Leeds and as far as Skipton it was in charge of what until 1967 was the North Eastern Region, but which became part of the Eastern Region also. From Skipton to Carlisle was again LMR territory, while north of Carlise, of course, Scottish Region control continued unchanged.

There were changes of route also. In the Midland Section timetable reorganisation of April 1966, as with a number of other expresses, the 'Thames-Clyde' was diverted from Trent to serve Nottingham, reversing there and rejoining the main line at Trowell. Then from May 1967 there was a change between Sheffield and Leeds, for the train left the former Midland main line at Swinton and used the one-time Swinton & Knottingley Joint Line as far as Moorthorpe, where it ran down the spur to join what was once the Great Northern main line, and so to reach Wakefield Westgate, where the up train stopped daily. To get back into Leeds City, use was made of the new spur line completed in 1967 to make possible the closure of Leeds Central. Lastly, whereas the speeds south of Nottingham and north of Leeds were faster than ever, with diesel haulage, the plague of pitfall subsidences between Nottingham and Leeds had made this section slower than at any time previously.

In its final years the down 'Thames-Clyde' took its place among the departures from St Pancras for Sheffield at ten minutes before each even hour, leaving at 9.50am for a 92min run over the 99.1 miles to Leicester; by 11.57am it was in Nottingham, with 7min there for reversal. Average speeds then dropped substantially, with a time of 40½min for the 28.3 miles from Nottingham to Chesterfield, though in view of the 4-mile climb at 1 in 100 to Bradway Tunnel, 16min for the 12.3 miles from Chesterfield to Sheffield did not leave much to spare. The slack-infested 38.6 miles from Sheffield via Moorthorpe and Wakefield to Leeds City needed no less than 71min (in 1939 the Sheffield-Leeds run by the best trains took 48min, and the 'Thames-Clyde' ran from Leicester to Leeds with one stop in two hours flat), and Leeds was reached at 2.20pm. From here, however, after a second reversal of the train, there was some improvement. With a stop at Settle in place of the former halt at Hellifield the 113-mile run from Leeds to Carlisle came down from the 136min of 1939 to 130min.

At Carlisle, except during the summer months, the train divided into three parts; there were six coaches for Glasgow and two for Edinburgh, and the two restaurant cars were detached, leaving passengers without any refreshments north of Carlisle; but this service was later restored. During the summer the Edinburgh coaches ran as a separate train throughout from London — the 'Waverley' — and the Glasgow portion then became an 8-coach train. The stops of the latter were as before save that Kirkconnel had replaced Mauchline, and that the terminus was Glasgow Central instead of St Enoch station, closed in 1966; 2hr 20min was still the overall time for the 115.5 miles from Carlisle. So Glasgow was reached at 7.05pm.

Southbound, the 'Thames-Clyde' was away from Glasgow at 9.35am, and into Carlisle, with the same stops, by 11.52am in winter and 5min later in summer, though not due to leave for the south until 12.09pm. Leeds was reached at 2.32pm and left 10min later; then, as mentioned previously, there came the new stop at Wakefield Westgate before the Sheffield stop (3.54-3.57pm); a halt at Chesterfield preceded that for reversal at Nottingham (5.05-5.10pm), and the final stage was a 97min sprint from Leicester to St Pancras, reached at 7.22pm. But 9¼hr northbound and 9hr 47min southbound for the through journey compared sadly with the 8hr 38min and 8hr 55min respectively in 1939, nearly 30 years earlier.

Further deceleration was to come, and in 1974 the train was 5min slower northbound, leaving St Pancras at 8.00am and arriving in Glasgow at 5.20pm. The name 'Thames-Clyde Express' was no longer used after the end of the 1974-75 timetable although there was still a departure from St Pancras for Glasgow at 8am. This train followed the West Coast Main Line north of Carlisle, with electric haulage from there to Glasgow Central. The new route and traction brought the train into Glasgow at 4.43pm but the advantage was short-lived and the service ended with the 1975-76 timetable. Anglo-Scottish trains connecting Kilmarnock and Dumfries with London then ran to and from Euston but a through Nottingham-Glasgow service still travelled by the Settle & Carlisle and G&SW route. In the 1982-83 timetable, however, the Settle & Carlisle line was reduced to a local service only and the Nottingham-Glasgow trains were rerouted to travel via Sheffield, Manchester, Bolton and Preston.

The Torbay Express

Little special distinction attached to the 'Torbay Express' of the GWR, other than that of being a fast and popular train. Before World War 1 it left Paddington at 11.50am, and followed the then prevailing GWR fashion of slipping coaches by having a slip portion on the tail as far as Taunton, for Ilfracombe, in the course of its 3hr non-stop run to Exeter. In the summer this Ilfracombe section achieved distinction by being the only slip portion in history to include a restaurant car in its four-coach formation. Just before the outbreak of war, the starting time was changed to 12 noon, and in the postwar recovery this became the permanent departure, though the Taunton 'slip' did not reappear.

Before the outbreak of World War 2, the 'Torbay', leaving Paddington at 12 noon, was due into St Davids station at Exeter at 2.49pm, having covered the 173.5 miles in 169min, at 61.6mph. A stop of 6min was scheduled here, and the 26.1 miles on to Torquay required 35min, making exactly 3½hr from London. From Torquay the London engine, almost invariably a 'King' 4-6-0, continued with the train, calling at Paignton, taking the train-staff for the single line at Goodrington Sands, calling at Churston, and descending the steep incline to Kingswear, to come to rest on the banks of the Dart opposite Darmouth at 4.05pm. The Goodrington-Kingswear stretch of 6 miles was probably the only piece of single track on the GWR used regularly by a 'King'. On Saturdays in summer the traffic for Torbay was sufficient to justify a non-stop run over 199.6 miles from Paddington to Torquay, and the 'Torbay Express' was allowed 3hr 28min to do it. Times beyond Torquay, however, were unchanged.

In the reverse direction, the 'King', after a level mile out of Kingswear, had first to tackle the nasty climb to Churston, including 2 miles at 1 in 66 and 1 in 75. The start from Torquay was even worse; it begins at 1 in 55 for ¾mile to Torre, and continues for another ¾mile at 1 in 73, so that banking assistance was often needed. Leaving Torquay at 12 noon, the Torbay was due in Exeter 35min later, and after 6min there, made the run of 173.5 miles to Paddington in 174min, at an average of almost exactly a mile-a-minute, arriving at 3.35pm. On summer Saturdays a non-stop relief was run from Torquay at 11.50am, taking 3¾hr, and the main train was allowed an extra quarter of an hour.

World War 2 at first saw the down 'Torbay Express' combined with the 'Cornish Riviera Limited', but the load of the combined train soon became too great for single engine haulage, and the 'Torbay' was split off and started separately at 10.40am. With additional stops at Taunton, Dawlish, Teignmouth and Torre, it was due in Torquay at 3.18pm and Kingswear at 3.50pm — only 15min before its peacetime arrival, when the start was 80min later. Going up, the 'Torbay' left Kingswear at 11.25am, as before the war, and Torquay 5min earlier, at 11.55am; at Newton Abbot it was linked up with a through portion which had started from Penzance at 8am, and the combined train, calling at Exeter, Taunton and Reading, was due in Paddington at 4.50pm. In the up direction, therefore, war added 1¼hr to the Torquay-London journey, but from 1 October 1945 the train was accelerated to arrive at 4.35pm.

In the summer of 1946 the old 12 noon departure from Paddington was restored, and with a non-stop schedule of 183min to Exeter, the down 'Torbay' was accelerated to reach Torquay in 3¾hr. The up 'Torbay' came down to a run of 3hr 50min from Torquay to Paddington.

The 'Torbay Express' maintained its separate existence until the Western Region timetable reorganisation of 1961, when it was decided that all West of England expresses, leaving Paddington at 30min past the even hours, should be made up of portions for both Plymouth and Torbay, including the 'Cornish Riviera Express'. The 'Torbay Express' thus became the 12.30pm departure from Paddington, but with stops at Reading, Westbury, Taunton and Newton Abbot added to its previous stop at Exeter only. Before this change the time from Paddington had come down to 3hr 25min, but this was now lengthened to 3hr 52min; and the up 'Torbay' similarly had its 3hr 35min timing from Torquay increased to 4hr 1min. In 1965 the 12.30pm from Paddington and the 10.55am up from Paignton lost their name, but from mid-May to mid-September the Torbay portion was split off from the 'Cornish Riviera Express' to form a separate train which carried the title 'Torbay Express'. This left Paddington at 10.50am, and ran non-stop over the 142.7 miles to Taunton in 124min; after a stop at Exeter from 1.31 to 1.35pm, passengers for Dawlish and Teignmouth had the privilege of a fast through service from London before the 'Torbay Express' stopped at Newton Abbot and was into Torquay by 2.22pm and Paignton by 2.30pm. On Saturdays the train did not stop at Taunton, but continued from Paignton to Kingswear, as in former days. Coming up, the 'Torbay Express' started from Paignton at 11.50am and from Torquay at 11.58am; with the same stops as in the other direction but an easier timing it arrived in Paddington at 3.35pm.

The Northumbrian

In the down direction the 'Northumbrian' was a train of war origin. Soon after World War 2 began, the passenger demands on the 1pm express from King's Cross to Edinburgh became so excessive that loads of 20 bogie coaches and over were being run almost every day. The limit was reached on 5 April 1940, when the streamlined A4 Pacific *Silver Link* headed a train of no fewer than 25 bogie vehicles; indeed, before starting, the engine was actually in Gasworks Tunnel, and a man had to be sent from the platform into the tunnel to give the driver the 'right away'. It may be added that the engine succeeded in getting this vast assemblage of stock to Newcastle without assistance and with no more than 15min loss of time, of which roughly half went in lifting the train up the initial climb to Finsbury Park.

But trains of such length, in addition to imposing unjustifiable strains on the locomotives, were most difficult to handle at intermediate stations, and notwithstanding the heavy wartime calls on motive power, division of the most heavily-patronised trains became essential. Thus the 12.45pm Newcastle 'relief' to the 1pm, until then booked to run on Saturdays only, became a daily service from the beginning of May 1940, and so continued with brief intermissions when train service cuts were made. At a later date it left King's Cross at 12.20pm, while the 1pm started at 1.15pm — in pursuance of the policy of spreading the long-distance services as evenly as possible, rather than 'bunching' them together — and the name 'Northumbrian' was conferred at the beginning of the 1949 summer train service. From October 1950, in pursuance of the systematic departure plan at King's Cross, the start became 12.18pm.

The 'Northumbrian' was a train of no special distinction. It called at Grantham from 2.22 to 2.28pm, and York from 4.07 to 4.13pm; then came the run over the Great Plain of York to reach Darlington at 5.04pm; there followed a stop at Durham, and the 'Northumbrian' reached Newcastle Central Station at 6pm. It was usually a train of about 13 bogie vehicles, including, of course, a set of restaurant cars.

The southbound 'Northumbrian' had a history going back to Great Northern and North Eastern days. Before World War 1 a restaurant car express left Newcastle at 10.28am for King's Cross, calling at Darlington; it was turned over by the North Eastern to the Great Northern at York, and became the latter's 'No 562 up', a heavy and rather lethargic train which left York at 12.15pm, called at Selby, Doncaster and Grantham (later, the Grantham stop was replaced by one at Peterborough), and rolled into King's Cross at 4.10pm. The North Eastern authorities ran a smart little connection from Edinburgh at 7.45am, with their own restaurant car attached; this called at Dunbar and Berwick, and was due in Newcastle at 10.19am, in nice time for a couple of through coaches to be attached to the London train. In this way a convenient early morning service was given from Edinburgh to London which foreshadowed the 'Morning Talisman' of much later years.

Between the wars the same service continued, and by 1939 had been slightly accelerated. The connection from Edinburgh now left Waverley at 8.05am, with a buffet car instead of a restaurant car, and reached Newcastle at 10.33am, connecting with the main train at 10.40am from Newcastle Central for the south. The Southern Area part of the run was but little less leisurely than before and required from 12.20pm out of York to 4.15pm into King's Cross to cover the 188.2 miles with stops at Selby, Doncaster and Grantham. In the many timetable reorganisations of later years the name 'Northumbrian' disappeared, and with it the identity of the train, which later has had many far more distinguished successors.

The Tynesider

For many years the night traffic between London and Newcastle was of sufficient importance to justify the running of an independent Newcastle sleeping car express and in the summer of 1950 this was added to the list of British titled trains by being given the name 'Tynesider'. At this time it was no flyer; leaving King's Cross a quarter of an hour before midnight, it was three minutes after six in the morning before the sleeper drew into the Central Station at Newcastle, but it had to make seven intermediate stops. Coming south, the 'Tynesider' schedule was six hours precisely — 10.35pm from Newcastle and 4.35am into London, but in this direction with stops at Durham, Darlington, York and Grantham only. At King's Cross the sleeping car passengers were not turned out in the small hours, of course, but as usual might remain comfortably in their berths until 7.30am.

By degrees the 'Tynesider' assumed such importance that by the 1960s it carried sleeping car passengers only. Although it did not leave King's Cross until one o'clock in the morning, passengers might take possession of their berths at any time from 11pm onwards, and on arrival might occupy them until 8am. The train comprised a brake-van and first class sleeper for Edinburgh; one first class, three composite and two second class sleepers and a brake-van for Newcastle; and two sleepers (one first class and one composite) for Darlington, with a brake-van for Middlesbrough, 12 vehicles in all with a tare weight of 454 tons. The run from London to Darlington was made non-stop in 4hr 5min, and after a stop at Durham, Newcastle was reached at a minute before 6am. The Edinburgh car was chiefly for the benefit of passengers for stations between Newcastle and the Scottish capital; it went forward with the 7am semi-fast from Newcastle and reached Edinburgh at 9.36am. Southbound, the 'Tynesider' was away from Newcastle at 10.45pm; after the Durham stop and the attachment of the Darlington car it left that station at 11.43pm, and a non-stop run brought it into King's Cross by 3.50 in the morning. It was a lighter train coming south than in the northbound direction.

The Ulster Express

For long years the Midland Railway cast envious eyes on the North of Ireland, and hankered to obtain its own share of the traffic between Great Britain and Belfast. It had a half-interest with the Furness Railway in the steamer service which operated between Belfast and the Ramsden Dock at Barrow-in-Furness, and ran through coaches to and from Barrow to connect with the boats; also it had a share in the service between Stranraer and Larne, as well as in the Portpatrick & Wigtownshire Joint Railway, running from Castle Douglas to Stranraer, over which through coaches and a sleeping car were run nightly from St Pancras. But finally the Midland ambitions were achieved by the completion in 1904 of the magnificent harbour and port installation at Heysham, near Morecambe; and the plan was carried even more thoroughly into effect by the Midland acquisition of the Belfast & Northern Counties Railway, thereafter called the Northern Counties Committee, in the previous year.

To connect with the Belfast boat at Heysham Harbour a through express was run from St Pancras at 6pm by way of Trent (the first stop), Sheffield, Leeds, Hellified and Lancaster; for the distance of 267.7 miles, including stops, a time of 5hr 52min was required. The train was booked to run non-stop from Leeds to Heysham, except for conditional stops at Skipton and Hellifield. In the reverse direction the boat train left Heysham at the uncomfortably early hour of 6.15am (at first an even earlier start was made, in the 'small hours' at 4.55am), and was due in St Pancras at 12.05pm. Competing with the Midland for the Belfast traffic was the service run jointly by the London & North Western and Lancashire & Yorkshire Railways between Fleetwood and Belfast, which also had a connecting boat train from and to London (Euston) by the LNWR route.

After the formation of the London Midland and Scottish group, it was soon realised that services from both Fleetwood and Heysham were an unnecessary duplication of facilities, and that considerable economies might be effected if the whole of the traffic were concentrated on one port; and as Heysham Harbour had more adequate space and more modern facilities, Heysham was chosen. Moreover, as the old LNWR main line offered a much more direct route from London than that of the Midland, it was arranged that the boat trains should run to and from Euston instead of St Pancras; the previous Midland connection from then on was run between Leeds and Heysham only, though with through coaches off the 5pm express from St Pancras; and the L&Y Leeds-Manchester-Fleetwood boat train was diverted to Heysham instead. Remodelling of certain connections at Morecambe made it possible for a train off the LNWR line to run to the Midland Promenade station instead of the LNWR Euston Road terminus, and to reverse in the former to reach Heysham Harbour. The distance from London was reduced from 267.7 to 239 miles.

The name of 'Ulster Express' was conferred on the Belfast boat train in 1927, when it was still running from Euston to Fleetwood, and remained with it when the transfer to Heysham Harbour took place. From the railway operating point of view the latter alteration meant relatively little difference, for the route from Euston as far as Preston, 209 miles, remained the same. Consequently, the starting time of 6.10pm at Euston remained unchanged. From here the 'Ulster Express', following the 'Lancastrian' and the 'Merseyside Express', ran non-stop to Crewe, 158.1 miles, in 167min; departure from Crewe was at 9.05pm, and the next stop at Preston, 51 miles further, was reached at 10.03pm; the last stage was from Preston, left at 10.08pm, to Morecambe Promenade, 25.2 miles in 30min, and Heysham Harbour was reached at 10.52pm, exactly one hour earlier than the previous 6pm from St Pancras.

For several seasons before the outbreak of war, however, a more ambitious plan was brought into operation. In summer the starting time of the 'Ulster Express' was altered to 7pm, and the entire distance of 234.3 miles from Euston to Morecambe Promenade was run without any intermediate stop. Arrival here at 11.12pm reduced the journey time from London to 4hr 12min, and the average speed rose to 55.8mph; 8min were allowed for reversal, and Heysham was reached at 11.30pm. In the up direction, the working of the 'Ulster Express' settled down ultimately to a departure from Heysham Harbour at 7am, and from Morecambe Promenade at 7.14am; from here there was a non-stop run over the 76.2 miles to Crewe in 89min, and then, after a 7min halt, another non-stop schedule of 165min to Euston, bringing the express into London at 11.35am. This was 75min quicker than the old Midland run to St Pancras.

After the diversion of the 'Ulster Express' to Heysham, both on the non-stop and the stopping schedule the run between Euston and Morecambe became a through locomotive working, and a 'Royal Scot' 4-6-0 was usually employed. Loads varied considerably according to season, and in the down direction the 6.10pm from Euston carried a through coach for Rochdale, detached at Crewe. For some years the first class end of the 'Ulster Express' included one of the first class lounge brakes — an open saloon furnished with leather-upholstered armchairs — built originally for the 'Royal Scot' service.

The onset of World War 2 played havoc with the 'Ulster Express' schedules. Both the train's name and, later, its restaurant cars were removed. At first it was altered to leave Euston at 4.50pm, and with stops at Rugby, Stafford, Crewe, Wigan and Preston, it reached Morecambe at 10.17pm; but the delays at the time of the *Blitz* were so severe that eventually the starting time was put forward to 3pm, and so remained until 1 January 1946, when it was altered to 3.35pm. In October 1946 the start from Euston went back to 4.55pm, and with non-stop running to Crewe, Morecambe was reached at 10 and Heysham at 10.15pm. In the up direction the train was booked away from Heysham at 8.25am, and from Morecambe at 8.50am; stops to set down passengers were made at Preston, Crewe and Bletchley, and Euston was not reached until 2.50pm. But from the beginning of 1946 the start was altered to 6.25am, and with stops at Morecambe and Crewe only the express was brought into Euston by 11.55am; from 7 October 1946 the Heysham start became 6.30am, and the London arrival 11.35am, as before the war. Restaurant cars in both directions returned on 1 October 1945.

Many changes were made in the running times of the 'Ulster Express' during the time when electrification work was in progress between Euston and Crewe. At one time, indeed, the down train achieved a record by being the only express which ever intervened between the 'Mancunian' and the 'Merseyside Express' on their northbound journeys; by starting at 6.10pm the 'Ulster Express' temporarily put the 'Merseyside Express' back to 6.20pm. In the up direction, however, the Heysham train consistently followed the 8am from Manchester to Euston at an interval of 10min. On completion of the electrification, the 'Ulster Express' departure northbound was very nearly back to the pre-war summer 7pm; it now left Euston at 6.50pm, and had the standard 121min non-stop timing to Crewe, where 14min were spent in picking up passengers and engine-changing. The next stop, after a run of 54min from Crewe, was for 2min at Preston (9.59-10.01pm), and the next after that at Morecambe Promenade at 10.32pm. After re-engining, a 10min run brought the 'Ulster Express' into Heysham Harbour at 10.47pm, with nearly an hour's grace before the steamer cast off for Belfast. Even including the 14min stop at Crewe, therefore, the 'Ulster Express' was 33min faster from London to Heysham than it was in its best prewar days. Passengers in the reverse direction, however, had a considerably less comfortable start, for they had to be into the train at Heysham Harbour before the 'Ulster Express' started at 5.55am. Coming south there was a stop at Lancaster but none at Preston; Crewe was reached at 7.45 and left at 7.55am; and with an additional stop at Rugby the scheduled arrival at Euston was at 10am, far earlier than ever previously in the history of the train. The time between London and Belfast had thus been brought down to 11hr 55min outwards and 25min longer coming back.

The 'Ulster Express' retained its name to the end, which came when the Heysham-Belfast service was withdrawn on 6 April 1975. Another casualty at the same time was a connecting service between Manchester Victoria and Heysham which was still shown in the timetable as 'Belfast Boat Express'. In earlier years the locomotive had carried a headboard and it had been the last steam-hauled named train on British Railways.

Today there is a Sealink service between the Heysham Sea Terminal and Douglas, Isle of Man, but the Heysham branch is closed to passenger traffic and coaches convey travellers between Lancaster station and the harbour.

The Waverley

It is strange to recall that the first access of the one-time Midland Railway to Carlisle was over London & North Western metals, and, moreover, by a route $1\frac{3}{4}$ miles shorter than the independent route via Appleby which the Midland built later. Indeed, the L&NWR, which the Midland reached at Low Gill Junction in Westmorland, by way of Hellifield, the Yorkshire Clapham Junction, and Ingleton, was so inhospitable to the Midland trains, from Low Gill over its main line on to Carlisle, that the latter company was practically forced to build and open in 1875 its Settle & Carlisle Railway. With its many viaducts and tunnels, and rock blasting throughout its length to find a foothold for the track, this 72-mile line was a very costly project, and the cost of operation has been on a commensurate scale in view of the extremely long and severe gradients leading to Ais Gill summit, of which the level of 1,169ft makes this the highest altitude reached by any main line in England.

Already the Midland had set about finding Scottish allies. To Glasgow the Glasgow & South Western Railway, with no other affiliations, was the natural partner; and this meant that the Midland trains, which had been to the east of the West Coast trains all the way to Carlisle, changed over, north of the Border, to the west side, when the L&NWR had handed over to its Scottish partner, the Caledonian. From Edinburgh the North British Railway had thrown out one isolated south-westerly tentacle to Carlisle; and although the NBR was one of the partners in the East Coast route, this connection between Carlisle and Edinburgh was a logical prolongation for the Midland, and a Midland and North British entente accordingly came about.

The result of these alliances was the building of jointly-owned stock, of Midland design, lettered M&GSW (Midland and Glasgow & South Western), and M&NB (Midland & North British) for these joint services. When the joint stock workings were abandoned, after the Grouping, the LNER took over a proportion of these vehicles, which for years afterwards explained the appearance of typical Midland stock in LNER colours, and, at the same time, the regular running of LNER sleeping cars into St Pancras, as well as LNER coaches on the through day trains over the Midland main line.

In the heyday of the Midland Scottish services, some remarkable trains were run between St Pancras and Edinburgh. Of special note was a summer night express to the Highlands, leaving St Pancras at 7.10 or 7.15 in different years, and carrying through coaches and sleeping cars for Aberdeen, Perth, Inverness and Fort William. In summer, too, what later became the 'Thames-Forth Express' was booked to run non-stop from Leeds to St Pancras, a distance of 196 miles, and for one or two summers the time for this run came down to 3hr 34min — the fastest ever scheduled over Midland metals between Leeds and London.

Various departure times were tried by the Midland for the morning service from St Pancras to Edinburgh, but in the LMSR era the start was fixed finally at 9.05am; the name 'Thames-Forth Express' was conferred in 1927. In the last years before the outbreak of World Ward 2 it became a very fast train, which was necessary if connection were to be made at Edinburgh with the LNER 'Flying Scotsman' to Dundee and Aberdeen; by 1938, however, this connection had been severed. Whenever possible, the LMSR had established a mile-a-minute standard over its main lines, and the down train therefore covered the 123.5 miles to Nottingham in 123min, arriving at 11.08am.

Curves, gradients and service slacks over colliery workings beyond Nottingham lowered the speed on to Chesterfield and Sheffield, where stops were made, and Leeds — $203\frac{1}{2}$ miles from St Pancras by the Nottingham and Sheffield loops — was reached at 1.05pm, in 4hr from London. A through coach from St Pancras to Halifax was left at Sheffield.

From Leeds to Carlisle the allowance of no more than 124min was the fastest scheduled over the route to date, and it included a 2min stop at Skipton, a very severe slack through Shipley, and the tremendous climb from Settle Junction to Blea Moor. Actually the time allowed for the 86.8 miles from Skipton to Carlisle was 90min, and required an average speed of 57.9mph — then an unparalleled requirement over such gradients. At the Border city of Carlisle the 'Thames-Forth' was due at 3.14pm.

Over the 'Waverley' route of the LNER, to which company's care the train was now handed over, some more formidable climbing was needed, from not far above sea level at Carlisle to 880ft at Whitrope, in the bleak Border hills, and again to 900ft at Falahill, between Galashiels and Edinburgh. From Newcastleton through Riccarton Junction to the former summit the ascent was almost continuously at 1 in 75 for 9 miles. In the years before the war, however, Pacifics had been introduced to this route, and made light of such inclinations, though the timings were easy relatively to those between Leeds and Carlisle. Stops were made at Hawick, St Boswells, Melrose and Galashiels, and the Waverley station at Edinburgh was reached at 5.45pm, just under $2\frac{1}{2}$hr having been spent on the final $98\frac{1}{4}$ miles.

Coming south, the 'Thames-Forth Express' was timed to leave Edinburgh at 10.03am, and making the same stops to Carlisle, ran into the Citadel station there at 12.37pm. Appleby and Hellifield were added to the Skipton stop, and with considerably less energetic running than on the northbound run the train reached Leeds at 3.08pm, and stood there 5min. Calling as before at Sheffield and Chesterfield to Nottingham, the up 'Thames-Forth' had one further stop — at Melton Mowbray — before setting out on a final mile-a-minute sprint to St Pancras, allowed 103min for the $105\frac{1}{4}$ miles. This brought the train into London at 7.20pm. The journey from Edinburgh to London had thus taken 9hr 17min, or 37min more than that in the reverse direction. In 1938 a Kettering stop replaced that at Melton, without change in the London arrival time.

Through most of the year the main set of cars between St Pancras and Edinburgh numbered five — third class brake, composite, kitchen and restaurant first, open third and third class brake — with the Halifax composite also between St Pancras and Sheffield, and another composite from St Pancras to Leeds only. One or two 'extras' were added by the LNER from and to Carlisle, and on the southbound journey the train was made up to a more substantial formation from Leeds. Over LMSR metals 'Jubilee' 3-cylinder 4-6-0s were normally used, and over the LNER, as already mentioned, a Pacific.

From the outbreak of war, the only day service between St Pancras and Edinburgh was by the 10am Glasgow train from St Pancras, and the 10.05am from Edinburgh Waverley, by which the overall times were spun out to $12\frac{1}{4}$hr northbound and $11\frac{3}{4}$hr southbound. Through Edinburgh coaches were still operated, however. In the down direction, for most of the war period, there was a 9.05am from St Pancras, but running only as far as Sheffield.

Through working of this train to Edinburgh was restored on 1 October 1945, including a non-stop run over the 113 miles from Leeds to Carlisle, which was reached at 4.30pm. Arrival in Edinburgh was at 7.21pm, 96min later than before the war. A much more drastic improvement came from 7 October 1946, when the old non-stop run from St Pancras to Nottingham was restored, though now with a start at 8.55am and a schedule of 142min. Edinburgh was reached at 6.46pm. Later, the train was badly slowed again; the start from London was altered to 8.50am, and additional stops at Luton, Kettering, Skipton, Hellifield and Appleby helped to extend the journey time to 10hr 32min; Edinburgh was not reached until 7.22pm. The corresponding southbound train left Edinburgh Waverley at 10.10am, and until mid-September 1952 took no less than 11hr 17min to complete its weary journey to St Pancras. A welcome improvement took place in the 1952-1953 winter service, when the start was altered to 1.05am, and all stops between Nottingham and London were cut out; St Pancras was then reached at 8.45pm.

When in 1957 a title was restored to this service, it was not 'Thames-Forth Express' but a more euphonious 'Waverley', suggested by the route that it followed north of the Border. This was accompanied by a very substantial acceleration; the train now left St Pancras at 9.15am, once again with a mile-a-minute run to Nottingham in 123min and a 40-minute acceleration to Carlisle, now reached at 4.02pm. New connections were made at Carlisle which made possible a 5hr journey from Leeds to Glasgow, and Edinburgh was reached 25min earlier, at 6.52pm. In the up direction the 10.05am 'Waverley' from Edinburgh also was put on to a 123min schedule over the final stage from Nottingham, and was brought into St Pancras by 7.48pm, 57min earlier than when the Nottingham-London run became non-stop five years earlier. Eventually, however, passenger patronage over the entire route declined to such an extent that the 'Waverley' began to be operated between St Pancras and Edinburgh during the summer months only, and over the remainder of the year no further north than Leeds and Bradford; during the winter period passengers to and from the Waverley route had to be content with a couple of coaches worked between St Pancras and Carlisle by the 'Thames-Clyde Express'.

The summer working of the 'Waverley' began at St Pancras at 9.05am, and the route followed differed considerably from that of the former 'Thames-Forth Express'. As far as Sheffield it was by way of Leicester and Derby, with stops at both towns and in addition at Luton and Chesterfield. Sheffield was reached at 11.56am and left 3min later. Then followed the same diversion as that of 'Thames-Clyde Express', from Swinton via the Moorthorpe spur to Wakefield, where a stop was made at the Westgate station, and on to Leeds City, reached at 1.11pm.

North of Leeds the schedule was distinctly leisurely; with stops at Skipton, Settle and Appleby the 'Waverley' was not into Carlisle until 3.45pm, and a time of 2hr 29min, with five intermediate stops, was needed to run the last 98.3 miles to Edinburgh, reached at 6.19pm after a 9¼hr journey. Southbound, however, with departure from Edinburgh not until 11.55am (nearly 2½hr later than that of the through coaches in winter for the 'Thames-Clyde Express'), and including the same five stops, Carlisle was reached at 2.22pm. From here the run to Leeds was 22min faster than in the northbound direction, for with three stops the 113 miles were allowed a tight 122min only. Leeds was reached at 4.28 and left at 4.36pm; stops were made at Rotherham, Sheffield, Chesterfield, Nottingham and Leicester, and the 'Waverley' was into London by 9.10pm, in exactly 9¼hr from Edinburgh. During the winter months the train ran between St Pancras and Leeds only, in the same times.

A St Pancras-Edinburgh service was last scheduled in the winter of 1968. On 6 January 1969 the closure of the Waverley route between Carlise and Edinburgh saw the end of the 'Waverley' expresses.

The West Coast Postal Express

If a claim were to be made as to which was the busiest train in Great Britain — not from the standpoint of carrying passengers and freight but from that of the work actually done on board — the 'West Coast Postal Express' in all probability would have headed the list. In the days when mail was picked up and dropped at lineside apparatus sites en route, the postal staff in the special sorting tenders numbered all but 50, and throughout the journey there was little respite in the work. Officially the train was the North Western Night TPO Down, but it was generally known as the 'West Coast Postal'. The train was put into its platform at Euston at about 7pm, and from then until departure a constant procession of Post Office motor-vans from all parts of London brought its quota of mail for the North.

As punctuality with a train of this description is even more essential than high speed, the 'West Coast Postal' was never distinguished for exceptionally fast timing. From Euston to Rugby, the time allowed in steam days for the 82.6 miles was 94min; and with departure from London at 8.30pm, Rugby was reached at 10.04pm. After a stop of 4min, the 'Postal' was booked to cover the 27.4 miles to Tamworth in 32min; here a heavy consignment of mail arrived both from the West of England and from Lincoln, Nottingham and Derby, by the Midland Division line, and had been transferred from the High Level to the Low Level station in readiness for the 'Postal's' arrival.

Leaving Tamworth at 10.47pm, the postal train ran the 48.1 miles to Crewe in 56min, arriving at 11.43pm. On this important traffic centre connecting mail trains had converged from various directions, and the heavy interchange of mails required a stop of 16min, releasing the 'West Coast Postal' at a minute before midnight. Some of the staff left the train here, to return to London with the up 'Postal'. It may be added that formerly this train did a certain amount of sorting of Irish letters, to relieve the small staff of the 'Irish Mail', which left Euston 15min later; the sorted mails were transferred from one train to the other by the simple expedient of delivering them to the ground apparatus at five different points en route, from which the sorting vans on the 'Irish Mail' picked them up at speed as it passed a short time after.

The next stop of the down 'Postal' was at Preston from 1.00 to 1.10am; then came the 90-mile run over Shap Summit to Carlise in 99min. At Carlisle, reached at 2.49am, a good many more of the hard-worked postal staff left the train, and were replaced by Scottish staff for the remainder of the journey. Up to this point, the pick-up apparatus had been in use 14 times and the delivery apparatus 9 times; simultaneous picking up and delivery had taken place at Wembley, Watford, Bletchley, Blisworth, Nuneaton, Warrington, Lancaster, Carnforth and Penrith. Formerly two Edinburgh vans were detached at Carlisle; by running this section separately, there was no need to stop either portion at Beattock for assistance to Beattock Summit. The Edinburgh vans left at 3.07am, and, calling only at Carstairs, reached the Scottish capital at 5.21am. In later years, however, the practice was reversed, and two sorting coaches for Edinburgh were attached at Carlisle.

Meantime the main portion of the 'Postal', after 10min at Carlisle, had left for the north at a minute before 3am, to run the 73.6 miles to Carstairs in 87min. Here a second division took place. After 4min the Aberdeen section was the first to leave, at 4.30am, followed by the Glasgow train at 4.35am. Latterly it had been customary for the 'Postal' to be one of the through Pacific locomotive workings between Euston and Glasgow, and the London engine therefore worked forward to Glasgow Central, stopping en route at Motherwell, and reaching the great industrial city at 5.15am. Ahead were the Aberdeen vans, in charge, most probably, of a 'Jubilee' class 3-cylinder 4-6-0, on a non-stop run to Stirling, which was reached at 5.20am. From here onwards, with only two of the mailvans remaining, the 'Postal' deigned to carry passengers. A passenger train, limited in weight to four bogie vehicles, had left Glasgow Central at 4.10am, and had been worked into Stirling at 5.11am; here the two were combined, and started away northward as a 6-coach train at 5.24am.

The weight restriction, which in Caledonian days with 4-4-0 locomotives had been even more severe, and permitted two passenger coaches only, was regarded as necessary in view of the tight timings of the Scottish run north of Stirling. Over Gleneagles summit, from Stirling to Perth, the 33 miles were allowed 38min only, and the 'Postal' was then worked forward over the 89.8 miles to Aberdeen, the only non-stop train of the day between these cities, in 99min. This brought the last remnant of the 'West Coast Postal' into Aberdeen at 7.52am, having taken 11hr 22min for the 540 miles from London.

In the reverse direction the first two vans of the 'Postal' began their journey at Aberdeen at 3.30pm, also as part of a passenger train, which in this direction was permitted to be made up a to total weight of eight bogie vehicles. A stop was made at Forfar from 4.38 to 4.42pm, and Perth was reached at 5.17pm. At one time in Caledonian days the run of 32.5 miles from Forfar to Perth was allowed 32min only. At Perth the passenger section was detached and the mailvans went forward alone at 5.24pm, calling at Stirling from 6.05 to 6.08pm, to the point where they reached the Glasgow to London main line at Law Junction, at 6.45pm. Here they stopped to await the main train, which with its Pacific at the head, working through to Euston, had left Glasgow Central at 6.35pm, and arrived at Law Junction at 7.03pm. For marshalling the train in right order, there was an allowance of 8min, and departure for the south was at 7.11pm. In this direction, as the approach to Beattock summit is on easier gradients than from the south, the Edinburgh vans, which had left the Scottish capital at 6.38pm, were attached at Carstairs, for which 6min were allowed, from 7.26 to 7.32pm. The 73.6 miles over Beattock summit to Carlisle then were covered in 81min. This brought the 'Postal' into Carlisle at 8.53pm.

More vans were attached here, and for the same considerable exchange of postal staff that had taken place on the northbound journey a total of 12min was spent at the Border town. Stops were made at Preston (11-11.10pm); Warrington (11.44-11.49pm); Crewe (12.19-12.31am); Tamworth (1.28-1.40am); and Rugby (2.14-2.22am); this brought the up 'West Coast Postal' into Euston at 3.55am, so that in the southbound direction the entire journey from Aberdeen had taken 12hr 25min. On this trip the deliveries and receiving apparatus were both in use simultaneously at Penrith, Carnforth, Lancaster, Stafford, Nuneaton and Tring, and delivery were made at five other stations also.

The onset of war did not bring to end the carriage of mails, of course, but it did compel considerable alterations to the working of the postal train, cutting out the exchanging of mail matter at speed, and almost all the sorting en route, so that the wartime 'Postal' consisted for the most part of ordinary vans. Additions of 71min were made to the northbound and 76 to the southbound times. But from 1 October 1945, the full postal working was restored, as well as the prewar speed; and apart from a minute or two of extra time over certain sections, the 'West Coast Postal' was one of the first British expresses to return to full normal peacetime working, speed included, after the war.

On the down journey the 8.30pm now called at Rugby 10.03-10.07pm; Tamworth 10.39-10.46pm; Crewe 11.42-11.58pm; Preston 1.03-1.13am; Carlisle 2.54-3.04am; and reached Carstairs at 4.32am. The Aberdeen portion was still the first from here, at 4.36am, stopping at Stirling (5.30-5.34am) to collect the passenger portion which had left Glasgow Central at 4.20am, and at Perth (6.14-6.25am). From Perth to Aberdeen the 89.9 miles were run in 95min, 4min quicker than before the war, and this 56.7mph sprint for the time being was one of the fastest scheduled runs on the LMSR. The Glasgow section of the down 'Postal' reached Central at 5.20am, and the Edinburgh portion was into Princes Street a minute later.

Coming up, with departures from Aberdeen at 3.30pm, Glasgow Central at 6.35pm, and Edinburgh at 6.38pm, the 'Postal' made the same stops as in the northbound direction, and was due in London Euston at 4am, 5min later than prewar.

At the beginning of June 1948, in an attempt to cure the then unpunctual running of the 'Postal', some alterations were made in the working. The connecting 4.20am from Glasgow Central became an independent train throughout to Aberdeen, leaving Glasgow 15min earlier, at 4.05am, making brief calls at Forfar and Stonehaven in addition to previous stops, and getting into Aberdeen by 7.46am, 16min earlier. The timings of the London train were eased to bring it into Perth by 6.29am, and starting away again at 6.40am, and with 2min added also to the Perth-Aberdeen allowance, the 'Postal' became due in Aberdeen at 8.15am. In 1952 the practice of attaching the Glasgow passenger coaches at Stirling was resumed, but any passengers in them were involved in a 48min wait at Stirling before their journey was continued.

While the departure of the southbound 'Postal' from Aberdeen at 3.30pm was not altered, the Glasgow start was put forward from 6.35 to 6.25pm, and with a departure from Carlisle 5min earlier at 9pm, the 'Postal' still was due in Euston at 4am. The additions in both directions were chiefly to the duration of the stops, for the 'Postal' was booked to make some smart runs in both directions, particularly the 35min allowance for the 32.5 miles from Forfar to Perth, and the 77min for the 73.5 miles from Carstairs to Carlisle. Latterly the 3.30pm from Aberdeen to Perth was raised to the dignity of Pacific haulage, for the Crewe engine which worked the Inverness sleeper from Crewe to Perth and back often filled in the intervening day usefully by making a run from Perth to Aberdeen and back, the return being on the 'Postal'. A start-to-stop run over the 32.5 miles from Forfar to Perth in 32min or even less in those days was nothing unusual.

Electrification between Euston and Crewe brought about a considerable change in the working of the 'Postal'. From April 1968 the Euston departure moved from its traditional 8.30pm to 9pm, the difference being easily recovered before Crewe was reached. But a greater change followed the bringing into operation of electric working between Rugby and Stafford via Birmingham and Wolverhampton. With a reversion to the 8.30pm London departure, the express was re-routed via Birmingham. The Rugby stop was abandoned; the train now called at Bletchley and next at Birmingham New Street, where the West of England and West Midland mails that used to be transferred at Tamworth were received. Next came halts at Wolverhampton and Stafford, and Crewe was reached at 11.41pm. A new connecting postal train left Peterborough East at 8pm, and running via Stamford, Leicester, Derby and Stoke-on-Trent got into Crewe by 11.18pm; the Central Wales train carrying mails for the North now started from Aberystwith instead of as formerly from Swansea, and reached Crewe by 11.34pm. With 20min allowed here for the heavy task of mail handling, the 'Postal' was away northwards at a minute past midnight. A stop at Warrington was added to that at Preston, and the Carlisle arrival was timed for 2.42am.

Out of London the load was eight postal vehicles and four vans; another van, detached at Preston, was added at Birmingham, and the leading van, for Liverpool, came off at Crewe. From Preston what had now become a 10-coach train was increased once again to 12 coaches by the addition at Carlisle of the Edinburgh sorting vans. So, leaving Carlisle at 2.54am, the 'Postal' continued with a fast 77½min run to Carstairs, where a break-up into three sections took place. First away, at 4.17am, were the six Glasgow vans, reaching Central Station at 4.54am; at 4.23am the four Aberdeen vans left; and the two for Edinburgh 2min later, arriving in Waverley at 4.54am. From March 1967 the Aberdeen section ceased to attach a passenger portion from Glasgow, and its stops at Motherwell, Stirling and Perth were therefore for postal purposes only. Perth was reached at 6.08 and left at 6.13am; the run from there to Aberdeen was still the only non-stop working of the day over this stretch and arrival at the Granite City was at 7.51am. From September 1967 however, with closure of the main line via Forfar, the train was re-routed from Perth via Dundee to Kinnaber.

Southbound the departure from Aberdeen was still at 3.30pm, and with one stop en route Perth was reached at 5.15 and left at 5.33pm. But in this direction also the route was now via Montrose and Dundee. As going north, there were halts at Stirling and Motherwell; then the Aberdeen section was into Carstairs at 7.24pm, preceding by 20min the main train, which had left Glasgow Central at 7.05pm. After a stop of 13min for marshalling, the 'Postal' then had a very healthy sprint in covering the 73.5 miles over Beattock Summit to Carlisle in 68½min, arriving at 9.05½pm. With a departure at 9.15pm, and stops at Preston and Warrington, this busy train had a stop of no less than 22min at Crewe, from 12.08 to 12.30am; subsequent halts were at Wolverhampton, Birmingham, Coventry, Bletchley and Watford before Euston was reached at 4am.

By this time the only remaining pick-ups or exchanges at speed south of the Border were at Harrow, Watford, Lancaster and Carnforth going north and at Penrith coming south. But in Scotland there was more extensive use; the apparatus was in action northbound at Carluke, Coatbridge, Carmuirs West Junction and Larbert in very rapid succession, and Alyth Junction. Southbound it was equally busy, being operated at Stonehaven, Laurencekirk, Dubton, Gleneagles and Carmuirs West Junction (Larbert).

The use of lineside apparatus was discontinued in 1971 but the train has continued to run between Euston and Aberdeen as a TPO (ie a train in which letters are sorted en route). Its present times of leaving Euston at 8.35pm and arriving Aberdeen at 7.20am reflect the faster running between Euston and Motherwell since electrification throughout in 1974.

The West Riding Limited

Last of the three London & North Eastern streamliners to go into service, in October 1937, was the 'West Riding Limited', and it had been running a little less than two years when the war broke out. In Great Northern days the pride of the Leeds service was the 2pm from Leeds Central to King's Cross, non-stop from Wakefield, and due into London at 5.25, or actually, according to the working timetable, at 5.27pm. It would have taken a bold man to prophesy a cut of three-quarters of an hour in this schedule; but the cut was duly made when the 'West Riding Limited' was inaugurated. Meantime, of course, the Pullman trains had been introduced, and the up 'Queen of Scots' had brought the Leeds-London time down by degrees to 3hr 10min.

Possibilities over this route had been demonstrated in November 1934 when an experimental run was made from King's Cross to Leeds and back with a four-coach train of 147 tons headed by Pacific No 4472 *Flying Scotsman.* On this trip, for the first time in history, the 156 miles to Doncaster were covered in no more than 2hr 2½min, and Leeds was reached in 2hr 32min, which long remained the record time over this course. The return journey was made in 2hr 37¼min, and with 208 tons a speed of 100mph was reached at Essendine — another LNER record up to that date. Coming up, the load had been increased to six coaches. It was thus proved that a greatly accelerated schedule would be practicable.

When the 'West Riding Limited' made its appearance, however, it was a train almost double the weight of the test train of 1934. But experience had been gained with the 'Silver Jubilee' and the 'Coronation', and above all the streamlined 'A4' Pacifics had now come into service, so that the allowance of 2hr 44min from King's Cross to Leeds, and 2hr 43min from Leeds to King's Cross, were both capable of punctual observance. The train was booked to run through to Bradord and for the London-Bradford journey the allowance was 3hr 5min each way.

A set of cars identical with that in use on the 'Coronation' was built for the service, consisting of four articulated 'twins' with a tare weight of 278 tons. Also two 'A4' Pacifics, No 4495 *Golden Fleece* and No 4496 *Golden Shuttle*, were allocated to the 'West Riding Limited', though a short time after its introduction other engines of the same class were taking their turns on the train.

Departure time from King's Cross for the down 'West Riding Limited' was fixed at the comparatively late hour of 7.10pm. Doncaster, 156 miles, was passed at 9.19pm, in 129min from London. The next difficult stretch, including the 1 in 150 ascent to beyond Hemsworth and the severe slowing through Wakefield, followed by 4 miles at 1 in 100 and 122 up to Ardsley and the extremely cautious approach necessary from Holbeck into Leeds Central, was allowed 34min for the 29.8 miles, and Leeds was reached at 9.53pm.

Here the reversal took place, and for the short run to Bradford two 0-6-2 tanks of the 'N2' class were backed on to the train — the only regularly rostered use on the LNER of a pair of tank locomotives on an express train. The necessity arose from the extremely severe gradients out of Leeds Central in the Bradford direction, and in particular the 1¼ miles at 1 in 50 from Holbeck up to Armley, followed by 5 miles up mostly at 1 in 100. The 9.3 miles from Leeds to Bradford were allowed 18min, and Bradford Exchange was reached at 10.15pm.

In the reverse direction the 'West Riding Limited' left Bradford at 11.10am, again with two 0-6-2 tanks at the head, and reached Leeds at 11.28am. Here the streamlined Pacific backed on to the opposite end, and leaving at 11.33am, joined the main line at Doncaster at 12.06pm, 17min behind the 'Silver Jubilee', after which the two flyers maintained a 15min space between them, the 'West Riding' being due in King's Cross at 2.15pm. This arrangement enabled a business man in Leeds or Bradford to have couple of hours at his office in the morning, and then to travel to London, spend all but five hours in the capital, and be back in his home city by or soon after 10pm — a much appreciated facility. The 'West Riding Limited' was withdrawn on the outbreak of war, in 1939, and was never reinstated.

In the spate of train naming that followed the nationalisation of Britain's railways, however, a new train was introduced in 1949 between King's Cross, Leeds and Bradford called the 'West Riding'. For many years there had been an express out of King's Cross at 4pm for these destinations, but making many stops en route, and the provision of an express at 3.45

in the afternoon non-stop over the 175.8 miles to Wakefield was certainly a novelty. This was the 'West Riding', and the experiment proved successful. As a special attraction, the front end of the train was composed in part of the beautiful cars used before the war on the streamlined 'West Riding Limited'. The 175.8 miles to Wakefield were run in 202min and Leeds Central was reached at 7.38pm, in 3hr 53min from London.

In the up direction the title 'West Riding' was conferred on the return working of the same stock, the 7.50am from Leeds, always a well patronised train. Intermediate stops south of Doncaster were cut out of the schedule, and the run of 156 miles to King's Cross was accelerated to a time of 182min, with an arrival at 11.49am, in one minute under four hours from Leeds. But a great deal more acceleration was needed to bring the speed up to that of the so-called 'Breakfast Flyer' of prewar days, which with additional stops at Retford and Grantham was into London 29min earlier, at 11.20am.

The year 1960 saw the title 'West Riding' transferred, in the down direction, to the morning express from London to Leeds which from its introduction in the middle 1950s had varied in starting time between 7.45 and 8.00am. Sixteen years were to elapse, however, before the speed of the prewar 'West Riding Limited' was restored by the eight-coach 'Deltic'-hauled 7.30am from Leeds to King's Cross and the 3.55pm in the opposite direction, which made the journey in 2hr 43min and 2hr 42min respectively but were no longer named.

The White Rose

In the days of the Great Northern Railway, and later of the London & North Eastern, there were two trains on the service between King's Cross, Leeds and Bradford that might be regarded as institutions. No matter how train services might be altered, or the tide of acceleration might swirl around them, nothing appeared to affect these 'fixtures', and year after year, both before World War 1 and between the two wars, they would carry on with schedules practically unchanged. Actually the two trains were one, a return working of the same set of stock; they were the 10.10am from King's Cross and the 5.30pm from Leeds. It was their successors which in the May, 1949, timetables, first received the title 'White Rose'.

In the earliest years of the present century, the principal morning express from King's Cross for the West Riding left at 9.45am, ahead of the 'Flying Scotsman', and made a non-stop run over the 156 miles to Doncaster in 169min; it reached Leeds in the smart time of 3hr 40min. At that time there was a 10.20am from King's Cross to Sheffield, calling at Peterborough and Grantham, and continuing by way of Nottingham and the Great Central line. When, a few years later, the 10.20am was withdrawn, it was decided that the Leeds train must make the Peterborough and Grantham stops, and the starting time from London was therefore changed to 10.10am. Leeds was now reached at 1.56pm, so no more than 6min had been lost by introducing the additional halts.

In London & North Eastern days the 10.10am down still continued, practically unchanged in schedule, right up to 1939, with the trivial variation that the Leeds arrival had now become 2pm, 4min later; also, to make room for the 10.05am. 'Junior Scotsman', as it was called, the 10.10 started at 10.15am during the summer months only. It had now grown into an extremely heavy train, with a through portion on the front for Hull, then the Leeds restaurant section, next a portion for Harrogate (worked between Leeds Central and Harrogate by the North Eastern Area), and finally the Bradford portion, detached on the outward journey at Wakefield.

Coming south, the timing of the trian had remained equally static, if not more so. From Leeds Central 5.30pm had been the absolutely unvarying departure time; at first, King's Cross was reached in the even four hours, but the arrival time was then brought forward to 9.25pm. There it remained even after a Peterborough stop had been added to that at Grantham, previously the only halt between Doncaster and King's Cross. As the years passed, Great Northern Atlantics gave place to Gresley Pacifics in the working of these trains, and well they might, for on my last prewar run with the 5.30pm from Leeds, on leaving Doncaster with the normal load, we were made up to 16 vehicles of 474 tons tare weight, or fully 500 tons loaded. I am not likely to forget that evening, for owing to a mishap we left Doncaster 18mins late, yet ran into King's Cross dead on time. The double-chimney streamlined A4 Pacific *Osprey* had whirled us over the 76.4 miles from Peterborough start to the dead stop in the terminus in 73min 44 sec

— a magnificient performance.

Included in the formation of these trains up to the war and on that run was a remarkable set of vehicles — a quintuplet restaurant car set designed and built at Doncaster in 1921 by Gresley specially for service on the 10.10am down and the 5.30pm up. The articulated formation comprised a kitchen car in the centre (the first in the country to use electricity exclusively for cooking), flanked by open first and third class restaurant cars, and with first class and third class brakes at the outer ends; a representation of roof-boards, lettered 'King's Cross and Leeds' in red, was painted on the roof of each vehicle. Why the designer should have wasted space on the two completely useless brake compartments was always a mystery to me; it would have been far more valuable to have additional compartments, or, still better, to have built the end vehicles as centre-corridor or open stock, and thus to have provided supplementary restaurant accommodation when necessary.

When in 1949 the name 'White Rose' was decided on, the train selected was a relatively new express, the 9.18am down, which was, in effect, a logical successor to the 9.45am of long ago, for once again it had become non-stop to Doncaster. The time allowed for the 156-mile run was 176min, and Leeds was reached at 1.11pm, so that the train had become 13min slower than the 9.45am of 1904. The 'White Rose' was for Leeds and Bradford only, except that on Tuesdays and Saturdays during the winter it carried as far as Doncaster a through restaurant car portion for Norwegian passengers travelling to Tyne Commission Quay. This had to be worked specially through from Doncaster to Newcastle by the North Eastern Region.

For some time after the name 'White Rose' had been conferred on the 9.18am down, the return working of the stock was on the counterpart of the prewar 5.30pm from Leeds, which by 1949 had become the 5.15pm up, making an extremely leisurely journey to London and taking 4½hr to do it. Then the return stock working was transferred to the 3.15pm up, an even more lethargic service calling at all principal stations, including even Hitchin, and not due until 7.56pm. This became such an exacting working, however, that in 1958 it was decided to cut out all stops south of Doncaster, and thereby to bring what had now become the 3.35pm out of Leeds into King's Cross 32min earlier, at 7.18pm. Acceleration of the 'White Rose' continued steadily until both down and up workings were timed at over a mile-a-minute between London and Doncaster. Then, in the summer of 1964, when with the cutting out of the journey north of Harrogate of the 'Queen of Scots' Pullman it became necessary to find a new name for that express, it took over the title 'White Rose'. But not for long, however, for with the March 1967 timetable the Pullman ceased to operate and the name became extinct.

The Yorkshire Pullman

Such was the success of the Harrogate all-Pullman train, when inaugurated in 1923, that the LNER soon began to cast about for similar sources of revenue in other directions. Sheffield appeared to offer attractive possibilities, and in June 1924 a five-car 'Sheffield Pullman' was introduced leaving King's Cross at 11.05am, 10min ahead of the 'Harrogate Pullman'. It was thought that the citizens of Nottingham might also be tempted by such luxurious facilities, and the train was therefore diverted from Grantham to Nottingham Victoria, running thence over the Great Central main line into Sheffield. The call at Nottingham was from 1.28 to 1.32pm, and Sheffield was reached at 2.20pm; after a wait just short of 2½hr, the 'Sheffield Pullman' set out on its southward journey at 4.45pm and was back in London by 8pm.

The new service failed to attract, however, and a month later the times were completely altered. The Pullman was now based on Sheffield instead of London; it left the Yorkshire city at 10.30am and reached King's Cross at 1.45pm; on the return journey it set out from London at 6.05pm — a popular departure time for Sheffield before the 1914-1919 war — and was back in Sheffield at 9.20pm. But the people of Nottingham still showed no Pullman interest, and in April 1925 it was decided to cut them out of the itinerary and to try Manchester instead. So the 'Sheffield and Manchester Pullman' was booked non-stop from King's Cross to Sheffield via Retford instead of via Nottingham — 161.2 miles in 177min, average 54.6mph — and continued non-stop from Sheffield to Manchester Central, which was reached at 10.12pm, in 4hr 7min from London. Returning at 9.50am, the Pullman ran to Sheffield in 70min, left there are 11.03am, and was into King's Cross at 2pm.

Unfortunately neither Manchester nor Sheffield

responded appropriately to these Pullman blandishments, and five months later both were deprived of their Pullman cars. For in September 1925 as mentioned in the 'Queen of Scots' chapter, the latter train began to run non-stop from King's Cross to Harrogate, and to serve Leeds and Bradford a new Pullman service was run 10min ahead, at 11.10am. For this the Sheffield and Manchester train was used. Leeds was reached non-stop at 2.35pm, and two cars continued to Bradford, arriving at 3pm. The Leeds cars were then worked empty to Harrogate to return at 11.15am to London via Leeds, where the Bradford cars, starting at 11.20am, were picked up; leaving Leeds at 11.50am, this service reached London at 3.15pm. Harrogate now had one daily Pullman train from London, but two in the reverse direction; also two complete trains were needed for the Leeds and Bradford service, as well as the two Edinburgh trains.

The arrangement was again altered entirely, however, in May 1928. When the 'Queen of Scots' was diverted once again to serve Leeds, the down working of the 'West Riding Pullman', as it now became, was changed from 11.10am to 4.45pm from London, giving Leeds, Bradford, Harrogate and Newcastle the much appreciated convenience of two fast Pullman connections with London twice daily each way. From September 1926 the 'West Riding Pullman' had been calling at Wakefield to detach the Bradford Pullmans, which from there had been worked direct through Batley to Bradford; from Bradford they proceeded through Queensbury tunnel into Halifax, giving the last-mentioned city a service in just under 4¼hr to and from London. This arrangement was continued with the 4.45pm down. One set of cars now sufficed for the return journey.

In 1935 it was decided to extend the Pullman facilities to Hull, which thus acquired, for the first time, not only Pullman cars, but also a 3½hr service to and from London. To detach and attach the Hull section, the 'West Riding Pullman' had to be stopped at Doncaster, and this resulted in the appearance of two very fast bookings in the timetable; the 4.45pm down was scheduled to run the 156 miles from King's Cross to Doncaster in 156min, at precisely 60mph, and the up train in one minute less. In view of the wider orbit of the train's operation, also, it now became the 'Yorkshire Pullman'; but with the advent of the 'Silver Jubilee' streamliner, the Harrogate section no longer worked through to Newcastle.

Two more changes have now to be chronicled. In the autumn of 1937 the 'West Riding Limited' streamliner came into service, and as this was given a mid-morning departure from Bradford and Leeds, there was no purpose in providing a Pullman service at much the same time. The Harrogate portion of the train, consisting of four cars and leaving at 11.15am, was therefore diverted to run via York to Doncaster, where it joined the two Hull cars and the two cars which had come from Halifax via Bradford and Wakefield. Eight cars was the minimum formation of the 'Yorkshire Pullman', but in later years it grew at busy weekends to as many as 11 or even 12. Normally, Pacific locomotives worked the train, but 2-6-2 engines of Class V2 often handled it successfully, especially in the up direction.

On its final schedule before the outbreak of World War 2 the 'Yorkshire Pullman' left King's Cross at 4.45pm, and made its first stop at Doncaster at 7.21pm; its various constituents reached Hull at 8.15pm, Leeds at 8.13pm, Bradford at 8.30pm and Halifax at 8.57pm. In the reverse direction the main train left Harrogate at 11.15am and York at 11.45am, and the Hull cars at 11.30am; in order not to compete with the 'West Riding Limited', the Halifax cars were worked quietly down to Doncaster as a non-passenger service. The combined train then left Doncaster at 12.25pm and made its way into King's Cross at 3pm.

During the war the 'Yorkshire Pullman' was withdrawn, but it came into service again on 4 November 1946, on a schedule allowing 4½hr each way between King's Cross and Harrogate. Departure from London was at 3.50pm, and from Harrogate at 10.20am. In September 1948 the start from King's Cross was altered to 4.45pm, and a year later the 'Yorkshire Pullman' changed places with the new 'Tees-Tyne Pullman', from now on to start at 5.30pm. An eleven-car train was now needed regularly, the Hull portion, which reached that city at 9.30pm, requiring four cars; the arrival time at Leeds was 9.16pm and at Harrogate 9.56pm, and the restored through Bradford section was due in that city at 9.42pm. The 156-mile run to Doncaster was allowed 172min. Coming south, the departures were at 10.07am from Harrogate, 10.15am from Bradford, 10.45am from Leeds, 10.30am from Hull and 11.50am from Doncaster, from which a run of 178min brought the 'Yorkshire Pullman' into King's Cross at 2.38pm.

The first major change in the working came with the turning over of the down express to 'Deltic' power in the autumn of 1961. At one stroke 30min was cut from the King's Cross-Doncaster time, from 175 to 145min for the 156 miles, and there was a total gain of 38min to Leeds; now starting out of London at 5.25pm, the 'Yorkshire Pullman' had a 3¼hr timing to Leeds, reached at 8.40pm and the Harrogate cars were into that town by 9.20pm. A year or two elapsed before 'Deltic' power became available for the up working also, with a similar speed-up. By the end of 1966 the down departure had become 5.37pm, and with a timing of 141min over the 156 miles to Doncaster, Leeds was being reached in 3hr 10min, Bradford in 3hr 30min, Harrogate in 3hr 50min and

Hull in 3hr 28min. In the up direction departures had become 9.52am from Harrogate, 10am from Bradford, 10.10am from Hull and 10.30am from Leeds, with a London arrival at 1.50pm.

Then, in March, 1967, there came the final change, which was the concession to Hull of its own independent 'Hull Pullman'. This made it possible for the main train to omit its Doncaster call; leaving King's Cross at 5.35pm for a non-stop run over the 175.8 miles to Wakefield in 159min, the 'Yorkshire Pullman' now required one minute over 3hr in which to reach Leeds City, 3hr 37min to Bradford and 3hr 44min to Harrogate. Coming up, departures were at 9.55am from Harrogate, 9.50am from Bradford and unchanged at 10.30am from Leeds, and with a time of 169min from Wakefield King's Cross was reached at 1.39pm, a journey 8min longer from Leeds than that in the opposite direction. The formation was four Harrogate cars and a brake van, followed by four Bradford cars with another brake van, ten vehicles in all and a considerably lighter formation than when the Hull portion was included.

The 'Yorkshire Pullman' continued to run as a King's Cross-Leeds-Harrogate train until the end of the 1977/78 timetable. Leaving London at 5.04, the time to Leeds with one stop at Wakefield was eventually 2hr 52min. The up train was allowed 2hr 55min for the same run.

The Yorkshireman

It is a singular fact that although non-stop services have been tried by three different routes between London and Sheffield, none of them ever developed sufficient traffic to justify continuance, and either the trains were taken off or additional stops were introduced. One outbreak of non-stop running followed the opening of the Great Central Railway's London extension in 1899. By 1904 the GCR was getting into its stride, and tabling some very fast trains. In summer the Midland, therefore, tried running its morning express to Glasgow non-stop to Sheffield, 158.3 miles, in 3hr 5min, and the Great Northern followed suit in 1905 with a special express from King's Cross at 6.10pm, taking only 2hr 50min for the 161.2 miles of the GN route. In the same year the Great Central, with the longest (164.7 miles) and hardest course of all three, brought the time of its afternoon 'Sheffield Special' down to 2hr 50min also.

After a couple of years, however, the Great Northern train had intermediate stops introduced. The Great Central train continued to run non-stop up to World War 1, but had its time increased to 2hr 57min. By 1906 the Midland had transferred its non-stop run to the 6pm down Heysham boat express from St Pancras, and in that year and 1907 was making the run in 3hr, but by 1909 10min had been added to this time, and this train was calling regularly at Trent. Then came the interruption of World War 1.

After the war, the GCR never resumed its non-stop running between Marylebone and Sheffield. But when the LNER had been formed, another attempt was made over the GN route, this time with the 'Sheffield Pullman' which had been introduced in 1924, and had run via Nottingham. In April 1925 this was altered to leave King's Cross at 6.05pm, and to run non-stop to Sheffield in 177min, with a similar run in the reverse direction, reaching London at 2pm. But these runs disappeared in 1927, and were not seen again.

Meantime the LMSR, in March 1925, had put on the train which shortly after was to receive the title of the 'Yorkshireman'. It was an entirely new service between Bradford and St Pancras, not serving Leeds but using the route via Thornhill which had been made avilable when in 1909 the former Midland Railway opened the connecting spur from Royston, on its main line to Leeds, to Thornhill, on the then Lancashire & Yorkshire main line from Wakefield to Manchester. The original intention was to build a railway through Bradford which would enable Midland Anglo-Scottish services to pass through that city, but it was never carried to completion.

A new route was made possible, however, between St Pancras, Sheffield and Bradford Exchange, and of this the 9.10am from Bradford to St Pancras, and the 4.55pm from St Pancras to Bradford, duly made use. A feature of the new service was that for the first time the LMSR assembled a train composed entirely of open vestibuled stock — third brake, third, first, kitchen car, two thirds, and third brake, seven vehicles in all. Later first and third class brakes with compartments replaced the previous two end vehicles. The time allowed in each direction was 3hr 10min between St Pancras and Sheffield, with an intermediate stop at Leicester, and 4¼hr between London and Bradford.

No further changes of note were made until the radical acceleration of the Midland services which took place in October 1937. Once again Sheffield was provided with a non-stop service to and from London, and the down 'Yorkshireman' was one of the two trains selected for the experiment. The old GC and GN times were nearly reproduced with an allowance of 2hr 52min for the run; the starting time was altered to 5.10pm from St Pancras, and Sheffield was reached at 8.02pm. Bradford was reached at 9.11pm, in a minute over 4hr from London.

Once again, however, it did not last. By 1939 the down 'Yorkshireman' was back to its old departure time, leaving St Pancras at 4.55pm, taking 106min to stop at Leicester, 3hr 5min to Sheffield, and as much as 4hr 20min to Bradford. In the up direction it was leaving Bradford at 9.05am and Sheffield at 10.13am, making an additional call at Chesterfield, and running from there to London by way of Nottingham, with a mile-a-minute run in 123min over the final 123.5 miles to St Pancras, reached at 1.21pm. Despite a journey of 205.5 miles as compared with 198.8 miles in the down direction and an extra stop, the up train therefore had the advantage of the down by 4min. The service was withdrawn on the outbreak of war, and could not be repeated afterwards, as the Royston-Thornhill line no longer carried passenger trains.

The Robin Hood

For many years one of the most popular trains between Nottingham and London left the Midland city for St Pancras at around about 8 o'clock in the morning. In the days before World War 1 it started from Sheffield at 7.20am, called at Chesterfield and, rather unusually for a London express, at Alfreton in the Erewash Valley; it then diverted from Trowell into Nottingham, where a stop from 8.20 to 8.25am preceded a non-stop run to St Pancras, 123½ miles distant, in 135 minutes — by an easy margin the fastest Nottingham-London schedule of the day. A coach was slipped en route at Kettering. Suspended during the war, the train reappeared in due course, still with the Sheffield start and the Chesterfield and Alfreton stops, and now also with halts to pick up passengers at Melton Mowbray and Manton, but no Kettering slip. By 1939 departure from Nottingham had become 8.23am, and arrival at St Pancras 10.35am.

In 1959, well after World War 2, the decision was reached to confer a name on this express, and in view of the proximity to Nottingham of Sherwood Forest, the title decided on was 'Robin Hood'. By now the Sheffield-Nottingham part of the journey had been cut out, for early morning passengers from Sheffield to London for the most part had transferred their custom to the Eastern Region's 'Master Cutler' Pullman. The Melton Mowbray stop also had been abandoned, leaving only the call at Manton. As yet little speeding up had taken place, for departure from Nottingham at 8.25am and arrival at St Pancras at 10.35am still left an elapsed time of 2hr 10min. In the later Midland accelerations, however, with the help of diesel power the time was reduced to 2hr, involving an overall average of over a mile-a-minute. The return working of the 'Robin Hood', during the brief period when this name was being carried, was at 4.45pm from St Pancras, a train of no great distinction making several intermediate stops and not due in Nottingham until 7.32pm.

An unnamed morning express from Nottingham at 7.55am continued, still travelling via Melton Mowbray and Manton after other Nottingham services to and from St Pancras had been diverted via Leicester. This reminder of the 'Robin Hood' ceased with closure of the Manton route to passenger traffic in 1967.

The Kentish Belle

In the year 1921 the then South Eastern & Chatham Railway tried the experiment of running a Sunday only all-Pullman express between Victoria and Ramsgate Harbour; leaving London at 10.10am, the 'Thanet

Pullman Limited' was booked non-stop over the 74 miles to Margate West in the fast time of 90min, and called at Broadstairs before terminating in the then Ramsgate Harbour station. The train continued to run for some time under Southern Railway auspices, but as the Pullman patronage was inadequate, ordinary coaches before long replaced some of the Pullmans, and by 1931 the Pullman accommodation had come down to a single car.

After the interruption of World War 2 an all-Pullman train from London to the Kent Coast once again came into operation in the summer of 1948. In conformity with the other Southern Pullman 'Belle' services it received the name of 'Thanet Belle'; leaving Victoria at 11.30am it called at Whitstable, Herne Bay, Margate and Broadstairs to Ramsgate, and the estimate of possible patronage extended to the provision of no fewer than 10 Pullman cars, two first class and eight third class. The starting time on Saturdays was fixed at 3.05pm. In the up direction the express left Ramsgate at 5.05pm from Mondays to Fridays, and at 6.15pm on Saturdays and Sundays. During the winter service of 1948-1949 the 'Belle' was replaced by an ordinary set of stock which included a couple of Pullman cars. The all-Pullman service reappeared in the summer of 1949, however, and in the following summer the experiment was tried of two round trips on Saturdays, at 7.55am and 3.05pm from Victoria, returning from Ramsgate at 11.15am and 6.15pm. The summer of 1951 saw the title changed to 'Kentish Belle', due to the introduction of through cars for Canterbury, which required a special stop at Faversham for these to be detached and attached; but this through working lasted for two summers only, and in 1952 the non-stop running between Victoria and Whitstable was restored.

With the inauguration in 1959 of the Kent Coast electrification east of Gillingham, and of standardised set trains, however, the 'Kentish Belle' ceased to exist, and subsequently there were no regular Pullman workings to or from Margate and Ramsgate.

The Man of Kent

The title 'Man of Kent' had but a short life. For some years between the wars the Southern Railway, with the help of the most capable Maunsell 'Schools' class 4-4-0s, had worked the 4.15pm from Charing Cross to Folkestone, Dover, Deal and Ramsgate as far as Folkestone Central in the fast time of 80min, including the Waterloo stop, and latterly as a corridor train with two Pullman cars in the formation. After World War 2 eight years elapsed before this booking reappeared in the timetable, but in the summer of 1953 the Folkestone Central arrival once again became 5.35pm, and in honour of the event the express received the title 'Man of Kent'. The return working of the stock, at 10.14am from Sandwich, carried the same name, and leaving Folkestone Central at 11.10am this express was due at Waterloo (East) at 12.27pm and Charing Cross at 12.30pm.

It needed hard work by the 'Schools' to maintain these times with trains of 350 tons and more in weight, especially on the long climbs from both directions to Knockholt summit, while over the straight and level stretch between Tonbridge and Ashford speeds of well over 80mph were common. Once again electrification terminated the use of a title; in 1961 electric trains took over the Folkestone and Dover service, and though there was still a 4pm from Charing Cross to Folkestone, Dover, Deal and Ramsgate, reaching Folkestone Central in 78min (inclusive of a stop at Ashford), it was one of an hourly series all uniformly timed, and so with no claim to a distinctive name.

The Trans-Pennines

In the days of the independent railways, before World War 1 three different companies operated through trains with their own locomotives from Liverpool and Manchester across the Pennines to Hull, all using North Eastern Railway metals to finish their journeys. The London & North Western Railway, by way of Stalybridge and Huddersfield, worked into Leeds New station and from there over the NER via Selby; the

Lancashire & Yorkshire ran via Wakefield Kirkgate and Knottingley to reach the NER at Goole; while the Great Central route was through Sheffield and Doncaster, joining the NER at Thorne Junction, and from there using NER metals through Goole. Of the three, the LNWR trains, over the most direct route, probably had the lion's share of the traffic; next came the Great Central; while the Lancashire & Yorkshire share, with no more than two through trains each way daily, was the smallest. After the grouping the Great Central route became London & North Eastern throughout; the other two routes brought the London Midland & Scottish and London & North Eastern Railways into association, and the LNER took over the former LNWR trains between Leeds and Hull. In the years between the wars the routes via Sheffield and Leeds were regarded as of sufficient importance for restaurant cars to be provided on the through trains.

At the beginning of the 1960 decade it was realised that this important cross-country service deserved special attention. It was therefore decided to introduce a series of diesel-powered set trains between Liverpool and Hull, choosing for the purpose the former London & North Western route as being the most direct, and to provide faster and more frequent trains than ever previously. The new sets were built at Swindon Works, and had many novel features; each was provided with a buffet and grill car. Most important of all, in view of the gradients through the Pennines, was the 1,840hp of the diesel engines, which with six-coach trains of no more than 228 tons weight made substantial accelerations possible. Between Leeds and Manchester, for example, the times came down from between 84 and 87min with two stops to 67min.

Eight trains each way daily carried the title 'Trans-Pennine'; six ran through between Liverpool and Hull, taking about 3hr, and the remaining two between Liverpool and Leeds only. The intermediate stops in almost all cases were at St Helens Junction, Earlestown, Manchester Exchange, Stalybridge, Huddersfield, Leeds and Selby, and in one or two cases at Brough also. It was at first intended to use similar trains for the service between Liverpool and Manchester and Newcastle, but this required more accommodation, and so was worked by locomotive-hauled nine-coach trains.

There were important developments in 1979 when the main Trans-Pennine service was restructured to run hourly between York, Leeds, Manchester and Liverpool, with a shuttle feeder between Leeds and Hull. The York-Liverpool trains and those running through to Newcastle were formed of air-braked, electrically-heated Mk 2 stock, and hauled by Class 47 locomotives. Vehicles from dmu Classes 123 and 124 were assembled into four-car units to form trains for the Hull-Leeds service. The Liverpool-York service has since been extended to and from Scarborough. An all-round improvement in speed and comfort such as this did not provide the opportunity to distinguish any particular train with a title and so 'Trans-Pennine' must be regarded as a brand name for a service in the same light as 'Inter-City 125'. From May 1983 certain trains were diverted from Liverpool to serve Llandudno or Bangor, leaving the Manchester-Liverpool line near Earlestown to join the West Coast main line at Winwick Junction.